Bitcoin Is Venice

Bitcoin Is Venice

Essays on the Past and Future of Capitalism

Allen Farrington and Sacha Meyers

BTC Media, LLC

Nashville, TN

Bitcoin Is Venice by Allen Farrington and Sacha Meyers

The authors and publisher give their permission to reproduce, distribute, or transmit this book, and this book only, in parts or as an unaltered whole for non-commercial uses. Please maintain author and publisher information, including this page and metadata, with any reproduction, distribution, or transmission, in whole or in part, whenever feasible.

All proceeds after costs from the sale of this book will be donated to the Human Rights Foundation's Bitcoin Development Fund.

ISBN 979-8-9857289-0-3 (Paperback)
ISBN 979-8-9857289-1-0 (eBook)

Published by BTC Media, LLC
438 Houston St. #257 Nashville, TN 37203
Address all inquiries to contact@btcmedia.org

Printed by Amazon
Cover painting by George Bodine
Formatting by RMK Publications, LLC

Hydra, sem a qual eu poderia ter escrito este livro mais rápido, mas sem a qual eu não teria querido. Você faz meu mundo girar. — Sacha

Емичка, моята катерица, моята принцеса, моята любов. Обичам те, нямам търпение да изживеем живота си заедно и се надявам да имаме много деца, които да прочетат тази книга и да я оценят като тъпа. — Allen

And from us both to our parents.

Thanks and Acknowledgments

We would like to extend our sincere thanks and appreciation for the contributions to the manuscript of: Alex Adamou, Saifedean Ammous, Robert Breedlove, Ben Carman, Nic Carter, Tuur Demeester, Russell Farrington, Ryan Gentry, Alex Gladstein, Michael Goldstein, Joe Kelly, Obaid Khan, Jamie King, Kelly Lannan, Hass McCook, Yorick de Mombynes, Robert Natzler, Pierre Rochard, Sven Schnieders, Clay Space, Alfonze Stier der Zeitkette-Meerkeßell, and Giacomo Zucco.

Thanks also to the BTC Media team for their tireless work bringing the manuscript to print. Thanks to George Bodine for the original painting used for the cover.

Thanks to Alex Gladstein at the Human Rights Foundation (HRF): Obviously for the important and inspiring work he and they do, but in our case, for arranging for the profit from sales of this book to go towards the HRF's Bitcoin Development Fund (BDF). In case the reader is unaware, the authors are not receiving compensation of any kind, either upfront or variably, based on sales. After the costs of the production and sale of this book, all proceeds will be donated.

In addition, the rights to the book are fully open-sourced. Not only do we allow piracy, we encourage it — *especially* if in the form of providing translations. If anybody would like to translate the book into a language other than English, as just mentioned we cannot stop you, but we may be able to help you and possibly to *pay you*. If this is of interest, please contact the authors for more information.

In the likely event that the reader did not personally pay for a physical copy of this book, in whatever form this text has taken as they find themselves reading it, and, in doing so, make a small donation already, we would encourage them to consider donating to the HRF, either the BDF or the general fund, as feels most appropriate.

Over and above those who helped with the process of writing, editing, publishing, and more, we would like to extend special thanks to Robert Natzler, Saifedean Ammous, Elizabeth Stark, and, of course, the global ecosystem of volunteers promoting this civilizational project.

Rob has been thanked above for contributions to this manuscript but has also been kindly and diligently editing *all* our writing for many years longer than we have been publishing, blogging, or attempting to be public figures of any kind. In a perfect world, he would have been a third co-author, but as we know well, the world is far from perfect. We can only hope that, post-hyperbitcoinization, his time preference will have lowered to the point he can be bothered putting pen to paper himself. Until such a glorious moment, it would be unfair not to acknowledge that an enormous amount of the intellectual content in this book originated in conversation with Rob. The few ideas that are original are probably originally his. Thank you, Rob.

Saifedean has also been thanked above as having generously lent his time to the writing and editing process, but he is owed an additional thanks far, far more important than this alone. Dr. Ammous taught us not just by his thinking but — as the best teachers do — by his example, to stop worrying about how others will receive our ideas, put them out there, and see what happens. Or, as Mrs. Ammous previously encouraged *him*, "*Stop Talebing and do it!*" (So, we suppose, thank you, Mrs. Ammous as well!) We acted on this inspiration long before committing to write this book, to be clear. But *this book* is the intellectually indebted, years-later output of the precedent set by his. Thank you, Saif.

Elizabeth is of a different stripe to Rob and Saif, and to us. She is likely of a different stripe to anybody else in the world, as a matter of fact. She is a force of nature. Her profession and skillset are entirely different to our own and her impact on the manuscript has been minimal. But her impact on our thinking and — sincerely and without exaggeration — our attitude to our work and to life has been profound. Her seemingly unbounded energy and enthusiasm helped us to keep going through dark times — for us, for Bitcoin, and as it sometimes seemed, for the world.

Her unwavering commitment to *just doing good* forces a continual reckoning with respect to our own motivations, and we wouldn't have it any other way. We believe in turn that she has coined the most important meme in Bitcoin history, or at least the most ethical, the most encouraging, and the most emblematic of the good we are all trying to do: *number of people go up*. And what better and more concise way to describe what we hope for from this book? It is very much helpful that our profession and skillsets are different because it means that, while her work will change the lives of billions, perhaps ours can reach the marginal thousand or so. Thank you, Elizabeth.

Finally, we thank all those who have contributed to Bitcoin voluntarily and at their own expense: developers, reviewers, writers, educators — everybody. The authors are in a position to promote human freedom and prosperity in a manner that aligns perfectly with our jobs. This is an incredible privilege and we do not take it at all lightly. We know most are not so lucky. Others have contributed more than we will ever be able to, at greater risk, and for less or no reward. If we have seen further, it is by standing on the shoulders of giants. Whatever success we have is due to them and should be theirs.

To whatever extent we can make this true by proclaiming it: Our success *is their success*.

Thank you, all, and we hope we have made you proud. Enjoy. ☺

A Note on the Composition of the Text

This book came about in an unusual way. Never conceived of as a single project, the content is fairly described as the intellectual preoccupation of the authors for the last four or five years, both personally and professionally. The idea to write in this medium *at all* came after the unexpected success first of *This Is Not Capitalism*, an essay cowritten by Sacha and Allen in March 2020, and which forms the basis of Chapter Three of the same name. Second, the essay trilogy *Wittgenstein's Money*, *The Capital Strip Mine*, and *Bitcoin Is Venice*, written by Allen from around June 2020 onwards and published between December 2020 and February 2021. This trilogy, likewise, forms the basis of Chapters Four through Six and were edited by Sacha and influenced by his ideas.

The book remains more a collection of related essays than a unified whole, and we use the word "chapter" more for ease of reference than absolute accuracy. In this light, it is fair to highlight that, as was just described for Chapters Three through Six, in the now complete collection, Chapters One and Eight (*Wrestling with the Truth* and *These Were Capitalists*) were written by Sacha and edited by Allen, while Chapters Two, Seven, and Nine (*The Complex Markets Hypothesis, A Capital Renaissance*, and *Global Money, Local Freedom*) were written by Allen and edited by Sacha. We have thoroughly enjoyed this process and firmly believe it has improved both of our writing and, indeed, our thinking. Although we use "we" throughout, this is more as an aid to the reader than a reflection of any authorial unity. The result is less a true synthesis and more a collection of essays from our individual points of view. We like that each author's voice retained its originality, even if it meant including material on which we disagree.

Table of Contents

Foreword

What if the year was 1400, and you stood at the brink of the Renaissance but didn't know it?

What if someone handed you a magical book that would explain what the coming Renaissance was, reveal the injustices and inefficiencies of the medieval system, and foretell why and how things would change in the coming decades?

What you have in your hands, dear reader, is a book that will do just this for you today, as we approach the Bitcoin Renaissance.

Humanity has potentially begun a historical transformation on par with the agricultural and industrial revolutions, and one with potentially even greater impact.

That may sound outlandish, but this book makes a compelling argument that it is, in fact, true.

In the same way that medieval Venice set the stage for the peoples of Europe to break free of the empire and transition from serfdom to liberty, and from financial slavery to financial sovereignty, today the Bitcoin network is the path to escaping the broken and unsustainable post-1971 political economy.

In newspapers and on television we are told not to worry about inflation, that employment is more important than saving, and that we can own nothing and be happy.

We should be satisfied, in other words, to work for those who own the assets, just as we watch their wealth continue to grow and concentrate, while we see the currency that we earn depreciate and see our way out of debt vanish.

This book is a stunning rejection of this emerging neo-feudalism and its administrators.

Over the past decade, governments, economists, and journalists have relentlessly hammered into the minds of their populations and audiences that Bitcoin is dangerous and risky. That it's for criminals. That it's a Ponzi scheme. That it's destroying the planet.

Time, however, has shown that it has been dangerous and risky to not hold bitcoin, which has been, since inception, the best-performing financial asset in the world.

But against the facts, Bitcoin users are still routinely told by authorities that their choice — opting peacefully into a new, fair, and neutral monetary system — is wrong, immoral, or even treasonous.

The reality, as the authors of this book argue, is that the world financial system is a cruel labyrinth, and we're all trapped inside, stuck in a situation where tomorrow is traded for today, where capital is strip-mined without consideration for the future, where our money is devalued by central planners, where our liberties are increasingly eroded, and where our behavior is spied on and used to engineer us to become more compliant and dependent.

Bitcoin fixes this and helps us escape but not by violence. It is "not a sword for Theseus to fight the Minotaur, but a thread to follow to exit the Labyrinth."

And exit we shall. We, after all, owe the Minotaur nothing. Let the beast starve. We'll find our own way out.

The way is through a new kind of Venice in cyberspace available to anyone in the world regardless of one's wealth, class, race, religion, gender, nationality, or occupation.

Where any of the billions with internet access can connect to this revolution, be a part of it, and even own a piece of it. That's what makes this revolution so much different from the ones that came before. Whereas those achieved change through new hierarchical structures, Bitcoin will change the world through decentralization.

As more and more people begin to realize that Bitcoin is monetizing right in front of our eyes, creating an alternative to the degenerate, fiat capitalist system that we have been forced to partake in, we should feel no debt to the old regime of short-term thinking, top-down planning, consumption-driven spending, growth obsession, central banking, bailouts, rent-seeking, regulatory capture, toxic bigness, risk transfer, globalism, and financialization.

Instead, we should turn our eyes to a future of long-term thinking, peer-to-peer collaboration, open-source architecture, nurturing, replenishing, risk sharing, localism, and growing productive capital, where the farmer plants his seeds instead of eating them and enjoys many harvests to come.

To understand what's coming, we need a guide. There could scarcely be one better than the book in your hands.

From the stunning realizations one receives when reading Chapter 3, This is Not Capitalism, to the illumination provided by Chapter 5, The Capital Strip Mine, the authors accomplish something extraordinary in the chapters ahead.

These lucid and lively pages explore all the nooks and crannies of the impact Bitcoin will leave on the world, especially in regard to investing, communications, culture, energy use, environmental sustainability, and how we build our communities.

In the book's crescendo, Chapter 6, Bitcoin Is Venice, we get a clarion call for a better future: more inclusive, less exploitative, filled with choice and reason and compassion. A financial system unrigged, with we, the people, at the controls. Digital gold, digital cash, and real property rights for all.

Perhaps you found it surprising that a human rights advocate be asked to write the foreword to a book about finance and economics. But read the book, and you'll understand why I've been tasked with preparing you for this journey.

This isn't simply about how money and finance works — though you'll learn a lot about that along the way — it's a book about how we can, and how we must, harness the power of Bitcoin to secure liberty in the electronic age.

Already as you read this there are tens of millions of people around the world who are peacefully opting into Bitcoin. Not just in dictatorships and broken economies, where 4.3 billion languish under authoritarians and 1.6 billion suffer under double- or triple-digit inflation, but in the West, too. Even the most hardened skeptics are admitting that yes, Bitcoin has a use case, somewhere.

But why? Why do, every day, more and more people exit the existing financial system into something new? This book explains the why: Individuals are leaving the old system of degenerate fiat capitalism, as the authors call it, as their money isn't theirs, it's someone else's, and the real owners are abusing the money printer.

This book is a guide to the system-wide effects of what happens when the money printer keeps going, when a preposterous global debt-to-capital ratio steals value from future generations, and when value is stealthily transferred from the have-nots to the haves.

But it's also, more importantly, an inspiring vision of a better money laying the foundation for a brighter future. As crazy as it may sound, the authors will explain why this is not just a dream and is something that can, and likely will — as the result of a beautiful incentive structure — be achieved. Most of the world just doesn't know it yet.

I feel comfortable saying that this book will be vastly more appreciated in five years, ten years, and twenty years, then today.

It will age very well.

Everyone else will get to appreciate it in due time. Today, you get a sneak peek of the future.

Enjoy the ride.

— Alex Gladstein

"Just as the technology of printing altered and reduced the power of medieval guilds and the social power structure, so too will cryptologic methods fundamentally alter the nature of corporations and of government interference in economic transactions."

— Timothy C. May, *The Crypto Anarchist Manifesto*

"This is your last chance. After this, there is no turning back. You take the blue pill — the story ends, you wake up in your bed and believe whatever you want to believe. You take the red pill — you stay in Wonderland, and I show you how deep the rabbit hole goes."

— Laurence Fishburne as Morpheus, *The Matrix*

Introduction

Quentin Skinner's monumental overview of the development of early modern political philosophy, *The Foundations of Modern Political Thought*, begins with the following lines:

> As early as the middle of the twelfth century the German historian Otto of Freising recognised that a new and remarkable form of social and political organisation had arisen in Northern Italy. One peculiarity he noted was that Italian society had apparently ceased to be feudal in character.

While Skinner's concern is political philosophy and not economic history, it is easy enough to identify that these social changes were made possible by a nascent form of capitalism. As the great medievalist Henri Pirenne commented on the period and region in his *Medieval Cities*:

> Lombardy, where from Venice on the east and Pisa and Genoa on the west all the commercial movements of the Mediterranean flowed and were blended into one, flourished with an extraordinary exuberance. On the wonderful plain cities bloomed with the same vigor as the harvests. The fertility of the soil made possible for them an unlimited expansion, and at the same time the ease of obtaining markets favoured both the importation of raw materials and the exportation of manufactured products. There, commerce gave rise to industry, and as it developed, Bergamo, Cremona, Lodi, Verona, and all the old towns, all the old Roman municipia, took on new life, far more vigorous than that which had animated them in antiquity.

Pirenne added that the rise of these cities, which was predicated on commercial and industrial expansion,

> Strongly stimulated social progress. It made no less a contribution in spreading throughout the world a new conception of labor. Before this it had been serf; now it became free, and the consequences of this fact, to which we shall return, were incalculable. Let it be added, finally, that the economic revival of which the twelfth century saw the flowering revealed the power of capital, and enough will have been said to show that possibly no period in all history had a more profound effect upon humanity.

And wouldn't you know it, but feudalism seems to be making a comeback. Joel Kotkin introduces his pithy tract, *The Coming of Neo-Feudalism*, anticipating this re-emergence:

> Of course it will look different this time around: we won't see knights in shining armor, or vassals doing homage to their lords, or a powerful Catholic Church enforcing the reigning orthodoxy. What we are seeing is a new form of aristocracy developing in the United States and beyond, as wealth in our postindustrial economy tends to be ever more concentrated in fewer hands. Societies are becoming more stratified, with decreasing chances of upward mobility for most of the population. A class of thought leaders and opinion makers, which I call the "clerisy," provide intellectual support for the emerging hierarchy. As avenues for upward mobility are diminishing, the model of liberal capitalism is losing appeal around the globe, and new doctrines are arising in its place, including ones that lend support to a kind of neo-feudalism.

Kotkin is more concerned with effects than with causes. His worry is, in essence, that the social fabric is rapidly unraveling. His argumentation repeatedly alludes to Shoshana Zuboff's notion of surveillance capitalism. While we agree with Kotkin (and by extension with Zuboff, and to really give credit where it is due, with Michael Goldstein) that it is important to give mimetically effective names to phenomena about which we intend to have productive discussions, we feel that the monolithic technology platforms this moniker is intended to capture are not the cause of neo-feudalism but are simply another awful effect of something deeper.

It is our belief that not all, but certainly some — and probably most — of the afflictions Kotkin cites can most sensibly be attributed to the regime of political economy dominant in the West since 1971, particularly acute since 2009, the roots of which can be traced to 1913 at the very earliest. Often lazily referred to as "capitalism," or sometimes sardonically as "post-capitalism," we think this is, in fact, another case of a poorly chosen name leading to a poorly framed discussion. If anything, the distinguishing feature of the economic circumstances from which these afflictions arise is the normalized devaluation and consumption of capital in the pursuit of ever more leveraged "growth." We will sometimes refer to the dominant regime of political economy but sometimes as degenerate fiat "capitalism" instead.

Those who do not own hard assets are increasingly tending to drown in debt from which they will realistically never escape, unable to save except by speculation, and unable to afford the inflation in the essential costs of living that does not officially exist. What amounts to an "official" message is the likes of Christine Lagarde (then-president of the International Monetary Fund and now of the European Central Bank) musing that "we should be happier to have a job than to have our savings protected," and the World Economic Forum suggesting that, by 2030, "you will own nothing, but you will be happy."[1] You will use things that somebody owns, mind you. But that somebody will not be you.

If we were to believe that these people mean what they say, and that the consumption of capital is not going to stop — perhaps we even realize that it cannot stop — we might be as similarly inclined as Otto of Freising to look for any sprouts of civilization that manage to advance beyond our rebooted feudalism. There may end up being a variety of reasons that different social units avoid this state. We think that, for some, the reason will be Bitcoin.

We *think* for some, but we *hope* for many, and we pray for all.

***

Bitcoin has gone through many cycles of popular conception, usually with high correlation with its cycles in price. From a wacky open-source project only known to a handful of mailing list participants and only understood by those proficient in C++ and steeped in cryptography, political philosophy, and monetary history, Bitcoin has since been dubbed just about every metaphor under the sun. It has also been written off more times than can easily be counted. The website 99bitcoins.com has a dedicated page for *Bitcoin Obituaries* which, as of the time of writing, lists 428 occasions on which a relatively mainstream media outlet declared Bitcoin "dead." And yet, as of the time of writing, its price in dollars is near its all-time high. Although impossible to quantify, we feel its reputation, its strength, and its potential are at all-time highs as well.

Most *serious* attempts by outsiders to grapple with Bitcoin over the years, even those unabashedly positive, have tended to view the phenomenon too narrowly in our estimation. And to be fair, often the authors will admit as much. We think Bitcoin is more than a cheaper payment rail or "digital gold," for example. It is more than a "digital ledger" and it is more than a solution to the Byzantine Generals Problem. It is certainly more than the "underlying technology" of "the blockchain," the primary value of which has turned out to be crystallized in consulting contracts to hapless conglomerates and the terrible books the savviest of these consultants would go on to write.

Of course, this is not an original insight. In recent years, it has become more generally accepted that Bitcoin is an inherently interdisciplinary phenomenon. To view Bitcoin solely through the lens of economics, say, or cryptography is to miss the forest for the trees. Bitcoin lies at the intersection of, at the very least, these two, as well as financial theory, history, political philosophy, theoretical computer science, distributed systems theory, game theory, and network and protocol design. Possibly even more that have escaped our own understanding. Arguably, the *inside* view is to work from the premise that it cannot be grappled with in its entirety but that perhaps some expertise can be brought to bear on some corner of its workings, necessarily constituting, at best, a humble contribution to a patchwork of thought. As Jameson Lopp famously put it, and which certainly set our minds at ease, "Nobody understands Bitcoin, and that's OK."

We do not claim to "understand Bitcoin", nor do we claim to have stumbled into the perfectly comprehensive and expansive framing. In fact, our framing is still fairly narrow in the scheme of things. We will barely mention the more technical topics of cryptography, theoretical computer science, distributed systems theory, game theory, or network and protocol design. There are many fine works on these topics we would recommend to the interested reader well ahead of any of our own thoughts.

But within the narrower confines of financial theory, economics, history, and political philosophy, we feel much more confident. We believe the popular understanding of Bitcoin can and should extend to these fields. We can only hope our contribution in these areas of our limited and relative expertise will be valuable.

***

When we say that the reason some social units can avoid collapse into neo-feudalism by embracing Bitcoin, what does that mean?

We are sure it seems hyperbolic to most, if not outright ludicrous, but it's actually fairly prosaic. It means that those social units that voluntarily choose to embrace Bitcoin — a global, digital, sound, open-source, programmable money — will be in a position to accumulate long-term–oriented capital at a disproportionate rate to those who do not. They will have a superior economic foundation from which to build healthy social and political institutions, which will contrast to those left behind as medieval Venice did to the remnants of the Western Empire. If it works, it will sort itself out. IF this system is

This is the thesis of the book in a nutshell. better of fue dude then those

*** who adopt will have more capital.

In Chapter One, *Wrestling with the Truth*, we provide a gentle introduction to the thesis of the book and the concepts with which we intend to grapple throughout via the allegory of mixed martial arts (MMA).

We argue that the philosophical essence of "competition" in economics and broader social affairs is a clash of alternative hypotheses as to what is really *true*. It is experimental but not scientific; combative but not violent; traditional but not frozen in time. We believe MMA demonstrates that the search for truth is unpredictable, dynamic, and accumulative of hard-earned knowledge. It is an essentially *human* endeavor that cannot be "modeled" with any intellectual honesty or seriousness. But it can be *understood*, and, as a metaphor, it can be usefully recycled.

In Chapter Two, *The Complex Markets Hypothesis*, we argue that academic economics has become overly mathematised and enamored with finance. First, this is in part due to the overwhelming mass of data financial markets throw off on which scientistic statistical analysis can be performed. Second, it's in part due to political interference in economic activity primarily and most destructively being directed through financial markets, creating an attractor for corruption — political and intellectual alike.

As professional investors, we think we are well placed to diagnose the shibboleths of modern finance as pseudoscientific obscurantism. Its tenets are designed to confuse outsiders and avoid and escape criticism for siphoning wealth and power to the already wealthy and powerful at the expense of the rest of society. Middle-class savers are hardest and most obviously hit, but everybody suffers in one way or another. We argue that the cornerstone of modern finance theory, the *efficient markets hypothesis* (EMH), is self-serving, vacuous nonsense.

Following Chapter One, *Wrestling with the Truth*, we build on our conceptual toolkit of unpredictability, dynamism, and accumulation of hard-earned knowledge to provide in place of the EMH a common-sense analysis of the workings of financial markets. These concepts will in turn serve us well in our analysis of economics in the chapters that follow.

In Chapter Three, *This Is Not Capitalism*, we switch our attention from the modern *theory* of financial markets to the modern *practice*. We diagnose the regime of political economy dominant in the West since 1971, and particularly acute since 2009, and alluded to earlier in this introduction. This regime is often called "capitalism," or, if acknowledged to have diverged a great deal from what "capitalism" once meant, is still felt to be somehow the inevitable end point of the dynamics of political economy that capitalism requires and creates.

We think this is deeply misleading. If "capitalism" means anything, it ought to at least include "the preservation and growth in the capital stock." We argue that the modern malaise and perpetual economic crises often attributed to "capitalism" follow from the implicit rejection of the ethos of nurturing, replenishing, and growing capital that is instilled by central banking, regulatory capture, and financialization.

Although we do not yet mention Bitcoin, we feel this is the political and economic background that made Bitcoin necessary in the first place. In fact, the acceleration of this regime in 2009 is precisely when *and why* Bitcoin was conceived and gifted to the world. Understanding the logic and dynamics of the regime is an essential starting point for grasping the emergence of a global, digital, sound, open-source, programmable money.

In Chapter Four, *Wittgenstein's Money*, we ponder that this emergence, while clearly instigated by central banking and financialization, and while of civilizational importance, has been largely ignored on the understandable yet comical grounds that it just doesn't *seem like* such a thing could ever happen.

We, therefore, ask an important question: What would it seem like if it *did seem like* a global, digital, sound, open-source, programmable money was monetizing from absolute zero? We find the mainstream economic understanding of the phenomenon rejects its importance by way of rejecting its existence on essentially semantic grounds: It isn't happening because it *can't* happen. It is not the kind of thing that happens.

We instead develop an analysis of money that is appropriately unpredictable, dynamic, and accumulative of hard-earned knowledge, as to capture that such a thing *can* happen and to give some idea of what it would *seem like* if it were happening.

In Chapter Five, *The Capital Strip Mine*, we consider the likely effects on the capital stock of a regime of political economy systematically ignoring the analysis of money just provided in Chapter Four, *Wittgenstein's Money*.

We establish that the primary purpose, utility, and benefit of money is to manage economic uncertainty, and that this assurance paves the way for the deliberate generation and embrace of yet more uncertainty brought about by directing time and energy towards the creation of capital. We argue that imposing an overly static view of money sets up a vicious cycle in which we are unwittingly incentivized to consume capital rather than create it, which destroys the benefits of money and disincentivizes capital formation further.

We predict such a system would evolve towards ever greater immediate consumption under ever more debt, and that if, by some unimaginable historical tragedy, money *itself* were to come to exist exclusively in the form of debt receipts, this vicious cycle could likely never be escaped.

In Chapter Six, *Bitcoin Is Venice*, we paint a far more optimistic picture of the future given Bitcoin *is not a debt receipt*: It is a pure asset with clear monetary utility. Moreover, it is historically unprecedented as a technology that offers virtually no potential utility towards violent ends whatsoever, and yet high defensibility against violence. These form an intellectual foundation for a radical reimagining of the monetary weave of the social fabric.

We predict, among a range of possibilities discussed in the chapter, more mobile capital than has ever existed, an associated shift in the geopolitics of citizenship, labor, and capital, a preeminent place for a close and novel variant of Islamic finance, and the collapse of most financial assets of the *Ancien Régime* into Bitcoin's growing gravitational pull.

In Chapter Seven, *A Capital Renaissance*, we turn our attention to the ways in which we predict a Bitcoin standard will enable a return to, and a normalization of, the nurturing, replenishment, and growth of capital. We will focus on highly tangible sources of capital — those where the effects of Bitcoin can be reasonably predicted in the not-too-distant future. We explore the likely effect of a return to sound money on the financial industry, internet infrastructure, and the environment.

In Chapter Eight, *These Were Capitalists*, we push further Hernando de Soto's brilliant abstraction of "capital" as not mere money — as originally introduced and explored across Chapter Four, *Wittgenstein's Money* and Chapter Five, *The Capital Stripe Mine* — but rather "economic potential energy."

We believe that nurturing, replenishing, and growing a stock of capital is a practice that is fundamental to all human affairs, not just economic exchange. Economic activity performed suitably creatively and responsibly — such as that described in Chapter Seven, *A Capital Renaissance* — may well be only a special case of a more general principle of social organization and behavior. It is a manifestation of a healthy society: the gauge of its health as observable with respect to its management and utilization of scarce resources and specialization of craft and output, among many other possible gauges.

We aim to make this plain by seeking to learn from those who fought to accumulate highly intangible sources of "capital" across three far more intangible stocks of capital than those previously discussed: the social fabric, the built environment, and cultural expression.

In Chapter Nine, *Global Money, Local Freedom*, we shift the topic of discussion away from, implicitly, voluntary cooperation across economic and cultural exchange.

We focus instead on the governing bodies that have nominal authority over this behavior and ask, very simply, what becomes of them under a Bitcoin standard? We think it is undeniable that sovereign corporations will simply have to adapt in terms of their constitution and functioning if they do not want to collapse into insolvency, both financial and societal.

We frame our discussion around the concept of *returns to violence* and aim to explore from first principles how the shifting returns to violence under a Bitcoin standard will change the role of the state, and, surely in turn, the opportunities for individuals to voluntarily cooperate.

***

Our various predictions for Bitcoin's path from this point on — for the optionality it offers to those social units that embrace it — could be true at any and every scale. It could be an individual, a family, a friend group, a neighborhood, a company, a city, an industry, a country, or the entire world. We will have to wait and see.

Of course, it could be nobody. It could fail altogether. We say this primarily to guard against accusations of blind faith, speculative mania, and fundamental unseriousness. But we don't say it to feign intellectual sophistication with post-hoc, unfalsifiable fence-sitting.

As if this wasn't entirely clear already, we are very happy indeed to be on the record as saying it is more likely Bitcoin will succeed than not. And so, while there are good reasons it might fail, "it's dumb" and "I don't like it" are not among them. In order to sensibly articulate the reasons why it might fail, you have to have at least tried to understand it in the first place.

Of course, nobody *fully* understands Bitcoin, and that's OK. But we can all put in the work to understanding it *more*, and we hope this book will help those who want to try.

Chapter One

Wrestling with the Truth
*Discovery and knowledge as aesthetic, codified,
and practical*

Let us begin with a thought experiment: Bitcoin's history mirrors the history of mixed martial arts (MMA).

Consider that prices emerge from action, and the truth of prices comes from experimentation. It is not dictated. It is discovered iteratively. Every transaction spreads knowledge, inching a price towards a better consensus, yet consensus itself is a moving target.

MMA has gone through many iterations from its roots in arts like judo to the form we know today, and it continues to undergo this process through the natural experiment every individual fight represents.

The power of prices is the process of dynamic discovery that underpins their emergence, not the fleeting consensus of a specific moment in time. *The price* is never right, but *prices* are as right as can be hoped for at that moment. Attempts to coerce prices without the ability to change the reality they communicate are, therefore, bound to run into trouble. And yet we do not seem capable to accept the truth of prices whenever it is inconvenient. To ensure that consensus can arrive at valid social truths, we require systems or institutions that withstand attempts at coercion and which tap into decentralized discovery.

Martial arts are a fitting case study, and an encouraging allegory for all that follows. A few decades ago, they were under the grip of bullshitting coercion. Today, they are thriving under a marketplace of ideas.

In the Beginning Was the Fight

"It's kind of crazy when you think about the history of martial arts. [...] Since the dawn of time, people have been trying to figure out better ways to fuck people up. Since they figured out language and figured out how to teach skills they've been working on techniques. [And not] until 1993 did we really know what worked."
— Joe Rogan, *The Joe Rogan Experience MMA Show #98 with Luke Thomas*

Wrestling is probably the oldest sport in the world. The earliest evidence for it dates from cave paintings in France over 15,000 years old. We also discovered that most holds practiced today were known in ancient times. Boxing is a little younger, depicted as far back as the third millennium BC in Sumerian relief. The reader might therefore be forgiven for believing there is little more to learn about the art of fighting. And yet, the modern world has only learned which fighting techniques are truly effective in the last thirty years. Few sports have evolved as much in recent decades, fewer still tracing their lineage to prehistory.

As Joe Rogan alludes to above, 1993 marks the birth of the Ultimate Fighting Championship. UFC spawned a free marketplace of fighting ideas called Mixed Martial Arts, or MMA. Before, charm and authority shielded much of martial arts from scrutiny. Competition was limited and the truth of stylistic superiority could not be definitively established. The UFC along with its famed fighting arena, the Octagon, created an environment where competing hypotheses could be systematically tested. With nowhere for falsehoods to hide, truth might finally stand a fighting chance.

The recent evolution of martial arts serves as a unique case study to understand the ways in which ideas are created, tested, and spread. Instead of arguing about a hypothetical judo versus karate fight with your mates after one too many pints, the UFC would run the experiment for all to observe. Instead of judging a given martial art by how cool it looked in a movie, it would have to prove its efficacy against a skilled, motivated, and resisting opponent. Deference to a sensei would no longer suffice. Mere decree would hold no value. Traditions would be questioned and schools humiliated. Others would emerge from unsuspected corners of the world. In that sense, we can say after 1993 fighting stopped being theoretical. It became practical.

We will evaluate the evolution of fighting using three settings: the Movie Set, the Dojo, and the Octagon. We will loosely link each with the three ancient Greek modes of persuasion: *Pathos* or emotion, *Ethos* or authority, and *Logos* or reason, and three different ways of learning: inspiration, rote, and praxis. We will see how ineffective ideas were spread and what would eventually combat them: ideally a front kick to the face. This is the story of how the UFC unleashed the competitive forces of free markets onto martial arts. It is, by extension, an allegory for the power of competition in incentivizing the search for and discovery of truth.

The Movie Set, or the Appeal to Emotions and Aesthetic Knowledge

"It is impossible for somebody to lie unless he thinks he knows the truth. Producing bullshit requires no such conviction."
— Harry Frankfurt, *On Bullshit*

Starting in the 1960s, Hollywood was largely responsible for the spread of Eastern martial arts to a Western audience. Many of today's greatest martial artists were drawn in by movies such as Bruce Lee's *Enter the Dragon* or Jean-Claude Van Damme's *Bloodsport*. The romantic image of a skilled fighter swiftly disposing of a dozen goons on his way to glory is more than enough to make most kids search for their nearest Kung Fu club.

Unfortunately, for many, their unrealistic expectations were rewarded only with bullshit. Hollywood looks to sell movie tickets, not rigorously test fighting techniques in realistic combat scenarios. Movies spread ideas and techniques of martial arts to resonate visually and emotionally with their audience and generate box office revenues.

Ancient Greeks dubbed this method for convincing people *Pathos*, an appeal to emotion. You believe me because you like me. What you learn you *know* (or you *think you know*) because of how it makes you feel; it *feels right*. It is a distinctly aesthetic way to acquire knowledge. It is pleasing. It is calming. Its forms are smooth, symmetrical, and flush.

Knowledge arrived at by this form of inspiration can of course be legitimate, but we can only know this by providing a proof. If practical, as opposed to deductive, a proof requires a test. But perhaps these fighting methods are never supposed to be tested, only admired. In fact, the point in these circumstances is precisely to avoid such a test at all costs. It is the *feeling* of knowledge that must be preserved; not the fact of it, or likely lack thereof.

No matter how good these movies are — and some are *bloody* good — they put form over function. A punch no longer travels the shortest distance to its target. It takes a dramatic looping detour. Street fights rarely end up on the ground. They are perfectly choreographed across streetscapes. The street ceases to be an interactive terrain of combat and becomes instead the inert setting of a melodramatic dance. If not the dance, then certainly the drama is compelling enough for the audience to suspend its disbelief, which is when the virus strikes. We buy some of the extravaganza because of how pretty it looks and we emotionally bond with the hero. Yet long after the credits have rolled and the lights turned back on, moviegoers will still associate karate with near superhuman feats. Most know it's all exaggerated, but we probably will still believe a black belt is someone to fear.

In moderation, a serious martial arts school might resort to breaking boards to attract new members, a useless practice never taught in a self-respecting regimen. Taken to the extreme, we get fake martial arts that teach you to channel life energy or chi into your strikes.

This is total fantasy. The emitters and receivers of these ideas alike are ambivalent as to their real effectiveness. Their assessment is based solely on how it looks and makes them feel. This is as divorced from empirical testing as it gets. The dynamics are like those of cult members accepting indoctrination purely for the sense of belonging it can bring.

The Dojo, or the Appeal to Authority and Codified Knowledge

"Education is an admirable thing, but it is well to remember from time to time that nothing that is worth knowing can be taught."
— Oscar Wilde

You must bow before entering the dojo. It's tradition. It's respect. It's Japanese. It is a show of deference to authority signaling a willingness to learn from the master. Unlike in fake martial arts, students of real martial arts believe in their teacher and her craft because of her accomplishments and standing in the wider community. This is akin to the trust we put in police officers and government officials. We might not be able to directly assess the veracity and deservedness of their claim, but it stands to reason that many others have done so. Ideas are tested for effectiveness through an intermediary.

The dojo spreads ideas by appealing to authority, or *Ethos*. The knowledge we derive we learn by rote. As a child might memorize her times tables by performing a kind of mental operation, so too she learns her karate steps by repetition of a physical operation. The knowledge has been codified and transmitted.

One of the greatest such teachers — or *sensei* — is Kano Jigoro, born in 1860, eight years before the Meiji Restoration when Japan began to industrialize. This period also marks the abolition of the samurai warrior class. Its three main disciplines were: sword fighting — or *kenjutsu* — archery — or *kyujutsu* — and unarmed combat — or *jujitsu*. As the samurai class began to fade, so did its knowledge. Enters Jigoro. While not a samurai, Jigoro trained in martial arts and became well known for his meticulous recording of the jujutsu techniques he deemed most effective. He described his work as *"keeping what I felt should be kept, and discarding what I felt should be discarded."* Old masters sought Jigoro to share their techniques in the hope they would not die out. These masters accumulated hard-won stores of capital in the form of knowledge gained through experimentation. Unable to maintain, let alone nurture, replenish, and grow these stocks themselves, the masters looked for someone they hoped would. They feared their knowledge would depreciate entirely, leaving nothing behind. Jigoro offered the means to avert such an epistemological disaster. He called his new school *judo*, the gentle way.

Given the task at hand and the high quality of the result, Jigoro seems to have achieved wonders. Judo remains one of the more effective martial arts and is a great foundation for aspiring fighters. But its flaws were inherent in Jigoro's method. By choosing what to keep or discard, *he* acted as the authority. We might say his doctrine acted as a server, and all who followed were merely clients. Of course, as a single server with no exposure to feedback, the doctrine itself invited self-induced vulnerability. The rigid structure Jigoro created shielded judo from outside criticism and internal experimentation alike. Students defer to their sensei and dojo rules prohibit using techniques from another tradition.

What if I punched you before you got close enough to grab my collar and throw me to the floor? It's not allowed. You may only compete against other practitioners of your art. As a result, the art slowly loses any grasp of the reality of consequential combat and turns into a game played against itself. Don't strike, don't grab the trousers, don't use leg locks, don't flick the genitals. Don't check if it works.

The rigid techniques and rules of a given school tend to lead it to evolve like a species trapped on an island. It becomes hyper-specialized for its environment. But what if the environment changes? The chink in a dojo's proverbial armor can appear during an exhibition match pitting two styles against one another. In 1963, boxer Milo Savage fought judoka Gene LeBell in a contest meant to show the superiority of American boxing.

Things didn't go as the organizers hoped. LeBell threw Savage to the ground and choked him unconscious. It was the first sanctioned mixed martial arts fight in the United States. When two very different hypotheses meet, we may get surprising results. There is in fact no way to know for sure without a fight. It must be tried empirically. We might say it cannot be modeled. Even if we could perfectly mathematize the fighters' abilities and parameterize the dynamics of the fight, the result would *still* be computationally irreducible. Why simulate the entire universe when the universe will happily simulate itself?[2] Why not just watch the fight?

Another seminal exhibition fight occurred in 1988 when kickboxer Rick Roufus fought Thai boxer Changpuek Kiatsongrit. The Thai fighter won with a single technique. He kicked Roufus's legs until they stopped working. The technique is common in Thai boxing but was rarely used in American kickboxing. After the fight, Rick's brother, Duke Roufus, said in an interview:

> I hope that people realize that Thais, if they fight our rules, they're not gonna win. And we're not gonna fight their rules. We experimented tonight but we found out it's not worth it. It doesn't take too much talent to kick to the legs.

Duke eventually became one of America's best Thai boxing coaches. He realized that kickboxing had not yet developed an answer to this simple but effective technique. It was fundamentally unpredictable, but now that an experiment had been run, the truth was out. The challenge now was to systematize such learnings.

The global martial arts community, nascent as it even was, had to find a way of testing techniques repeatedly by running empirical tests rather than aesthetic comparisons or thought experiments. Only then could we hope to discover the truth.

The Octagon, or the Appeal to Reason and Practical Knowledge

"A true partnership between the people on the ground managing holistically and the researchers supporting their efforts needs to start with mutual respect. But since the time of Descartes, and the beginning of modern science, society has so elevated the status of the academic researcher and so lowered that of the land manager that generally the researcher speaks with more authority on management today than the person actually managing the farm from day to day and producing food. And this is so even though farmers and pastoralists were the ones who discovered which plants and animals could be domesticated, and then bred thousands of varieties from them several millennia before scientists existed."

— Allan Savory, *Holistic Management*

The Gracie Challenge was an open invitation to martial arts schools in the Los Angeles valley: Come fight a member of the Gracie family. Kung-fu, judo, and karate practitioners all rose to the challenge hoping to demonstrate the superiority of their art. The grainy footage, most of which dates from the early 1990s, shows a consistent story. The Gracies took their opponents down to the ground and submitted them with a choke or joint lock. Pretty kicks and punches were no match for someone versed in ground fighting. The Gracies' art is now known worldwide as Brazilian Jiu Jitsu. BJJ is a cornerstone of modern mixed martial arts training. But in the early 1990s, it was virtually unknown.

Brazilian Jiu Jitsu's story starts with a roaming Japanese emigrant named Mitsuyo Maeda. Born in 1878, Maeda studied judo under its founder, Jigoro. He traveled the world, reportedly winning over 2,000 professional bouts, many against practitioners of other arts. He eventually settled in Brazil where he taught a version of judo with a high emphasis on ground fighting. He called it *jiu jitsu*. One of Maeda's students was named Carlos Gracie. The art spread through the family and was for a time known as Gracie Jiu Jitsu.

Although BJJ's techniques are like judo's, its culture and training methodology are not. BJJ encourages playful experimentation. New techniques are constantly developed and tested by the community. In comparison, judo has an official list of techniques that can only be edited by an official body. Whereas judo operates on a client/server model, BJJ is truly a peer-to-peer martial art; whereas judo focuses on competition within its community, BJJ was from the start focused on testing itself against other arts; whereas judo seems intent on honing an aesthetic equilibrium, BJJ is a dynamic process: never settling, always looking to discover its own flaws and improve.

The veracity encoded in judo must be trusted; the veracity encoded in BJJ can be verified. The measure of BJJ's success has always been *effectiveness*. It does not bow to authority nor look to convince with aesthetics. It appeals to reason, or *Logos*, and it grants knowledge in the form of what James C. Scott calls *mētis*, in his magisterial *Seeing Like a State*, which we reference repeatedly. Of this form of knowledge, Scott writes,

> Mētis is most applicable to broadly similar but never precisely identical situations requiring a quick and practiced adaptation that becomes almost second nature to the practitioner. The skills of mētis may well involve rules of thumb, but such rules are largely acquired through practice (often in formal apprenticeship) and a developed feel or knack for strategy. Mētis resists simplification into deductive principles which can successfully be transmitted through book learning, because the environments in which it is exercised are to complex and nonrepeatable that formal procedures of rational decision making are impossible to apply. In a sense, mētis lies in that large space between the realm of genius, to which no formula can apply, and the realm of codified knowledge, which can be learned by rote.

Mētis — hard-won, discovered, evolving practical knowledge — is needed to *act,* and where the necessity for human action exists, the knowledge it allows the actor to generate comes about in a helpfully, practically reflexive manner. Scott writes,

> We might reasonably think of situated, local knowledge as being partisan knowledge as opposed to generic knowledge. That is, the holder of such knowledge typically has a passionate interest in a particular outcome. An insurer of commercial shipping for a large, highly capitalized maritime firm can afford to rely on probability distributions for accidents. But for a sailor or captain hoping for a safe voyage, it is the outcome of the single event, a single trip, that matters. Mētis is the ability and experience necessary to influence the outcome — to improve the odds — in a particular instance.

The mixed martial artist does not want to win a *moral* or an *aesthetic* victory, nor does he want to win *the hypothetical* or the *median* fight; he wants to win *this fight*. He has a passionate interest in the particular outcome of his own victory and the avoidance of the physical pain that would come with his own loss. He is deeply motivated to learn in the moment; to treat every action and reaction as an experiment that can improve his performance. He does not want merely to observe the outcome: He wants to *influence* it.

Back in Los Angeles, Rorion Gracie was looking to reach a wider audience. The family's wins against local martial arts schools spread its reputation across the valley, but not far beyond. In 1993, Rorion created the Ultimate Fighting Championship. It would have "no time limit — no rules" just like the Challenges.

Fighters from all styles would be invited. The Gracie family enlisted Royce Gracie not because he was their best but because his slim frame would make his victory even more of a statement. Royce went on to win the first UFC, defeating bigger and stronger opponents with techniques most had never seen before. BJJ's effectiveness could no longer be denied.

In the twenty-eight years since, much was established — almost none of which could have been predicted, and certainly not modeled from mathematical models of fighting. Entire arts like Aikido were shown to be ineffective and flashy striking arts like Kung-fu or karate were outcompeted by more prosaic wrestling or boxing. Arts mostly unknown a few decades ago like Brazilian Jiu Jitsu or Russian Sambo[3], both descending from judo, are now considered among the most effective. Today still, new techniques are emerging like the calf kick, which looks to cripple the opponent's leg by hitting a nerve behind the knee.

Each time two fighters step in the Octagon, an experiment ensues. Techniques from all arts are empirically tested for effectiveness. Success means victory. It is not a popularity contest, nor do authority figures decree what does and doesn't work. The mat doesn't lie, as the BJJ saying goes. Try it and see. It's the only test that matters, and only the truth will emerge.

Going for the Finish, or the Tap Out

"Stop trying to hit me and hit me!"
— Laurence Fishburne as Morpheus, *The Matrix*

The rules of the UFC have drastically increased the cost and reduced the returns of peddling fake martial arts. Bullshit artists can now be called out and the "arts" they espouse have been unequivocally shown to be ineffective. It is not enough for an art to hide behind a veneer of respectability. Authority first needs to prove itself in combat lest it be ignored or even ridiculed.

By introducing a space where fighting ideas could be empirically tested against a creative, motivated, and resisting opponent, the UFC heralded a Golden Age of discovery. The result called Mixed Martial Arts is ever evolving, never static. It is not a destination, but a process. It is not a list of techniques but a mindset to test ideas and adopt any that proves effective in combat. It took Jigoro's insight of "keeping what I felt should be kept, and discarding what I felt should be discarded" and scaled it beyond one man to a community of purposeful actors.

The UFC established new incentives to discover, preserve, and protect truth in a combative but respectful way. Even though its fights are violent affairs, it convinces through non-violent means. It appeals to reason. Unfortunately, until recently in human history non-coercive means of convincing others were necessarily social. And as such, they suffered from Karl Popper's *paradox of tolerance* where the tolerance of intolerance leads to rule of the latter. In a society of pacifists, the lone dissenter becomes the king.

Violence has only ever been prevented by one of three means: inherent human goodness, perceived benefit from cooperation, or credible or enacted threats of violence greater and more terrifying still. An appreciation for elements of all three is precisely the rationale for learning martial arts, and self-defense in general: That the good and the brave might defend not only themselves, but can cooperate with those who *cannot defend themselves*, by threatening the malicious with greater inflicted costs than they expect in illegitimate gains.

This may all sound intellectually impressive at first glance but is really nothing more than pointing out that civilization is superior to a state of nature. That the encouragement of capital and deterrent of morality (i.e., "civilization") have historically been the best and last defenses against violence has given the immoral a clear incentive: Stigmatize and ridicule morality, demonize the honest formation of capital, or infiltrate the institutions intended to support either (voluntarily established or otherwise), and their prospective violence might generate higher returns.

But now this equation features a novel variable, and one tinged with historical irony at that: After millennia of compounding technological advances taking us from the sword and shield to the longbow to the trebuchet to the handgun to the tank to the dreadnought to the fighter jet to the atomic bomb, humanity has discovered a technology that only resists and disincentivizes violence, and has no other use.

In short: Bitcoin fixes this. In long: the remainder of this book.

Chapter Two

The Complex Markets Hypothesis
Markets are subjective, uncertain, complex, stochastic,
adaptative, and fractal ... but not efficient

Modern academic economics is beholden to mathematics so complex, so obscure, and so removed from the reality it purports to describe and explain as to be effectively impervious to satire.[4] It is Poe's Law in departmental form. As investors, we, the authors, are professional capital markets participants. But in a past life, we were academically trained not in economics or finance, but in physical geography, environmental systems engineering, hydrology and water resources management, mathematics, philosophy, and computer science, across our various credentials. We believe this unusual combination of knowledge and experience gives us a worthwhile insight into why modern academic economics is such a comical disaster.

We think it is a vicious interplay of three factors, each as unfortunate as the last, each feeding and fed by the others. First: physics envy. This is well understood and is not an original insight. Second, a more specific, material effect of physics envy in this realm: It pushes academic economists to search for what can be measured and quantified, rather than what can or should be understood. Financial markets throw off torrents of data, particularly in recent decades with the advancement of computation and networked computers. Third, and as will become clearer as we develop our thesis in later chapters — in particular Chapter Five, *The Capital Stripe Mine* — financial markets are positioned directly adjacent to the fiat spigot of artificial money. The metaphor may even be more accurate if expressed as financial markets *being the spigot*. There is no other channel by which counterfeit money can be or ever is pumped into society at large. That is to say, the authors are repentant Cantillonaires, although we really are doing our best to throw off this mantle and reposition ourselves in advance of a Bitcoin standard.

The relevance of this third point — spigot proximity — is simple: funding and power. In a sense, these are really the same thing in different guises. If there are billions and billions of dollars,[5] siphoned primarily from middle-class savers none the wiser, sloshing around an industry that has grown ever more comfortable wielding covert political power, it makes eminent tactical sense for the industry to try to buy legitimacy from an unsuspecting civil society. And at what cost? Basis points, in the scheme of things? Basis points of basis points? Probably more iterations are required. Finance has become nationalized and nations have become financialized. This extractive dance leaves two symbiotic parasites thriving on whatever productive capital survives their ravaging. Tarek El Diwany writes in the preface to the third edition of *The Problem with Interest*, published just after the global financial crisis,

> No industry other than the banking industry could have raised such huge sums of capital, loans and guarantees in a few short months. That these funds should have been provided with such little conditionality is incomprehensible unless one accepts that some of the most important decisions of government are in fact taken by the banking lobby. At the height of the crisis, one leading public official at a well-known bank remarked to me that "the bankers are in the bunker with the government". Meaningful change cannot be achieved in these circumstances and one is forced to conclude that the present establishment is incapable of reforming itself.

What El Diwany describes may seem circumstantial but is only a single, specific case — one of which he was personally aware and could knowledgeably comment on — of a general issue in no way British or contemporary. When Andrew Jackson refused to recharter the Bank of the United States on philosophical and ethical grounds essentially identical to those for which we advocate in this book, the Bank called in all its loans in order to create a recession. Jackson's speech on the matter is as harrowing as it is instructive:

> The distress and alarm which pervaded and agitated the whole country when the Bank of the United States waged war upon the people in order to compel them to submit to its demands cannot yet be forgotten. The ruthless and unsparing temper with which whole cities and communities were oppressed, individuals impoverished and ruined, and a scene of cheerful prosperity suddenly changed into one of gloom and despondency ought to be indelibly impressed on the memory of the people of the United States.
> If such was its power in time of peace, what would it have been in a season of war, with an enemy at our doors? No nation but the freemen of the United States could have come out victorious from such a contest; yet, if you had no conquered, the government would have passed form the hands of the many to the few, and this organized money power, from its secret enclave, would have dictated the choice of your highest officials and compelled you to make peace or war, as best suited their own wishes.

Besides literal political corruption, an obvious yet subtler way to buy legitimacy is to infiltrate the academy and astroturf the meme that "finance" is deeply scientific, needs to be conducted by a professional managerial elite, and needs to be culturally and politically integrated with the institutions of science, engineering, and mathematics. Further, it can even be infused with any self-important thinker of deep thoughts like poets and playwrights, too, if any are up for it or need a quick buck and if none of the regular "scientists" are available. By whatever sneakily propagandistic means necessary, finance must be obfuscated into a *systemically important meta-institution* to which no respectable person would object.[6]

Spoiler alert: It is not. This is bullshit. Finance is simple, or at least it should be: You take capital from savers and pass it on to investment projects; you try not to lose it and you try to give back more. You don't get paid a lot for this because it's not hard. The end.

El Diwany brashly but justly opens the preface to the *second* edition of *The Problem with Interest* with a brief discussion of premodern medical quackery such as leeches, lack of ventilation, and urine soaking, before his segue to modern academic economics as follows:

> Orthodox views have often proved all-pervasive and wrong, even in the light of facts that state otherwise, established assumptions have an uncanny knack of surviving. It is my contention that such is the case in the field of Western economic debate today. Where once the student asked "does raising the interest rate reduce inflation?" he now askes "by how much must we raise the interest rate in order to reduce inflation?" These are the complacent assumptions of the new "consensus economics."
>
> Many developing nations now reach for the medicines that consensus recommends. But treatments involving "shock therapy" and IMF austerity packages are uncomfortably reminiscent of the remedies of the quacks: extreme in their side effects and of ambiguous benefit. Sometimes, there appears the assertion that things would be worse under any other economic regime, of course, the assertion is untenable because on can never relive the past to know the difference. Meanwhile, consensus economics extends its grasp, and society is increasingly coming to accept pollution, the business cycle, inflation and gross inequalities in wealth as the unavoidable facts of economic life.

The complacent assumptions of the new economic consensus must be, and are, zealously and unrelentingly incepted into the public consciousness in order to obfuscate that finance has gradually shifted over the twentieth century from what we might call a peer-to-peer model to a client/server model. We used to be allowed to learn by experiment by having a good old scrap with our financial competitors. Now we are told what is to be done by decree. Client/server models of *any kind of social organization* are typically objectionable on the basis of fragility, single points of failure, lack of feedback, and simple *unfairness*: Who gets to be the server? Who guards the guards? Finance now has an aesthetically minded design that patently *doesn't work*, and what's more, nobody seems to be bothered that it doesn't work, as if *working* isn't even the point. Pondering all this for any length of time leads one to realize it goes well beyond finance or economics and arrives at political and moral philosophy. El Diwany would argue it is ultimately a question of religion, and we would be hard-pressed to disagree.

It is a special case of: *Is this just?* The answer is, of course, *no, this is highly unjust*, which is why its propagandistic obfuscation is an institutional imperative. Federal Reserve board member Jeremy Rudd recently mused along the same lines, slipping in as a footnote to his September 2021 paper, "Why Do We Think That Inflation Expectations Matter for Inflation? (And Should We?)":

> I leave aside the deeper concern that the primary role of mainstream economics in our society is to provide an apologetics for a criminally oppressive, unsustainable, and unjust social order.[7]

There is unfathomable institutional power at risk over this being more widely and clearly understood. And while there is a decent case to be made that *Bitcoin fixes this*,[8] our goal in writing this book is very simply to *make this more widely and clearly understood*, such that Bitcoin can fix things *faster*. As alluded to in the acknowledgements section, the most important meme in Bitcoin is — or certainly should be, we think — *number of people go up*. Bitcoin is software, a protocol, an app, a network, a language: We will get to all of this in due course. But arguably, most importantly, it is a *community*. None are sufficient but all are necessary. We need "number of people to go up," and we hope we can contribute.

Bitcoin is peer to peer in every sense; it is so by design and it could not be any other way. As free and open source, it is peer-to-peer software; as consensus-driven software, it is a peer-to-peer protocol; as a censorship-resistant protocol, it is a peer-to-peer app; as a distributed app, it is a peer-to-peer network; as a communications network, it is a peer-to-peer language; and as a peaceful language, it is a peer-to-peer community.

The client/server fiat finance and monetary model is none of these things, cannot be any of these things, and will never be any of these things. It is a closed-source, non-consensual, censorial, centralized, incomprehensible, violent system. It is unsurprising, therefore, that its system administrators would prefer to muddy the waters on how, exactly, it all works.

In light of all this, we think that finance is a natural place to begin our analysis. This serves three distinct purposes. First, we suspect most readers are more familiar with the likes of banks, brokers, stocks, and bonds than they are with the more abstract concept of "capitalism." If so, this may be a gentler introduction before we get into the meat of our argument.

Second, we intend to shatter false idols as early and as dramatically as we possibly can. The financial services industry hides behind nonsensical mathematical obscurantism in order to shield itself from criticism from the regular people, whom it has convinced no longer really understand what they are trying to criticize and don't really know how to express their criticism in a way that even makes any sense.[9]

But this is easy: *It is nonsensical mathematical obscurantism.* This chapter will walk the reader through a forensic deconstruction of the discipline's crowning glory: the *efficient markets hypothesis* (EMH) from which *modern portfolio theory* flows and, by extension, pretty much all of contemporary academic finance. We will go into much more detail later in this chapter, but the EMH may be reasonably, if satirically, characterized as: *The price in a financial market is by definition correct.* Hopefully, the reader cringed at the flagrantly self-serving nature of this preposterous claim, never mind its illogical, epistemologically questionable, and radically unscientific form.

The third purpose of beginning with finance loops back to the first few paragraphs of this chapter: In a perversely rational attempt to satisfy misplaced physics envy, access never-ending reams of irrelevant data on which statistical analysis can nonsensically be performed, and remain as close to the money spigot as possible, modern academic economics has spontaneously reorganized itself around the kind of self-serving thinking implicit in the EMH — and academic finance around *this very idea.* Similar to our desire to ease the reader into the *subject matter,* analytically demolishing this shibboleth also serves to ease the reader into our *mental models and toolkit.* We will go on to reapply more or less the same concepts in analyzing money, financial capital, social capital, Bitcoin, and more in later chapters. We have already done so in mixed martial arts.

Our overall thesis can arguably be reduced to a handful of dichotomies contrasting approaches to the study of human action and the configuration of human relations in all their forms: design versus evolution, stasis versus dynamism, equilibrium versus process, modelling versus experimentation, trust versus verification, decree versus discovery, and rationality versus heuristics. Modern academic economists may not think they are interested in *how to price securities,* but they *are* intensely interested in designing static equilibrium models, trusting this methodology, and decreeing all else to be irrational. Hence, whether they like it or not, modern academic economists have been seduced by the idea that the question of how to price securities can even be answered.

Our argument in this chapter will go through the following propositions, which serve as headings for their own sections of discussion: Value is subjective; uncertainty is not risk; economic complexity resists equilibria; markets aggregate prices, not information; and, markets tend to leverage efficiency. We will offer commentary on Andrew Lo's *adaptive markets hypothesis,* Benoit Mandelbrot's interpretation of fractal geometry in financial markets, and George Gilder's discussion of information theory. We will also occasionally invoke the concepts of "reflexivity," as articulated by George Soros in *The Alchemy of*

Finance, and several simple heuristics such as "skin in the game" and "robustness."

This might seem like an excessive coverage list just to offer a counter to the claim that markets are "efficient," which seems pretty reasonable in and of itself. If it is at all reassuring to the reader before diving in, we don't think our thesis has five intimidating-sounding propositions, so much as one quite simple idea, from which many related propositions can be shown to follow. We think that, fundamentally, the EMH is contradicted by the implications of value being subjective, and that some basic elements of complex systems are helpful, in places, to nudge the reasoning along. If it isn't too arrogant, we think this insight can be helpfully extended to all of economics, which we will do in much of the rest of the book. And if the reader suspects this *is arrogant*, our immediate retort would likely be that this does not reflect that we are clever, but that economics is simple, albeit perhaps not easy.

As for this chapter, and helpfully referring to the split just mentioned, there is an important point we want to stress that is implicit in much of the book: Finance is utterly broken with or without Bitcoin. It has increasingly become a self-referential game that enriches only its participants by moving money yet destroying wealth. It is so desperately, irreparably broken that its insidious influence has infiltrated not just modern academic economics — as just claimed and as argued in later chapters — but, via the financialization of everything ... everything. It is as much a cancer of the discourse as of the markets. A society in which barely literate, degenerate options traders spouting garbled charlatanic bullshit are revered as purveyors of ancient wisdom is surely broken and decadent by any sound assessment. The rare few financiers who are committed to the *actually ancient and wise* practice of taking capital from savers and passing it on to investment projects, trying not to lose it and trying to give back more, sadly suffer with the rest of us. And this assumes it is even possible to perform this role successfully in the first place. Often, it is not.

Although Chapter Three, *This Is Not Capitalism*, tackles this more directly, while this chapter is really more of a theoretical debunking, we ask the reader to remember that the theory only exists in the first place to retroactively justify the practice. Incidentally, this lends itself to autobiographical detail: This is how the authors first came to appreciate Bitcoin. Before we thought it might be *possible* that Bitcoin can finance, we knew that it was *true* that finance needed to be fixed.

A common criticism of Bitcoin, albeit naïve and superficial, is that it is a solution looking for a problem. This is what we aim to debunk. The problems are terrifyingly real, and for reasons we will explain in later chapters, many lead back to money — which is to say, to finance, in one way or another. In the client/server model of finance, they are one and the same thing. The reader is encouraged to keep in the back of their mind an aphorism beloved of Bitcoiners the world over, should the following at times seem a little *too* theoretical:

Fix the money, fix the world.

Value Is Subjective

"Not everybody's gonna dig what I dig, but I reserve the right to dig it."
   — Whoopi Goldberg

You shouldn't compare apples and oranges, except that sometimes you have to, like when you are hungry. If apples and oranges are the same price, you need to make a decision that simply cannot be mathematized. You either like apples more than oranges or vice versa. And actually, even this may not be true. Maybe you know full well you like oranges, but you just feel like an apple today, or you need apples for a pie recipe for which oranges would be *très gauche*. This reasoning is readily extended in all directions — which is *objectively* better — a novel by Dickens or Austen? A hardback or an eBook by either or anybody? And what about the higher order capital goods that go into producing apples, oranges, novels, Kindles, and the like? Clearly, they are "worth" only whatever their buyer subjectively assesses as likely to be a worthwhile investment given the (again) subjective valuations of others as to the worth of apples, oranges, novels, and whatnot ....

This is all fine and dandy and readily understood since the marginal revolution of Menger, Jevons, and Walras in the 1870s rigorously refuted cost and labor theories of value. As Menger put it in, *Principles of Economics*, probably still the best theoretical introduction to economics,

> Value is thus nothing inherent in goods, no property of them, nor an independent thing existing by itself. It is a judgment economizing men make about the importance of the goods at their disposal for the maintenance of their lives and well-being. Hence value does not exist outside the consciousness of men.

Fair enough. But the first seductive trappings of the EMH come from the rarely articulated assumption that such essential subjectivity is erased in financial markets because the goods in the market are defined only in terms of cash flows. There may not be an answer as to whether apples are better than oranges, but surely $10 is better than $5? And surely $10 now is better than $10 in the future? But what about $5 now or $10 in the future?

There are (at least) two reasons this reductionism is misleading. The first comes from the mainstream treatment of temporal discounting, which is to assume that only exponential discounting can possibly be "optimal." The widespread prevalence of alternative approaches — hyperbolic discounting, for example — is then usually treated via behavioral economics, as a deviation from optimality that is evidence of irrational cognitive biases.

This has been challenged by Alex Adamou, Yonatan Berman, Diomides Mavroyiannis, and Ole Peters, in their paper, "The Microfoundations of

Discounting,"[10] in which the authors argue that the single assumption of an individual aiming to optimize the growth rate of their wealth can generate different discounting regimes that are optimal relative to the conditions by which their wealth grows in the first place. This in turn rests on the relationship between their current wealth and the payments that may be received. Sometimes the discounting that pops out is exponential, sometimes hyperbolic, sometimes something else entirely. It depends on their circumstances.

We would editorialize here that an underlying cause of confusion is that people value time itself, and, naturally, do so subjectively.[11] It may be fair enough to say that they typically want to use their time as efficiently as possible — or grow their wealth the fastest — but this is rather vacuous in isolation. Padding it out with circumstantial information immediately runs into the fact that everybody's circumstances are different. As Adamou said on Twitter shortly after the paper's first release, "Not many ninety-year-olds play the stock market." It's funny because it's true.

And it is easy to see how this result can be used as a wedge to pry open a conceptual can of worms. In financial markets, there are far more variables to compare than just the discount rate — and if we can't even assess an objective discount rate, we really are in trouble! In choosing between financial assets, we are choosing between uncertain and non-deterministic streams of future cash flows, as well as (maybe, who knows?) desiring to preserve some initial capital value. Assume these cash flows are "risky," in the sense that we can assign probabilities to their space of outcomes.[12] There can be no objective answer because different market participants could easily have different risk preferences, exposure preferences, liquidity needs, time frames, and so on.

Time frames are worth dwelling on for a second longer because this points to an ill definition in our hasty setup of the problem: To what space of outcomes are we assigning probabilities, exactly? Financial markets do not have an end point, so this makes no sense on the face of it. If we amend by suggesting (clearly ludicrously) that the probabilities are well defined for every interval's end point, *forever*, then we invite the obvious criticism that different participants may care about different sequences of intervals. Particularly if their different discount rates (which we admitted they must have) have a different effect on how far in the future cash flows have to come to be discounted back to a value that is negligible in the present. Once again, people value *time itself subjectively.*

In the readily understood language employed just above, market participants almost certainly have different *circumstances* to one another, from which different subjective valuations will naturally emerge. What seems to you like a stupidly low price at which to sell an asset might be ideal for the seller because they are facing a margin call elsewhere in their portfolio,[13] or because they hold too much of this asset for their liking and want to rebalance their exposure. Or perhaps some price might seem stupidly high to buy, but the buyer has a funding gap so large that they need to invest in something that has a non-zero probability of appreciating by that much. If you *need* to double your money, then the "risk-free asset" is infinitely risky. There is no right answer, because value is subjective.

Uncertainty Is Not Risk

"Many idle controversies involving the nature of expectation could be avoided by recognizing at the outset that man's conscious actions are the reflection of his beliefs and nothing else."
— Nicholas Georgescu-Roegen, "The Nature of Expectation and Uncertainty"

"Risk" characterizes a non-deterministic system for which the space of possible outcomes can be assigned probabilities. Expected values are meaningful and hence prices, if they exist in such a system, lend themselves to effective hedging. "Uncertainty" characterizes a non-deterministic system for which probabilities *cannot* be assigned to the space of outcomes. Uncertain outcomes cannot be hedged. The proposition is meaningless.[14] This distinction in economics is usually credited to Frank Knight and his wonderful 1921 book, *Risk, Uncertainty, and Profit.* In the introduction, Knight writes,

It will appear that a measurable uncertainty, or "risk" proper, as we shall use the term, is so far different from an unmeasurable one that it is not in effect an uncertainty at all. We shall accordingly restrict the term "uncertainty" to cases of the non-quantitative type. It is this "true" uncertainty, and not risk, as has been argued, which forms the basis of a valid theory of profit and accounts for the divergence between actual and theoretical competition.

Keynes is often also credited an excellent exposition,

By "uncertain" knowledge, let me explain, I do not mean merely to distinguish what is known for certain from what is only probable. The game of roulette is not subject, in this sense, to uncertainty [...] Or, again, the expectation of life is only slightly uncertain. Even the weather is only moderately uncertain. The sense in which I am using the term is that in which the prospect of a European war is uncertain, or the price of copper and the rate of interest twenty years hence, or the obsolescence of a new invention, or the position of private wealth owners in the social system in 1970. About these matters there is no scientific basis on which to form any calculable probability whatever. We simply do not know. Nevertheless, the necessity for action and for decision compels us as practical men to do our best to overlook this awkward fact and to behave exactly as we should if we had behind us a good Benthamite calculation of a series of prospective advantages and disadvantages, each multiplied by its appropriate probability, waiting to be summed.[15]

The conclusion of the Keynes passage is particularly helpful as it gets at why it is so important to be clear on the difference, which otherwise might seem like little more than semantics: People need to act. They will strive for a basis to treat uncertainty as if it were risk so as to tackle it more easily, but however successful they are or are not, they must act nonetheless.

Knight hints at the direction of the argument of *Risk, Uncertainty, and Profit*, which we will summarize here: Profit is the essence of competitive uncertainty. Were there no uncertainty, but merely quantifiable risk in patterns of production and consumption, competition would drive all prices to a stable and commoditized equilibrium. In financial vocabulary, we would say there would be no such thing as a *sustainable competitive advantage*. The cost of capital would be the risk-free rate, as would all returns on capital, meaning profit would be minimized. In aggregate, profit would function merely as a kind of force pulling all economic activity to this precise point of strong attraction.

But of course, uncertainty is very real. In the economic realm uncertainty is a direct consequence of subjective value; in engaging in pursuing profit, you are guessing what others will value. As Knight later writes, "With uncertainty present, doing things, the actual execution of activity, becomes in a real sense a secondary part of life; the primary problem or function is deciding what to do and how to do it."

So far, we have danced around the keyword and concept here, but this "deciding what to do and how to do it," and "pursuing profit," we call *entrepreneurship*. In a world with uncertainty, the role of the entrepreneur is to shoulder the uncertainty of untried combinations of capital, the success of which will ultimately be dependent on the subjective valuations of others. This is not something that can be calculated, simulated, or *modeled*, as any entrepreneur will tell you.[16] It is a process of dynamic discovery. As Ross Emmett noted in his centennial review of *Risk, Uncertainty, and Profit*, it is no coincidence that the word "judgment" appears on average every two pages in the book.[17]

You can't just *imagine* starting a business; you have to actually do it in order to learn anything. And, in order to do it, you have to expose yourself to your own successes and failures. Your experiment changes the system in which you are experimenting, and you will inevitably have a stake in the experiment's result.[18] This is fertile ground in which to plant Soros's theory of reflexivity. As briefly as possible, and certainly not doing it justice, Soros believes that financial markets are fundamentally resistant to truly scientific analysis, because they can only be fully understood in such a way that acknowledges the fact that thinking about the system influences the system. He writes that the scientific method,

> Is clearly not applicable to reflexive situations because even if all the observable facts are identical, the prevailing views of the participants are liable to be different when an experiment is repeated. The very fact that an experiment has been conducted is liable to change the

perceptions of the participants. Yet, without testing, generalizations cannot be falsified.[19]

All potential entrepreneurial activity is uncertain (by definition), but the fact of engaging in it crystallizes the knowledge of its success or failure. The subjective valuations on which its success depends are revealed by the experiment, and you can't repeat the experiment pretending you don't now know this information. Alternatively, this can be conceived of in terms of the difference between thinking and acting, or talking and doing. In a reflexive environment, you can't say *what would have happened had you done something*, because, had you done it, you would have changed the circumstances that lead to you now claiming you would have done it. As Yogi Berra (allegedly) said, "In theory there is no difference between theory and practice, but in practice, there is."

We can also now invoke "skin in the game," a phrase of dubious origin — possibly originating in a 1986 Wall Street Journal article[20] — and indicating a financial stake of some or other kind, exposing somebody to the consequences of their actions, good or both. "Skin in the game" is often advocated for in both a moral sense of those making the decisions deserving the outcome, but also in the sense of optimal system design, in that such an arrangement encourages people to behave the most prudently out of all possible incentive schemes. Braving the wild uncertainties of entrepreneurship requires capital. It requires a stake on which the entrepreneur *might* get the upside of profit but *might* get the downside of loss. We say "might" because you cannot possibly know the odds of such a wager. It relies not on risk but on uncertainty.

The combined appreciation of "judgment" and "skin in the game" is key to understanding what entrepreneurs are actually *doing*. They do not merely throw capital into a combinatorial vacuum; they are intuiting the wants and needs of potential customers. As the economist Alex Tabarrok says, "a bet is a tax on bullshit. Or, don't talk: do."

The aforementioned Emmett review of *Risk, Uncertainty, and Profit* also noted that the very concept of *Knightian uncertainty* re-emerged in the public consciousness around a decade ago due to two events: The role ironically played by financial risk instruments in the financial crisis, which neo-classical economists had up until that point insisted would reduce uncertainty in markets,[21] and Twitter celebrity and former practitioner of late-stage fiat finance Nassim Taleb publishing the bestseller *The Black Swan*. Emmett writes,

> Taleb did not suggest that uncertainty could be handled by risk markets. Instead, he made a very Knightian argument: since you cannot protect yourself entirely against uncertainty, you should build robustness into your personal life, your company, your economic theory, and even the institutions of your society, to withstand uncertainty and avoid tragic

results. These actions imply costs that may limit other aspects of your business, and even your openness to new opportunity.

But enough about entrepreneurship, what about financial markets? Well, financial markets are readily understood as one degree removed from entrepreneurship. With adequate mental flexibility, the reader can think of them as markets for negotiable *fractions* of entrepreneurial activity. Entrepreneurship-by-proxy, we might say. If you want, you can use them to mimic the uncertainty profile of an entrepreneur: Your "portfolio" could be 100% the equity of the company you wish you founded. Or 200%, with leverage, if you are really gung-ho! But most people think precisely the opposite way: Markets present the opportunity to tame the rabid uncertainty of entrepreneurship, as it always naturally exists in isolation, and skim some portion of its aggregate benefit.[22]

There is an additional complication. The fact of such markets usually being liquid enough to enable widespread ownership creates the incentive to think not about the underlying entrepreneurship at all, but only about the expectations of other market participants — to ignore the fundamentals and consider only the valuation. There are shades of Soros's reflexivity here. The market depends to some extent on the thinking of those participating in the market *about* the market. This is sometimes called a Keynesian beauty contest, after Keynes's analogy of judging a beauty contest not on the basis of who you think is most beautiful, but on the basis of who you think others will think is the most beautiful. If everybody is doing that, then you really need to judge on the basis of who you think others will think ... others will think — and so on — is the most beautiful.

Unlike the entrepreneur, who must only worry about the subjective valuation of his potential customers, participants in financial markets must worry, in addition, about the subjective valuation *of this subjective valuation* by other market participants. This might induce grumbling at this point that this represents "speculation" as opposed to "investment," and we certainly believe that, over time periods long enough to reflect real economic activity allowed for by the investments, such concerns will make less and less of a difference. As Benjamin Graham famously said, "In the short run, the market is a voting machine, but in the long run, it is a weighing machine." But the voting still happens. It is clearly real and needs to be accounted for. Risk is once again useless. Uncertainty abounds.

This range of possibilities is intriguing and points to a deeper understanding of what financial markets really *are*: The aim of a great deal of finance is to grapple with the totality of uncertainty inherent in entrepreneurial activity — equally well understood as "investment of capital," given the need for a "stake" — by partitioning it into different exposures that can sensibly be described as *relatively* more or less "risky." The aim of doing so is generally to minimize the cost of capital going towards real investment by tailoring the packaging of uncertainty to the "risk profiles" of those willing to invest, as balanced by escalating transaction costs if this process becomes too fine-grained.

This is the essence of a capital structure: The more senior the capital claim, the better defined the probability space of outcomes for that instrument. Uncertainty in aggregate cannot be altered, nor can its influence be completely removed from individual instruments, but exposure to uncertainty can be unevenly parceled out amongst instruments.

This suggests a far more sophisticated understanding of "the risk/reward trade-off" and "the equity premium" than is generally accepted in the realm of modern portfolio theory, and, by extension, the EMH: Bonds are likely to get a lower return than stocks not because they are less "risky" (which in that context is even more questionably interpreted as "less volatile"), but because they are engineered to be less uncertain. The burden of uncertainty is deliberately shifted from debt to equity. You don't get a "higher reward" for taking on the "risk/volatility" of equities; you deliberately expose yourself to the uncertain *possibility* of a greater reward in exchange for accepting an uncertain possibility of a greater loss.

It is worth pondering for a second that this is arguably why the "equity risk premium" even exists and why modern academic economists are so confused about how much it differs from what their models and theories predict, while financial professionals are not in the slightest. If there really were no uncertainty in investment and every enterprise — and hence every financial instrument linked to it — had a modellable risk profile, then price discrepancies derivable from expectation values could be arbitraged away. There would be no equity risk premium nor a risk premium of any kind on any asset. Everything would be priced correctly and volatility would be zero. That volatility is *never* zero clearly invalidates this idea. We suggest that the distinction between risk and uncertainty provides at least part of the explanation: Unless, by remarkable coincidence, every market participant's opportunity costs (of exposure, liquidity, time, etc.) and perception of uncertainty (of fundamentals, others' perceptions of fundamentals, others' perceptions of others' perceptions, etc.) is all identical, and remains so over a period of time, price-altering trading will occur.[23]

An important formal concept to appreciate in the context of uncertainty is that of "heuristics." This is a worthwhile loose end to tie up before moving on from uncertainty, along with that of, "randomness and unpredictability."

This is quite a simple idea that originates with Herbert Simon and has been taken up with force more recently by Gerd Gigerenzer.[24] Simon's framing began by assuming that individuals do not, in fact, have perfect information, nor the resources to compute perfectly optimal decisions. Given these constraints, Simon proposed that individuals demonstrate *bounded rationality*; they will be as rational as they can, given the information and resources they actually have. This probably sounds straightforward enough — perhaps tautological — but notice it flies in the face of behavioral economics, which tends to cover for neo-classical economics by saying, effectively, that since information and competition are perfect, risk is always defined and the optimal decision can always be calculated, but the reason people don't do so is that they are hopelessly irrational. We have always thought this is quite silly on the face of it, but it is clearly also seductive. Anybody reading the likes of *Thinking, Fast and Slow* immediately gets the intellectual rush of thinking everybody is stupid except themselves.

Bounded rationality encourages the development of "heuristics," with which the reader may be familiar, if only due to behavioral economists frequently railing against the concept. A heuristic is a rule of thumb for dealing with an uncertain environment that you are pretty sure will work even if you can't explain why, precisely. The classic example is that of a dog and a frisbee, or an outfielder in baseball catching a flyball: The outfielder *could* solve enough differential equations to calculate the spot the ball will land, but the dog certainly can't. And it turns out that neither do: In real life, they adjust their running speed and direction such that the angle at which they see the frisbee or ball stays constant. And it works. No equations required.

The implied simplicity of heuristics has subtle mathematical importance as well. A more technical way of specifying this is to say that they have very few parameters — discrete, independent information inputs to the decision procedure — and, ideally, they could even have zero. In a purely risky environment, a decision procedure ought to have *as many* parameters as are needed to accurately model the underlying probability distribution. But the more uncertainty you add to such an environment, the more dangerous this becomes, essentially because what you are doing is fine-tuning your model to an environment that simply no longer exists. Eventually you will get an unforeseen and unforeseeable fluctuation so large that your overfitted model gives you a truly awful suggestion.

Heuristics are *robust* to such circumstances in light of having very few parameters to begin with. Think back to the outfielder: Imagine they solve all the necessary fluid dynamical equations, taking account of the fly ball's mass, velocity, and rotation; the air's viscosity; the turbulence generated; and so on and so forth. If there is then a gust of wind, they're screwed. Their calculation will be completely wrong. But if they embrace the heuristic of *just looking at the damn ball* this won't matter!

Gigerenzer is fond of pointing out that Harry Markowitz — considered the founder of modern portfolio theory — didn't actually use any Nobel Prize–winning modern portfolio theory for his own retirement portfolio; he used the zero-parameter 1/n approach. If one were being especially mean-spirited, one might say that he didn't want his own bullshit to be taxed. And as it turns out, in order for the Markowitz many-many-many-parameter approach to investing to consistently outperform 1/n, you would need around 500 years of data to fine-tune the parameters. Of course, you also need the market to *not change at all* in that time. Good luck with that.

Since markets feature multitudes of interrelated uncertainties, it is reasonable to expect participants to interact with them not with the perfect rationality of provably optimal behavior, but with the bounded rationality of heuristics, which are selected on the basis of judgment, intuition, creativity, etc. Basically, people mostly are not stupid. And if they are, they have skin in the game, so they get punished and possibly wiped out. To paraphrase John Kay and Melvyn King's discussion in *Radical Uncertainty*, organizations that understand the irreducibility of uncertainty focus on resilience and adaptability. They aim to at least survive and ideally benefit from uncertainty. Those that believe in the neo-classical model of rational expectations emphasize forecast accuracy and operational efficiency. The Global Financial Crisis empirically demonstrated how brittle a banking system guided by complex risk models really was.

A cute conceptual corollary to *risk is not uncertainty* is, *unpredictability is not randomness*. There can be unpredictable events that are not random, and randomness that is not unpredictable. And, moreover, we would argue these are not even binaries, nor ends of a spectrum, but strictly untranslatable given uncertainty is a psychological characteristic and randomness a mathematical one. The random can be so fundamentally complex as to only be comprehensible by a human mind as uncertain, and the uncertain can defy modelling as random because it is more than merely complicated: It is creative, intuitive, *human*.

The difference essentially comes down to *causation* — a concept with which modern academic economists are deeply uncomfortable — and the ability of humans to intuit causation and confirm their intuition via sound experimentation. Think of biological evolution, to which we will return as a useful metaphor several times. This is, strictly speaking, a random process. Genes do not *think*. Yet, the mechanism by which a given species evolves is so incomprehensibly complicated that any *human* attempt to treat it as "random" — to model it and to deduce and statistically quantify its potential paths — cannot be taken seriously.

Or think of Keynes's example of the obsolescence of a new invention. This is "unpredictable" not because it is subject to an extremely complicated probability density function, but because the path of causation that would lead to such a situation involves such obvious genuine uncertainty as to defy probabilistic causality. Or think even of the bitcoin mining process. The time series of the first non-zero character in the hash of every block is certifiably random, but it is not unpredictably random. It is the result of a highly coordinated and purposeful effort. Because we understand the causal process by which this time series emerges, we can predict this randomness very effectively.

A key building block of the EMH is the "random walk hypothesis": The idea that you can "prove," using statistical methods, that stock prices follow "random walks" — a kind of well-defined and genuinely random mathematical behavior. But you can do no such thing. You can prove that they are *indistinguishable* from random walks, but that is really just saying you can use a statistical test to prove that some data can pass a statistical test. If you *understand* what *causes* price movements, you will arrive at no such nonsense as claiming that the moves are, themselves, random. They very probably *look* random because they are fundamentally unpredictable from the data. And they are fundamentally unpredictable from the data, because they derive from the incalculable interplay of millions of market participants' subjective assessments of the at-root uncertain process of entrepreneurship.

None of this is based on randomness, nor "risk," nor "luck." It is based on the unknown and unknowable reinvested profit that results from intuiting the results of untried and unrepeatable experiments and backing one's intuition with skin in the game.

Before moving on, we think it is worth tying all of this to where it is more tangibly sensible. A big deal was made around the turn of 2020 about Netflix being by far the best performing US mid-to-large-cap stock of the 2010s. Netflix is useful as an example because of the scale of its success, but note the following argument does not depend on scale at all. While the reader could craft an explanation as complicated as they like, we think saying, *streaming is better than cable*, pretty much does it, once added to all the circumstantial factors to do with the competitive and technological environment.

Now imagine an investor in 2010 whose thesis was that streaming is better than cable and would likely win in the long run, who surveyed the competitive environment, and decided Netflix would be a good investment. Is their outperformance over the next ten years "luck"? Was all the "information" "in the price" in 2010? Would the Capital Asset Pricing model have told them what the price *should* have been? Did the stock go for a nice little random walk to the moon?

This is clearly an insane interpretation. Consider the alternative: The investor better intuited the subjective values of future consumers than did the average market participant. Very likely they justified this on the basis of a heuristic or two. They staked capital on this bet — which was not risky and random but uncertain and unpredictable — and exposed themselves to a payoff that turned out to be huge, *because they were right*! And for that matter, all successful long-term investments can frankly be reduced to *one parameter* (how's that for a heuristic?): *X is going to change.*

For Netflix, X was "the consumption of video content." For Amazon, X was "the default choice for consumer purchasing." For Bitcoin, X was, and still is, "money." One *could* model absolutely everything under the sun and pop out the "correct" price of Netflix on February 9, 2034, but one needn't do so — and for that matter, one probably shouldn't. A little numeracy certainly wouldn't hurt, but, otherwise, judgment, intuition, creativity, and heuristics will do just fine.

To the peddlers of the EMH, rational expectations, perfect information, and the like, this obviously sensible interpretation is utterly heretical.

Economic Complexity Resists Equilibria

"In equilibrium systems, everything adds up nicely and linearly. It is trivial to generalize to many agents; this simply corresponds to connecting more glasses of water. The effect on the water level from adding several drops of water is proportional to the number of drops. One does not have to think about the individual drops. In physics, we refer to this kind of treatment where only a global macrovariable, such as the water level, is considered as a "mean field approximation." Traditional economic theories are mean field theories in that they deal with macrovariables, such as the gross national product (GNP), the unemployment rate, and the interest rate. Economists develop mathematical equations that are supposed to connect these variables. The differences in individual behaviour average out in this kind of treatment. No historical accident can change the equilibrium state, since the behaviour of rational agents is unique and completely defined. Mean field treatments work quite well in physics for systems that are either very ordered or very disordered. However, they completely fail for systems that are at or near a critical state. Unfortunately, there are many indications that economics systems are in fact critical."

— Per Bak, *How Nature Works*

The link between profit and entrepreneurship can be tugged at ever-so-slightly further and invites a brief detour into the basics of complex systems. The argument goes more or less as follows: The discussion on uncertainty needn't be interpreted as a call to abandon mathematical analysis altogether — just the sloppy mathematics of risk and randomness that has no connection to the real world. There is an alternative mathematical approach, however, which directly addresses and contradicts the standard neoclassical formalism.

Israel Kirzner is widely considered one of the foremost scholars of entrepreneurship. One of Kirzner's theses in his best-known book, *Competition and Entrepreneurship*, is a positive argument that has roughly two parts, as follows: First, entrepreneurship is by its nature non-exclusionary. It is a price discrepancy between the costs of available factors of production and the revenues to be gained by employing them in a particular way — aka profit. In other words, it is perfectly competitive. It does not rely on any privileged position with respect to access to assets; the assets are presumed to be available on the market. They are just not yet employed in that way, but could be, with capital that is presumably homogeneous.[25] Anybody could do so. The only barrier is that of the willingness to judge and stake on uncertainty. He writes, "The entrepreneur's activity is essentially competitive. And thus, competition is inherent in the nature of the entrepreneurial market process. Or, to put it the other way around, entrepreneurship is inherent in the competitive market process."

This notion of what "competition" really means is highly antithetical to the neo-classical usage. In fact, it is more or less the exact opposite. Rather than meaning something like "tending towards abnormal profit and hence away from equilibrium," the neo-classicals mean "tending towards equilibrium and hence away from abnormal profit." Kirzner bemoans this,

> Clearly, if a state of affairs is to be labelled competitive, and if this label is to bear any relation to the layman's use of the term, the term must mean either a state of affairs from which competitive activity (in the layman's sense) is to be expected or a state of affairs that is the consequence of competitive activity […] [Yet] competition, to the equilibrium price theorist, turned out to refer to a state of affairs into which so many competing participants have already entered that no room remains for additional entry (or other modification of existing market conditions). The most unfortunate aspect of this use of the term "competition"; is of course that, by referring to the situation in which no room remains for further steps in the competitive market process, the word has come to be understood as the very opposite of the kind of activity of which that process consists. Thus, as we shall discover, any real-world departure from equilibrium conditions came to be stamped as the opposite of "competitive" and hence, by simple extension, as actually "monopolistic."[26]

Kirzner's second positive argument is that correcting this conceptual blunder leads one to realize that a realistic description of competitive markets would be not as constantly at equilibrium, but rather as constantly *out of equilibrium*. As Ludwig von Mises is well known for saying in his English lectures at NYU, in a rather thick Austrian accent, *"zee mahket eez a process!"* We might equivalently say they are not *linear* — they do not have a multivariate solution — but rather that they are *complex*.

Complex systems are commonly associated with the Santa Fe Institute (SFI) and popularized by W. Mitchell Waldrop's fantastic popular science book, *Complexity*. Waldrop focuses, for the most part, on one of the SFI's first-ever workshops held between a group of physicists and economists in 1987. Our thinking here comes from the very first paper of the workshop, W. Brian Arthur's now somewhat infamous work on increasing returns.[27] To get a sense of what we mean by "infamous," consider the following from Waldrop:

> Arthur had convinced himself that increasing returns pointed the way to the future for economics, a future in which he and his colleagues would work alongside the physicists and the biologists to understand the messiness, the upheaval, and the spontaneous self-organization of the

world. He'd convinced himself that increasing returns could be the foundation for a new and very different kind of economic science. Unfortunately, however, he hadn't much luck convincing anybody else. Outside of his immediate circle at Stanford, most economists thought his ideas were — strange. Journal editors were telling him that this increasing-returns stuff "wasn't economics." In seminars, a good fraction of the audience reacted with outrage: how dare he suggest that the economy was not in equilibrium!

Arthur's paper at the workshop, *Self-Reinforcing Mechanisms in Economics*, is a breath of fresh air for anybody who has had the displeasure of slogging through the incessant cargo cult math of modern academic economics. It is frankly just all so sensible! Sure, there are a few differential equations, but only after ten pages of things that are obviously true, and only to try to frame the obviously true observations in the absurd formalism of the degenerate economic mainstream.

To begin with "conventional economic theory is built largely on the assumption of diminishing returns on the margin (local negative feedbacks); and so, it may seem that positive feedback, increasing-returns-on-the-margin mechanisms ought to be rare." Mainstream economic theory assumes competition pushes all into equilibrium, from which a deviation is punished by the negative feedback of reduced profits. So far, so good.

> Self-reinforcement goes under different labels in these different parts of economics: increasing returns; cumulative causation; deviation-amplifying mutual causal processes; virtuous and vicious circles; threshold effects; and non-convexity. The sources vary. But usually self-reinforcing mechanisms are variants of or derive from four generic sources: large set-up or fixed costs (which give the advantage of falling unit costs to increased output); learning effects (which act to improve products or lower their cost as their prevalence increases); coordination effects (which confer advantages to "going along" with other economics agents taking similar action); and adaptive expectations (where increased prevalence on the market enhances beliefs of further prevalence).

Now we are getting into the meat of it. An example or two wouldn't hurt before applying this to entrepreneurship and markets.

Arthur likes Betamax versus VHS, which is a particularly good example in hindsight because we know that VHS won despite being mildly technologically inferior. Point number one: If a manufacturer of VHS tapes spends an enormous amount on the biggest VHS (or Betamax) factory in the world, then the marginal costs of producing VHS will be lower from that point on. Even if the factory as a whole is loss making, the costs are sunk, and so the incentive is to pump out VHS by the gallon. The fact that this can be done so cheaply makes consumers more likely to choose VHS over Betamax, which will in turn justify the initial expense and contribute positive feedback (via profit).

Point number two: Doing so may give the owner of the factory the experience to learn how to do so even more efficiently in the future. By the same eventual mechanism as above, this contributes positive feedback via lower prices.[28]

Points number three and four: If more people seem to be buying VHS tapes than Betamax, then producers of Betamax *players* are incentivized to shift production towards VHS players instead. Cheaper VHS players incentivize consumers to buy more VHS *tapes*. The *appearance* of VHS winning this battle causes economic agents to adapt their behavior in such a way that makes VHS more likely to *actually* win.[29] Arthur writes,

> If Betamax and its rival VHS compete, a small lead in market share gained by one of the technologies may enhance its competitive position and help it further increase its lead. There is positive feedback. If both systems start out at the same time, market shares may fluctuate at the outset, as external circumstances and "luck" change, and as backers manoeuvre for advantage. And if the self-reinforcing mechanism is strong enough, eventually one of the two technologies may accumulate enough advantage to take 100% of the market. Notice however we cannot say in advance which one this will be.

While Arthur mostly considers realistic examples in economics which have discrete end states that are then "locked into," such as settling on VHS over Betamax, or Silicon Valley over Massachusetts Route 128, our contention would be that every one of these features describes a part of the process of entrepreneurial competition. The fact of staking capital at all towards an uncertain end represents a fixed cost which must be matched by competitors, and after which, unit costs fall.

As we have mentioned several times, entrepreneurs learn from the result of their experiments and improve their own processes. There is a clear coordination effect for customers in the default assumption of doing whatever other customers are doing. And adaptive expectations are likewise fairly straightforwardly applied: We tend to assume that businesses will continue to exist and that we can continue to act as their customers. Businesses tend to assume the same of their customers within reasonable bounds of caution. The specific positive feedback as a result of each individual effect is that of "profit" — it is positive in the sense that it can be reinvested in the enterprise and allow it to grow.

Of course, it is possible that these effects would diminish and the marginal feedback become negative. But what we are more tangibly proposing here is that any once-existing competitive advantage has been completely eroded away. This only happens when the product itself becomes either obsolete in light of a superior competitor or completely commoditized. The former is simply more of the same at the macro level, but the latter we can in turn explain by uncertainty becoming so minimal that we can more or less safely assume it is merely risk. Such circumstances are few and far between. Uncertainty is prevalent in all aspects of economic life, as we have discussed. So, too, are increasing returns and positive feedback loops.

To bring in Arthur one last time:

> If self-reinforcement is not offset by countervailing forces, local positive feedbacks are present. In turn, these imply that deviations from certain states are amplified. These states are therefore unstable. If the vector-field associated with the system is smooth and if its critical points — its "equilibria" — lie in the interior of some manifold, standard Poincaré-index topological arguments imply the existence of other critical points or cycles that are stable, or attractors. In this case multiple equilibria must occur. Of course, there is no reason that the number of these should be small. Schelling gives the practical example of people seating themselves in an auditorium, each with the desire to sit beside others. Here the number of steady-states or "equilibria" would be combinatorial.

Recall there is no way to know from the starting point which steady state will be settled into. And of course, Arthur is only talking about specific economic circumstances, not the aggregate of all economic behavior. The aggregate will likely have shades of evolution in a competitive environment (another concept we will soon encounter in more detail): Many, many such interdependent sub-systems, always moving towards their own steady state, but almost all never getting there. There is a solid mathematical basis to saying that economic behavior in aggregate is wildly uncertain.[30]

Moreover, there is also a solid mathematical basis to saying that the standard neo-classical formalisms are meaningless gibberish dressed up to *look like* science. It betrays a concern only for superficial visual pleasure at the expense of even *attempting* to understand the mess of order and causation embedded in the system.[31] William Whyte excoriates the idea of reducing even *all of man's social behavior* to a *"finite, embracing science,"* never mind just his economic activity, in *The Organization Man*, writing,

> Part of the trouble lies in our new-found ability to measure more precisely, and the idea that the successes of natural science were due in large measure to the objectiveness of the phenomena studied eludes social engineers. There are, of course, aspects of man's behavior that we can properly measure and we learn much by doing so. But how fascinating, alas, it all is! Here, it would seem, we can at last be rid of the bugbear of values. The median income level of a hundred selected families in an urban industrial universe correlated .76 with population density — not .78 or .61 but .76, and that's a fact. The next step beckons: having measured this far, it seems there is nothing that can't be

measured. We are purged of bias, and somehow by the sheer accumulation of such bias-free findings, we will have the basis of a theoretical formula that describes all. Just like physics.

Contrary to the endlessly proliferating theorems on theorems on theorems of modern academic economics, we contend that the most important mathematical result in the history of economics is Henri Poincaré's proof of the insolubility of the three-body problem. Properly understood, it shows that all mathematical results besides itself are not important in economics and are likely dangerous. To produce relevant *theorems*, one must have a well-founded *theory*. And yet, if the purely mechanical dynamics of *n* spherical cows in a vacuum cannot be solved for *n* greater than or equal to three, then it seems rather unlikely that the physical *and psychological* dynamics of *all human activity* can be meaningfully solved for either.

The authors advise this not even be attempted. The economist who couches his incomprehensible model of nothing whatsoever with such caveats as "*all else equal*," or "*holding these factors constant*," reveals first and foremost his mathematical illiteracy, for he is attempting to model the kind of thing for which such caveats graduate his model from wrong to *not even wrong*. Or, to quote Nobel Prize–winning theoretical physicist and founder of the study of complexity science, Murray Gell-Mann, "Imagine how difficult physics would be if particles could think."

Markets Aggregate Prices, Not Information

"How happy is the blameless vestal's lot!
The world forgetting, by the world forgot.
Eternal sunshine of the spotless mind!
Each pray'r accepted, and each wish resign'd."
— Alexander Pope, "Eloisa to Abelard"

Even the framing of the EMH is nonsensical. You don't really need to get into subjective value, uncertainty, complex systems, and so on, to realize that in reading the proposition, *prices reflect all available information,* you have already been hoodwinked. What does "reflect" mean?

A common and dramatic improvement upon this can be made by suggesting instead that markets *aggregate information.* We noticed this is typical of many more enlightened critiques of EMH, and it serves as a far better starting point in at least *suggesting* a mechanism by which the mysterious link between information and price might be instantiated. Unfortunately, we think the mechanism suggested is simply invalid. It is not realistic at all and it implicitly encourages a dramatic misunderstanding of what prices really are and where they come from.

In making sense of this, we have to assume some kind of "function" from the space of information to price. We think it is acceptable to mean this metaphorically for the sake of exposition, without implying the quasi-metaphysical existence of some such force. We might really mean something like, *the market behaves as if operating according to such and such a function* or, *such and such a function is a reasonable low-resolution approximation of market dynamics.* Adam Smith's famed *invisible hand* is an instructive comparison. For the time being, we will talk as if some such function *exists.*

We can maybe imagine information as existing as a vector in an incredibly high-dimensional space, at least as compared to price, which is clearly one dimensional. We could even account for the multitudes of uncertainty we have already learned to accept by suggesting that each individual's subjective understanding of all the relevant factors and/or ignorance of many of them constitutes a unique mapping of this space to itself, such that the *true information vector* is transformed into something more personal for each market participant. Perhaps individuals then bring this personal information vector to the market, and what the market does is *aggregate* all the vectors by finding the average.[32] Finally, the market *projects* this n-dimensional average vector onto the single dimension of price. If you accept the metaphorical nature of all these functions, we can admit this model has some intuitive appeal, in the vein of James Surowiecki's *The Wisdom of Crowds.*

The problem is that this is clearly not how anybody actually interacts with markets. You don't submit your n-dimensional information/intention vector; you submit your one-dimensional price. That's it. The market aggregates these one-dimensional price submissions in real time by matching the flow of marginal bids and asks. This understanding captures the mechanics of how we know price discovery in markets *actually works*. There is no mysterious, market-wide canonical projection function — no inexplicable "prices reflect information" — there are just prices, volumes, and the continuous move towards clearing.

This understanding also implies a perfectly satisfactory and not at all mysterious source of the projection of information into price: Individuals who make judgments and act. Any supposedly relevant "information" is subject both to opportunity cost and uncertainty. Individuals alone know the importance of their opportunity costs, and individuals alone engage with uncertainty with heuristics, judgment, and staking. If individuals are wrong, they learn. If they are very wrong, they are wiped out. Effective heuristics live to fight another day.

We are genuinely surprised that this confusion continues to exist in the realm of the EMH, given that, as far as we are concerned, Friedrich Hayek cleared it up in its entirety in *The Use of Knowledge in Society*. A superficial reading of Hayek's ingenious essay might lead one to believe something like *prices reflect information*. But, to anachronistically borrow our function metaphor once more, Hayek points out that the projection from the n-dimensions of information to the one dimension of price *destroys an enormous amount of information*. Which is the whole point!

Individuals are incapable of understanding *the entirety of information in the world*. Even the entirety of individuals is incapable of this. Thanks to the existence of markets, nobody has to. They need only know about prices. "Perfect information" is once again shown to be an absurdity. Of the "man on the spot," whom we might hope would make a sensible decision about resource allocation,

> There is hardly anything that happens anywhere in the world that might not have an effect on the decision he ought to make. But he need not know of these events as such, nor of all their effects. It does not matter for him why at the particular moment more screws of one size than of another are wanted, why paper bags are more readily available than canvas bags, or why skilled labor, or particular machine tools, have for the moment become more difficult to obtain. All that is significant for him is how much more or less difficult to procure they have become compared with other things with which he is also concerned, or how much more or less urgently wanted are the alternative things he produces or uses. It is always a question of the relative importance of the particular things with which he is concerned, and the causes which alter their relative importance are of no interest to him beyond the effect on those concrete things of his own environment.

Hayek proposes this be resolved by the price mechanism:

> Fundamentally, in a system in which the knowledge of the relevant facts is dispersed among many people, prices can act to coordinate the separate actions of different people in the same way as subjective values help the individual to coordinate the parts of his plan.

Perhaps ironically, this points to the only sensible way in which markets *can* be called "efficient." They are efficient with respect to the information they manipulate and convey: As a one-dimensional price, it is the absolute minimum required for participants to interpret and sensibly respond. Markets have excellent social scalability;[33] they are the original *distributed systems*, around long before anybody thought to coin that expression.

There is a kind of amusing category error at play in the degenerate mainstream understanding that this explanation dissolves entirely: It is fashionable and faux profound to say that "prices are information" — and this is true, in a sense. Prices *are* a form of information, but we can get at the root of the problem by observing that information is not a form of price. Therefore, it is fallacious to interpret the "are" in "prices are information" as a bijective relationship and is precisely what forces us to have to try to take the nonsense of *market-wide canonical projection functions*, and so on, seriously.

Provided with information, individuals can, and do, produce a price. But given a price, nobody — never mind a third-party observer or even the entire market — can (re)produce the information that created it. And this is the whole point. The "function" from information to price is not random, not ill-defined, and certainly not an "aggregation." Rather, it is a very specific kind that serves a very specific purpose: It is the *perfect compression* of economically relevant information. It strips the noise of subjective values, preferences, and interpretations of reality down to pure objective signal, the same for everybody, and hence that the algorithm of the market *can aggregate*, entirely indifferent to its source or what went into its construction.

If trade is a kind of speech act, and subjective value the speakers' interpretations of the acts of others, then prices are the text and the text alone. A price, much like a sequence of words, may *mean different things to different people*, but it nonetheless must be communicated in a medium of minimally yet universally comprehensible syntax for these differing interpretations to work from in the first place.

This all meshes nicely with the complex systems approach to economics associated with W. Brian Arthur at SFI, and perhaps more specifically with John Holland. His paper at the aforementioned inaugural economics workshop, "The Global Economy as an Adaptive Process," at seven pages and zero equations, is well worth a read. Holland recounts many, now familiar, difficulties in mathematical analysis of economics that assume linearity, exclusively negative feedback loops, equilibria, and so on, before proposing that *the economy* is best thought of as what he calls an *adaptive nonlinear network*. Its features are worth exploring, even if they require some translation:

> Each rule in a classifier system is assigned a strength that reflects its usefulness in the context of other active rules. When a rule's conditions are satisfied, it competes with other satisfied rules for activation. The stronger the rule, the more likely it is to be activated. This procedure assures that a rule's influence is affected by both its relevance (the satisfied condition) and its confirmation (the strength). Usually many, but not all, of the rules satisfied will be activated. It is in this sense that a rule serves as a hypothesis competing with alternative hypotheses. Because of the competition there are no internal consistency requirements on the system; the system can tolerate a multitude of models with contradictory implications.

We could easily translate "rule" as "entrepreneurial plan" or similar. Entrepreneurial plans can contradict one another, clearly, and — if they are bidding on the same resources for a novel combination —can and do compete with one another. Clearly, such plans are hypotheses about the result of an experiment that hasn't been run yet. Holland then says,

> A rule's strength is supposed to reflect the extent to which it has been confirmed as a hypothesis. This, of course, it's a matter of experience, and subject to revision. In classifier systems, this revision of strength is carried out by the bucket-brigade credit assignment algorithm. Under the bucket-brigade algorithm, a rule actually bids a part of its strength in competing for activation. If the rule wins the competition, it must pay this bid to the rules sending the messages that satisfied its condition (its suppliers). It thus pays for the right to post its message. The rule will regain what it has paid only if there are other rules that in turn bid and pay for its message (its consumers). In effect, each rule is a middleman in a complex economy, and it will only increase its strength if it turns a profit.

Much of this does not need translating at all: We see Menger's higher orders of capital goods, and value of intermediate goods resting ultimately with the subjective value of consumers, who pass information up the chain of production. We see agents that learn from their experience. We see skin-in-the-game of staked capital in "bidding part of its strength" and we see uncertain gain or reward ultimately realized by profit or loss. But most importantly, we see agents who have no such fiction as "perfect information," but rather responding solely to prices in their immediate environment, and whose reactions affect prices that are passed to other environments. In *Complexity*, Waldrop quotes Holland's frustration with the neo-classical obsession with well-defined mathematical problems:

"Evolution doesn't care whether problems are well-defined or not." Adaptative agents are just responding to a reward, he pointed out. They don't have to make assumptions about where the reward is coming from. In fact, that what the whole point of his classifier systems. Algorithmically speaking, these systems were defined with all the rigor you could ask for. And yet they could operate in an environment that was not well defined at all. Since the classifier rules were only hypotheses about the world, not "facts" they could be mutually contradictory. Moreover, because the system was always testing those hypotheses to find out which ones were useful and led to rewards, it could continue to learn even in the face of crummy, incomplete information — and even while the environment was changing in unexpected ways.

"But its behaviour isn't optimal!" the economists complain, having convinced themselves that a rational agent is one who optimises his "utility function."

"Optimal relative to what?" Holland replied. Talk about your ill-defined criterion: in any real environment, the space of possibilities is so huge that there is no way an agent can find the optimum — or even recognise it. and that's before you take into account the fact that the environment might be changing in unforeseen ways.

Hayek gives us the intuition of prices conveying only what market participants deem to be the most important information and actually destroying the rest, and Holland shows how this can be represented with the formalism of complex systems. But note that the EMH forces us to imagine that the information is somehow *in the market itself.* It is honestly unclear to us whether the EMH even allows for honest or "rational" disagreement given it implies that the price is "correct," and all other trading is allegedly "noise."[34]

By our account (Hayek's and that of everybody sensible and not beholden to the cargo cult math of degenerate fiat economics), people can clearly disagree. That's why they trade in the first place; they value the same thing differently. This is not at all mysterious if we realize that engaging with markets requires individuals to compress the economic signal nascent in the n-dimensions of their information, heuristics, judgments, and stakes, and project it onto the single dimension of price, and that markets do not project the aggregates; they aggregate the projections.

Markets Tend to Leverage Efficiency

"The path is smooth that leadeth on to danger."
— William Shakespeare, *Venus and Adonis*

We know that entrepreneurial efforts will tend towards positive feedback loops if successful, which is a fancy way of saying, they will "grow." And we know that the diversity of compounding uncertainty in markets for securities linked to these efforts will likely generate substantial volatility. But can we say anything more? Can we expect anything more precise?

It turns out that we can, and here we finally get to Alex Adamou, Ole Peters, and the Ergodicity Economics research program. The goal of the program is to trace the repercussions of a conceptual and algebraic error regarding the proper treatment of "time" in calculations of "expectation value" that pervaded mainstream academic economics over the course of the twentieth century.[35]

In *Holistic Management*, Allan Savory gives a delightful example of a non-ergodic system that speaks entirely to everyday experience. Most interestingly of all, he has nothing remotely like *ergodicity* in mind (at least, as far as we know),

> The following example illustrates how timing may fundamentally change the quality of an event. Suppose you have a small house on a hill, and you and your donkey fetch water daily from the stream below. After one year of trampling the same path day after day a substantial gully forms, and the stream bank where you load the water cans becomes a trampled out bog. In this instance you could say that we had had 365 donkey-days (1 donkey x 365 days) of trampling ...
>
> Now, suppose you took a herd of 365 donkeys down the hill and hauled a year's worth of water in one morning. In this instance you would again have 365 donkey-days of trampling. Though a passerby that afternoon would remark on severe trailing and trampling of the streambank those "wounds" would have 364 days of plant growth and root development to heal before you had to come back. When you did, you could expect to find both the trail and the loading place completely overrun by new growth. In fact both might well be greener and healthier than before with the old grass removed and the dung and urine deposited, though they had still borne 365 donkey-days of traffic per year. Thus time, rather than animal numbers, was the critical factor in trampling.[36]

With more technical detail then, the *conceptual and algebraic error* is as follows: Imagine some variable that changes over time, subject to some well-defined randomness. Now imagine a system of many such variables, whose "value" is just the sum of all the values of the variables. Now imagine you want to find the "average" value of a variable in this system in some pure, undefined sense.

How do you make sense of an "average" of a system that will be different every time you run it? Well, you could fix the period of time the system runs for and take the limit of where individual variables get to, as attained by running the system over and over and over to infinity. Or, you could fix the number of systems (preferably at "one" for minimal confusion) and take the limit of where individual variables get to attained by running the system further and further into the future, to infinity.

These are called, respectively, the "ensemble average" and the "time average," and they are easily remembered as the *x average* achieved by taking *x* to infinity and holding the other fixed. "Ensemble average" is commonly known as "the expectation" but Adamou and Peters resist this terminology because it has nothing whatsoever to do with the English word "expectation." You shouldn't necessarily *expect* the expectation.

These values might be the same. This means you can measure one of these even if what you really want is the other. If so, your system is called "ergodic." The concept first developed within nineteenth-century physics when Ludwig Boltzmann wanted to justify using ensemble averages to model macroscopic quantities such as pressure and temperature in fluids, which are strictly speaking better understood as time averages over bajillions of classically mechanical collisions. His justification rested on his separate argument that the observables we wanted to calculate were ergodic.

One line of attack that *Ergodicity Economists* can and do take against mainstream academic economics is to point out that a great deal of financial modelling uses techniques — most notably expectation values — which would only be appropriate if the corresponding observables were ergodic. But they are not. Almost none of them are, to a degree that is both obvious and scary once you grasp it in its totality: Clearly the numbers in finance are causally dependent on one another and take place in a world in which time has a direction.

However, our intended usage is more cheerful. We want to direct the reader's attention to another of Peters and Adamou's papers on the topic: "Leverage Efficiency."[37] Imagine a toy model of the price of a stock that obeys geometric Brownian motion with constant drift and volatility that varies by random draws from a normal distribution. It turns out that the growth rate of this price — clearly a useful variable to know something about — is not an ergodic observable. Its time average is different to its ensemble average. And clearly what we care about is the time average, as we don't tend to hold stocks across multiple alternate universes, but rather across time in the actual universe. In particular, in turns out that the ensemble average growth rate is equal to the drift, while the time average growth rate is equal to the drift minus a correction term.

This becomes important when we introduce leverage via a riskless asset an investor can hold short. Let's call the model drift of the stock minus the stipulated drift of the non-volatile riskless asset "the excess growth rate." Then we can say that the ensemble average growth rate in situations with variable leverage is the growth rate of the riskless asset, plus the leverage multiplied by the excess growth rate. However, the time average has a linked correction, as above. As it is difficult at this point to continue the exposition in English, compare the formulae below:

$$g_e(l) = \mu_{riskless} + l * \mu_{excess}$$

$$g_t(l) = \mu_{riskless} + l * \mu_{excess} - \frac{(l * \sigma)^2}{2}$$

The relevance of the difference is that the latter formula is not monotonic in l. In other words, you don't increase your growth rate unboundedly by levering up to infinity. This might seem intuitively obvious, and, in fact, the intuition likely strikes in exactly the right spot: In reality there is volatility — and not because people are irrational, recall but because entrepreneurship is uncertain. The more and more levered you are, the more you are susceptible to total wipeout for smaller and smaller swings.[38] In fact, we can go further and observe that we can, therefore, maximize the growth rate as a function of leverage, implying an objectively optimal leverage for this toy stock:

$$l_{opt} = \frac{\mu_{excess}}{\sigma^2}$$

What might this optimal leverage be in practice? Well, Adamou and Peters propose the tantalizing alternative to the EMH: the *stochastic markets hypothesis*. As opposed to the EMH's *price efficiency*, they propose *leverage efficiency*: It is impossible for a market participant without privileged information to beat the market by applying leverage. In other words, real markets self-organize such that the optimal leverage of *1* is an attractive point for their stochastic properties.

Adamou and Peters gather data from real markets to establish what the optimal leverage would, in fact, have been:

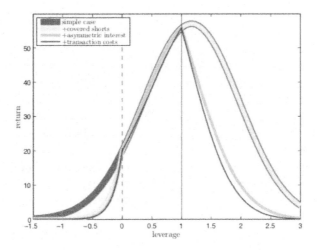

Figure 1. Total return from a constant-leverage investment in the S&P500, starting August 4, 1955, and ending March 10, 2017, as a function of leverage. From the paper, Leverage Efficiency, by Ole Peters and Alex Adamou (Source: https://arxiv.org/abs/1101.4548)

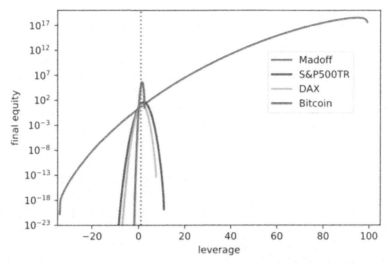

Figure 2. Annualized growth rate of indicated assets over individualized holding periods for the selection of assets indicated in the legend, as a function of leverage.

If we assume that the excess return of the stock price is generated by real economic activity in the long enough run,[39] this would seem to suggest that a certain amount of volatility is actually natural. Were a stock to consistently generate an excess return above that of the riskless asset, investors would lever up to purchase it. This mass act would (reflexively!) cause its volatility to shoot up as the price shoots up. In the inevitable case of a subsequent drop in price for any reason whatsoever becoming self-fulfilling by forcing sales to satisfy the constraints of precisely these levered positions, volatility would increase further still.

This is a somewhat naïve and hand-wavy explanation, but the gist is that the lack of volatility in the short run will tend to generate excess volatility in the medium run, such that a natural level is tended to in the long run. Or, markets are "stochastically efficient." We leave it to the reader to mull over what all this implies. If interventions in financial markets are targeted solely at reducing volatility as a worthwhile end in itself, the rationale of which makes no mention of growth or leverage. We will return in Chapter Five, *The Capital Strip Mine*, to the consequences of market-wide obliviousness to *optimal leverage* and *the stochastic markets hypothesis* in the pursuit of neverendingly expanding unbacked credit. (Spoiler alert: They are not good.)

This has a final interesting implication that we teased earlier: the resolution of the so-called "equity premium puzzle." That, according to such-and-such behavioral models from the psychological literature, the excess return of equities "should be" much lower than it really is. Cue the behavioral economists' claims of irrational risk aversion, and so on and so forth. Adamou and Peters provide an alternative with no reference to questionably scientific models of human behavior at all. The difference between the growth rates of the risky (l=1) and riskless (l=0) assets is the excess return minus the volatility correction.

If markets are attracted to the point at which leverage efficiency equals 1, then it follows by substituting the definition of the equity risk premium in terms of risky and riskless assets into the equation defining optimal leverage, that the equity premium ought to be attracted to the excess return over two. Adamou and Peters delightfully write, "Our analysis reveals this to be a very accurate prediction [...] we regard the consistency of the observed equity premium with the leverage efficiency hypothesis to be a resolution of the equity premium puzzle." *Quod erat demonstrandum.*[40]

We knew from previous sections that volatility is *likely*. It will exist to some extent due to the teased-out implications of subjective values and omnipresent uncertainty. But now we know that it is *necessary*. It is not noise, irrationality, panic, and so on, around a "correct price." It is, at least in part, inevitable, reflexive rebalancing of leverage around whatever the price happens to be.

Adaptation, Information, and Fractals

"The war between the centrifuge of knowledge and the centripetal pull of power remains the prime conflict in all economies reconciling the two impulses is a new economics, an economics that puts free will and the innovating entrepreneur not on the periphery but at the centre of the system. It is an economics of surprise that distributes power as it extends knowledge. It is an economics of disequilibrium and disruption that tests its inventions in the crucible of a competitive marketplace. It is an economics that accords with the constantly surprising fluctuations of our lives."
— George Gilder, *Knowledge and Power*

As mentioned in the introduction to this chapter, of all the dissenting work on the EMH, we most recommend, by far, Andrew Lo's "The Adaptive Markets Hypothesis" — the original paper[41] and the follow-up book of the same name — as well as the various thoughts of Benoit Mandelbrot on fractals in financial markets — strewn across numerous academic papers but lucidly conveyed in the popular book, *The (Mis)behavior of Markets* — and George Gilder's *Knowledge and Power*.

Lo argues that a handful of concepts from evolutionary biology provide a far better base for understanding the behavior of markets than does the EMH. Rather than a kind of mathematical game that "perfectly rational" agents can win, Lo encourages the reader to think of agents as only imperfectly perceiving only their immediate environment, acting on heuristics, competing with others, and adapting both to competition and to changes in the environment itself. And of course, evolution (or perhaps more accurately "mutation") is the result of entrepreneurial experimentation.[42]

Our main critique of Lo is simply that he doesn't take uncertainty seriously enough. In covering the academic history surrounding the EMH, he only gives Simon a page or so, and Gerd Gigerenzer, a paragraph. The key point of failure, in our view, is his treatment of the Ellsberg paradox. Or rather, the fact that he concludes his otherwise rigorous discussion of uncertainty at this point.

The problem here is that the uncertainty in the Ellsberg paradox is confined to the odds, whereas we know from the previous discussion that the uncertainty in economics exists in the outcomes. This means that the odds aren't just unclear, they are non-existent: not just unknown but unknowable. By stopping here, Lo passes off the results of running the experiment that gives rise to the so-called paradox as simply indicating ambiguity aversion, which he presents as a kind of irrational bias — then a segue to behavioral economics. This prevents Lo from exploring the implications of so-called "Knightian" uncertainty on entrepreneurship and competition, and ultimately, gives him little ammunition to take on the EMH directly. In fact, he acknowledges that he never really does — he just proposes something he thinks is better.

That said, we agree that his model is better. Far better! Adaptation is a fascinating concept to employ here, which comes through very naturally in the complex systems approach. We find the basic intuition of changing circumstances and responding agents compelling. As do, it would seem, several thinkers we have already cited in this chapter. Consider this passage from Israel Kirzner,

It is necessary to introduce the insight that men learn from their experiences in the market. It is necessary to postulate that out of the mistakes which led market participants to choose less-than-optimal courses of action yesterday, there can be expected to develop systematic changes in expectations concerning ends and means that can generate corresponding alterations in plans.

Also, there is a tradition of referring to formal heuristics as *ecologically rational*, and the biological analogy is no coincidence. This passage from Waldrop's *Complexity* on John Holland's conversion to complex systems thinking in his study of genetics is striking in the almost simple obviousness of the comparison drawn to economics (again, not at all a coincidence):

It bothered Holland that [R.A.] Fisher kept talking about evolution achieving a stable equilibrium — that state in which a given species has attained its optimum size, its optimum sharpness of tooth, its optimum fitness to survive and reproduce. Fisher's argument was essentially the same one that economist use to define economic equilibrium: once a species' fitness is at a maximum, he said, any mutation will lower the fitness [...] but that did not sound like evolution to me.

[...] to Holland, evolution and learning seemed much more like — well, a game. In both cases, trying to win enough of what it needed to keep going. In evolution that payoff is literally survival, and a chance for the agent to pass its genes on to the next generation. In learning, the payoff is a reward of some kind, such as food, a pleasant sensation, or emotional fulfilment, but either way, the payoff (or lack of it) gives agents the feedback they need to improve their performance: if they're going to be "adaptive" at all, they somehow have to keep the strategies that pay off well, and let the others die out.

One thing we especially like about Lo's approach is his idea of "evolution at the speed of thought," often rhetorical as much as anything else. We think this provides a useful conceptual tool to deal with what we deemed to be the only consistent deficiency in the material we covered on complex systems: Arthur, Holland, et al., seem to us so focused on the comparison to biological evolution, and on shifting the comparative conceptual framework from physics to biology as a whole, that they forget the role of purposeful human beings in all of this.

Economic "mutation" is not random, it is creative, intuitive, and judgmental. It happens at the speed of thought because humans think *on purpose*. They do not cycle through the space of every thought that can possibly be had until they hit on one that happens to be a business plan.[43]

To put this in a wider context and loop back to previously cited thinkers, we think W. Brian Arthur is best read alongside Kirzner, and indeed Kirzner is best read alongside Arthur. Particularly in *The Nature of Technology*, which is otherwise an excellent book, Arthur perfectly grasps *how* change happens, but not *why*. In *Competition and Entrepreneurship*, Kirzner perfectly grasps *why* change happens but not *how*. Both the why and the how rely, in part, on understanding economic evolution as an essentially human phenomenon, because genes mutate, but humans *think*.

Gilder picks up on similar concepts in *Knowledge and Power*. Gilder's argument is roughly that markets are best understood through the lens of *information theory*. Truly free markets minimally disrupt the *signal* of economic reality and preserve the low entropy surprise and subsequent disorder of human creativity as manifested in entrepreneurship. He writes,

> At the heart of capitalist growth, however, is not the mechanistic homo economicus but conscious, willful, often altruistic, inventive man. Although a marketplace may work mechanically, an economy is no sense a great machine. The market produces only the perfunctory denouement of tempestuous drama, dominated by the incalculable creativity of entrepreneurs, making purposeful gifts without predetermined returns, launching enterprise into the always unknown future. The market is the conduit, not the content; the low-entropy carrier, not the high-entropy message. Capitalism begins not with exchange but with giving, not with determinist rationality but with creation and surprisal.

We believe the idea of information, signal, noise, and interference is a powerful one to employ.[44] Economically relevant *information* is discovered from experimentation, not deduced from a model.[45]

But the following quote from the *Knowledge and Power* nicely links Lo to Mandelbrot:

> Information theory is the nemesis of those who would reduce markets to material laws. As manifestations of the interplay of human minds, markets are more analogous to biological phenomena. As the controlling knowledge of economics resides deep inside the companies that make up the market. You cannot predict the future of markets or companies by examining the fractal patterns of their previous price movements. There is no information there.

While Gilder's commentary on fractals is only really in passing, Mandelbrot's ideas on the topic in finance are thorough and iconoclastic, to say the least. The mildly boring part of *The (Mis)behavior of Markets* is Mandelbrot showing that, empirically, financial data does not seem to fit the Brownian motion of the random walk hypothesis — and hence the EMH. The juicy part is his explanation of *why*. To avoid getting into any really tricky mathematics and essentially rewriting his book, we will summarize his argument as, *this isn't random enough*. More suggestively, *it is too predictably random*.

Mandelbrot thinks that prices in financial markets are, up to a certain granularity, fractals. If true, this has many fascinating implications, but the most relevant here is that the self-similarity this implies means that any randomness in their fluctuation must be irregular. It should not be possible to ascertain any regularity just by changing the time span because they look the same on *every* time span. The randomness must itself be pretty random. And that randomness must be random, and so on. There are no genuinely normal distributions in finance, Mandelbrot believes, but rather they all tend towards Cauchy. Within the realm of Strange Finance (as opposed to *Normal* Finance, which is a fiction of modern academic economists), let us propose the Farrington-Meyers law: The tails are always fatter than you think, even when you take into account the Farrington-Meyers law.[46]

What then of Gilder's dismissal of the idea? We think the two have much more in common than the extract above might suggest. At precisely the risk outlined in a previous endnote of taking the "information theory" metaphor a little too seriously, consider the following from Gilder,

> Stanford University's Thomas Cover, the leading information theorist of the day, put Mandelbrot's set — the colorful filigreed whirls of intricate design and apparent complexity of Mandelbrot's fractal printout — on the jacket of his canonical book, Elements of Information Theory. From movie posters to book covers to power point décor, graphic artists often use the Mandelbrot set as a symbol of dense information. But information theory itself is full of surprises. Inside the jacket of his book, Cover writes, "The information content of the fractal on the cover is essentially zero." If the measure of complexity is the number of lines in the computer code needed to produce the effect, Mandelbrot's fractal, the product of a simple computer algorithm, bears virtually no content at all. It is all froth on a core of simple algebra.

What does any of this have to do with "complex" markets? Neither Gilder nor Mandelbrot fully explore this idea, and we may be going out on a limb here, but we think Gilder's criticism can essentially be reconciled with Mandelbrot's by suggesting the following: Financial data may look like a fractal up to a certain granularity, but beyond that granularity, it is more complex still. And besides, Mandelbrot would very likely agree given his concern has always been how to *model* markets, not how to *predict* them. His entire point is that the only remotely sensible way to model them *precludes prediction.*

This synthesis is almost exactly what you would expect if you thought markets were maximally uncertain, so to speak. If risk were predictable, then it could be hedged against. If it were unpredictable in and of itself, but were distributed predictably, then *that* could be hedged against. And so on and so forth. This all lends itself to a hand-wavy inductive proof by contradiction.

We know that nothing can be perfectly hedged because it derives from profoundly incomprehensible uncertainty, and uncertainty on uncertainty, and uncertainty on *that* uncertainty, and so on. Financial markets can shift uncertainty around and selectively parcel it into more and less risky instruments, but uncertainty itself cannot be removed. Participants only have information that may or may not motivate them to act. If others act first, they must adapt — at the speed of thought.

Simply Too Complex

"One problem that confronts the modern economist is the sheer complexity of the system that he seeks to describe, this complexity makes any attempt to model the system extremely difficult, and without some kind of model no scientific attempt at forecasting can be undertaken. In building an economic model, the econometrician must identify the precise starting values of every variable in the economic process and describe the exact nature of those processes and their inter-relationships. Meteorologists know how complex a task this is. Yet where the meteorologist works with precise and measurable physical laws, economists deal in uncertainty and unquantifiable propositions, and where meteorologists hesitate to predict weather patterns more than one week ahead, the bold economist may stretch his own horizons over several years. Though economic forecasts over short time periods are sometimes broadly accurate, over longer periods they are usually inaccurate.

"The chaotic system is simply too complex for the economist to understand let alone to model on a computer. It would be quite an achievement if forecasters could reliably predict the direction of change, never mind its amount. Whilst physicists, doctors and chemists can predict the events of their own domain with some success, there are no economists whose modelling efforts are as reliable. I do not wish to belittle economic forecasters for many are extremely able. I shall simply wish them good luck in their endeavours and proceed in my own direction."

— Tarek El Diwany, The Problem with Interest

The authors wish economic forecasters well, too, because why not? They probably *mean well*. But we also wish very much to belittle them because the road to hell is paved with good intentions — or as Blaise Pascal said, "Whoever wants to act the angel, acts the beast."

They must be mocked mercilessly and their ideas made to be so obviously embarrassing that they are ashamed to speak in public at all. Why is it understood we cannot predict the weather more than two weeks in advance, yet we can predict *the product of all human behavior* to infinity, or thereabouts? The weather can't even think. Economic forecasting should be at least as embarrassing as us telling the reader that, on February 9, 2034, it will rain with 30% humidity, and Amazon's stock price will be $472.34 and 5/8 (having accounted for stock splits, of course). Should this come about, the ground will be clear for the layman not to fall for such scientistic charlatanism and instead to *understand* at least the following:

Value is subjective, which means uncertainty governs all economic phenomena. This creates a complexity that resists equilibria and is constantly changing besides. Within such a system, prices convey the minimal possible information necessary for economic agents to purposefully react. They do so with judgment and heuristics, not "perfect information," which is nonsensical, as is "perfect competition" and "rational expectations."

For these reasons, prices may pass statistical tests for randomness, but they are not themselves random (although it is plausible that their randomness is random, and that randomness is random, and so on) but rather are unpredictable on the basis of market data alone. They are, however, predictable to the extent that the predictor accurately assesses the future subjective valuations both of economic agents and fellow market participants, and backs up this prediction with staked capital. This act of staking changes the uncertainties at play, rendering any attempt at genuinely scientific analysis futile. You *can* beat the market, it's just hard, and it depends on understanding *people*, not data. And it's meaningless if you do it in theory but not practice.

Markets have many characteristics. We suggest they are subjective, uncertain, complex, stochastic, adaptive, fractal, reflexive — really any clever-sounding adjective you like — just not efficient. This means there is no "correct price" and strongly suggests that degenerate fiat finance is self-serving bullshit. Having tackled the relatively more practical concept of *capital markets*, what of *capitalism* itself? Is it self-serving bullshit too?

It depends what you mean by "capitalism."

Chapter Three

This Is Not Capitalism
This is your brain on central banking,
regulatory capture, and financialization

If we had to pick a moment in time in which we entered the final stages of degenerate fiat "capitalism," we would likely pick March 2020, when it seemed very much as if the everything bubble had popped.

In the end, P/E ratios didn't implode under their own stupendous highs, nor did the conceptual insanity of negative rates trigger bank runs. The euro didn't fall apart (yet) and there was no hyperinflation (yet). It was an "exogenous shock" *wot done it*, and it was magicking one quarter of all money in existence out of thin air *wot staved off* a catastrophe since made all the more inevitable.

We encourage readers to read the phrase, "exogenous shock," with maximal eye-rolling sass and to recall when we discuss the kind of nonsensical economic theorizing that got us into that mess, which works perfectly well in every conceivable circumstance other than contact with the real world.

This put us in a tragicomic position. In order to deal with this "exogeny," we seemingly had to go into overdrive on the exact same measures that made us vulnerable in the first place: We needed to print money like there was no tomorrow and throw it at everything that moves. That was literally the plan. That's how we deal with emergencies now.

This chapter is about the bizarre reaction we noticed from a solid majority of the professional commentariat to the effect that this is the inevitable result of capitalism run wild. We are not sure what these people mean, or even think they mean, by "capitalism." If they mean, "the regime of political economy dominant in the West since 1971 and particularly acute since 2009," then they are correct on a technicality, but they are abusing the word.

If "capitalism" means anything, that meaning ought to at least include the notion of preserving and growing capital. It can include other nasty bits and bobs, for sure, but it must at least include this. We are mindful of Eli Heckscher's concluding remarks in *A Plea for Theory in Economic History*:

> A special warning, I think, it necessary against the promiscuous use of the concept of "capitalism" — *das Wort das sich immer zur rechten zeit einstellt, wo volkwirtschaftliche Begriffe fehlen* [the word that always comes in at the right time, where economic terms are missing], to adapt

a famous phrase from the *Faust* of Goethe. By this it is, of course, not intended to infer that some rational and distinct meaning cannot be expressed through the word "capitalism," but simply that it is far too often made an excuse for muddled thinking.

The aim of this book could well be concisely captured as *providing* such a rational and distinct meaning and analyzing how the concept so captured is affected by the emergence of Bitcoin.

But before we get to global, digital, sound, free, open-source, programmable money, we will build our theoretical foundation around this effort precisely because such a rational and distinct meaning seems very much absent from the public discourse. In particular, *the preservation and growth of capital* is not happening, nor has it happened since before the dominance of the regime now misleadingly bearing this name. Reflecting on how this regime came about, Andrew Redleaf and Richard Vigilante write in *Panic: The Betrayal of Capitalism by Wall Street and Washington*, "The ideology of modern finance replaced the capitalist's appreciation for free markets as a context for human creativity with the worship of efficient markets as substitutes for that creativity. The result was a divorce of entrepreneurial knowledge from economic power."

George Gilder comments similarly on this phenomenon in *Knowledge and Power,* arguing that the Great Financial Crisis "has a clear and identifiable cause. That cause is a prevailing set of economic ideas that can be summed up as capitalism without capitalists — capitalism dominated by financial hypertrophy rather than technological vision and innovation."

It is somewhat concerning to us that people seemed, and still seem, to be lining up to both defend and attack "capitalism," when the object of discussion could hardly be further from any worthwhile meaning of the word but is rather better described as: To boost aimless consumption, primarily with uncollateralized debt, by destroying the price signals for capital and depleting its stock.

We humbly suggest the following schema for categorizing both the attacks and defenses. To borrow an expression from James C. Scott's *Seeing Like a State* that we will use throughout the book, the attackers tend to be "high modernists," concerned with aesthetic knowledge and emotional persuasion: They dislike what they think capitalism is because it *feels wrong*, and they want to redesign it from the top down. Scott introduces "high modernism" as follows,

> It is best conceived of as a strong, one might even say muscle-bound, version of the self-confidence about scientific and technical progress, the expansion of production, the growing satisfaction of human needs, the mastery of nature (including human nature), and, above all, the rational design of social order commensurate with the scientific understanding of natural laws. It originated, of course, in the West, as a by-product of unprecedented progress in science and industry.

High modernism must not be confused with scientific practice. It was fundamentally, as the term "ideology" implies, a faith that borrowed, as it were, the legitimacy of science and technology. It was, accordingly, uncritical, unskeptical, and thus unscientifically optimistic about the possibilities for the comprehensive planning of human settlement and production. The carriers of high modernism tended to see rational order in remarkably visual aesthetic terms. For them, an efficient, rationally organized city, village, or farm, was a city that looked regimented and orderly in a geometrical sense [...]

[...] High modernism was about "interests" as well as faith. Its carriers, even when they were capitalist entrepreneurs, required state action to realize their plans.

Those who attack "capitalism" unfortunately tend to be exceptionally high modernist. They undoubtedly require state action to realize their plans and, in many cases, this is what they are openly agitating for. And they are partly right: Degenerate fiat "capitalism" *is* wrong. Yet while their diagnosis might be sound, their prescription would do nothing for the disease and would kill the patient besides.

The defenders are degenerate fiat financiers, concerned with codified knowledge and authoritative persuasion. They are *in no way right*: They are the most inadvertently inhumane and destructive people alive — one is tempted to say they are *evil* in the Arendtian sense of the banality of their inhumanity and destruction. They mindlessly repeat the exact dogma that has caused all the problems to date, and in the course of lobbying for more power to fix the problems their power has caused.

We, on the other hand, and Bitcoiners in general, neither attack nor defend "capitalism" — in scare quotes so as to distinguish degenerate fiat "capitalism" from actual capitalism — but rather question the premises and do our best to clarify what we are talking about in the first place. We are concerned with practical knowledge and logical persuasion. We value experimentation, such that it might lead us to discover some sliver of informational signal that can, in principle, be independently verified, provided the dynamic process being analyzed has not changed too much in the meantime, although it probably has. But this is all far too sensible for so early in the book. We will get to this in due course. This chapter focuses on attacking what the *defenders* in particular get wrong about "capitalism," which they think they are defending when really, they defend only themselves.

This is your brain on central banking, regulatory capture, and financialization. This is not capitalism.

Money Is a Story

"When a medium of exchange is generally accepted in society, it is called "money." How does a commodity such a gold or silver turn into money? This happens through a gradual process, in the course of which more and more market participants, each for himself, decide to use gold and silver rather than other commodities in their indirect exchanges. Thus, the historical selection of gold, silver, and copper was not made through some sort of a social contract or convention. Rather, it resulted from the spontaneous convergence of many individual choices, a convergence that was prompted through the objective physical characteristics of the precious metals."
—Jörg Guido Hülsmann, *The Ethics of Money Production*

There is a vast literature on the question of "what is money?" We present a simplified version for the sake of what is key to this chapter. Our account is by no means exhaustively wide nor exhaustively deep, but it is correct enough within the realms of what we cover. We will go into this question in much more detail in Chapter Four, *Wittgenstein's Money*, with implications in all chapters that follow.

Money is a story. It is a story of what work has been done on credit that is yet to be redeemed. It is the Schelling point for universal credit. It is an IOU that everybody is willing to redeem (primarily *because* everybody is willing to redeem it) and hence that, at every instance of its transfer, it is re-ordained with the ascription of economic value to work actually performed. Note that money is *not* a *social construct*, a *collective delusion*, or any other such denigration that snidely implies that nothing about money really matters and we could reinvent it all tomorrow if we wanted to. Money may be a story, but the qualities of the story matter a great deal. The truer the story, the better.

By "true," we ought to mean that the process of transferring money has, and is trusted to have always had, the characteristics of censorship resistance and integrity assurance. We can think of this in cryptographic terms, as there is a ready analogy to be made to ensuring the security and validity of network communications. Transferring money *is* sending a message through the network of economic exchange. It is "censorship resistant" if Alice knows her message is *to Bob and only Bob*; it is not diverted to Charlie, nor is it destroyed. It is "integrity assured" if Bob knows the message is *from Alice and only Alice*; it is not really from Charlie, nor also to Dorothy, nor really from nobody at all.

When money is printed — whether this be bank notes or lines in a database — this is violating integrity assurance. It is equivalent to the printer extending themselves credit on the unwilling, and mostly unknowing, behalf of everybody. No work has been done that anybody is willing to redeem. No economic value has been created, or contracted to be created, to match the token now in circulation. Bob does not know his message of value transfer is *from Alice and only Alice*; it is not from anybody. The issuer has executed a man-in-the-middle attack on the structure of economic exchange.

And note this isn't an *old man yells at cloud* rant against money creation in general in which we insist all economic activity must be conducted with gold. The money created by credit extension *can be* perfectly legitimate if the risk of the maturity transformation is priced freely by interest, borne by the equity holders of the lending institution, mitigated with collateral they understand, and accepted in exchange by willing economic actors.[47] But it is not if the risk is priced by political expediency, borne by nobody, collateralized by everybody, and forced into continual use and reuse by the threat of state violence.

It also doesn't hurt to have the lenders know and consent to what is happening with their deposits, rather than suffering from the collective delusion that their funds are "in the bank." Note also this is not a moral claim: *Violating integrity insurance* may be immoral to whatever extent the reader considers lying to be immoral. But we use this expression in purely economic terms. The informational signal the money *ought to* represent is fraudulent. It is interference with the economic and social truth.

We will return below to the implications of ignoring the importance of integrity assurance. For now, bear in mind as we continue that money is universal credit and that its supply and value in a free market is a reflection of the reality of how much valuable work has been done and not redeemed. As Oliver Wendell Holmes put it, "We must think things not words, or at least we must constantly translate our words into the facts for which they stand, if we are to keep the real and the true."

There will likely always be the straightforward political incentive of lust for power to compromise the censorship resistance or integrity assurance of money. But there will be consequences. People will believe a story that simply isn't true and will act as if it is.

Stocks and Flows

"Imagine for a moment two people, Bill and Ben. Bill is a banker and earns $200,000 a year at Goldman Sachs. OK, he's miserably paid by banking standards, but bear with me. Ben is a gardener and earns $20,000 pruning roses and trimming hedges. Who is better off? If you measure the income each receives, then Bill is clearly richer, in fact precisely ten times richer. This measurement is the equivalent of GDP; it tells you about the 'flow' of income each receives in a year. But, just like GDP, these numbers don't reveal much about the true wealth of Bill and Ben.

"To discover more, you'd need to know about their stock of assets. Did I forget to mention that Ben the gardener recently inherited a huge country estate in Long Island worth $100 million? In truth, he works in his own vast garden as a bit of a hobby on Tuesday afternoons and pays himself a token wage. But he plans to sell off the estate next year, move into somewhere more modest in Manhattan and live off the interest from investing the $95 million or so he'll have left over.

"Poor Bill, meanwhile, is up to his neck in debt. He has to fork out half his salary each month on his mortgage, which has another ten years to run. He has car payments on his (scratched-up) Porsche and a troubling bank overdraft that he's acquired to maintain his highfalutin lifestyle. Unfortunately, he's also pushing fifty (Ben is nineteen by the way) and the bank is going to have to let him go.

"Now who looks better off, Bill or Ben?"
—David Pilling, *The Growth Illusion*

Another decent definition of money is the most liquid form of capital. Although this is rather a circular definition, as "liquidity" is traditionally conceived of as a measure of how quickly and easily an asset can be converted to "money." It still tautologically works, as money can be converted to money in zero time and with zero difficulty, but it deserves to be padded out.

We can say that money is the most *salable* asset: The asset that emerges with the property of being the most widely accepted in exchange for other assets, not to be consumed, but to retain value for later exchange.[48] Note that, in a barter economy of only consumable goods, money adds little value beyond the administrative: It becomes easier to calculate exchange rates. Where money adds immense social value is in calibrating the exchange rates of goods that *cannot be consumed*, but rather are used to create consumable goods, or are used to create goods that are used to create consumable goods, and so on.

This all points to a higher analysis; money itself is not the most important aspect of capitalism. Nor is trade, nor markets, nor profits, nor even assets, but *capital*. *Goods that are used to create consumable goods* are a form of capital, but really, we mean something less tangible than any of the former; a kind of economic potential energy stored in the transformation of materials into higher and higher forms of complex good, but always ready to be rereleased to work again the same process of transformation. Seen this way, capital is not any particular thing or even behavior. It can exist only as an emergent property of a social system in which the exchange of shares of ownership of private assets is seamless.

Capitalism — an economic system respecting and encouraging the nurturing, replenishment, and growth of *capital* — thus requires a delicate balance of the extremity of social interdependence. We must not be so loosely connected as to be unable to form no nascent markets in which capital can be made more or less liquid, but not so tightly connected as to disallow differentiation in these markets. People need to agree enough to be able to trade but also *disagree enough* to be *willing* to trade.

The consensus enabled by price discovery in a market really is *a discovery*, not rhetorically, but in fact: It is a distributed discovery of a social truth. Individuals do not find their own private truths in isolation, nor is a politically correct truth dictated and imposed on all. Price is the maximally compressed signal of economically relevant information. Entrepreneurs react to what information they think might be captured by the signal — what about broader economic reality they think this signal might *mean* — by manipulating whatever capital they can bring under their control.

Capital is a stock. Its dimension is currency. It exists (and in theory could be measured) at any instantaneous point in time. Money and assets are also stocks, meaning they too can be measured at any point in time. But the numbers alone cannot have any independent meaning because they are dependent on the unit chosen to measure the dimension: dollars. The number will be different in euros, yen, or bitcoin.

Such measures as "revenue," "profits," and with a little leeway even "trade" are flows. Their dimensions are currency over time. There is no such thing as instantaneous profit. Profit happens over time. This means that the numbers representing profit, as with all flows, are sensitive to changing the unit measuring the currency, and the unit measuring the time.

This might seem like pointless semantics, but the distinction is key as follows: You need stocks to create flows, and you need flows to replenish stocks. Our entire analysis of how bankrupt (morally as well as factually) the contemporary financial system is can more or less be derived from the appreciation that this simple maxim is not widely understood. What does it mean more practically?

"The economy" is an aggregation of businesses, which can be helpfully split into the financial and non-financial.[49] Financial businesses oversee the allocation of liquid capital by matching the preferences of contributors of capital with regards to perceived risk, timeframe, and so on, with non-financial business projects with appropriate characteristics.[50] Non-financial businesses turn liquid capital into illiquid capital — higher and higher forms of complex good — in an attempt to satisfy a perceived customer demand. If they make revenue, they are correct in a demand existing for such a good or service. If they make a profit, they have satisfied this demand efficiently; they have produced more than they have consumed. If they make a sufficient return, they have earned enough of a profit (i.e., flow) on the capital (i.e., stock) supplied to satisfy their investors. Profit is both payment to the providers of capital, and the opportunity to reinvest without requiring further external financing.

Non-financial businesses cannot create either revenues or profits without first being provided with capital. This might be as simple as saying that you can't sell goods without first buying them or making them, and you can't pay for the raw materials before you have made a profit unless you first have financing. Or it might be more complicated but also more obviously linked to wealth creation, in that you need to buy a machine (a higher order capital good) that takes raw materials as an input and churns out something more complicated and more valuable. Clearly you don't want the machine for its own sake; you want it for what it will produce. The machine has to be purchased with liquid capital, and then exists as illiquid capital. It can be liquidated if desired (i.e., sold for cash), but its primary value is as a form of economic potential energy. It is a stock that creates flows.

You need stocks to create flows, and you need flows to replenish stocks. You need financing to start a business, and you need profits to maintain one. Profits are required to pay back the financing, and will eventually give the business owner the ability to eschew financing entirely and maintain the business's capital requirements sustainably and internally. This is as true for a single business as when aggregated to "the economy."

The health of a single business, and the health of the aggregation of all businesses, should not be measured by "growth" in revenue, or in profits, or even in capital, but in the ratio of profits to capital. The rate of return. And ideally, it should be (geometrically) averaged over a very long time — not only can no meaningful investment take place over a single year[51] but the length of credit cycles will obscure what is really happening over as long as ten or twenty years. A high rate of return is a high flow to stock ratio. If all the flow is reinvested, it will be the rate of increase of the stock, and reflect the meaningful growth of "the economy."

Recall once more the "dimensionality" argument: The ratio of profit one year to profit the year before is not even "growth." It is an "increase."[52] Return on capital is a growth rate. Its units are one over time. Economic well-being and sustainability can only be sensibly measured with aggregated return on capital. Unsurprisingly, this is not at all how anybody does so.

"GDP Growth" and Other Useless Metrics

"Over a period of generations, the goods and services which constitute national output change so much that statistical comparisons can become practically meaningless, because they are comparing apples and oranges. At the beginning of the twentieth century, the national output of the United States did not include any airplanes, television sets, computers or nuclear power plants. At the end of that century, American national output no longer included typewriters, slide rules (once essential for engineers, before there were pocket calculators), or a host of equipment and supplies once widely used in connection with horses that formerly provided the basic transportation of many societies around the world. What then, does it mean to say that the Gross Domestic Product was X percent more in the year 2000 than in 1900, when it consisted largely of very different things at these different times? It may mean something to say that output this year is 5 percent higher or 3 percent lower than it was last year because it consists of much the same things in both years. But the longer the time span involved, the more such statistics approach meaninglessness."

— Thomas Sowell, *Basic Economics*

Widespread misunderstandings of money and capital, and of stocks and flows, come together to form a dangerous cocktail with *GDP growth*. In understanding how GDP is commonly discussed, and why that discussion betrays a stunning ignorance of money and capital, we will be in a position to evaluate the likely final phase of degenerate fiat "capitalism" into which we have recently entered.

As we see it, there are (at least) three problems with "GDP growth": (1) the "economic well-being" it claims to measure is in fact unmeasurable, (2) the "economic well-being" it claims to measure is politically and socially irrelevant, and (3) it is not a "growth rate" at all.

1. The "economic well-being" it claims to measure is in fact unmeasurable.[53] GDP is the total monetary value of goods and services produced in a region over a period of time. If somebody says "the economy" grew by 2%, they likely mean that the quantity of goods and services produced increased by that amount. Of course, not every quantity grew by exactly that amount. Some might even be shrinking. What matters to the measure is the total monetary value. When there is one fewer unit of A, costing $1, but one more unit of B, costing $2, GDP still increases by $1.

So far, so good. This certainly seems "measurable," so what's the problem? Over time, human ingenuity comes up with new or improved goods and services. When that happens, there isn't merely one more of A or B. There is something else entirely: C. GDP, which so far tracked how much the production of A and B increased, now also tracks C. Given enough time, demand for A, B, and C might disappear, so that GDP only consists of X, Y, and Z — none of which existed when records started. How can we then say that "the economy" grew when it doesn't make more of what it used to?

The unsatisfactory answer is that when C was invented, it had a market price which could be compared to those of A and B. Conceived of this way, the comparison is indeed meaningful. But this exchange rate between A and C only came into existence *after* C was invented. Beforehand, no amount of money could buy C. Innovation expanded the opportunity set so that capital could be allocated to the production of something new. The price of C only reflects the opportunity cost of its production and consumption after its discovery, not the value embedded in the discovery itself.[54] There are no exchange rates to the future.

The value of discoveries compounds over time. A practical illustration of long-term "GDP growth" makes its nonsensical nature plain. According to GDP, a Vietnamese on average earns as much today as an American did in the 1880s. Yet the Vietnamese have the same life expectancy as Americans did in the 1980s. Today's Vietnamese live in a world of smartphones and penicillin, whereas 1880s Americans lived in an age of candlelight and often-fatal bacterial infections. The monetary value of their income might be considered comparable by economists, but that is because they do not, and cannot, measure the constant improvements brought upon by human ingenuity.

Economies do not grow, they change. And you can't measure counterfactuals in dollars.[55]

2. The "economic well-being" it claims to measure is politically and socially irrelevant. GDP growth is the growth in wealth of the average person, rather than the average growth in wealth of a person. This is Ole Peters's proposal for "DDP," or *Democratic Domestic Product*.[56] GDP growth is a plutocratic measure, that is indifferent to the higher moments of the distribution from which it is drawn. It is entirely possible for the wealth of every single person bar one to go down, while GDP growth goes up. In fact, something not too dissimilar to this seems to have happened in Europe and the United States since the Global Financial Crisis. GDP keeps on climbing while median measures of income, disposable income, assets, net financial wealth, and more, have gone sideways or even down. The gains have increasingly been concentrated in higher and higher brackets of existing wealth, to the point where, at certain cut-offs, *more than 100% of the gains have gone to some upper bracket*. In other words, some groups are in fact getting poorer, but other groups are getting richer at a faster rate, such that GDP still grows.

While there is reason to believe that technological changes and geopolitics have contributed to this phenomenon, as will be touched on in part in later chapters, we will explain below why we think this can largely be explained by state enforcement of the dominant regime of political economy, and its abject ignorance of the principles of money, capital, and returns.[57]

3. It is not a "growth rate" at all. It is an "increase." It is a difference between two flows. A growth rate is a return; a flow over a stock. Moreover, GDP isn't even the correct flow one would need to compute a relevant return, because it is the aggregation of revenue, not of profit. By religiously focusing on this entirely irrelevant metric, it is almost trivially easy to end up doing both of the following:

- encouraging profitless revenue, which indicates a real demand, but an inefficient use of resources in satisfying that demand. Capital is one such resource — possibly the most important — hence:
- encouraging destruction or consumption of capital; or, a short-term high of consumption at the expense of the long-term ability to produce what we might like to consume. Think of a farmer eating seed rather than planting it. His consumption increases, but eventually he loses the ability to consume *at all*.

Equally useless without the proper context is stock market capitalization. Obviously, it is more or less a good thing for stocks to go up, because it means that lenders of capital are getting a return, and companies that are proving the viability of their economic proposition can raise capital more cheaply. But there must be underlying economic success for this to be justified. Individual companies can always see their valuations grow out of line with their fundamentals, either on hype or entirely on merit as their prospects for the future are seen to be improving. But if valuations *across the board* are marching upwards vastly out of line with rates of return on capital, never mind with increases in cash flows or book value of equity, something is wrong.

There are two obvious contenders for what might be wrong and which have the potential to reinforce one another in a deadly spiral: inflation and speculation.

By inflation, we mean to ignore such bullshit euphemisms as "quantitative easing" and "market support" and to direct the reader's attention to the simple fact of artificial money being pumped into financial markets to increase prices beyond what reality is doing its best to get them to show. When prices go up because a currency is being debased, that is inflation. It might make a social and political difference if the price increases are in milk and bread, or housing and healthcare, rather than in financial assets, but economically it is irrelevant. It reflects only what the artificial money was first used to buy (also known as the *Cantillon effect*, after Richard Cantillon, the French-Irish economist who first described it). Eventually it will dissipate to all goods and services. We will return below to the broader consequences of artificial money being directed specifically to financial assets, but for the time being, we simply mean to point out that the prices are fake. They do not reflect reality.

By "speculation" we should be clear that we do not mean anything intrinsically negative. Speculation is usually rolled out by financially illiterate opportunistic rabble-rousers as a culprit for the consequences of intervention-induced market collapses, when in fact it is more than likely that speculation was trying to direct prices to reflect reality while artificial money or some other kind of coercion was pushing in the other direction. We mean simply that financial market inflation can induce a certain kind of speculation that is unhealthy. If it becomes clear enough to market participants that the artificial money firehose will not be turned off, this actually reduces the incentive to speculate *against* the fake signals being provided by inflation and start contributing to inflation instead.

Say you are a pension fund that needs an 8% return to meet its liabilities without difficulty. And say that stocks have been inflated to the point that you can in all honesty expect only a 2% return over the long run from here given reasonable assumptions about valuation metrics returning to something sensible at some point. You might be tempted to look for other asset classes that are not so corrupted. But if you are reasonably sure that artificial money will keep pushing prices up for longer than the time horizon over which you would otherwise expect a reversion, then it might actually be sensible to stay invested and get your 8% from inflation alone. This way, those who might otherwise be incentivized to contribute to correcting the effect of price manipulation are actually incentivized to contribute to reinforcing it, if the manipulation is strong enough in the first place.

When this vicious cycle gets into full gear, the idea of measuring "economic well-being" solely by the *increase* (not growth) in stock market valuations, may be even more misguided than by that of GDP "growth." It is not a returns metric. It says nothing about sustainability and in this specific scenario (the one we have been in for at least thirteen years) it is virtually guaranteed to be concealing highly unsustainable misdirection of capital, if not its outright destruction.

Natural resources are also stocks, and the rates at which we extract from them, and at which they naturally replenish, are flows. This makes the idea of measuring solely the rate of increase (not growth) of consumption (not investment) all the more horrifying because it could well be the irreplaceable destruction of natural resources that is being nominally counted as contributing to economic well-being. This is clearly insane and is the height of high time preference, short-term thinking. As Elinor Ostrom writes of such *common pool resources* in *Governing the Commons*,

> The term "common pool resource" refers to a natural or man-made resource system that is sufficiently large as to make it costly (but not impossible) to exclude potential beneficiaries from obtaining benefits from its use. To understand the process of organizing and governing CPRs, it is essential to distinguish between the resource system and the flow of resource units produced by the system, while still recognizing the dependence of one on the other.

We will return to this in much greater depth in Chapter Five, *The Capital Strip Mine*, and again in Chapter Seven, A *Capital Renaissance*, but it is not just economics that requires a proper understanding of stocks and flows. It is the maintenance of the natural world. A more accurate interpretation of contemporary practice might be that it contrives to ignore the natural world as a mere "externality" to be discounted against growth in GDP, or other useless metrics. Given it does so as a matter of course, it follows that the dominant regime of political economy is not only financially bankrupt, but morally bankrupt and likely ecologically bankrupt as well.

What Would Happen in an Economically Healthy Capitalist Society

"The modern obsession with growth, and leverage to achieve that growth, is fundamentally philosophically at odds with the notion of creating a harmoniously balanced society, leading as it does to repeated cycles of debt-fuelled lunacy. Like a long-suffering father bailing out his son's gambling debts, governments have become accustomed to entertaining moral hazard by subsidizing risk taking by their financial institutions."

—Harris Irfan, *Heaven's Bankers*

Lots of things would happen in an economically healthy capitalist society. We will go through some of them relatively quickly as they are more or less common sense and fall out naturally from the previous discussion.

You would be able to preserve wealth in money. Money is the stored and accepted value of work done in the past, redeemable for goods and services in the present or future. Money should not constantly decline in value. There are considerations regarding the conditions of credit extension and systemic leverage that make the issue more complicated over shorter periods and that we want to avoid for now and will return to in Chapter Five, *The Capital Strip Mine*. But, all else equal, over a long enough period of time you would expect the purchasing power of money to increase roughly in line with aggregate return on reinvested capital, because the same past work done now has access to a greater amount of goods and services.

This means you would only lend capital to risky enterprises because you want to, not because you have to in order to have any hope of preserving your wealth. This in turn means capital would be priced so as to accurately reflect society's preferences for saving and consumption, and investment projects would be coordinated accordingly.

Governments would either run surpluses, borrow on an open market that prices risk freely, or it would be acknowledged and accepted that they could institute emergency taxes. Printing money is a stealth tax on wealth that disincentivizes holding money, as above. It has the same first-order effect on wealth transfers but has hidden second-order effects of misdirecting capital due to political expediency and cowardice.

Relatedly, governments would (or should), therefore, be always incentivized to act in the public interest. They should not be beholden to stoking financial market inflation at all costs. They should not be "bought" by Wall Street, nor have their banking laws written by bankers and their airline safety regulations written by unsafe airlines.

Investment decisions could legitimately include greater social and environmental considerations without risking fiduciary liability. Not to appease woke Twitter mobs on the one hand, while lobbying to preserve access to slave labor on the other; but out of genuine concern for community and preservation of the natural world. If you are constantly incentivized to increase short-term profits, you will consider firing everybody and moving production to China. If you are incentivized to increase long-term returns, you can double down on investment in your existing workforce and stomach the costs of more environmentally friendly inputs to production. The latter is clearly a broader social good but is still easy enough to motivate and justify given the effects would otherwise be worst felt in the local communities where the workforce is based.

Individuals and businesses would buy a lot more insurance. Preservation of wealth would be more important than the desperate need to grow it to stay ahead of inflation, and so the prudence of insurance against any and every "exogenous" disaster would be incentivized. Or, rather, it is obviously sensible in the first place, and so it wouldn't be incentivized *against*.

There would be no bailouts. Nothing would be "systemically important" because disasters — even "exogenous" ones — would be adequately insured against. When a business fails, its (willing) contributors of equity would be wiped out, its (willing) contributors of debt would not make whole, and its remaining liabilities would be covered by insurance. Government could even take a far more expansive role in protecting consumers in such cases given, (1) it can afford it, and (2) there is no competing incentive to side with business, nor a moral hazard to side with both but encourage recklessness nonetheless.

Company executives would be incentivized by long-term measures of growth in real value, not short-term measures of increases in per-share value. To be clear, buybacks are, in theory, a valuable tool to price capital properly. We do not argue against them in general, but we acknowledge that, in practice, they are often used as a means to enhance the latter rather than the former. We argue below this behavior is entirely a pathology of the dominant regime of political economy of which this book is a critique.

What Has Happened in Real Life

"In exactly the same way that all of us sit in our citizenship stadium and get nudged to hold up a card creating a common knowledge display of 'Yay, military!' so do all of us sit in our investor stadium and get nudged to hold up a card creating a common knowledge display of "Yay, capitalism!"
—Ben Hunt, *This Is Water*

We have spent the past ten years working on the assumption that the supply and price of money is unimportant, that maximizing the *increase* in GDP and stock market valuations is best for "the economy," that it doesn't matter that these numbers do not represent rates of reinvested return, and that "the average person" is a meaningful concept whose economic well-being we can measure. This is your brain on central banking, regulatory capture and financialization. As George Gilder writes in *Knowledge and Power*,

> The prevailing theory of capitalism suffers from one central and disabling flaw: a profound distrust and incomprehension of capitalists. Capitalists are owners who understand intimately what they own. For the last decade, the chief endeavor of capital markets has been to weaken all the disciplines of ordinary ownership.

In short, then, *what has happened*, is that the disciplines of ordinary ownership have been weakened tremendously successfully. We detail just three of the most obvious consequences:

Everybody gets levered up the wazoo. If you can't save because money does not retain value, then you have to be fully invested. If capital has all been misallocated such that price signals are unreliable and losses are artificially sustained, then any minor advantage has to be levered to achieve a satisfactory return. And if interest rates are artificially low, this might even seem like it makes good business sense.

If all your competitors are levered to the hilt and you aren't, even though you can optically afford it, you will be outcompeted. So, you have to do it, too. You can't compete prudently in the long run if your competitors spend you to death on cheap capital in the short run. Even if there are no competitive pressures, there will be pressures from shareholders. As with speculation and buybacks above, there are perfectly sensible ways for businesses to use leverage to beneficially affect capital allocation, for themselves and for the market at large. But usually, this is because the company has visibility on likely variations in cashflows and slack to absorb shocks — not *despite* having no visibility and no slack.

There are forms of leverage other than debt. You can think of leverage more abstractly as an induced vulnerability to shocks — "exogenous" or otherwise — in exchange for a magnified gain in their absence. The more debt you have, the more vulnerable you are to shocks to cash flow, because you have no choice but to pay the interest. But in many ways, other vulnerabilities to shocks can be even more dangerous. At least debt is relatively transparent: You can infer from the financial statements how much of a shock you can afford. Other vulnerabilities are less inherently knowable. Supply chain decisions can be a form of leverage: To get the absolute lowest costs that can be sweated out your setup, you could choose a single supplier (say, in China) and instruct them to deliver *right on time* to drive your carried inventory to effectively zero.

Of course, this means that any shock to this setup whatsoever will break it entirely. There is no slack. It is exceedingly fragile. Entire sectors grind to a halt because they are operationally levered to the eyeballs towards one specific task and cannot adjust to even mildly different circumstances.

Declining to hold a cash balance is a form of leverage *by omission*, as is declining to purchase insurance it would really be prudent to hold. If the need to be levered gets desperate enough, many will even consider *selling* insurance as a way to top up returns, clearly indifferent to the long-term implications of this insanity, because the short-term pressures are too intense to care. The behavioral pull here should not be underestimated. If absolutely everybody is selling insurance, you might want to consider buying some, and yet this takes a special resolve.

The Cantillon effect is justified as a public good. *The Cantillon effect* refers to the phenomenon that newly debased money is not distributed equally throughout society all at once but is introduced in a specific place, giving its initial holders illegitimate purchasing power at everybody else's expense. By the time the inflation washes through "the economy," those who receive the artificial money last have had reduced purchasing power for as long as it takes them to at best catch up with everybody else. Also, as this is done sneakily, the new money isn't priced in properly either, giving the Cantillon insiders an additional advantage. This is all rather amusing when you consider the likely hyperbolic response of financial elites and economists to the idea of "helicopter money." For all its obvious flaws, helicopter money is a substantially better *and fairer* idea than quantitative easing.

As per the dominant regime of political economy, the artificial money is introduced to the financial sector by means of "open market operations" in which central banks purchase financial instruments on the market to add to their balance sheets in order either to boost the prices of these assets, lower the borrowing costs of corporations, or both at once. This is justified because "growing GDP" and "supporting the stock market" are thought to be legitimate political goals — price signals, capital allocation, and rates of return be damned. Don't even think about taking account of the social fabric or ecological disaster. And if you do care about the environment, the solution is obviously to print a lot more money anyway.

This means that those whose income derives from the face value of financial instruments benefits at everybody else's expense. There is a decent argument to be made that, actually, an enormous number of pensions (public and private alike) dependent on these valuations, which justifies the social and political goal in the first place. But this obscures a crucial point: There is an important difference between benefitting from increases in valuation because your wealth is tied up in those assets, and because your income derives from periodically skimming the value of those assets. Those in the latter position are actually in charge of all of this financialized, regulatorily captured mess, and yet when challenged will wax lyrical about the savings of all those hardworking men and women in the former camp, pulling on your heartstrings until they snap. This is not to suggest vast conspiracy: We honestly aren't sure at all how many in the latter camp really understand any of this. They strike us as being primarily driven by straightforward self-interest, from which follows cognitive dissonance and incoherent justifications of things they merely want to be true.

Of course, this camp tends to be exceedingly well-off already — bankers, market makers, hedge funds, mutual fund managers; the derivative professional services of each of the above — lawyers, accountants, corporate managers; corporate *executives* incentivized by options, hence in turn incentivized to buy back stock — not because the stock is undervalued and capital pricing in aggregate will benefit from this decision, but because valuation is not considered at all, and the intention is to temporarily boost the stock price in time for the options to mature and be cashed in. Each of these people makes out like bandits while little old retired schoolteacher grandmas are left holding the bag when markets inevitably collapse and their pensions evaporate.

And of course, when that happens, who can we expect to go on CNBC and beg Congress for bailouts but precisely the corporate executives, bankers, and the like, whose maintaining of this regime of political economy caused it all in the first place. In dire enough straits, some executive teams will even have the stone-cold cojones to buy back $3 billion of stock with more or less the entirety of their company's free cash flow, take combined options packages worth over $10 million marked-to-market[58] *in one fiscal year*, no doubt boosted higher in time for payday by all these buybacks, and then hold their employees' jobs hostage in their negotiations for government bailouts.

These people's wealth is determined almost exclusively by how high they can push flows — stocks and rates of return be damned. Everybody else is left with low or negative real returns and depleted stocks of capital and wealth. This is why GDP growth can be positive, while almost everybody feels poorer. Almost everybody *is poorer*. Objectively so. Their savings have been stealthily taxed and handed to the already rich, while their everyday costs have gone up to reflect the dissipation of this inflation. Democratic domestic product growth (or lack thereof) would capture this, but nobody cares about DDP. GDP all the way, baby! Look at that S&P go!

Hey, wait, what happened?[59]

Financialization. In a world with only apples and oranges, bananas are new. But so are securities backed by mortgages on the properties of apple and orange farmers. Leading up to the last financial crisis, banks selling mortgage-backed securities (MBS) were *contributing to GDP growth*. They were incentivized to do so because their income came from skimming flows rather than growing stocks, and they were allowed to flagrantly lie about the risks of doing so by captured regulators. Of course, the products themselves were largely highly toxic — not only did they not create any real wealth, they encouraged the staking of real wealth against synthetic versions of the same underlying toxic assets. Capital was depleted, but only in the very long run, long after the banks had taken their cut and passed on the hot potato (well, most banks).

But that cut was growth! GDP went up! Bank stocks went up! Bonuses went up! Everything went up until suddenly it went down to lower than where it started. This might seem hopelessly irrational, and in one sense it is. But that is not the sense in which anybody is incentivized to behave in a world in which returns must chase inflation, insurance must be sold rather than bought, and you know full well you will be bailed out if (or when) you blow up. And not this is not just banks: United Airlines was, in early 2020, in an arguably conceptually identical position. It financialized its balance sheet (woohoo growth!) for little reason other than to enrich its executives, blew up (but … but … but exogenous!) and then wanted a bailout, which it duly received.

Nor is it *all* banks. It is perfectly possible to run a bank responsibly amid such insanity. It just takes ethics and guts. Legendary BB&T CEO John Allison wrote an entire book, *The Financial Crisis and the Free Market Cure: Why Pure Capitalism Is the World Economy's Only Hope*, about how flagrantly unethical banking and regulatory practices caused the previous crisis while he ran his bank well, including being subject to a Treasury shakedown to take TARP funds it didn't need in order to help the likes of Citigroup and Merrill Lynch look less like dangerous lunatics.[60]

Readers might see the unfortunately suggestive title of this book and think Allison is solely proposing greater privatization of gains. It is far more accurate to say he is proposing less socialization of losses. Amen to that. Ever eager to prevent the last crisis (or to *be seen* to have retroactively and heroically prevented the last crisis) much of the pre-GFC financialization has since been made illegal. And yet financialization continues apace. Imagine what grifting, off-balance sheet, 2010s shenanigans are on the cusp of seeing the light of day!

Figure 3. Source: US Bureau of Economic Analysis, prepared by the authors.

Consider Figure 3 of finance as a proportion of US GDP. Something is wrong here. Finance certainly ought to grow: If done properly, it contributes enormously to societal well-being by helping allocating capital efficiently. This is all well and good. But it should not grow *faster* than everything else, because it typically charges a percentage fee of the face value of the assets or securities that pass through its allocating hands. For finance to consistently grow as a proportion of GDP, either it is simply upping its take — which might be reasonable within bounds, but raises questions of adequate competition in the sector and of possible regulatory capture — or it is making more and more MBS-like time bombs. It is spinning off flows of toxic financial exposure, of whose values it is taking a cut but not a stake, that don't actually contribute to real economic returns, and hence to the aggregate growth in the stock of capital.

Once again, it isn't just banks. In recent years this attitude seems to have firmly entrenched itself in just about every industry. Credit card income represented 40% of Macy's profit before its recent bankruptcy.[61] Patreon is now basically a payday lender.[62] These aren't extraordinary cases. They are exactly what you would expect when interest rates are artificially low for long enough: Any business with enough customers and enough data on their customers' purchasing behavior can very likely borrow at low (fake) rates and effectively lend to customers at higher ones.

This arbitrage can even give them the leeway to make a loss on their actual good or service, furthering the widespread misallocation of capital away from things that can be sustainably profitable and towards facilitating indebted consumption of garbage

The obsession with GDP growth that fuels financialization also leads us to forget that inventing new things to produce tomorrow is as important, if not more so, than increasing what is produced today. So-called capitalists in such a regime can resemble the Soviet Union apparatchiks who focused exclusively on increasing output at the expense of managing the inputs or improving the quality of anything produced. Since the value of genuine innovation can't be measured, it tends to be discarded in a world focused exclusively on forever increasing such meaningless statistics as GDP and stock market capitalizations with no understanding of why these numbers ought to go up. In many ways it is like a cargo cult: When good things happen, stocks go up — so stocks going up *must be a good thing*! As visualized in Figure 4, official government policy from now on is for stocks to go up.

The effect of all this is that we make more of A, B, and C, and then move on to securitizations of A, B, and C, and synthetic securitizations of A, B, and C, and so on, until it all collapses. We never get to see X, Y, or Z. We never even think about what they might have been.

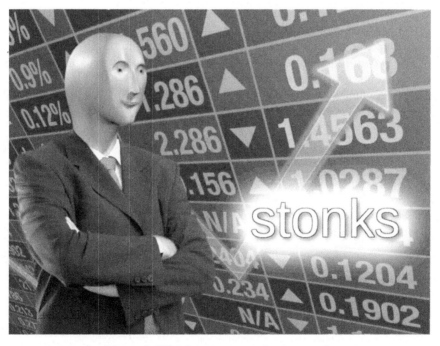

Figure 4. Official government policy in meme form.

Accelerated Descent

"What does Wall Street get out of financialization? A valuation story to sell. What does management get out of financialization? Stock-based compensation. What does the Fed get out of financialization? A (very) grateful Wall Street. What does the White House get out of financialization? Re-election. What do YOU get out of financialization? You get to hold up a card that says 'Yay, capitalism!'"
—Ben Hunt, *This Is Water*

The dominant regime of political economy in the West since 1971, and particularly acute since 2009, has been built on a set of related economic fallacies: There are no adverse consequences to manipulating the price and supply of money; economic well-being can be measured by increases in flows of revenue rather than the growth rate of profit over capital; such measures as GDP growth and stock market capitalization ought to be maximized at all costs; and the growth rate of the average matters but not the average growth rate.

Had we built a capitalistic society on the principles of sound money and long-term returns, a great many institutions and incentives would likely be radically different to what we see today. The structure of economic production would be far more robust to shocks, far more inclusive in its creation and distribution of wealth, and far less corrupting in its rewarding of political cronyism.

The factors we falsely deem to cause economic well-being are, in fact, fine-tuned to accelerate our inevitable descent into ever greater fragility, inequality, extraction, and financialization, and, ultimately, to the total depletion of capital. This is your brain on central banking, regulatory capture, and financialization. This is not capitalism.

But what would it seem like if it were?

Chapter Four

Wittgenstein's Money

*What would it seem like if it did seem like a global, digital,
sound, free, open-source, programmable money was
monetizing from absolute zero?*

"'When I use a word,' Humpty Dumpty said in rather a scornful tone, 'it means just what I choose it to mean — neither more nor less.'

'The question is,' said Alice, 'whether you can make words mean so many different things.'

'The question is,' said Humpty Dumpty, 'which is to be master — that's all.'"

—Lewis Carroll, *Through the Looking Glass*

Ludwig Wittgenstein once asked a friend, "Tell me, why do people say it is more natural to think that the sun rotates around the Earth than that the Earth is rotating?" The friend said, "Well, obviously, because it just seems like the sun is going around the Earth." Wittgenstein replied, "Well, what would it seem like if it did seem like the Earth were rotating?"

This is not capitalism. That much we know. Whatever it is — what we call *degenerate fiat "capitalism"* — seems to be collapsing in slow motion. Even were it not for its own miraculous traits and merits, which we will discuss in due course, this is reason alone to brace ourselves for the wider world's sudden and ill-informed interest in Bitcoin, because Bitcoin probably fixes this.

A great many newcomers will arrive with an open mind — as we all did once — but so, too, will many representatives of the incumbents to this disruption emerge from the woodwork to insist that what we can see with our very own eyes isn't actually happening because, according to their theory, it can't.

Bitcoin can't be a store of value because it *has no* intrinsic value. It can't be a unit of account because it is too volatile. It can't be a medium of exchange because it is not widely used to price goods and services. These are the three properties of money. Therefore, bitcoin can't be money. But bitcoin has no other basis for being valued, therefore, it is valueless.

We call this argument, *semantics therefore reality*. Its proponents are too used to appeals to emotion or authority to be open to an appeal to reason; they are too used to aesthetic or codified knowledge to be open to knowledge that must be arrived at practically.

And what could possibly — *practically* — falsify this? It is, at root, a claim about the material world; about what will, or in this case *won't*, happen in real life. And yet it looks rather like it relies entirely on the meanings of words. In discussing dollarization in Ecuador — the instructive process of an "official" money being spontaneously replaced by a simpler superior money — Larry White says of those who deny by definition that such a thing can even happen that they, "Are only looking at the blackboard and not at what is happening outside the window."[63] Bitcoin doesn't *feel like* it makes sense, and it is nowhere to be found in the textbooks, therefore it doesn't. This is a curious approach to understanding novel phenomena, that, in general, we would not recommend. Reality doesn't care how you describe it.

But there is also a softer, slipperier, more agnostic form of the semantic theory that acknowledges that *something* is happening. That bitcoin is not *nothing*, but that it surely cannot be money because it is so dissimilar to the standard (semantic) conception of what money should be and how it should behave that the proposition is too uncomfortable to accept.

It certainly seems like a network of some kind: It is global, digital, sound, free, open, and programmable. And it has undeniably increased in value from a point in the past when it was worth nothing at all. But does this distinguish it from a regular old financial bubble? Can "money" be reconciled with bubble-like behavior? And is bitcoin's digital nature such a plus? Doesn't the internet enable a speed and potency of virality that is arguably finely tuned to inflate a bubble in anything deemed openly, programmably digital? Bitcoin may be something — maybe the "blockchain technology" it runs on? — but, obviously, it just *seems like* bitcoin isn't money.

Wittgenstein would be most unimpressed. He would likely ask, "What would it seem like if it did seem like a global, digital, sound, open, programmable money was monetizing from absolute zero?"

Let us ask that too.

The Times, They Are A-Changin'

"Everybody is so terribly sensitive about the things they know best."
—Norton Juster, *The Phantom Tollbooth*

The semantic theory is alarmingly static. This stasis is rooted in its semantic chicanery: Many languages have different verbs to distinguish between "being" as in having some property intrinsically or circumstantially, such as *ser* and *estar*, respectively, in Spanish. English does not. We *are* male just as we *are* hungry. But in which sense *is* Bitcoin volatile? Is it *intrinsically* volatile or is it volatile at some moment, in some circumstances, relative to some standard? Are goods and services somehow fundamentally resistant to being priced in Bitcoin? What happens if you try to do so? Is it like dividing by zero?

Imagine if all respectable business knowledge had been derived from studying large, established companies because there had never been a start-up in living memory. If a start-up then came along, people might well say, *"That's not a business because it doesn't make a profit,"* or *"That's not a business because it doesn't have a defined business plan."* Clearly, this would be ill-advised. That is not to say that their models and definitions would be perfectly wrong instead of perfectly right, but rather that things are not so binary. Reality is messy, and it is reality we should care about, not our theories of reality that, it turns out, have never really been tested.

In this chapter, we propose we should reject the arrogance of *knowing* that a new money cannot emerge because reality follows from our semantics. We hope that by instead embracing ignorance and uncertainty, by focusing on plausible behaviors and circumstances, and by looking to discover rather than to decree, we will have the tools to recognize Bitcoin's emergence rather than rejecting it out of hand as a disprovable theorem. We will probe what it might seem like if it did seem like bitcoin was money.

In Chapter Five, *The Capital Strip Mine*, we will paint a dire picture of what we could expect to happen to the ability to create and sustain capital when a monetary regime is contrived to ignore — or even go against — the ideal characteristics we are about to explore. In Chapter Six, *Bitcoin Is Venice*, we will take substantial poetic license in charting the course for recovery from such a disaster — what it might seem like *as it is seeming like* a global, digital, sound, open, programmable money is monetizing from absolute zero. In Chapter Seven, *A Capital Renaissance*, we will look at where this is already leading, and in Chapter Eight, *These Were Capitalists*, we will speculate as to where it will lead next. But first, how we get there.

Apples, Zebras, and Knowledge

"Knowledge is at the heart of dynamic civilization — but so is surprise. A dynamic civilization maximizes the production and use of knowledge by accepting widespread ignorance. At the simplest level, only people who know they do not know everything will be curious enough to find things out. To celebrate the pursuit of knowledge, we must confess our ignorance; both that celebration and that confession are central to dynamic culture. Dynamism gives individuals both the freedom to learn and the incentives to share what they discover. It not only permits but encourages the incentives to share what they discover. It not only permits but encourages decentralized experiments and competitive trial and error — the infinite series by which new knowledge is created. And, just as important, a dynamic civilization allows its members to gain from the things they themselves do not know but other people do. Its systems and institutions evolve to let people develop, extend, and act on their particular knowledge without asking permission of a higher, but less informed, authority. A dynamic civilization appreciates, protects, and nurtures specialized, dispersed, and often unarticulated knowledge."
—Virginia Postrel, *The Future and Its Enemies*

Let us start with a thought experiment. Imagine you could see the future in a very peculiar and economically relevant way: You know how everybody will value everything at every point in time. You are certain of it, and you are never wrong. Would you ever need money?[64]

If you know how you will value things then you know what *you* will want to buy at any given point in the future, say Alice's apples. Now, normally you would need money because Alice might not value whatever you had that you wanted to trade, say zebras. But in this case, you know how Alice will value zebras because you know how she will value everything. If that's enough to buy the apples, great. If not, find something else she values more highly, say beer, and then go find Bob. Now, if Bob also doesn't value your zebras, that's fine too because you can just keep doing this until you close the loop, given you know all these valuations. You can instantaneously grasp the best path from zebra to apple and trade all the way to what you want. If these valuations flap around over time (which you will also know), you can plan to orchestrate your trading across time to get the best rates.

An obvious objection might be that all this excess trading would be a massive nuisance. Maybe you wouldn't actually *need* money, but it would still save you time and energy because rather than having to deduce and execute the highest value trading loop in advance of every purchase, you could jump immediately to who valued zebras most, get the money, and go back to Alice. And in fact, you could do even better, because you would sell the zebra when its value peaked and keep the money for however long happens to pass before wanting to buy the apples. Fair enough, money is still useful.

But now imagine that *everybody* had this superpower. Everybody knew what everybody else valued at every time. Now would you need money? Let's ring up Alice and find out. You go to Alice with your zebras to get some apples. Does it matter that Alice doesn't want zebras? We don't think it does anymore because Alice now has the superpower, too. If she doesn't want zebras herself, she knows that Quintin does. If she wants Quintin's quiches, perfect. If not — if she really wants Peter's pies — then luckily Peter also knows that Quintin wants zebras. If he wants Quintin's quiches, perfect, if not … what happens is that the previously inconvenient highest value trading loop doesn't now need to be executed — it merely needs to exist at all in order for everybody to establish the relevant exchange rate between whatever they have and are trying to buy, or whatever they want and are trying to sell. This knowledge would make money moot.

If we were at all tempted to believe that some particularly economically astute individual could, in theory, know all others' future valuations, we would be forced to admit they also knew all future events as well. How could they know how Alice will value things at an arbitrary point in the future if we don't know *what things there are to value*?

This is the key to unwinding the thought experiment. Nobody can know all future events, nor the whims of all perfect strangers. Arguably, we can barely know *any* future events or the whims of *any* strangers. We may be reasonably sure of events close to us in time and circumstance, but as we get further away from our own familiarity, further into the future, or both, we obviously can claim to know less and less. Hence, we might be able to guess what we ourselves or others close to us value *now*, but others we know less well, or anybody at all further and further into the future, we cannot know. If we did know this, we would not need money. But we can't, therefore money is useful. Money conveys *information* in the form of *prices* that we otherwise would not and could not know.

What this shows is that a "double coincidence of wants" that makes barter untenable at any worthwhile scale has little to do with "convenience" and is first and foremost a product of knowledge. We can only have a limited appreciation of others' valuations, and this appreciation diminishes the further removed from us they are in circumstance and in time. And note, this includes our future selves: We do not know for sure what we will value in the future because we do not know what will *happen to us* in the future. Money is useful to us because of economic uncertainty: Our fundamental inability to know much at all about what all others think and about what is going to change.[65]

Money would ideally give its users a sense of certainty about the future. A kind of tacit agreement with the rest of the economic network precisely because next to nothing else can be known surely enough to be agreed upon in advance. But if a new money were to emerge, it would very much be challenging the agreement, and hence would be fraught with uncertainty over the period of its emergence. Its very existence would represent a kind of *disagreement* that would seem confusing and disorienting.

We could point to this engendered uncertainty as clear-cut evidence against the new money, and reason by extension that the necessary network effects will fail to materialize. But this would be to avoid the legitimate question as to whether accepting greater uncertainty in the short run is worth gaining greater certainty in the long run, and if network effects could develop on this basis instead. This would depend on the real-life merits. There would be no textbook answer; no equation to solve; no oracle to consult; no definitions to check against. Particularly not definitions that are only absolutely valid in precisely the case of zero competition, maximal certainty, and static time — a kind of inexplicably non-entropic universe. A new money could not be helpfully described as providing utility as a "medium of exchange" from its beginnings — although, in the long run, being *digital* certainly wouldn't hurt its chances in this regard.

What it would seem like if it did seem like a new money were emerging would be a promise of superior certainty in the future, with an admission of increased uncertainty in the present. It would seem as much like a dangerous and exciting narrative and experiment as a provable guarantee.

Purchasing Power in a Changing World

"The quantities of consumption goods at human disposal are limited only by the extent of human knowledge of the causal connections between things, and by the extent of human control over these things. Increasing understanding of the causal connections between things and human welfare, and increasing control of the less proximate conditions responsible for human welfare, have led mankind, therefore, from a state of barbarism and the deepest misery to its present stage of civilisation and well-being, and have changed vast regions inhabited by a few miserable, excessively poor, men into densely populated civilized countries. Nothing is more certain than that the degree of economic progress of mankind will still, in future epochs, be commensurate with the degree of progress of human knowledge."
—Carl Menger, *Principles of Economics*

But *how usefully* can money fill a demand for certainty? We should think about what it would mean for money to be more or less useful in this way, but attempting to measure this utility brings us to the precipice of a philosophical pickle. Given this utility is understood as an emergent reaction to constant and unpredictable change, we must be careful to choose a measure that is invariant to this change. We don't want to use a stretchy ruler. We must dig a little deeper lest we fall back into the semantic theory and demand money be a "store of value" without further exploration of what *being a store of value* could practically consist of.

As a starting point, let us assume it means that a candidate money retains its purchasing power over time, that it will not intrinsically depreciate — like a tool that we need to repair or food that will rot — or that will lose value for more intangible reasons, in the sense of going out of fashion — like clothes or jewelry, or real estate in a declining area.

We immediately run into problems: Notice that whether or not any such item "retains its purchasing power" is precisely subject to the change we admit we cannot predict. It is circumstantial, behavioral, and depends on the subjective valuations of other market participants. A depreciated tool may nonetheless become *more valuable* if a new use for it is discovered and it turns out to be in short supply. Rotted food may command a higher price as compost — perhaps there is a dire compost shortage — or maybe it is discovered that it actually tastes *better* at a certain maturity. Clothes, jewelry, or real estate might come back into fashion and appreciate just as easily as they once went out.

There is yet another difficulty: Surely, we want a failure to maintain purchasing power to capture some way in which the money ends up being valued less relative to what we might want to purchase, but not some way in which everything else ends up costing more? In other words, that the money is less useful, not that everything else is more useful. In the latter case — say a war or a natural disaster that causes all real costs to soar — it hardly seems reasonable to describe the probable resultant price increases in terms of money's decline in value rather than on things having become much more costly to produce. Taken to an extreme, it seems nonsensical to expect that money's ability to "store value" will entitle its holder to consume some good that may not even end up being produced — or some quantity of goods greater than everything that *is* produced.

But it gets even worse: What if an entirely new good or service is invented over the period across which we intend to maintain purchasing power? Has our candidate money's purchasing power increased *infinitely*? What if a good stops being produced or sold on the market altogether? Has our purchasing power decreased infinitely? What to make of all this?

It might have first seemed natural to mean specifically that a candidate money "retains purchasing power" if, at t_0, it can purchase a given quantity of every other good or service in the market, then, at t_1, it can still purchase this same quantity in each case.[66] Upon probing, however, this seems naïve — in the case of a new invention, "infinite" seems an amusing but entirely unhelpful answer. In the case of natural disaster, we can't expect to purchase the same amount because we can't expect there to have been *produced* the same amount, which seems not to be a negative attribute of the money, but rather the money accurately reflecting a negative change in the economic network. Perhaps we could track the changes in a "basket" of goods, but then how do we decide how to weight the inputs and how do we adjust for quality improvements? Any choice will be arbitrary and will better reflect the reality of some economic actors than others.

But even in what we might think of as more "regular" or "normal" economic circumstances, it proves tricky to pin down. Imagine that some good, a widget, hasn't changed at all between t_0 and t_1, but that some new invention, a fidget, has superseded it. Nobody wants widgets anymore because fidgets are far better, so widget makers stop producing widgets, and the suppliers to widget makers stop producing widget-making squidgets, too. Now, with nobody making squidgets, it becomes very expensive to make widgets and although far, far fewer are made, their price becomes much higher than at t_0, pre-fidget. So, has the money with which all these prices have been quoted "lost purchasing power"?

If you still want to buy widgets, then yes, you have lost desirable purchasing power. If you prefer fidgets, then no, you have gained purchasing power. But crucially, these are connected at root by decisions to shift real, scarce resources from producing one good to another. Hoping for an answer that can be sensibly relative only to our individual demands is myopic because the prices will be dictated by the aggregation of *all demands* (and for that matter, all supplies — people who *sell* widgets and squidgets have a stake in this too!). If *any* demands or supplies change — due to discovery, taste, costs, or opportunity costs elsewhere — any circumstance or behavior anywhere — then the allocation of scarce resources to try to match supply to demand will almost certainly change, too, and in a way that will wrap back around eventually to affect the original demands and supplies.

Can we grapple with this? And can we coherently describe *why* it is difficult to grapple with? Even before resolving this, it is worth pointing out that money itself will be subject to these same forces — it will just be a lot less natural to point out whenever there is no legitimate monetary competition because we are using it as our measure in the first place. The binaries of the semantic theory seem to absolutely apply. This money *would be* a unit of account, and while we can assess *how* it is accounting for units, it means little to ask if it is doing so *well*. And even this begs the question, "*Well* relative to *what*?"

But were a new money to emerge, it would naturally have to emerge in a specific place, at a specific time, in a given locality of the economic network. It would not appear everywhere, all at once, and hence could not be helpfully described as providing utility as a "unit of account" from its beginnings — although, in the long run, being *global* certainly wouldn't hurt its chances in this regard.

It would present different utilities to different people depending on their circumstances, their behaviors, their beliefs, and its price. Its entry into the web of supply and demand would change the allocation of scarce resources in ways that would wrap back around and eventually affect its own supply and demand. Hoping for an explanation of its value that can be sensibly relative to individual demands is myopic.

What it would seem like if it did seem like a new money were emerging would be widely disparate views, rapid change, and no consensus, with sentiment ebbing and flowing unpredictably as the relative merits of the promise of future certainty from the challenger and the supposed failures of this promise from the incumbent were constantly being weighed and re-weighed by the market.

Time, Energy, and the Triangle Game

"Life ... uh ... finds a way."
— Jeff Goldblum as Dr. Ian Malcolm, *Jurassic Park*

Have you ever played the Triangle Game? Here's what you do: Get in a big group and instruct everybody to mill around aimlessly. While this is happening, instruct everybody to pick two other people but keep their choice to themselves. Then, on a signal, tell everybody to move to form an equilateral triangle with the two people they chose. Then, watch chaos ensue. Even if the activity of the network as a whole ever seems to calm down, it can just as easily spiral out of control again with one step because one person moving may be reacted to by others, which may be reacted to by others still, and so on. Every individual decision has effects that permeate unpredictably through the entire network, unevenly over time, while every individual decision-maker is only immediately aware of the dynamics in their small locality, just like in a network of economic exchange.[67]

Asking an individual to evaluate an invariant of the economic aggregate in terms of only their own supplies and demands is rather like asking a participant in the Triangle Game to explain the average speed of every player solely in terms of their own next step. You can't even begin to explain it. You can't even conceive of what such an explanation might consist of. And that's holding just about everything we can constant in a small environment: If millions of participants started periodically changing their choice of vertices and entering and exiting the game, all while the geography on which the game was being played was shifting under their feet, that might start to better resemble real economic activity.

Notice also that this does not mean there is no order and pure chaos: To each participant there is clear, and even *simple*, order. They are not inventing motions on the spot they aim to be random. They are obeying simple rules, without creativity and without chance. That a system is predictable does not mean it is deterministic — such is the key insight at the heart of statistical mechanics. But perhaps less intuitively obvious to many is that the inverse also fails: That a system is deterministic does not mean it is predictable. The triangle game is fully determined in the minds of its participants and yet fundamentally unknowable at any more macroscopic scale. Jane Jacobs makes a related observation in *The Death and Life of Great American Cities*, writing,

> To see complex systems of functional order as order, and not as chaos, takes understanding. The leaves dropping from the trees in autumn, the interior of an airplane engine, the entrails of a rabbit, the city desk of a newspaper, all appear to be chaos if they are seen without

comprehension. Once they are seen as systems of order, they actually look different.[68]

The Triangle Game is precisely complex enough to require that we cannot pretend we can understand it as a whole, yet neither can we insist that no parts of it are capable of being understood. Scale matters. Moreover, *minds matter.* The difference between a rabbit and a newspaper editor is that a rabbit does not understand its intestines whereas the newspaper editor understands their desk. To reflect the language of a few paragraphs up: The process by which their desk ends up in a given state is likely too complex for another mind to grasp merely by *looking* — due to complexity, sure, but also due to *both creativity and chance.*

Humans *act* in ways that make sense to them. This simple axiom is practically a tautology and is certainly at least obviously true from experience, and yet contemporary academic economics has somehow contrived to ignore its consequences: A human being necessarily understands what they are doing, but another human being almost certainly does not understand what the first is doing; in most cases will not, and in many cases *cannot.*

This does not bode well for understanding economic cooperation! How to cooperate at all if nobody can understand anybody else on philosophical principle? A naïve answer might be: *It doesn't matter because we have prices.* There is some Hayekian insight here in terms of tapping into the magic of the clearing of markets, but we must be more rigorous as there is a sense in which this is not an answer at all: We have swapped out one unexplained phenomenon for another — possibly an *even more complicated one*!

What do humans collectively take prices to *mean* when they are purposefully acting? What opportunity cost do they all have in common?

Consider that rather than accepting a price that is dependent on *literally every other demand and supply in the network,* you could always make the widget yourself. If there are literally no widgets for sale anymore, you needn't assume your purchasing power has "infinitely decreased" if the inputs can still be purchased and the knowledge of how to combine them still exists and can be accessed. You can still "purchase" a widget, and you can still sensibly conceive of its cost: The initial purchase of the inputs, plus the opportunity cost of your own time and energy, since any time and energy you devote to making a widget you can't devote to making or doing anything else that might later be traded for money.

If, on the other hand, widgets are still mass produced, you will very likely find that the difference between the cost of the inputs versus the available market price of the finished widget is one you cannot reconcile as a viable opportunity cost of your time and energy turning one into the other. Since so much effort has been put into minimizing this exact opportunity cost of time and energy on the part of the widget manufacturer as a requirement to stay competitive, you will probably rather pay the difference than commit this time and energy yourself.

Upon reflection, this process and mentality is exactly the same for anybody who transforms one good or service into another in order to later sell at a profit: The price is deemed by buyers to be an acceptable equivalent of their time and energy, that the costs were treated in the same way by the (current) seller, and that the hoped-for profit is deemed the best use of their time and energy in transforming one into the other. In setting out to make our own widgets, whoever we buy the squidgets from will have gone through the same thought process and calculations. The gwidget-makers (you need a gwidget to make a squidget) will have done the same.

And so on, all the way down to the absolute origin of the supply chain of every good or service. If a good, extracting raw materials, which, if you own the land, takes only time and energy; if a service, only time and energy; if, in either case you nonetheless require tools, back into the loop you go. The entirety of the chain of prices across *all exchanges* is shown to be a series of independent and real-time decisions about how to value one's own time and energy and best guesses as to how others value theirs.

We can readily imagine, if you go back to trying to create your own widget, just how long it would take if you were committed not to use money to pay *any* upfront costs for inputs but to spend only your own time and energy fashioning everything required from beginning to end. The difference between however you value this presumably enormous amount of time and energy and the cost you actually pay for the inputs, is exactly the value created by money intermediating a much more specialized series of exchanges.

Back to our original circumstances, if the prices of widgets have gone up because resources have been pulled from squidgets, and so on, what this really means is that a great many economic actors no longer believe their time and energy to be best allocated to widget making. Although we can articulate their reasons for believing this, we cannot say it is objectively right or wrong. It is as "right" as they end up profiting by how they allocate their time and energy instead. The invariant measure we require is therefore not of widgets, specifically, but of the aggregate contribution of time and energy to productive enterprises as collectively valued by their output. Widgets might matter to you, but we can tell by the fact of their being produced far less (or not at all) that they no longer matter as much to the network. Time and energy matter to the network, but circumstances and behaviors have changed what time and energy can be transformed into.

Readers may have noticed we sneakily begged the question when we originally introduced natural disasters: We said this would cause "real costs" to soar. But what is a "real" cost? If we aren't measuring costs in money, then what are we measuring them by? Now we have our answer: in human time and human energy. In the case of a natural disaster, we are assuming a great deal of intermediate resources of production is destroyed, and we have to devote time and energy to rebuilding it all if we hope to maintain the same output. Whatever output we achieve will cost more money *because* it will take more time and more energy.

And so, "maintain purchasing power" as a property of money can only sensibly mean: If, at t_0, it can purchase a given proportion of the whole output of the economic network, then, at t_1, it can purchase that same proportion. Regardless of what has inevitably changed in the meantime, money is useful to the extent it lets us contribute time and energy to the network at one point in time knowing that our claim will not be diluted, and that at any future point in time we can receive the same proportion back.

The semantic theory leaves us hanging with ungrounded promises of "storing value." Value as decreed by whom? And stored relative to what? It is far more fruitful to understand money as preserving a contribution of time and energy relative to the economic network that utilizes it. A new money could not be helpfully described as providing utility as a "store of value" from its beginnings — although, in the long run, being *sound* certainly wouldn't hurt its chances in this regard.

Even if it is clear its contribution will be preserved, it will not be at all clear what will happen to the network itself and hence how valuable this preservation really is in the wider scheme of things. But the better a money can preserve such contributions and protect them from dilution, the greater the chances its network will attract time and energy, and hence value. Money is the minimal information that captures the social truth of the value of time and energy. The question is how to make this information as scarce as time and energy themselves.[69]

The semantic theory assumes the incumbent money's network is mature and total, and hence can't make any worthwhile sense of a challenger "gaining share" of "time and energy stored." If it is messy and confusing in real life, then of course, it is messy and confusing from the perspective of such static and limited definitions.

What it would seem like if it did seem like a new money were emerging would be superficially extreme uncertainty masking such a substantial improvement in the promise of protection from dilution that the nuisance of the uncertainty of the period of emergence could credibly claim to be outweighed.

Money, Capital, and Social Scalability

"Capital, as I argued earlier, is therefore not created by money; it is created by people whose property systems help them to cooperate and think about how they can get the assets they accumulate to deploy additional production. The substantial increase of capital in the West over the past two centuries is the consequence of gradually improving property systems, which allowed economic agents to discover and realise the potential in their assets, and thus to be in a position to produce the noninflationary money with which to finance and generate additional production."
—Hernando de Soto, *The Mystery of Capital*

Do we necessarily *want* the same proportion of time and energy back at some point in the future? What if some proportion of time and energy will produce *less* in the future than it does now? What kind of garbage utility is that giving us?!

To set the stage nicely for Chapter Five, *The Capital Strip Mine*, we want to explore arguably the direst flaw of the semantic theory. The economic change catalyzed by money has important consequences *for money*. A theory of money that ignores the possibility of experimentation, dynamism, and change blinds itself and its adherents to the most interesting aspect of its own alleged subject matter. A new money that advantageously plays to these possibilities will have an ace in the hole for the long term that may help it overcome the uncertainty it generates for itself in the short term — all of which will fly completely under the radar of the semanticists.

Let us start by thinking about how and why such garbage utility could come about. A natural disaster is perhaps a clean example once again. What we assume has been destroyed is essentially *tools*. If we once had a tractor that was battered by a hurricane, we will now need to use a plow, which will take much more time and energy to yield the same output. Given any constraints on time and energy, we will have to accept a lower yield. Trading our earlier time and energy for what it currently produces seems like a raw deal. If the plow has also been washed away, and the hoe and digging sticks for that matter, we are almost back at a state of nature in which the *tools* we desire need to come from raw time and energy itself, with no intermediation.

Working forwards, then, from this original state, we see that it is precisely this commission of time and energy to creating tools that not only increases potential output, but frees up time and energy to perpetuate this very process by using these tools to create yet more complicated tools. We can consider making squidgets instead of just widgets. If we free up enough time and energy with squidgets, we can redirect the surplus towards gwidgets. With so many productive options beyond putting time and energy directly into the bare necessities, we can forget about our worries and our strife and start to specialize in using these increasingly complex tools. Money very likely emerges at some point in this process of complexification, as the accompanying uncertainty this complexity generates across circumstances and time creates a reciprocal demand for certainty that money fulfills.

Of course, the process of *making* the more complex tools is by no means clear-cut from the perspective of value. We risk the time and energy being wasted on an output that is no more productive than existing tools or not productive *at all*. Or perhaps it is productive, but the output is no longer valued. But equally, we can think of the time and energy provided by previous tools as buying the cushion to absorb such a risk. That might manifest literally or, of course, via money: We trade time and energy, however indirectly, for money, that we save up to see us through a patch of experimentation of tool development such that we can afford not to rely on its outcome.

However, there will come a time when individuals' skills become so specialized, the tools we incrementally desire become so complex, and the uncertainty inherent in their development so great, that we cannot rely on individuals to create them. Realistically, no single person has the knowledge to build a tractor all on their own (or a pencil for that matter),[70] never mind the time. But equally, the minimum collection of those with the necessary skills may not be equally willing to take on the risk that their time and energy committed to inventing a tractor comes to naught.

Money can save the day: those who *are* willing to take the risk can pay for the contribution of those who are not. This might seem so straightforward as to be banal, but notice we are using money in an essentially new way: not because we want to guard against the consequences of uncertainty, but because we want to embrace them. The uncertainty in question will not be an accident of our circumstances — it will be entirely deliberate. We want to tempt others to engage in economic behavior, the output of which is uncertain, at the opportunity cost of behavior that is presumably much more certain. In effect, we are buying uncertainty with certainty.

More precisely, we are creating *capital*. Capital is not *just* complex tools, nor is it the money used to motivate their creation, but could be thought of as the extent to which the two are fluid. We believe Hernando de Soto has by far the best appreciation of the true subtlety of the concept, from his brilliant, *The Mystery of Capital*:

> Capital is not the accumulated stock of assets but the potential it holds to deploy new production. This potential is, of course, abstract. It must be processed and fixed into a tangible form before we can release it." Later he adds, "capital, like energy, is also a dormant value. Bringing it to life requires us to go beyond looking at our assets as they are to

actively thinking about them as they could be. It requires a process for fixing an asset's economic potential into a form that can be used to initiate additional production.

De Soto focuses on the sociological importance of property rights in providing for such a process. For our purposes, we can be ever-so-slightly more abstract and see the ultimate *point* of property rights and the role they play as providing a certainty of economic relevance that can be measured with money and bargained against the uncertainty we want to exploit. Money provides a means to motivate embracing the risk of the opportunity cost in time and energy of exploring our assets' potential in the hopes of realizing even greater production. Highly certain money and highly uncertain complex tools are both *capital* to the extent they can be seamlessly exchanged.

The emergence of capital has at least three notable effects. Firstly, the more capital we succeed in creating — the process is risky, remember, and we can't guarantee we will create any — the more specialized we are likely to individually become, meaning the less our understanding of supply and demand helpfully extends beyond our own circumstances and into the future. Secondly, the more capital we merely try to create, the more uncertainty we directly invite into the network. Thirdly, the possibility of creating capital in future rather than just deferring consumption means that the uncertainty we want to brace against with money need not imply a risk but an opportunity as well.

That capital creation is more or less dependent on human creativity means that the chance to take part in capital creation could arise at any moment. Wanting to ensure we are able to do so if or when the opportunity arises further increases money's utility, which, of course, further enables capital creation. For all three reasons, fundamental economic uncertainty will increase. Money, having allowed for the circumstances for capital to emerge, therefore, becomes all the more useful the more capital proliferates.

Humans act in ways that make sense to them: ways that have *meaning*. But entrepreneurs must act in ways they predict will have meaning to others. There is something deeply social about this act. As we argued in Chapter Two, *The Complex Markets Hypothesis,* the entrepreneur does not, *cycle through the space of every thought that can possibly be had until they hit on one that happens to be a business plan.* That is to say, the creation of capital is not a mathematical or a probabilistic exercise. It requires creativity, intuition, and judgment. It requires a theory of mind and an empathy for the subjective preferences of others.

But in particular it requires a delicate balance of old and new. Capital creation must not be so old as to offer only more of the same, likely at greater expense and poorer quality. But it must not be so new as to confuse and alienate potential customers; not a single tone and pitch of signal — a single, unchanging bit of information — nor white noise either — utterly random information, incomprehensible and irreproducible. Not order, and not chaos, but complexity.

If economic activity is a language, trade a speech act, and prices the compressed signal of syntax, then entrepreneurship bears a remarkable resemblance to authorship. Great works of literature must strike a similarly delicate balance. They must not be so traditional as to be dull, yet not so novel as to be jarring. They must be traditional *enough* to be intelligible, yet novel enough to present a challenge. They accept a literary form, then they stress its conventions.

Yet try as they might to be original, they find themselves always within a canon; that they communicate in a publicly shared language at all means that, while their syntax may be simple and rulebound, their semantics beg to be experienced subjectively: to connect with and resonate in an also-thinking, also-feeling mind. The author must respect the humanity of her audience and in doing so, she must take a leap of faith. In *After Babel*, George Steiner beautifully captures this tension, its extremities, and its potential for resolution,

> An analogy with chess may clarify the issue. It is estimated that the number of possible board-positions is of the order of 10^{43} and that there are, within the constraint of accepted rules, some 10^{125} ways of reaching these. Until now, it is thought, men have played fewer than 10^{15} games. There is, therefore, no practical limit to the previously untried moves still to be made, or to the number which the opponent can understand and reply to. But despite this boundless potential for novelty, the occurrence of genuinely significant innovation, of inventions which in fact modify or enlarge our sense of the game, will always be quite rare. It will always be in a miniscule proportion to the totality of moves played or playable. The man who has something really new to say, whose linguistic innovation is not merely one of saying but of meaning — to poach on H.P. Grice's distinction — is exceptional. Culture and syntax, the cultural matrix which syntax maps, hold us in place. This, of course, is the substantive ground for the impossibility of an effective private language. Any code with a purely individual system of reference is existentially threadbare. The words we speak bring with them far more knowledge, a far denser charge of feeling than we consciously possess; they multiply echo.

As there cannot be a private language, nor can there be a private money, nor private capital, nor a private economy. Like an author, the entrepreneur also must take a leap of faith and create something they believe will be valued by an independent mind. The dry syntax of price and the momentary act of a trade might suggest a transience to the enterprise, but its semantics is in its capital: The stored time and energy of all prior successful attempts to forge connections of value between independent minds. The capital stock is a literary corpus that likewise ought to be learned and respected so as to ensure it can be nurtured, replenished, and grown. It has brought us all to where we are now and it forms the bedrock of understanding of any economically thinking and acting human. However transient or disconnected one's actions and decisions might momentarily seem — however inconsequential an act of consumption or pointless an act of destruction — they have meaning and can in principle be understood only as following from the irreducibly complex context from which they were produced.

Alternatively, Ludwig von Mises's socialist calculation problem applies also to literary analysis. There can be no socialist overlord of literature capable of unilaterally determining what a given text *means*. And it is not even that they *should not*, but that the proposition itself is philosophically incoherent: To propose it is to misunderstand the nature of subjective value. An official price set by a socialist and an official interpretation set by a literature tsar are the same kind of arrogant, incoherent untruth: It is a proclamation of the shared content of everybody else's minds. It doesn't matter what it says: It is wrong.

The process of an author and an entrepreneur alike is fraught with irresolvable uncertainty. To assume it can be known, never mind that it can be reduced to mathematical formalism, is so stupid and so arrogant as to be comical. To "model" an "economy" is strikingly similar to having a computer "simulate" the next great novel or the course of fashion in clothing, music, or poetry.[71] If pushed far enough, there are shades of outright blasphemy. To presume that fallen man can know such a thing is an insult to God; for the polytheistic or the religiously disinclined it is at the very least an insult to collective human intelligence.

As James C. Scott put it in *Seeing Like a State*, it is a distinctly high-modernist stupidity and arrogance. It is a kind of stupid arrogance the reader would be hard-pressed to source prior to, perhaps, the late eighteenth century, and originating anywhere besides north-western Europe. Religious tradition the world over is unanimous in rejecting this profound lack of humility before God, *the gods*, Mother Nature, the Universe, the truth, even culture and society — regardless of metaphysical premise, whoever or whatever is rightly appreciated as being greater than any individual. Understood this way, "uncertainty" is not some mathematical or psychological curiosity; it is obvious. It could not be any other way.

In capital accumulation and authorship alike, a successful contribution will serve to further this uncertainty by deepening the canon of meaning. And it is surely from the canon that such simple building blocks *as the syntax* emerge. Trade and poetry — speech acts in different realms — necessarily draw on their respective capital stocks, but if others subjectively value them highly enough, they contribute as well.[72] Hence they deepen uncertainty and make the signal of syntax all the more necessary to navigate a world of social meaning.

Let us make can make the following holistic proposal, mindful that we could very probably shift back again from economics to literature by replacing "money" with "text" and "capital" with "literature": *Money emerges from uncertainty, capital emerges from money, and uncertainty emerges from capital.*

Thankfully, this cycle holds to the extent time and energy is becoming increasingly valuable — that is, to the extent capital is generating a yield. If money is useful to the extent it lets us trade time and energy to the network at one point in time knowing that at any future point, we can receive the same proportion back, then we *should want* the same proportion back in the future. If the money is genuinely *useful*, this "same" in time and energy will be more, better, or both, in "value."

A given money may have qualities that lend it to more or less sustainable formation of capital. This provides another, more oblique, avenue to judge its utility: how sustainable is the proliferation of capital that is forming with this money at its base? If money has characteristics that, for whatever reason, are understood to be encouraging reactions to economic uncertainty with reckless or net-value-destructive risk-taking, this undermines the utility of any certainty implicitly guaranteed in the first place. This is reason to believe the economic network it serves will, over time, generate less, worse, or both. Its yield may be less than its depreciation.

That uncertainty has such a key causal role shows that the network created by money is far more complex than the kinds we are normally used to, and that its "network effects" are far more nuanced as well. When you use Facebook, Twitter, Telegram, email, or whatever, you understand the nature of your relationship to the network. It facilitates your talking to whomever you want to talk to. Beyond that, you don't really care how it works, nor does it really affect you.

But with money, not only do the mechanics of the network intimately affect your interaction with it, you *can't* know how it works. All around you, actors in the network are embracing uncertainties you don't understand so that you don't have to.[73] We are back in The Triangle Game. How it affects you is determined by how *everybody else behaves*, with everybody else in the same intractable position. In his essay, "Money, Blockchains, and Social Scalability," Nick Szabo explains the titular concept of *social scalability* as follows:

> The ability of an institution — a relationship or shared endeavor, in which multiple people repeatedly participate, and featuring customs, rules, or other features which constrain or motivate participants' behaviors — to overcome shortcomings in human minds and in the motivating or constraining aspects of said institution that limit who or how many can successfully participate. Social scalability is about the ways and extents to which participants can think about and respond to institutions and fellow participants as the variety and numbers of participants in those institutions or relationships grow.

Money provides a clear and stable way for participants in the network of economic exchange to think about and respond to their circumstances, precisely as capital formation follows from growth in the variety and numbers of participants. This growth creates a fundamental uncertainty that exceeds the cognitive capacity of any individual human to grasp and hence to respond to directly. While simpler networks create value for their users by allowing channels of communication that would likely have been too costly to establish otherwise, money allows channels of communication that could not be comprehended otherwise.

If, as in a *social* network, we knew with whom we were dealing in economic exchange, we could perhaps base this communication in the simpler medium of trust than in money. But since we mostly do not, the specific social scalability conferred by money allows for what Szabo calls "trust minimization," or, "reducing the vulnerability of participants to each other's and to outsiders' and intermediaries' potential for harmful behavior," adding:

> Most institutions which have undergone a lengthy cultural evolution, such as law (which lowers vulnerability to violence, theft, and fraud), as well as technologies of security, reduce, on balance, and in more ways than the reverse, our vulnerabilities to, and thus our needs to trust, our fellow humans, compared with our vulnerabilities before these institutions and technologies evolved.

Given money bridges the likely lack of trust we have with direct economic counterparts, and the certain lack of trust we have with the entirety of an economic network, it is crucial that we trust the money itself. A functioning money "reduces vulnerabilities to, and thus our need to trust, our fellow humans."

It is worth being as clear as possible that *money is not capital*. Money is the right to time entirely in general. It is liquid and fungible. Capital is time that has been crystallized towards a specific end. It is illiquid and nonfungible. This should also elucidate that *savings is not investment*. Savings is money, and investment is capital; savings is clearly required for investment, as time in general is required to then be crystallized by specific allocation and direction. But fungible savings must be transformed by purposeful action; savings become "investment" by wrestling with uncertainty and seeking to create productive capacity with the potential to increase the capital stock, and ideally eventually reward the original contribution of the saver.

This in turn raises two more points that are likely helpful to appreciate but which we feel are not at all commonly understood. The first is that the point of "profit" — in a more leadingly philosophical sense, its *meaning* — is the enablement of investment. Hence "profit" in any absolute sense or by any absolute measurement is, in effect, meaningless. It is *returns* that matter.

As was discussed at length in Chapter Three, *This Is Not Capitalism*, "growth" is only meaningful if reflecting a flow over a stock. "Profit" is the flow that allows the stock of "capital" to be grown. Treating "revenue growth" (by which the speaker unknowingly means "increase") as solely important instead of profit and returns invites the belief that the costs of facilitating that growth are solely *unimportant*. This may manifest in a variety of ways, but obviously telling examples include depreciation and interest.

If we optimize for *increasing* — not growing — revenue *right now* — not over the long term — then we are likely indifferent to the longevity and fragility of the stock that generates that revenue. A short-lived capital stock will manifest in accelerated depreciation and a fragile capital structure will incur an undue interest charge. Both depreciation and interest will affect (accounting) profits, and both depreciating real assets and increased leverage will affect (accounting *and real*) capital value, but neither will affect revenue. Unsurprisingly, this is precisely what degenerate fiat finance optimizes for and encourages.

The second is that the proper distinction between money and capital provides a clear means of dispelling a common yet silly trope regarding the supposed "danger" of "deflationary" currency. Never mind that deflation is the natural result of the capital accumulation that follows technological progress, the trope goes as follows: Capital accumulation *itself* will grind to a halt because savers will get their return purely from saving and won't need to invest.

There are two dire flaws in this illogical complaint. The first is a clear ignorance of what "returns" are and where they come from. If there is no capital accumulation then savers will clearly *not* get a return solely from saving. We go into much more detail on this point in the following chapter, *The Capital Strip Mine*,[74] but deflation is not a metaphysical constant; it is the result of human action and decision-making. In particular, the lowering of prices is a decision made by a merchant who has decreased her own costs or increased the longevity of her capital base such that lowering her prices will be effective in attracting customers from competitors and will actually boost her profits and returns. The ability to lower costs likely derives from technological progress or novelty in business design — both forms of capital formation that require crystallizing money from savers in illiquid and uncertain forms.

The second is that money is the right to dictate what capital is formed, but it is not *itself* capital. We are honestly not entirely sure what the objectors even think they mean in making this objection, but it may be something along the lines of: *If everybody merely saves rather than invests, then all that capital is wasted.* This is absurd. "Capital" will reflect as much time as people collectively are willing to devote to deferred rather than immediate consumption; to crystallizing uncertain effort in illiquid form rather than cashing in on the efforts of others right now. Money merely bids for this time and directs it to one end or another, but it cannot be "wasted" by not being spent; it is not capital. There is no such thing as "hoarding," except in the minds of degenerate fiat economists attempting to moralize their own predilection for appropriation.

What will actually happen in an environment that encourages savings is very simply that everybody will retain the ability to cash in on others' time in a private emergency, which is obviously a social good. This is only problematic if everybody tries to do so at the same time, but it is worth being exceptionally clear on *why* and tracing the causes as best we can rather than assuming the force of metaphysical constants. This is *bad* precisely because it means many people will simultaneously look to consume rather than invest, which necessitates that prior to this emergency, *they were investing*, in addition to saving! Otherwise, what is the shift in behavior the emergency dictates?

And this makes perfect sense too: Investment is by definition uncertain. It may fail. Of course, an individual will want a store of fungible, liquid value to fall back on in case their non-fungible, illiquid, *hoped-for* value turns out to be valueless. It is only in the mind of a degenerate fiat economist who believes that consumption is a cause of prosperity rather than an effect, and that leverage is unequivocally good because it always and everywhere "stimulates investment" that keeping separate non-invested savings and investment seems strange at the level of the individual, and damaging at the level of society. It is neither. It is natural, healthy, and sane.

What it would seem like if it did seem like a new money was emerging would likely be a focus by its proponents on the qualities of capital that are totally absent from the semantic theory. In the semantic theory, money doesn't change in any sense worth pondering, and so capital formation happens however it happens. In the real world, the operation of money might become more or less trustworthy, uncertainty might become more or less dangerous, and capital formation might become more or less healthy. A new money would be much more likely to emerge if it *seemed like* all these characteristics of the incumbent were getting worse and worse. If the new money were free and open source and programmable, that certainly wouldn't hurt its chances either.

What It Would Seem Like

"Every step and every movement of the multitude, even in what are termed enlightened ages, are made with equal blindness to the future; and nations stumble upon establishments, which are indeed the result of human action, but not the execution of any human design."
—Adam Ferguson, *An Essay on the History of Civil Society*

What would it seem like if it did seem like a new money was emerging? It would depend on the relative merits of the challenger and the incumbent, but also on how the perceptions of these merits spread, how perceptions of these perceptions spread, and so on. As the opportunity cost is absolute, the challenger money cannot merely be dabbled in, like a novel social network, but must be sincerely *believed*. Hence the challenger's emergence may for a time depend on how individuals in the network think about money itself.

An adherent of the semantic theory would dismiss the challenger out of hand. If it isn't acting as a medium of exchange and a unit of account then it won't acquire the network effects to ever do so, meaning it won't store value either, and it can't be money.[75]

But a more sophisticated observer might be less interested in definitions and in codified knowledge and look to the circumstances of competition between the two in real life. She would realize money has value on the basis of economic uncertainty, and that the greater the uncertainty we have around its operation, the less useful it becomes; that the demand for certainty it reciprocally fulfills means its value is primarily derived from perceived utility in exchange in the future rather than in the present; that it should support healthy and stable capital formation and that its mechanism should trustworthily capture true scarcity without dilution.

Turning to the challenger, they might be put off by the lack of immediate utility and the uncertainty this unfavorably invites. Nonetheless, they might recognize the value of the essential trustworthiness of its mechanism, and its transparent and limited dilution as providing a useful *future* certainty that respects the time and energy it aims to preserve. They might be encouraged by its prospects for healthy capital formation and the early signs of such capital formation taking place, and notice that the perception of its utility is spreading, steadily self-perpetuating the size and strength of its network. They might, in summary, be humble enough to realize that perhaps those using the challenger possess some practical knowledge they do not.

As for the incumbent, they might worry its highly dilutive mechanism could not be trusted at all; that the capital formation it supports is toxic and unstable; that its overall operation is highly uncertain and that, as this perception seems to be spreading, its long-term utility and the size of its network is in increasingly serious question. They might reason that, like Esperanto, its elaborate design may make it pleasing to its designers yet fragile and encumbered in the real world, whereas natural languages and natural moneys emerge and evolve to fulfill a decentralized demand. They suit a coarse reality, not clean semantics. That these designers seem to have no conception of the importance to money of time, uncertainty, knowledge, and capital might make them more nervous still about the likely quality of their design.

But regardless of their own appreciation of the merits, our observer cannot escape that they will also need to pre-empt others' realization of the merits, and *their* appreciation of others' realizations of the merits, and so on. The challenger money's success will be subject to precisely the uncertainty that generates its potential utility. This is not just a trade-off in the minds of economic actors but a likely source of dynamic instability.

As with any good, we may grasp our own demand and supply for the challenger money right at this moment, but we can only have a limited appreciation of others' valuations or our own in the future, and this appreciation diminishes the further removed from us they are in circumstance and in time. As we act on this valuation, this decision will have effects that permeate unpredictably through the entire network, unevenly over time. We might be aware of the dynamics of the network in our small locality, but we can have next to no idea of the consequences of our actions on the dynamics of the network *as a whole*.

This is all to say that if it did seem like a new money was emerging, it would likely seem extremely volatile, irrational, and unpredictable. From any individual's perspective, it would be. But we are back playing the Triangle Game: The individual's perspective tells us nothing. It possibly tells us less than nothing because it might *seem* informative as a snapshot of the dynamics of the network as a whole. It might *seem* like this volatility, irrationality, and unpredictability destroys the challenger's utility as money. But their individual perception is irrelevant to the whole. If it is acted on, by an individual, it affects the whole in volatile, irrational, unpredictable ways, and loops back around to affect his later perception.

If it did seem like a new money was emerging, we propose it would *seem* more like it were tracking an evolving and messy narrative than obeying a fixed and clean equation. It would *seem* like a continuous experiment, the outputs of which flow back in as inputs as the experimenters continuously discovering a new and evolving social truth. It would be slow, and it would be sporadic. It would not be the smooth exponential of a hot new social network, because the nature of its "network effects" would frankly be far more complex. It would be, in essence, the erratic and ever-changing spread of a contrarian belief about the nature of money itself. In the short run it would be a (literally) chaotic mess, but in the long run it would tend towards the merits of the belief.

In Chapter Five, *The Capital Strip Mine*, we will evaluate the contemporary incumbents and evaluate the effects of their characteristics on the formation of capital, and in Chapter Six, *Bitcoin Is Venice*, we will evaluate the challenger. In Chapter Seven, A *Capital Renaissance*, we will anticipate the many kinds of tangible capital that we hope will once again flourish under the monetary regime we have proposed is emerging in this chapter, and in Chapter Eight, These *Were Capitalists*, we will articulate the benefits of a healthy societal attitude towards stocks of intangible capital that go well beyond the merely economic.

But for now, we will conclude by saying that if it did seem like a global, digital, sound, free, open-source, programmable money was monetizing from absolute zero, we guess it would seem a lot like this.

Chapter Five

The Capital Strip Mine
Leverage, knowledge, and the uncapitalizing of America

The most egregious falsehood regarding economic health that is nonetheless widely believed is surely that we ought to measure it by the magnitude of goods and services consumed. This is dangerous nonsense. Consumption is the result of a complex web of individual commitments of time and energy towards uncertain ends. The result is delayed, and the greater the complexity, the greater the uncertainty, the greater the delay, and the more plentiful the result is likely to be. To measure the health of such a system only by its tangible output and not its internal workings is like measuring the health of a tree by its size. Small trees can be vibrant and large trees can be dead.

A better analogy — perhaps the perfect analogy — is a farm. A planted seed is foregone consumption. The farmer invests time and energy, made uncertain by the vagaries of pests and weather, in nurturing the delayed but more plentiful bounty of harvest. The wealth of the farmer is not the magnitude of the harvest, but the capacity of the land to produce harvests indefinitely. Indeed, this is the origin of the word "yield." The farmer could always choose to maximize his consumption by eating his seed rather than planting it; by selling his soil rather than tending it. But patently, this would decrease any sane measure of his wealth.

In, *The Unsettling of America*, Wendell Berry laments the gradual shift in attitudes to agriculture in the United States from that of nurturers to exploiters:

> I conceive a strip-miner to be a model exploiter, and as a model nurturer I take the old-fashioned idea or ideal of a farmer. The exploiter is a specialist, an expert; the nurturer is not. The standard of the exploiter is efficiency; the standard of the nurturer is care. The exploiter's goal is money, profit; the nurturer's is health — his land's health, his own, his family's, his community's, his country's. Whereas the exploiter asks of a piece of land only how much and how quickly it can be made to produce, the nurturer asks a question that is much more complex and difficult: what is its carrying capacity? (That is: How much can be taken from it without diminishing it? what can it produce dependably for an indefinite time?) The exploiter wishes to earn as much as possible by as little work as possible; the nurturer expects, certainly to have a decent

living from his work, but his characteristic wish is to work as well as possible.

We contend that under degenerate fiat "capitalism," an analogous transformation is happening to the capital stock as Berry bemoans of the agricultural stock; that this is driven by an obsession with immediate, quantifiable consumption rather than delayed, uncertain investment; and that this is fueled by dysfunctional money that does not calibrate certainty and uncertainty as it should. In our ignorance, impatience, and arrogance, step by step we are turning the farm into a strip mine.

In Chapter Four, *Wittgenstein's Money*, we explored the consequences of failing to appreciate the role of time, ignorance, and uncertainty in understanding the function of money, and how its function can change. We pushed the reasoning to an embrace of the role of capital — that the certainty provided by money allows for increasingly uncertain endeavors to create increasingly complicated tools and organizations, and the extent to which the creation of capital is successful sets the stage for further economic uncertainty still.

The more capital we accumulate, the more specialized we are incentivized to become in our own economic contribution, which increases our vulnerability to unpredictable changes in all other supplies and demands. Also, the more surplus we are likely to be able to create, some portion of which can be diverted towards further experimentation, which makes changes in supply and demand more unpredictable still. This makes money that actually functions the way its users expect it to all the more valuable. Money emerges from uncertainty, capital emerges from money, and uncertainty emerges from capital.

In this chapter, we will explore what we can expect to happen to this potentially virtuous cycle if we ignore the link between money and uncertainty; if we fail to grasp the importance of capital and suppose maximizing consumption to be our most important collective goal; and if we are indifferent to the money underpinning the cycle becoming highly uncertain and dysfunctional.

The *Semantic Theory of Money* we satirically articulated in Chapter Four has a spiritual counterpart here: That by all manner of semantic contortions, we can convince ourselves that we can consume more than we produce, reap more than we sow, borrow more than we repay. As Ludwig Wittgenstein said in *Philosophical Investigations*, "philosophy is a battle against the bewitchment of our intelligence by means of language." Let us not be so bewitched but cut through this nonsense and call a spade a spade.

In Chapter Six, *Bitcoin Is Venice*, we will get rather more excited about putting all this behind us. But for now, let's get our hands dirty.

How to Increase Consumption

"Profit arises as a result of the constantly changing environment within which economic activity is carried on and the associated uncertainty concerning the outcomes of alternative courses of action. Profit is the residual, if any, left for the entrepreneur after he pays out the contractual incomes agreed upon for the factor he hired. The entrepreneur is identified as being ultimately in control of the venture, ultimately responsible for all receipts and all outlays, and thus subject to the uncertainty which surrounds the amount and sign of the difference between them. Profits are not seen as uncertainty-bred differences between the anticipated value of resource services and their actual value. The profits won by any particular entrepreneur depend on his own ability and good luck as well as upon the general level of initiative and ability in the market."
—Israel Kirzner, *Competition and Entrepreneurship*

There are three ways to increase consumption. One is to commit more human time and energy to producing stuff to consume. Another is to consume existing capital rather than *use* it. Clearly, neither of these first two options is sustainable. There is a maximum of time and energy it is possible to commit, and a point well below the maximum beyond which committing any more is undesirable. And there is a finite stock of capital which, if consumed rather than used, will eventually be depleted.

The absolutely only way to *sustainably* increase the economic output that is available for consumption is to grow the capital stock above its natural rate of depreciation. If we have more capital, the same amount of human time and energy will create a greater output available for consumption. Hence it ought to take less human time and energy to exchange for a given proportion of this output.

The tricky thing about growing the capital stock is that it is by its nature an uncertain process. It cannot be automated, nor reduced to an algorithm. It is necessarily experimental. New capital is as much discovered as invented. This is why money is so important to efforts to create capital: These efforts themselves take time and energy that might otherwise have gone towards more certain avenues of production. Only some small group may have the knowledge and skills to credibly experiment with creating a particular new tool or new organization, and they may not be willing to take the risks required. Some other group may have the willingness to take the risks but not the knowledge or skills to do so. Money provides a means for coordinating the risks of attempting to create capital such that those contributing to the risk taking are not necessarily those bearing the risks.

By disconnecting the bearing of the risk from its execution, we incentivize those willing to bear risk to seek out those risks whose reward seems the greatest, unburdened by their own particular circumstances. We will collectively run not only more experiments that have the potential to increase our economic well-being, but we will also prioritize running the best experiments. Functional money facilitates all this parceling up and trading of risk. What we must try to understand next is that this process has reflexive effects on the functioning of money.

In pondering the flow of money around the creation of capital, we think it is helpful to be rigorous in keeping track of accounting identities and thinking about how they evolve across time. Trading certainty for uncertainty in the form of experiments in capital creation results in a very particular accounting transformation. It pulls forward potential value from the future and crystallizes it as value in the present, while we create a separate financial asset to reflect the future value we hope will one day be realized. We might call this *financialization*. We pay for production capital with financial capital.

For example, say we take $100 of savings and make an entrepreneurial investment. That is to say, we buy some capital goods, some raw materials, and hire some workers, and put them all to work over time to try to churn out a product we will attempt to sell for a profit. This $100 which was originally intended for future consumption will now very likely lead to present consumption, as our workers and suppliers will be $100 better off and may very well decide to consume. This will happen *first*. It will take time for us to make a profit, but we will have to make our payments upfront as we are the ones willing to bear these risks, not our employees and not our suppliers.

This $100 has become a $100 liability of equity finance and probably less than $100 of assets with the remainder as an expense. If we succeed in making a profit above these expenses, we will earn cash as an asset, which we balance with retained earnings as a liability. But we can't know that until it happens. *At the very start*, we have simply spent $100 in exchange for a collection of assets and promises. We have swapped certainty for uncertainty. Our workers and suppliers have crystallized $100 in present value in exchange for future value, the risk of which we have decided to bear over the period of its attempted realization.

This could all be more complicated still. Rather than owning a stake in the uncertain output of an entrepreneurial venture, a provider of capital may prefer to be entitled to an agreed-upon return, provided it is received first among the venture's profits. This may be efficient all-round as such a provider of capital may willing to embrace *some* uncertainty, but not quite the level they think this entrepreneurial venture entails in its entirety, and would prefer to trade potential upside for surety and priority of repayment. The entrepreneur may agree to this as they may be unable to reach the required $100 of financing otherwise. In another scenario, they may be confident enough of the relative certainty of the return on the project that accepting the need to divert the first profits is worth it to boost their own returns on equity.

Of course, we have just described debt — hardly a revelation. But once again, let us track the accounting identities: The debt provider started with $50 of savings and gave it all to the entrepreneur. Now the debt provider has a liability of $50 equity finance and $50 of credit assets. There is some uncertainty surrounding the true value of this credit, but it will only become clear as the venture is carried out. Hopefully, it will lead to a profit such that retained earnings top up assets as cash. Possibly, the venture will fail so badly that even the $50 provided cannot be recovered from the remaining assets. The debtor and creditor weighing up these possibilities in their own minds, and comparing them to their respective other opportunities, will determine the level of interest — the *cost* of this capital.

The entrepreneur is in a similar accounting position to previously: $100 of assets of entirely uncertain value, but now $50 of equity liability and $50 of debt, with an additional cost going forward of interest on this debt. Once again, this total of $100 of savings has been crystalized as present value, transferred, and very possibly spent currently, while the future value for which it was traded remains as-yet-unrealized and uncertain.

The final complexification possible is that financial capital and production capital are sufficiently decoupled such that it is possible to purely intermediate financial capital without ever directly investing. That is to say, to take savings from those seeking a debt-like return and to make credit investments — that is, a bank. Once more, the accounting identities are that of the business will be the same, but now we introduce an intermediary with, let's say $40 of debt financing, $10 of its own equity, and the $50 credit to the business, but now underlying savers who have $40 of equity and a $40 credit to the intermediary.

Again, this will hardly be a revelation. We run through these possibilities in such granular detail so as to make three points as clearly as possible. The first is to make plain the accounting balance: No matter how complex this gets, the same underlying uncertainty is still there. It cannot be escaped. It cannot be financialized away. We cannot use accounting to conjure up more time or energy. The capital structure financing the endeavor may be unboundedly complex, but there will always be $100 of expenditure of subsequently uncertain value that traces back to $100 of equity, *somewhere.*

The second is to make clear that while this underlying uncertainty cannot be removed by different financializations, the parceling up of risk *can* affect the experiment. This can be made clear in two ways. First of all, from the entrepreneur's point of view, the more debt is used as finance, the more their potential equity returns are boosted, but the less room they allow for variability in the success of the venture. There are lower and closer bounds of the level of profitability that will be acceptable for the experiment to continue before her equity value is wiped out and the experiment ends with asset write-downs. Equivalently, at the macro level, we can see the proliferation of assets as we introduce more and more debt to the system. More and more (perceived) value is tied to the same underlying experiment. Debt gives greater perceived safety to the provider of financial capital by sucking safety from the rest of the system and making the real experiment more fragile. It is useful — but only to the extent this transfer of risk is what everybody really wants.

Financialization and Prices

"Nonfinancial corporations are increasingly engaging in financial activities themselves in order to secure the highest possible returns. The fact that this model is unsustainable — resting as it does on rising leverage and increasing profit distribution over investment in future production — is beside the point. Production was never the point of the capitalist enterprise — profit was. And the financialization of nonfinancial corporation has been an excellent way to maximize profit. "Certain households have also been able to extract peculiar benefits from the financialization of the economy. Globalization was a convenient excuse for wage repression in many parts of the Global North. The problem of overaccumulation this created — that is, when workers aren't paid enough to buy what capitalists produce — was solved by the proliferation of debt. The dramatic increases in consumer lending between 1979 and 2007 improved people's subjective sense of prosperity and allowed them to purchase luxuries like cars, iPhones, and laptops produced by hyper-exploited labor in the Global South."
—Grace Blakeley, *The Latest Incarnation of Capitalism*

The third, and most important, point is what will happen to prices. Note that we are very deliberately *not saying,* what will happen to "inflation," as this word has two distinct meanings that may be related to one another, but may not. We will shortly consider what happens if "the money supply" changes — call this "monetary inflation" — but in what follows, we assume it does not, and we face only "price inflation."

It is instructive to think about *why* prices might increase as a result of decisions made by real people, rather than assuming this is a fact of life or some metaphysical constant (it is neither). Prices are set by sellers at the level they best judge will not be so high as to lead to customers going to competitors and leaving their own inventory unsold, but not so low that they can't still make a desired profit and return. These decisions depend crucially on uncertainty and time. Profits, returns, and depletion of inventory cannot be known in advance and can only be judged and reacted to with respect to how they unfold over time.

Sellers will, therefore, decide to increase their prices for one of two reasons: (1) their own costs have increased and they can no longer make the desired profit or return otherwise, or (2) customers start to buy *faster,* such that inventory is depleted before it can be replaced, suggesting that more potential customers exist than can be serviced and unit profits can be increased without risk. Likewise, sellers will decide to decrease prices if, (1) costs have decreased and the increase in customers gained by lowering prices will more than offset the fall in unit profit, leading to an increase in aggregate profit and returns, or (2) customers start to buy *slower*, such that inventory is not being shipped as fast as it is being bought in.

The speed with which inventory can be moved is really a function of how much capital has been devoted to its production in the first place. Increasing or decreasing prices is the appropriate short-term response to positive or negative strains on inventory and more liquid and abstract forms of working capital. But the appropriate long-term response *may be* more or less capital investment, such that real supply can be increased or decreased. The wisdom of such a decision will depend on whether the source of the faster or slower purchasing is fundamentally sustainable. Capital investment is essentially an experiment that must be financed and will take time, whereas prices can be changed on the spot.[76]

This all raises a fascinating and more complex question: What will be the effect on prices *of financialization to create capital*? If we pull forward value from the future and crystallize it in the present, what will happen to prices? On the face of it, this turns savings that would not have been used to consume into income, some portion of which probably will. Therefore, goods will start to be bought *faster*.

But we must remember this $100 of present value only exists because it has been traded for an experiment of entirely uncertain value. What happens with this experiment is key. If the experiment fails: Those who financed it will have $100 less than they had accounted for at the time of failure and therefore will be forced to consume less, meaning customers will buy *slower*. Recall, however, that capital naturally depletes, and so if it is not replaced, its ability to turn time and energy into a relatively increased output will diminish, meaning costs will steadily increase.

If the experiment succeeds: There will be no asset write-offs that destroy the ability to consume and so the $100 brought forward will not be perfectly balanced out. However, the financialization will have to be unwound, which will turn newly created income back into savings. Over the period this happens, consumption will once again be slower. But more importantly, the capital created by the experiment will then allow time and energy to produce more of some or other output, meaning goods and services can be created at relatively lower cost.

Of course, we must aggregate all such behavior as no single experiment will impact *all prices* (or probably even *any* prices), hence in the above three paragraphs we referred only to costs of production and speed of purchasing, not to prices. But it is straightforward enough to realize that the *timing* of all experiments is all that really matters in determining to what extent the impact of a single experiment can be generalized. Let us look in turn at the immediate effect of crystallizing future value, then the delayed effect of changing the capital stock.

Financialization will always lead to immediate faster consumption but later slower consumption as the financialization is unwound. If the unwinding follows from a successful experiment, the slower later consumption will be somewhat transient as the capital will likely be recycled; if a failed experiment, the slower later consumption will be permanent as the capital allowing for this consumption has been destroyed. But there will be slower later consumption of some variety due to *this financialization alone* in either case.

We must then look across *all financializations*: If the experiments are conducted in perfect synchrony, we can be fairly certain prices will rise dramatically in the short term. If they are perfectly desynchronized, then the unwinding of completed financializations will tend to cancel out the setting up of new financializations. Hence, it is fair to say that the effect of financialization *alone* on price will reflect the rate at which aggregate financialization is increasing or decreasing.

Changing the capital stock will have a simpler and more fundamental effect: The capital stock naturally depletes, causing costs to rise and hence prices to rise. Hence the *successful* creation of new capital will cause costs to fall and prices to fall, with an unpredictable lag reflecting that this aggregate is only meaningful insofar as it follows individual decisions and flows of information. We might summarize by observing that, in the short run, prices will respond to accelerating or decelerating financialization, but in the long run will respond to the inverse of the change in productive capital. In the medium run, it seems unlikely these processes will be perfectly synchronized *or* perfectly desynchronized, and hence prices may well be volatile as per accelerating and decelerating financialization, but following a trend as per net capital accumulation.[77]

The desire to create capital at the level of individual such experiments will probably always follow, in one way or another, from the entrepreneur's assessment of the sustainability of the movements in price she is seeing. There will never be a right answer — it will depend on knowledge, judgment, and appetite for risk. We must recognize that these decisions to create capital will affect prices in turn. If financial capital and production capital are adequately decoupled, the relationship in aggregate can quickly become complex and the feedback profound.

A farmer may well be able to fashion a plow with time he consciously decides not to devote to tilling. But pledging some portion of a hoped-to-be-more-plentiful harvest against the tractor that will provide it — and which in no amount of time could he have possibly built himself — is another matter altogether. As is the possibility this pledge could then be traded on. Judgment pertaining to prices will affect decisions to experimentally create capital, but so too will decisions to experimentally create capital affect prices. We must bear all this in mind in charting the health of the capital stock.

The more we financialize, the more experiments we are able to run. The incremental experiment will probably be the next riskiest, and the more its financialization is steered towards debt, the greater the risk becomes still. As we need *some* level of experimentation to avoid the entropic decay of the capital stock and the collapse of civilization, there emerges an ever-important question of, *how much risk do we want to take?* and, derivatively, *who is deciding to take these risks, and who is bearing them?*

So far, the assumed answers to these questions have been something like, *we take as many risks as individuals desire to and whoever decides to take the risks bears the risks*. We haven't assumed anybody is taking risks they don't want to or that they aren't bearing, and we *certainly* haven't assumed that the aggregate magnitude of consumption features in anybody's calculations. Unfortunately, to make the analysis more applicable to our degenerate fiat reality — to make clear why we might be incentivized not to create capital but to consume it; not to cultivate the land but to strip mine it — we will have to explore both.

Maximizing Consumption

"When the decision point of investment is heavily influenced by not wanting to hold dollars, you get financialization. Similarly, when consumption preferences are guided by the expectation that money will lose its value rather than increase in value, investments are made to cater toward those distorted preferences. Ultimately, short-term incentives beat out long-term incentives; incumbents are favoured over new entrants, and the economy stagnates, which increasingly fuels financialization, centralization and financial engineering rather than productive investment. It is cause and effect; intended behaviour with unintended but predictable consequences.

"Make money lose its value and people will do dumb shit because doing dumb shit becomes more rational, if not encouraged. People that would otherwise be saving are forced to take incremental risk because their savings are losing value. In that world, savings become financialized. And when you create the incentive not to save, do not be surprised to wake up in a world in which very few people have savings. The empirical evidence shows exactly this, and despite how much it might astound a tenured economics professor, the lack of savings induced by a disincentive to save is very predictably a major source of the inherent fragility in the legacy financial system."
—Parker Lewis, *The Great Definancialization*

What if we foolishly do not think that economic health rests on growing the capital stock but rather on the instantaneous magnitude of consumption? If we grow weary of the hard work of farming and think the path to happiness lies instead in feasting on our seeds? How will our analysis differ?

First, we will see financialization as unequivocally good and be totally indifferent to the risks and the fragility it creates. When prices naturally increase as present value is crystallized and exchanged, we will have little choice but to conceive of this inevitability as an intrinsically *good thing*, since increased consumption is a good thing, and increased prices can't help but follow.

In particular, we will encourage entrepreneurs to assume any increase in purchasing is fundamentally sustainable, regardless of what their judgment and their knowledge tells them, because this will motivate capital investment in increasing the production of whatever is being purchased. If more such investment can be financialized, all the better, because that starts the loop all over again. Financialization is good. Pumping out more stuff is good. "Number go up" is good.

Because we don't care about the risks of these experiments failing — only that they are attempted — we will be in a curious position when they do fail. What we will *see* will be asset write-downs that mean purchasing power evaporates and consumption slows. This slowing down will force sellers to lower prices, at least for the period over which capital can be re-allocated to reflect this change. Hence, we will have little choice but to conceive of decreasing prices as an intrinsically *bad thing*, since decreased consumption is a bad thing, and decreased prices can't help but follow.

The solution, naturally, will be financialization. We replace the uncertain value that has since proven to be *certainly* valueless with more crystallized value traded for future uncertainty and go back to step one. Financialization is good. Pumping out more stuff is good. "Number go up" is good. All the while the natural depletion of the capital stock is not offset, and the price increases that follow from real costs increasing is mistaken as a sign of health.

Depressing as this would be, this is actually a much rosier picture than reality because there is still an alignment between those taking and bearing the risks. What we are effectively assuming is that willing contributors of capital waste it on ill-advised experiments over and over and over again until they have none left. This is still unideal because the ability to increase output for the same input of time and energy is universally positive. But it is only indirectly bad for those that do not contribute to such financialization and simply save instead. The output they can purchase may have fallen, but at least they will retain entitlement to a given share of it.

This also shows why it is unlikely: It relies on capital providers and entrepreneurs being neverendingly stupid. They must make poor judgments about the sustainability of their investments over and over and over again, and take more and more risk with less and less realistic likelihood of the risks paying off. They suffer by far the most from their own folly. To understand why reality is far worse than this, we must return to the question of the creation and supply of money.

What If Money Were Debt?

"Money has been the oil that has kept the wheels of society turning and allowed the complexity of our present civilization to develop, but credit, the centralized creation of money, interest, and particularly compound interest, have seriously destabilized the relationship between money and the goods and services, or wealth, it originally represented."
—Allan Savory, *Holistic Management*

We must be clear on how money is created in real life. Our sense is many have the impression that fiat money is created by central banks. This is partly true, but is not an exhaustive explanation, and is actually misleading in isolation. It is true that "quantitative easing" involves creating new central bank reserves for member banks, but this is not the only way, nor the most common way. The majority of "new money" is created by commercial banks making loans. Contrary to popular belief, modern banks do not "intermediate between depositors and lenders." As is nicely explained in *Money Creation in the Modern Economy*, the quarterly bulletin from the Bank of England,[78] when a bank makes a loan, it wills into existence a deposit that is the debtor's asset and its own liability. In fact, it is more accurate to say that *loans create deposits* than it is to say that *deposits create loans*.

This might seem bizarre, but the explanation requires being clear on what fiat money *even really is*: It is a fungible pan-bank liability. Other than the tiny minority of modern money that exists as cash, there is simply no such thing as a dollar, a pound, or a euro, that is not a right to claim that amount of cash from a bank — which, of course, nobody does because it is far, far safer to keep cash in a bank, and far, far easier to make almost all payments by instructing your bank to just change the title on that amount of its liabilities. If the payee has liabilities with bank B, then bank A must transfer that value of its central bank reserve assets to bank B, so bank B can create a matching liability. Banks tend to have accounts with one another so they don't have to resort to this so often, and it is central bank reserves that are the ultimate mechanism for value settlement.

There are two peculiarities with all this. First, there will almost certainly be far more debt than there is any real appetite for because it is not possible to save outside of financialization. The only way to save is to accumulate the residual of credit that has already been issued completely outside your consent or approval. You might think that holding others' debt can still be worthwhile if it is paid back. But the situation here is far more perverse: Your asset with the bank is the bank's liability, matched by a loan somewhere else. That loan is that person's liability. That person may accumulate their own assets in the form of bank liabilities, which means the bank has been transferred reserves assets to balance these liabilities. This person may then pay off the loan, at which point the bank cancels the two. But you get nothing. All that happens then is that the bank uses the new reserve cushion to justify making more loans. Your credit might exist because the bank made a loan, but it is not *in that loan*; it is in the never-ending recycling of one loan into another into another.

The second peculiarity is that those signing off on the risks are not those bearing the risks. In fact, the reader will be forgiven for having completely lost track of the real risk here because it is so well obscured. If enough loans go bad that the bank's equity cushion is wiped out, then the central bank will be forced to create reserves to ensure the bank's liabilities can still be met (i.e., money can still function, payments can still be made, and savings won't entirely evaporate). But the original liability will now never be netted off, meaning there are permanently more such liabilities, which means there is permanently more money, which means everybody's money is worth less. This will be true in both senses of "inflation": It is true by definition in terms of share of the total, but it will be true for prices as well, as the local slowing in consumption that would have paired the initial quickening due to financialization simply never happens. Don't let any nasty Bitcoiners tell you that the dollar isn't backed by anything, when we all know full well it is backed by self-referentially mispriced toxic loans and stabilized by a military and commodity cartelization pact with Saudi Arabia.

Lyn Alden explains in her wonderful and detailed essay, "The Fraying of the US Global Currency Reserve System,"

> In the early 1970s, there were a variety of geopolitical conflicts including the Yom Kippur War and the OPEC oil embargo. In 1974, however, the United States and Saudi Arabia reached an agreement,[79] and from there, the world was set on the petrodollar system; a clever way to make a global fiat currency system work decently enough.
>
> We think of this as normal now, but this five-decade period of global fiat currency is unusual and unique in the historical sense. Imagine trying to architect a way to make an all-fiat currency system work on the global stage for the first time in human history. In doing so, you have to somehow convince or force the whole world to trade valuable things for foreign pieces of paper with no guarantee from the paper-issuing governments that those papers are worth anything in particular, in relation to an amount of gold or other hard assets.
>
> With the petrodollar system, Saudi Arabia (and other countries in OPEC) sell their oil exclusively in dollars in exchange for US protection and cooperation. Even if France wants to buy oil from Saudi Arabia, for example, they do so in dollars. Any country that wants oil, needs to be able to get dollars to pay for it, either by earning them or exchanging their currency for them. So, non-oil-producing countries also sell many of their exports in dollars, even though the dollar is completely fiat foreign paper, so that they can get dollars for which to buy oil from oil-producing countries. And, all of these countries store excess dollars as

foreign-exchange reserves, which they mostly put into US Treasuries to earn some interest.

In return, the United States uses its unrivaled blue-water navy to protect global shipping lanes, and preserve the geopolitical status quo with military action or the threat thereof as needed. In addition, the United States basically has to run persistent trade deficits with the rest of the world, to get enough dollars out into the international system. Many of those dollars, however, get recycled into buying US Treasuries and stored as foreign-exchange reserves, meaning that a large portion of US federal deficits are financed by foreign governments compared to other developed nations that mostly rely on domestic financing.

The petrodollar system is creative, because it was one of the few ways to make everyone in the world accept foreign paper for tangible goods and services. Oil producers get protection and order in exchange for pricing their oil in dollars and putting their reserves into Treasuries, and non-oil producers need oil, and thus need dollars so they can get that oil. This leads to a disproportionate amount of global trade occurring in dollars relative to the size of the US economy, and in some ways, means that the dollar is backed by oil, without being explicitly pegged to oil at a defined ratio. The system gives the dollar a persistent global demand from around the world, while other fiat currencies are mostly just used internally in their own countries.[80]

Hopefully we will not be tarred and feathered as fiat apologist no-coiner shills for making the following observation, but we contend that this setup does not *absolutely necessarily* lead to catastrophe. If a central bank is run such that the moral hazard of its relationship to member banks and bankers is taken seriously; if banks are kept as small and as systemically *unimportant* as possible; if the pain of systemic deleveraging and the ecstasy of systemic leveraging are insulated from political interference; if retention of adequate reserves is mandated and is eaten into by bad credit; all with an eye towards faithful risk pricing and a healthy capital stock … then things *might* be okay. It should also be noted that money is a technology that has no platonic form, and that relative to most *real-life* alternatives, fiat has the dramatic advantage of vast payment reach and inexpensive settlement that count in its favor at all the times it isn't imploding.

However, if the prevailing sentiment of those responsible for such a setup foolishly believe that economic health rests not on growing the capital stock, but rather on the magnitude of consumption, then slow-motion disaster will be next to inevitable. Let us explore the mechanics of such a catastrophe.

Gradually, Then Suddenly

"The dislocation of the monetary and credit system that is nowadays going on everywhere is not due — the fact cannot be repeated too often — to any inadequacy of the gold standard. The thing for which the monetary system of our time is chiefly blamed, the fall in prices during the last five years, is not the fault of the gold standard, but the inevitable and ineluctable consequence of the expansion of credit, which was bound to lead eventually to a collapse. And the thing which is chiefly advocated as a remedy is nothing but another expansion of credit, such as certainly might lead to a transitory boom, but would be bound to end in a correspondingly severer crisis."
—Ludwig von Mises, *The Theory of Money and Credit*

To start with, the oversupply of debt forces the price of debt down to clear the market.[81] The ranking of experimental viability that the market might have carried out to allocate scarce capital becomes irrelevant and all prospective experiments are carried out. This juncture is key. These experiments are, by their nature, uncertain. The price of the capital they would faithfully attract can hardly be better described than a crowd-sourced best guess as to their risk relative to the opportunity set. It is possible that these guesses are conservatively false and that all will succeed. But it is likely that more bad experiments will fail than would have otherwise, hence more debt will tend to mean more *bad* debt.

And not only this, but the experiments' financial capital is all bidding against each other for real production capital — which cannot be artificially increased as can the debt to finance the experiments — hence the costs of running the experiments go up just as the cost of financing them goes down. The effect is akin to redistributing the mean risk created by the marginal risky experiment to the entire ensemble. We get more individually bad debt *and* more averagely bad debt.

And of course, we must not confuse the nominal interest rates forced upon economic actors by artificial debt creation with *real* time preference. A low rate on a manipulated market reflects neither an abundance of available funds for investment nor creates that which it is pretending to be.[82] Or, perhaps more provocatively: An interest rate *should be* a discount rate; it *should reflect* the balance of time and opportunity cost. But high time preference incentives create high discount rates, which viciously recreate high time preference incentives in the form of short-term investment horizons.[83] Low interest rates do not solve what is essentially a character flaw, and in fact they exacerbate it by providing the unknowingly flawed not only with no negative feedback that might be of character-building value, but also with an abundance of artificially cheap capital to waste on their high time preference nonsense. And it can get even worse if the costs of this are socialized.[84]

Consider Elinor Ostrom's analysis of *common pool resources*, any communal resource that is rivalrous, and hence depleted by usage, in *Governing the Commons*. We will discuss this book in far more detail in Chapter Seven, A *Capital Renaissance*, and as mentioned already in Chapter Three, *This Is Not Capitalism*. For now, however, we intend to draw solely on her insights on discount rates. She writes,

> Discount rates are affected by the levels of physical and economic security faced by appropriators. Appropriators who are uncertain will discount future returns heavily when traded off against increasing the probability of survival during the current year. Similarly, if a [common pool resource] can be destroyed by the actions of others, no matter what local appropriators do, even those who have constrained their harvesting from a [common pool resource] for many years will begin to heavily discount future returns, as contrasted with present returns. Discount rates are also affected by the general norms shared by the individuals living in a particular society, or even a local community, regarding the relative importance of the future as compared with the present.

In other words, common pool resources by necessity need to be approached with a low time preference if they have any chance of being preserved rather than pillaged or — as the case may *literally* be — strip mined. Such is the extent of the insidious influence of mispricing capital. Private experiments fail, but public experiments fail also — likely without anybody fully cognizant of the fact that public resources are being experimented on and nobody is privately assuming that risk.

All this ought to lead to persistent lower later consumption to reflect the capital that has been destroyed, but in our brave new world, such politically incorrect outcomes are not to be tolerated. Consumption cannot slow! Consumption is wealth and well-being! The central bank will first buy the bad debts with newly created reserves. That means banks are not forced to write down their own assets, as doing so would threaten the quality of their liabilities and the entire systemic functioning of money, causing consumption to collapse even further. Then, the central bank will lower the rate paid on its reserves, meaning banks must create more (probably bad) loans to maintain their profitability. It may combine both efforts and buy toxic credit assets on the open market, freeing up the balance sheets of capital market participants beyond just banks to take on these new loans.

By this series of machinations, we emerge with more financialization, borne not of the opportunity to create capital, but the necessity to stabilize money, and the desire to increase consumption. We get more dilutive equity and yet no redemptive deleveraging, as financialization cannot decelerate and any deflation, however transient and coincidental, is deemed *bad* and triggers further panicked intervention. We get short-term price increases in response to the crystallized value of financialization that become permanent inflation as no matched future value ever materializes. We get official proclamations that this inflation is *good* and ought to be *targeted*. And from the starting point of an oversupply of debt we get … an oversupply of debt.

Believe it or not, it gets even worse. It is *possible*, however unlikely, that the originally expanded set of experiments *all work* despite their risks being systemically mispriced. But if the nearly inevitable long-term inflationary features of such a system are widely enough appreciated, this will distort the incentives of those trying to create and preserve value. A risky entrepreneurial endeavor making a return below this inflation rate will no longer be creating wealth for its owners but losing it — not as fast as holding fungible pan-bank liabilities (money), admittedly, but then money on its own is thought to have no risk. The point of the risk of entrepreneurship is to get a real return.

Hence all return-seeking capital assets are unnaturally incentivized to lever up to stay ahead of inflation. Of course, all that is really happening here is that by swapping equity for debt, the experiments themselves are forced to become riskier than they ought to be. They become more fragile, which creates more bad debt, which will eventually require permanentizing inflation. It also makes a corrective rate rise prohibitively systemically risky because more and more debt can only be sustained at progressively lower rates. If rates rise, debt fails, and if debt fails, money fails.

The slim possibility of all experiments miraculously working evaporates as experiments are forced to be bad and get worse. From the starting point of the widespread belief of systemically necessary inflation we get … the widespread belief of systemically necessary inflation.

Behavior and Incentives

"It is harder to ignore the enormous increase in indebtedness and overhead that has accompanied the enlargement of farm technology. Mr. Billard quotes an Iowa banker: "In 1920 […] $5,000 was a big loan, and people hesitated to borrow. Now a $40,000 loan is commonplace, and having mortgage after mortgage is an accepted thing. I occasionally wonder whether the average farmer will ever get out of debt.

"The Iowa banker's statement, doubtful as it may seem out of context, is made in praise of credit. Nowhere is there a question of the advisability of basing so large on enterprise on credit, or of the influence of routine indebtedness on a people's character. Nowhere is there a suspicion that there might be any worth in the old rural values of solvency and thrift."
—Wendell Berry, *The Unsettling of America*

What really matters in all of this — what the financial terminology ought to elucidate but can just as easily obfuscate — is what is happening to the incentives individuals face to devote their time and energy to economically useful behavior. Are they incentivized to nurture, replenish, and grow the capital stock or not? We can think of four obvious changes in relative incentives, although we are sure there are countless more.

First, there will be an incentive to find some asset other than money to save with. Likely candidates are real estate and equity and bond indices. Inflation in these asset classes will march upwards with the threat of inflation in general, distorting the price information they otherwise both create and rely on and further misdirecting capital to ends that are only as sustainable as the inflationary regime. Anybody who wants these assets for their actual economic function — somewhere to live, stable cash flows, whatever — ends up at the mercy of this regime: Unable to own anything unless they lever up too, which of course just exacerbates the problem.

Second, those who hold return-seeking capital assets but who do not lever up are comparatively disadvantaged if their competitors do. And if they don't get politically preferential access to the front of the queue for new loans, they may have to sell to those who do. The oldest company in the world, Kongō Gumi, was run by fifty generations of the same Japanese family before selling out to conglomerate Takamatsu in 2006, when it "succumbed to excess debt."[85]

Third, this constant and pointless demand for financialization will create political and business opportunities to better facilitate it. Financial capital will increasingly be directed towards the very business of financialization at the expense of creating real productive capital. Those in on such schemes will do very well indeed, but this is clearly not economically useful. Matt Stoller describes this process in equal parts entertainingly and depressingly, as industries as odd and diverse as portable toilets, prison phones, and dentistry are financialized to absolutely nobody's benefit other than those orchestrating, "a form of legalized fraud shifting money from the pockets of investors and workers to the pockets of financiers."[86]

Fourth, this artificially expanded opportunity will favor general bigness and concentration in finance itself. Berry's insight of the optimal organization of agriculture we think once again transcends his domain and is a valuable commentary on credit and capital:

> In a highly centralized and industrialized food-supply system there can be no small disaster. Whether it be a production "error" or a corn blight, the disaster is not foreseen until it exists; it is not recognized until it is widespread. By contrast, a highly diversified, small-farm agriculture combined with local marketing is literally crisscrossed with margins, and these margins work both to allow and encourage care and to contain damage.

In other words, the financial system will tend towards a structure that makes crises all the more devastating when they inevitably occur. And if we recall the idea of *leverage efficiency* from the Ergodicity Economics school and first introduced in Chapter Two, *The Complex Markets Hypothesis*, we realize that this is no mere rhetorical claim. We do not use the word "inevitable" to be dramatic, but rather to be accurate: Leverage efficiency tends to one in the long run. Leverage creates volatility that wipes out leverage. Systemically excess leverage *will* end badly. Not *might*, will.

And finally, an obvious consequence of all four is accelerating inequality between those who do and do not own capital, who are and are not able to get to front of the queue for artificial finance, and who do and do not make malinvestments in their own human capital on false price signals. Given the focus of this chapter is to elucidate the dynamics of the capital stock, we will leave the connection at the following musing: If the popular reaction to such spiraling inequality and unaccountable overseeing of proliferating crises is to whip up anti-capitalist sentiment and/or demand compensatory money printing, will the incentives to channel time and energy towards nurturing, replenishing, and growing the capital stock get better or worse?

The Uncapitalizing of America

"We are faced with a choice between continued expansion of debt on the one hand and widespread business and personal bankruptcy on the other. The increase in the money supply that results from the creation of new debt can and often does encourage general price inflation, but, since almost every developed economy nowadays suffers from such inflation, this is widely regarded as an acceptable fact of modern life."
—Tarek El Diwany, *The Problem with Interest*

Does it ever end? If so, where? When? How?

It is likely impossible to say because the impetus is politically variable, *and* there will always be the countervailing force of successful experiments propping the whole thing up. We can interpret their significance from multiple angles. By definition, they add to the capital stock and may or may not offset its natural rate of depletion. They contribute to deflation which may or may not offset the inflation caused by the perversity of the monetary regime. Most critically, they offer a means of natural deleveraging — even within the ideological obsession with consumption — because the lower later consumption that balances their financialization will be relatively less impactful.

But that the opportunity to deleverage exists does not mean it will be taken. Successful investment and capital creation may not pull hard enough and may only delay the inevitable. The never-ending march to greater and greater leverage will meet its final boss at the zero-lower bound of interest. It is difficult to overstate the importance of appreciating the ZLB from first principles.

If you are offered a negative interest loan, what this means is that you can spend it on an investment project that loses money and still make money yourself. This financialization allows you to crystallize future value that *will never come to exist*. In other words, it encourages not even the relative waste of capital, but its direct consumption. Imposing negative interest rates is strip-mining the capital stock. It is eating the seeds rather than planting them. It is utter insanity, but it is an insanity with no alternative if we can't deleverage and yet we must consume.

Berry's analysis of the tragic logic of the accelerating pillaging of the agricultural stock we think translates practically word for word. It may even be more accurate to say that it *generalizes*, as the agricultural stock is but one form of accumulated capital — the original:

It is no doubt impossible to live without thought of the future; hope and vision can live nowhere else. But the only possible guarantee of the future is responsible behavior in the present. When supposed future needs are used to justify misbehavior in the present, as is the tendency with us, then we are both perverting the present and diminishing the future. But the most prolific source of justifications of exploitative behavior has been the future. The future is a time that cannot conceivably be reached except by industrial progress and economic growth. The future, so full of material blessings, is nevertheless threatened with dire shortages of food, energy, and security unless we exploit the earth even more "freely," with greater speed and less caution. The obvious paradoxes involved in this — that we are using up future necessities in order to make a more abundant future; that final loss has been made a calculated strategy of annual gain — have so far been understood to no great effect. The great convenience of the future as a context of behavior is that nobody knows anything about it. No rational person can see how using up the topsoil or the fossil fuels as quickly as possible can provide greater security for the future, but if enough wealth and power can conjure up the audacity to say it can, then sheer fantasy is given the force of truth; the future becomes reckonable as even the past has never been.

To say this *sheer fantasy* "ends" here is likely presumptuous. It gets abjectly worse here, but nobody knows when it ends. When all capital has been consumed? When leverage is infinite?

What about if or when savers revolt against the obvious tax on their savings that negative rates require? Inflation may be a stealth tax that is unavoidable as far as they are concerned, but surely this obnoxiously direct tax can be avoided by removing deposits? Unfortunately, this will do little more than trigger a liquidity crisis that will have to be patched by long-term inflationary reserve creation, from which yet more short-term inflationary leverage will predictably metastasize. And if you think about it, this nuisance would be rather solved by simply banning cash, introducing purely digital state money, or both, such that fungible pan-bank liabilities are not liabilities against anything in particular, besides the loans that created them. It would be jolly good for banking stability to protect it from the animal spirits of the rabble. We wonder if anybody has considered this.

In Chapter Four, *Wittgenstein's Money*, we stressed that money is useful not because it fits some or other semantic scheme that holds up if and only if nothing in real life changes, but because real life does change, and money provides certainty in an uncertain world. But this is not to say that uncertainty is harmful. Capital formation is by necessity highly uncertain but greatly beneficial. Money provides a means of socially scaling the embrace of this uncertainty, *provided* it gives us certainty in the first place. The more capital we create, the more complex the economic environment gets, and the more valuable the certainty of money becomes. Money emerges from uncertainty, capital emerges from money, and uncertainty emerges from capital.

This progression towards order and complexity can be reversed if perturbed with enough economic misinformation. If the value of money becomes increasingly uncertain, it will create increasingly worthless capital, which will mean money is less valuable anyway. If you break money, you break capital, and if you break capital, you break money. If you break money badly enough, you have to start strip mining capital to reclaim enough certainty to function at the level of civilizational complexity achieved to that point. But as this complexity depends on this capital, this is clearly not a sustainable proposition.

If we believe, or merely suspect, we are heading towards this outcome, can it be stopped? Can we opt out? Does anything … *fix this?*

What would it *seem like* if it did *seem like* we could fix this?

Chapter Six

Bitcoin Is Venice
Rhapsody on a theme of Nakamoto

In the Introduction, we wrote that Bitcoin will be one means of escaping rebooted feudalism. This could be true at any and every scale. It could be an individual, a family, a friend group, a neighborhood, a company, a city, an industry, a country, or the entire world. We will have to wait and see.

While there are good reasons it might fail, "*it's dumb*," and, "*I don't like it*" are not among them. In order to sensibly articulate the reasons why it might fail you have to understand it in the first place. Most do not. As we explained in Chapter Four, *Wittgenstein's Money*, most do not even know what it is they are looking at. Nor are they likely to any time soon because they don't want to see it. As philosopher of science Norwood Russell Hanson might say, their perception is *theory-laden*. Also, their theories are wrong. Oops.

And so, in the spirit of such colorful outrage as "it's a Ponzi scheme," "it's a waste of energy," and "it's backed by nothing,"[87] we will present our own set of colorfully outrageous metaphors to try to help people understand *what is actually happening right now*, and why things seem exactly like they should.

So outrageous they might just be accurate.

Bitcoin Is Ariadne

"Anyone who accumulated large amounts of wealth while remaining independent of military-political command structures faced the problem of safeguarding what he had gained. Unless a merchant could count on the protection of some formidable man of power, there was nothing to restrain local potentates from seizing his property any time his goods came within reach. To gain effective protection was likely to be costly — so costly as to inhibit large-scale accumulation of private capital."
—William McNeill, *The Pursuit of Power*

Bitcoin is often framed as "competing" with fiat currency. This is true in a sense but we fear there is a rhetorical danger of invoking the wrong kind of "competition." It is not a *fight*, for example. There is no conflict. Bitcoin is not trying to damage or sabotage its opponents, because it isn't *trying* anything and it knows no opponents. It has no awareness whatsoever of who might oppose it or why. It is simply an alternative, an exit valve, an opt-out. It is competing only insofar as it is proving to be a far superior alternative. It is not a sword for Theseus to fight the Minotaur, but a thread to follow to exit the labyrinth.

Bitcoin is Ariadne.

There will be tremendous value in normalizing this rhetoric amid the likely growing chorus of opposition desperate to smear Bitcoin as inherently nefarious or even hostile. Opponents must be forced to explain what is wrong with people interacting freely, and why true goodness can only follow from coercion, in their understanding. Should those who have found a way out of the unbearable labyrinth of capital strip mining not take it? What do they owe the Minotaur?

Does anybody really believe that, having fully understood the choice they face, any individual would choose to save in a self-referentially mispriced toxic loan rather than a provably sound digital bearer asset? Or, more simply still, that they will think it makes less sense to hold money that is a pure asset than money that is literally *defined as* a liability? Why not opt into a financial system that is built on trustless verifiability rather than unverifiable trust?

Threats of violence, perhaps? After all, the only way to "seize" properly secured bitcoin is through torture. In *The Pursuit of Power*, William McNeill interprets efforts in early modern Europe to industrialize and standardize weaponry and military drill as having the effect that "the magnitude and controllability of organized violence per tax dollar went up — spectacularly." It seems reasonable to suggest the potential for a similarly spectacular *fall* in such returns of late.

It is worth working through the optics of any decision to engage with Bitcoin in a truly hostile manner, because it is certainly coming. McNeill reminds us that, even some seven-hundred-or-so years ago, "the breakdown of established patterns of conduct always appears deplorable to a majority of those who witness it." By no means do we have a utopian outlook on this subject — rather, it is something of an intellectual rite of passage to accept the nonzero utility of dystopian paranoia. Bitcoin will be banned, many times, in many places. But a ban is an open admission of practical and moral failure and is arguably the best advertisement of all. A ban is the Berlin Wall. Fragments of any ban will one day become souvenirs of the folly and cruelty of repression. Bitcoin doesn't force anybody to stay. They come, and then they stay, because they want to — because it is both practically and morally superior.

As with East and West Berlin, it is also worth working through the likely ripples on society at large of the foundational difference of valuing and enshrining voluntary interaction. Yes, Bitcoin has different mechanics — we will get to this in later sections of this chapter — but from these mechanics follow different behaviors; from these behaviors, different cultures; from these cultures ... who knows?

We don't profess to know, but we can offer some ideas. First, we are wholly unprepared for the societal implications of making most wealth and much capital *entirely* mobile. We have been edging in this direction for decades as *software has eaten the world*, as Marc Andreessen famously put it.[88] Andreessen's article, "Why Software Is Eating the World," remains probably the most important treatise on finance written this century, and yet many in finance have not read it, and many who have think it is not about finance but about tech. It is only about tech insofar as by "tech" you mean "software," by "software" you mean "everything," and by "everything" you mean "finance." So, you are right, but in at least three different wrong ways. Maybe more.

Our preferred philosophical abstraction of Andreessen's argument would be something like the following: Software is productive capital for which the raw ingredients are coherent human thoughts. This has recreated the independent skilled-laborer-cum-entrepreneur as a class of economic agent whose capacity for capital creation is human, not financial. This class has arguably been minimized in the economic landscape at large since the Industrial Revolution morphed the Renaissance Italian blueprint of capitalism to its vastly more complex and socially ubiquitous successor stage dependent on organizing and directing labor around immobile capital.[89] Economic historian N. S. B. Gras was remarkably astute writing in 1942 in *Capitalism: Concepts and History*,

> Behind capitalism then, there is a will to save, to plan, to advance, to accumulate, and to attain security (for the investing capitalists and for the administrators). All persons, including workers, may join the ranks of the capitalists, if they save part of their income and plan their lives. In fact, a large number of workers are psychologically capitalists and, in a small way, actually capitalists. This existence of small owners of capital infuriates the intellectuals who would lead the proletarians into socialism or communism. Most hated by socialists and communists, in

fact, are these petty bourgeois who are many in number and firm in their faith in saving and planning and managing. There is no greater error than identifying workers with the proletariat.

If capital is something created by the administrative effort of men, large and small, and if capital to be effectively used must, like labor, be administered, then the essential element in the system of capitalism is administration.

Software arguably takes Gras's argument to an extreme even he would not have imagined: Software engineers are not merely *psychologically* capitalists, nor is it surprising they are *actually* capitalists. They are *clearly* capitalists. There is no doubt. The product of their entirely mental labor is transparently capital. Such agents have vast bargaining power over financial capitalists, which they tend to exercise currently by demanding equity. But note, the equity stake grounds capital creation in the existing financial system. This power was only ever forward-looking — such workers could bargain over and make mobile wealth they were yet to create.[90]

But Bitcoin has severed the final link. Vastly more capital is, in theory, now mobile as it no longer needs to be moored to a given financial system. By "everything," we need not mean "finance" but can actually mean "everything," particularly since a silver lining of the nightmare of lockdowns seems to have been normalizing knowledge work from just about wherever the workers want rather than a handful of unlivable metropoles. Joel Kotkin laments,

> Rather than a base for upward mobility, the great cities have largely become magnets for those who are already well-to-do. Few working-class or middle-class families can now afford to move to places like Paris, London, Tokyo, New York, San Francisco. Many former residents, like Chicago's black middle class, have left to make their future elsewhere. Many who still work in those cities are forced into intolerably long commutes. As the middle class dwindles, it leaves behind a marginal urban population who depend on the city for a livelihood but often can barely get by.

But likely no longer. And of course, wherever this high-skilled, newly mobile capital-cum-labor recongregates, all other forms of work will be viable as well — this need not be understood at surface level as an elitist prediction, but rather as baby steps towards feasible localism, at long last, and as we will discuss in much more detail in Chapter Seven, A *Capital Renaissance*, and Chapter Nine, *Global Money, Local Freedom*.

Physical capital still matters, clearly. So does cultural capital. These are so obvious as to be weird to need to point out, and we will go into much more detail on Bitcoin's likely impact on these stocks of capital, respectively, in Chapter Seven, as just mentioned, and Chapter Eight, *These Were Capitalists*. But those in a position to extract protection rents on physical capital, likely with the allure of cultural capital, will need to adjust to this new reality. Sticks are out, carrots are in. What are you gonna do about it? Build a wall? Good luck with that.

In the remarkable essay, "Economic Consequences of Organized Violence," Frederic Lane emphasizes the importance of sovereign competition in using and controlling violence in an era of more mobile capital than we are used to today:

> If all the tribute was used for conspicuous consumption, a term which seems particularly appropriate for the court of a prince of the ancièn regime, growth was slowed by lack of investment. Merchants who gained protection rents from international trade and colonization, although not entirely inconspicuous in their consumption, probably had a lower propensity to consume. If so lower profits for governments and higher profits for trading enterprises meant more capital accumulation and more growth.

McNeill similarly observes that in the wake of the eleventh-century upsurge of Venetian and Genoese private commercial activity in the Mediterranean,

> Rulers of old-fashioned command societies were simply unable to dominate behavior as thoroughly as in earlier times. Peddlers and merchants made themselves useful to rulers and subjects alike and could now safeguard themselves against taxation and robbery by finding refuge in one or another port of call along the caravan route and seaways, where local rulers had learned not to overtax the trade upon which their income and power had come to depend.

We may well be heading back to such a dynamic, with the wilds of the internet the spiritual successor to the high seas.[91]

But what does finance look like in such a society? It certainly doesn't follow from the above that finance *disappears*. Surely it just changes — but to what? We think there are two helpful strands of answers. The first is *programmable*, which, by its nature is unpredictable except by its potential. Analogies to the early web are cliché, but with perfectly good reason. With open access and a programmable interface, who knows what will be invented? Who knows how quickly inventions will be iterated and combined? The second is *Islamic*.

Bitcoin Is Halal

"An individual can be arrested for 'manufacturing' money in his own home but the commercial banking system is given the full protection of law in doing what amounts to the same thing. There is no justice in this [...] There are those who say that we must develop an Islamic alternative to modern commercial banking. But why must we do so? The Islamic alternative to the cigarette industry is no cigarette industry, and were we to remain true to our principles we might realize that the Islamic alternative to commercial banking is no commercial banking."
—Tarek El Diwany, *The Problem with Interest*

That Bitcoin can potentially be considered concordant with the teachings of Islamic finance is an insight we owe to conversation with Saifedean Ammous. What we mean by this is since bitcoin is a digital bearer asset and not a debt instrument, its natural state of safe custody is outside financial institutions. Also, without the ability to mint new bitcoin as and when politically convenient, deposit insurance is impossible and loan origination requires the prior provision of liquid capital. Hence prospective intermediaries would not be able to guarantee investor protection from loss arising from the debtor's activities.

In combination, it becomes comparatively much less likely that contributors of capital will accept a fixed upside and unlimited downside, particularly given the near-certainty of deflation rather than the contemporary norm of price inflation that must be forcefully chased with low-volatility capital appreciation. Would-be depositors will either save unilaterally or demand the shared upside of equity, for the most part. Supply will contract and swathes of demand for leverage will be priced out of whatever market is left.

What remains of interpersonal, non-programmatic banking is likely to look very similar to the proscriptions of Islamic finance, with a dramatically reduced role for debt, and a focus on *risk sharing* rather than *risk transfer*. Bitcoin is halal.

To be clear, the reasoning that arrives at this outcome is quite different. In Islam, interest on monetary debt (riba, الربا) is unlawful (haram, حرام) on ethical grounds, whereas we suggest it is unlikely to emerge to any great extent in a bitcoin standard on purely economic grounds given the risks will (finally!) be properly priced, hence can be legitimately shared rather than dishonestly transferred. Even still, the resulting behavior has a clear ethical resemblance to the cultural norms in the Bitcoin community, centered first and foremost on low time preference. Consider the Islamist scholar Abul Alā Mawdūdī's (ابو الاعلى مودودى) exhortation in *First Principles of Islamic Economics*,

It is incumbent on every member of the Muslim community to live within his means. He is forbidden to let his expenditure exceed his income, thus compelling him to stretch his hands out to others in order to sustain his extravagance, use unfair means to grab the wealth of others or become indebted to others to help finance his unending needs and, by consuming his resources in clearing his debt, eventually join the ranks of the destitute.

And even if we contest the underlying ethical objection, more similarities in attitude at a higher level are readily forthcoming. We might think, for example, that even in a bitcoin standard there will still be *some* willing supply and demand for interest-bearing, at-risk capital; why then should consensual exchange be prevented? The Islamic response hinges on the *haram* feature of what is deemed "speculation"; given the inherent uncertainty of entrepreneurship, the commitment to pay interest on monetary debt finance is unavoidably fraudulent given the debtor does not *and cannot* really know she can meet her obligations.

Only *pari passu* equity stakes are fair and honest, and furthermore, introduce no disharmony of incentives or outlooks between the capital providers. Once more, we may differ in our understanding of the ethics of such contracts, but Mawdūdī's reckoning of the consequences of the proliferation of such "speculation" has a clear appeal:

> Due to the absence of a reasonable and healthy relationship of participatory cooperation between the capitalist [creditor] and the entrepreneur [debtor], the global economy suffers tremendously and faces alternative highs and lows that adversely affect the world's economic health. The capitalist's stranglehold had helped to boost the spirit of speculation and minting of money through interest. this has naturally poisoned the bilateral relationship between capital and enterprise, and the raising and lowering of interest rates are now done in such a way as to keep the entire world's economic health always in risk.

By simply substituting out "all debt" for "money as debt" and similarly tracing out the consequences, Bitcoiners would likely agree entirely. Economist and noted Islamic Finance scholar Mohammad Siddiqi dryly makes this connection in, *A Vision for the Future of Islamic Economics*,[92] noting that, "almost all money in circulation is interest bearing debt transferring wealth from fund users to the owners of capital. It is not technically necessary for society's means of payment to play this role."

In *The Problem with Interest*, Tarek El Diwany makes a strikingly similar point to our own in Chapter Five, *The Capital Strip Mine*, all the more remarkably from an entirely different basis, that "polluted rivers, festering rubbish tips and resource-depleted seas may be just the first instalment of the price that is paid for entering in to a race with compound interest."

To a limited extent, believe it or not, the IMF seems to agree as well. In a 2010 working paper titled, *The Effects of the Global Crisis on Islamic and Conventional Banking: A Comparative Study*, Maher Hasan and Jemma Dridi conclude that Islamic banks' asset-based, rather than debt-based, operations, "make their activities more closely related to the real economy and tend to reduce their contribution to excesses and bubbles." The paper also includes the unintentionally hilarious deadpan explanation,

> The profit/loss-sharing nature of investment deposits provides Islamic banks with an additional buffer. However, this feature was not tested in the crisis given that most banks remained profitable. In addition, in the context of the crisis and given the loose monetary stance in most countries, this feature is likely to put Islamic banks' profitability at a disadvantage compared to conventional banks.

The closest analogues to "loans" as we might think of them are qard al-hasan (قرض الحسن), a straightforward interest-free, benevolent loan, and sukuk (صكوك), a kind of pooled, fixed-term equity investment — curiously more like the *colleganza* than any common contemporary instrument, originating in Venice but soon thereafter inspiring slight modifications across medieval Italy, France, and Spain.[93] Collateral is uncommon in either case but where it is taken there is a final intriguing comparison to be made: The collateral must be transferred to the possession of the creditor for the term, hence in the case of default, no repossession occurs.

As with everything in Islamic finance, the ultimate rationale is simply fairness and justice; those who default on a mortgage are not kicked out of their home because the home is in possession and use by the debtor and could not have been *halal* collateral to begin with. The connection to bitcoin is the likely incentive in a healthily deflationary environment not to recourse to hard assets to store value over the long-term, combined with an increased background incentive in financial transactions for all parties to access and retain sound money.

It is interesting to compare the prescriptions of Islamic finance — and arguably the difficulty Muslims have in living up to these prescriptions — with the development of commercial finance in medieval and Renaissance Mediterranean Europe. In short, we see essentially the same ethical starting point leading to a gradual diversion (one might say *temptation*). Frederic Lane writes in, *Investment and Usury*,

> As soon as any appreciable amount of liquid capital was accumulated in the hands of retired merchants, widows, or institutions, they sought ways of making their wealth yield income. In such cities as Venice, where investment in land had limited possibilities, they put their money with someone who could promise a return. Practical necessities of commerce and the traditions rooted in Roman law shaped the forms of contracts. When the moralists and the canon lawyers examined their contracts they denounced as usurious all loans bearing a fixed interest even if the interest charge was very moderate and even if contracted between businessmen as commercial investments. But if there was risk and

uncertainty about the return, the transaction would probably be approved as a partnership. In practice, loans to consumers were at a fixed rate and secured by collateral. Businessmen were better able to obtain funds without pledging specific security and without specifying the yearly return. Therefore loans to businessmen more generally escaped being obviously usurious. A distinction between productive loans and those that were merely exploiting consumers was recognized in the fourteenth century by the nobles of Venice and by some Roman lawyers.

And far more recently, Allan Savory comments disdainfully on what he evidently thinks of as declining communal standards in the crossover between ethics and commerce, writing in *Holistic Management*,

> In my lifetime alone, the distinction between wealth and money has probably become more blurred than at any time in history. High interest was usurious when I was a child; now that's seen as quaintly old-fashioned. Major banks move headquarters to states with more lenient usury laws and still retain customer confidence. Where it was once acceptable for lenders to advertise or engage in aggressive promotion, it is now commonplace. Money itself has become a commodity (like grain or oil) that earns money and can be traded internationally. The use of credit cards and the electronic speedup of monetary transactions has blurred the distinction further.

One need not personally subscribe to all, or any, tenets of Islamic finance to appreciate a broader — essentially ethical — point than its admittedly tenuous connections to bitcoin. The study of Islamic economics and finance is intriguing as it is, to our minds, the only systematized, contemporary, and *successful* alternative to what we might call "Western" financial precepts, now, of course, near-globalized and seemingly omnipresent in commerce. Note, for example, the IMF describes "Islamic banks" as opposed to "Conventional banks."[94]

A common difficulty with the conceptual challenge posed by Bitcoin is that the omnipresence makes it difficult to think rigorously in terms outside the framework of mainstream Western finance at all. Western finance *is water*. But perspective *can be* achieved, and precepts *can be* challenged. Mawdūdī, Siddiqi, and El Diwany challenged them, Nakamoto challenged them, and the reader owes it to themselves to challenge them, too. Elevating morality above perceived efficiency makes for a profound starting point.

El Diwany makes a fascinating point on the relationship between his faith and his economic beliefs in the preface to the second edition of *The Problem with Interest*, writing,

> So often we hear that religion should not interfere with science. I maintain that science should not interfere with religion. If God says that

interest is prohibited, who are we to disagree? And it is hardly plausible to argue that Muslims should not interfere with modern economics, since men of other religions have most clearly done so already. It's just that people don't refer to Ricardo, Marx, Keynes, and Friedman as Jewish economists. Instead they speak of Classicism, Marxism, Keynesianism and Monetarism. Islamic economics is not like this. In the very name of our discipline, we announce who we are, and in our work, we set out clearly what we are trying to do for the world.

While we absolutely understand this rightful pride, and while we certainly mean no offence, we cannot help but think this attitude is a bit of a shame. It is in the nature of a religion to be exclusive in terms of social membership. One cannot be both a Muslim and a Catholic, and certainly not a Muslim and an atheist. And yet, we feel that almost all of what El Diwany discusses *just is true*. One needn't be a Muslim to realize this; one need only be curious, intelligent, and humane.

We predict that Islamic banking, finance, and economics alike will soon be taken far, far more seriously than they are currently or arguably ever have been in the past. And the reason why is rather amusing in light of El Diwany's quote above: because of *science*! Or at least because of the methodology of science properly applied: The tenets of Islamic finance will be absolutely necessary as a starting point to understand what on earth is going on. This is not exclusive in terms of social membership.

This will affect everybody in the world, whether Muslim, Catholic, atheist, or whatever else. It is a testament to the vitality of Islamic thought: It conveys profound truth and wisdom accessible to all humanity.

Bitcoin Is Gravity

"An amount of money lent to a government, and the interest amount charged, is assumed to be risk-free because it is in turn assumed that a government can tax, borrow, or print further amounts of money to pay its debt. These three options are indeed available to a modern government, but one must not ignore the fact that the government has no access to risk-free rates of return when investing the borrowed money. The above-mentioned options are in fact nothing more than means of passing on the bill to others when the fact of a non-risk-free physical system eventually reasserts itself."
—Tarek El Diwany, *The Problem with Interest*

To date, it has been very difficult to conceptualize what value, exactly, has peacefully opted out of fiat and into bitcoin. Pricing only happens at the margin, and marginal fiat exchanged for bitcoin is just a bank liability that the bank relabels. Bitcoin exchanged at the margin likely engenders lower time preference, as discussed above, hence lower consumption of garbage, but which is conceivable only counterfactually.

This will change when people start selling not just their fiat, and not just their time, but when they start liquidating real assets. Gold will probably be the first victim, for readily understandable reasons as bitcoin is an upgrade in almost every respect. But gold is not systemically important. This shift will be noticeable but not otherwise impactful. When the accumulation drive hits short-term credit, real estate, and passive equity, that is when the party will really start.

These three are artificially large asset classes given they are de jure productive, hence cash generative and priced on yield, yet de facto speculative savings instruments given long-term saving with fiat is impossible. But more vitally still, they *are* systemically important. Their prices, in aggregate, affect capital formation. An overly concise summary of Chapter Five, *The Capital Strip Mine*, might be that these prices are wrong, and hence the capital is being strip-mined as quickly as it is being formed. Reversing this is the long-term hope, but anticipating the short-term mechanics of this reversal is another matter entirely.

The key insight is that if these assets were *actually* priced on yield, the kind of flows we anticipate would have no impact on long-term holders beyond minor disappointment. But because they are not, any substantial outflow can easily become a self-fulfilling prophecy. Corporations use short-term credit as ersatz cash with an inflation-hedging yield, however minuscule these days. But this is not an "investment." There is no upside but just sure-enough downside protection. If the downside protection disappears then the entire proposition evaporates — and note this could easily happen without substantial selling but simply a neglect to continue buying, given the whole point of short-term credit is that it continuously rolls over. What would likely happen next is central banks stepping in to "support" these markets with asset purchases, which, of course, is the best imaginable endorsement of bitcoin's utility.

Behind all of this is the seemingly straightforward question of bitcoin's "fair value." There will always be a hesitancy to shift savings from something as well understood and naturally priced as short-term credit to bitcoin on the basis of being entirely unsure of how to compare bitcoin's price to its "fundamentals."

What will gradually be realized is that, with bitcoin, the traditional relationship is inverted. we do not think it is quite accurate to say that bitcoin's price *is* its fundamentals, but certainly its price is a largely reflexive function of its fundamentals: As the price goes up, the fundamentals go up (and we must be mindful also that as the price goes down, the fundamentals go down. Sustained attack that drives the price down for long enough is by far the biggest risk). Bitcoin was weakest when smallest, but less so the more time passes.[95] Bitcoin is a black hole sucking unsustainably artificial value beyond its event horizon. As it grows, so does its pull. Bitcoin is gravity.

The "store of value realization" argument for its gravitational pull is by far the most obvious, the least creative, and is only scratching the surface of its likely continued evolution. Consider the implications of deepening liquidity, which, note, is subtly different from "price" alone. This is a necessary precondition for increasingly large purchases in the first place. MicroStrategy could not have done what it did a year earlier. Apple and Berkshire (dare we say?) still cannot do what they likely one day will.

But market deepening has far more interesting implications. It enables Strike, for example, Zap's soon-to-be widely copied, soon-to-be annihilation of FX markets. Strike combines ever-tightening spreads on fiat liquidity pools with Lightning's instant settlement and relative programmability to offer unmatchable foreign exchange transfers. There are several astonishing features here that it is worth making absolutely sure we understand.

First, this service cannot be matched within the fiat settlement infrastructure. We don't mean that it is difficult; we mean that it is impossible. Interbank payments with the same currency and within the same jurisdiction can be more or less free and instant, and in many places are, since all this amounts to is relabeling a bank liability or, at worst, a net flow between mutual counterparty banks that can be batched and properly settled at enormous scale, hence offered to the end-users at low or zero cost. But across currencies, jurisdictions, or both, this is impossible — fundamentally *because* fiat is a debt instrument. What we might think of as a simple "payment" in this context is really more like a credit relay. Each party needs to trust the next party in the chain, and price not only the operational expense but this perceived risk, before passing it on, given the actual claim will be settled much, much later. And payment *streaming*? Fuhgeddaboudit. Not in your wildest dreams. With Strike, none of this is relevant.

Lightning has no lower bound on value and settles instantly, and that's the end of that.

This service does not expose the user to the price of bitcoin *at all*. And yet, the fact of its existence and usage deepens the markets, which directly contributes to bitcoin's fundamentals, hence price, increasing. And if heavy users of this system one day decide they'd prefer to keep the transfers they receive in sound, free, open source, programmable money, well, that makes the process even simpler still.

It doesn't even end there. The Lightning infrastructure is still young and small and it needs staked value to grow. What better way to put bitcoin-denominated capital to work than seeking a return on competitive liquidity and routing? As bitcoin's fiat value grows, so do the incentives to contribute to scaling Lightning, which increases the efficiency of fiat payments routed via Strike-and-others over Lightning, which increases the depth of the fiat markets for bitcoin. And the more Lightning scales, the more the prospect of payment streaming opens up opportunities for better funding decentralized infrastructure — for example, incentivizing running Tor exit nodes, the storage and routing building blocks sought by the likes of Sci-Hub, accessible and portable economies in gaming, off-platform content monetization and advertising-free content-driven apps, but also things literally nobody has yet imagined. All of which increases Lightning's utility, which increases Bitcoin's utility. The more falls into this orbit, the bigger the orbit gets. The Jevons paradox in the metaverse!

Deeper markets also indirectly legitimize lending fiat against bitcoin reserves. While nominally tailored to allowing synthetic institutional leverage, normalizing this service will reduce the incentive for anybody to ever sell, in inverse proportion to how widely accepted bitcoin is for regular payments at a given time. It will be Pierre Rochard's speculative attack,[96] but without even requiring awareness or intention. It will just be the sensible thing to do. If or when miners are able to access this service to pay for electricity, even partially, marginal supply will evaporate. Many miners have already discovered the hack of tapping capital markets at the farcically low costs of capital that are inevitably downstream of relentless central bank intervention to cover their costs, not need to sell their winnings, and effectively becoming long/short hedge funds with anomalous energy expenditures. Increasing depth will also make increasingly viable credit card rewards programs, salary allocations, and, once again, things literally nobody has yet imagined, which might read as negligible in nominal terms, but are more about buying mindshare than fiat. Small buys lead to big buys.

Properly sophisticated, grown-up, Ivy League MBA, *CFA-accredited* readers might liken this entire line of reasoning, and our enthusiasm for it, to GameStop, the fiat finance hilarity of early 2021, in the sense of uppity retail thinking they are sticking it to the man but really just blowing their savings on a practical joke from which Citadel will be the ultimate winner (not our reading, to be clear, but a common one. Ours is that these people knew exactly what they were doing and that you can prove it if you are willing to just *look*). We would encourage such readers to think more seriously about the game theory involved in all of this, particularly if gold and then short-term *government* credit fall into Bitcoin's orbit.

You might think this leads precisely nowhere at all, but the central banks of Venezuela, Iran, North Korea, Singapore, and El Salvador would disagree with you, that we know of so far. Central bank accumulation will become the defining macroeconomic issue of the decade, and advocacy for accumulation by the tech-savvy one of the defining political issues. Entirely mobile, unseizable capital will be attracted to, and will compound physically, wherever it is most welcomed, as will the human capital that likely comes with it. Countries with geopolitical rivals who decide to ban Bitcoin will be cutting off their nose to spite their face. When China starts to pay Russia for natural gas first in dollar stablecoins on Bitcoin, then *in bitcoin*, don't say we didn't tell you to think about it a little more than not at all.

Come to think of it, even GameStop can be non-ironically tied to this discussion. It has turned out a decent amount of faux-populist rancor was misplaced and the real culprit for screwing the little guy wasn't shady backroom deals between Citadel, Sequoia, the SEC, and the Fed, but rather the limitations of equity clearing and settlement given the mechanics of counterparty risk. Try to imagine, if only for a moment, tokenized equity certificates pegged to a secure digital bearer asset, with no counterparties, that settle in T + *right now*. Can you imagine that? Citadel might be the short-term winner in all this, but the long term is all about tokenized equity on sidechains.

Bitcoin Is Logos

"To imagine a language is to imagine a form of life."
— Ludwig Wittgenstein

LinkedIn founder Reid Hoffman infamously said on the Tim Ferris podcast that Bitcoin is like a Wittgenstein language game,[97] with no elaboration whatsoever! Were we to pick up the baton, we would refer to *Philosophical Investigations* and the dictum that, "the meaning of a word is its use in the language." In other words (no pun intended), Hoffman is characterizing Bitcoin as understandable only by interpreting the actions of the participants as essentially consisting of communication with other participants, hence expressing in a codified grammar what they *mean* and relying on this grammar to understand what others *mean*.

We think it is worth invoking Norwood Russell Hanson once again to appreciate the position of a functionally illiterate outsider in the presence of such a language game; an adherent of the (admittedly satirical) semantic theory of money. If perception is theory-laden, and if our theory invalidates the possibility of a new money monetizing from scratch, and that money takes the form of a language we don't speak, and we won't learn this language because we think it can't exist ... we are just about *guaranteed* not to understand it.

That Bitcoin can be thought of as a language game clarifies why it is inherently peaceful. Money is an information system that records and updates who has done work that is valued by others, such that credit can be universalized and socially scaled.[98] Frederic Lane and Reinhold Mueller note in *Money and Banking in Medieval and Renaissance Venice* that "both 'medium of exchange' and 'standard of value' are sufficiently ambiguous to make 'moneyness' a matter of degree," and that, "conceptually and historically the two are separable."

To consider just how far we have come from what was once considered common sense, consider Luigi Einaudi's musings in his essay, "The Theory of Imaginary Money from Charlemagne to the French Revolution,"

> If one reads books on the monetary subjects that were written in the period from the sixteenth to the eighteenth century, one frequently encounters the concept of "imaginary money." Other terms used are "ideal money," "political money," moneta numeraria, "money of account." What these terms meant was not very clear even to contemporaries. The most authoritative writer among the historians of French monetary vicissitudes, François Le Blanc, resigned himself to defining as imaginary any kind of money which, "properly speaking, is but a collective term comprising a certain number of real moneys.[99]

In what is surely the final nail in the coffin of the *semantic theory of money* and proof that its proponents really are rather historically clueless, Einaudi later writes,

> The key, needed to interpret the apparent confusion of the monetary treatises written prior to the eighteenth century is the distinction between a monetary unit used as a standard of value and of deferred payments and another monetary unit used as a medium of exchange.
>
> There was, then, a monetary unit used only as a standard of deferred payments (promises to pay) or for the purpose of keeping accounts. This was the function of a money of account, an imaginary or ideal money. The public made contracts, kept books, established mortgages, or stipulated rents in pounds, shillings, and pence. In the time of Malestroit and his "Paradoxes" (1565), an ell of velvet was valued at 10 pounds tournois; a measure of wine; at 12 pounds; a pair of shoes, at 15 sous; the daily wage of a laborer; at 5 sous; the annual rent of a gentlemen, at 500 pounds; and a town-house or farm, at 25,000 pounds.
>
> Although it was possible to make contracts or to keep accounts in imaginary money — that is, in pounds, shillings, and pence — it was impossible to make actual payments in these monetary units, since they had not been coined for several centuries. Payment was made in real currency, that is, in gold coins, white money or silver coins, black money or low-grade silver, vellon or copper coins.

What Einaudi identifies here is essentially the tension presented by money increasingly taking on the character of information removed from specie, as webs of capital and trade extend further in space and time than it is convenient to be accompanied by physical coinage. Economic information in the form of price *signals* is kept the truest by the scarcity of precious metals. But their *broadcast* — the recording and updating of the canon of economic activity — is limited by this same factor. This recording and updating is a technical problem, and candidate technical solutions ought to be evaluated not on how and how well they fit *sufficiently ambiguous* definitions, as Mueller and Lane would surely criticize, but on *how and how well they work;* be they Rai stones, gold ducats, or dollar-denominated bank liabilities; real or imaginary, physical or digital; instantiates or abstract; pure asset or debt. The solution provided by Bitcoin is in some sense the purest yet conceived in that it captures this information *as speech* — we only use software to check the grammar.

It also clarifies a crucial reason why it is winning and will likely continue to win: It is organic. Inorganic languages, such as, notoriously, Esperanto, necessarily fail in the long run without their adoption being coercively enforced. Despite their alleged perfect, calculated — even *scientific* — design, they have no informal resonance, no literature, no idioms, no metaphors, no jokes, no vernacular, no traditions, and no practical history on which to draw. They are linguistic analogues of socialist command economies, and they fail for essentially the same reasons. As James C. Scott writes in *Seeing Like a State*,

> Any attempt to completely plan a village, a city, or, for that matter a language is certain to run afoul of [...] social reality. A village, city, or language is the jointly created, partly unintended product of many, many hands. To the degree that authorities insist on replacing this ineffably complex web of activity with formal rules and regulations, they are certain to disrupt the web in ways that they cannot possibly foresee.

Although often framed as the genius, quasi-miraculous, and possibly religious creation of Satoshi Nakamoto, the reality is that Bitcoin has been "made" and continues to be made and remade, by unknowably many individuals. It is free and open-source software. Which is to say — literally — that *it is* a language. While code, a program, an app, a network, and a community — all accurate in some or other sense — Bitcoin is probably more helpfully described as *linguistic commons*.[100]

Languages change and evolve organically. But it is perhaps paradoxically necessarily that languages must remain *mostly* unchanging — mostly *common* between their speakers — such that change can be recognized and contextualized, rather than simply disorienting. Saifedean Ammous's framing of "salability across space" and "salability across time" — it seems now firmly in the lexicon[101] — is worth teasing out further in the context of understanding Bitcoin as language, and money as an information system. The essence of temporal salability is soundness; the essence of spatial salability is portability. Prior to Bitcoin, the two were in inescapable tension; economic development induces a market demand for money to be increasingly purely informational, as commerce itself becomes more complex than movement of specie can efficiently support. But information is, by its nature, not scarce at all, and so retaining some semblance of scarcity in informational money, hence temporal salability, requires trust in a centralized source of truth.

Note this does not imply "fiat," but rather "fiduciary," from the Latin *fiducia*, for *trust*. With *relatively* sound specie held in reserve by *relatively* prudent bankers, "bank money" — payment purely by debit and credit of accounts with a bank—in thirteenth-century Venice was *relatively* trustworthy, and in fact dominant and thriving. Not to mention in Genoa, Florence, Barcelona, and Bruges, interoperable via bills of exchange; all a little less temporally salable, perhaps, but vastly more spatially salable.[102] But of course, Bitcoin resolves the underlying tension entirely. It is digital (that is, *informational*) scarcity. We get the portability of email with no trust, just verification.

A Bitcoin transaction is a global speech act that means, roughly, *I am provably entitled to this portion, x, of the money supply, and am now transferring it to somebody else*, in a language that everybody remembers forever and which can't be used to lie. This is why efforts to ban Bitcoin, while they will certainly be attempted, will also almost certainly fail. Bitcoin is the ultimate samizdat.

Bitcoin is logos.

We cannot help but feel that there is something deeply spiritual about the conceptual elevation of monetary exchange beyond the merely transient and transactional that is implied by our insistence that money is language. *Consumption* strikes of the material and individual, but *communication* is an intellectual and social act. *Homo economicus* might navigate a world of utility maximizing automatons, but human beings engage, trust, and cooperate, *so as to then more productively trade*. A trade *might* be sensibly conceived of as a one-off — an act removed from time and place — if, as pure, meaningless consumption, nothing comes of it. But it might be in the course of creating capital, in which case the act's relationship to time, to circumstances, and to the community of fellow actors matters deeply. As George Steiner says of language in *After Babel*,

> One thing is clear: every language-act has a temporal determinant. No semantic form is timeless. When using a word we wake into resonance, as it were, its entire previous history. A text is embedded in specific historical time; it has what linguists call a diachronic structure. To read fully is to restore all that one can of the immediacies of value and intent in which speech actually occurs.

First discussed at length in Chapter Four, *Wittgenstein's Money*, Steiner's thesis in *After Babel* is that *all language is translation*, as evidenced in the following concise extracts:

> Any model of communication is at the same time a model of translation, of a vertical or horizontal transfer of significance. No two historical epochs, no two social classes, no two localities, use words and syntax to signify exactly the same things, to send identical signals of valuation and inference. Neither do two human beings.

And a few pages later,

> Thus a human being performs an act of translation, in the full sense of the word, when receiving a speech-message from any other human being. Time, distance, disparities in outlook or assumed reference, make this act more or less difficult. Where the difficulty is great enough, the process passes from reflex to conscious technique.

We have already argued that we think this extends naturally and valuably to understanding trade and capital accumulation as a form of linguistic exchange, drawing on a literature, but always creating incrementally new meaning. What does positive-sum trade from a foundation of subjective value *mean* if not an always-personal imprint of revealed preference on the corpus of all past imprints? Is Steiner's thesis in linguistic philosophy and literary criticism not radically subjectivist and methodologically individualist? Is Steiner not a Misesian? Is *After Babel* not the *Human Action* of language?

So, too, is to invest; to tap into the values and intentions of fellow human beings and to realize one's place in a growing corpus of meaningful productive activity — not forgettable gibberish but *a diachronic structure.*

This is all a source of great optimism given prevalent legal and social commitments to protecting politically undesirable speech. Naïve as we are sure it will seem to some; we think one of the most important US Supreme Court cases of the next twenty years will be the ruling that the right to broadcast Bitcoin transactions is guaranteed under the First Amendment. Prior to this, while the legality is still up in the air, we fully expect a sitting congressperson to invoke congressional privilege and "broadcast" a transaction by dictating its hexadecimal representation on the floor of the House or Senate.

This will probably be followed by tweeting one, working one into a public deposition, embedding one in a flag — which will end up on t-shirts and lapel pins, as well as fully physically to be waved around as a staple at protests. *Don't Tread on My Node!* You either make countably infinite sets of numbers, letters, and colors illegal — whatever that even means — or you accept that Bitcoin is going to happen.

Bitcoin Is Techne

"The Venetians were not thinkers: they were doers. Empiricists par
excellence, they mistrusted abstract theories."
  —John Julius Norwich, *A History of Venice*

Recording and updating the speech act of transferring value is a technical
problem, to which Bitcoin is a technical solution. It is not an idea about how
things *ought to work*. It is a real thing that *does work*. Although the observation
may seem flippant, the distinction is enormously important.

Nic Carter put it to Frances Coppola on Peter McCormack's podcast *What
Bitcoin Did* that in order to make an apple pie from scratch, you have to first
invent the universe,[103] by which he was conveying that if you want to create a
robust, fast-settling, online payments system with finality, you need to create
Bitcoin. No alternative has ever *actually worked*. Given the problems Bitcoin
solves are very clearly *not just academic* but are core to human
civilization, *actually working* is rather important. Bitcoin is techne.

We think this captures what is likely the biggest hurdle for most newcomers
who do actually make an effort to understand the details, because, on the face of
it, Bitcoin is completely absurd as an engineering construct. *Miners do
WHAT?!? Coins are stored HOW?!?* and so on — we've all had these
conversations. Even the mathematically inclined who enjoy toying with the
cryptographic primitives may very reasonably think, should they lack the wider
context, *this is completely ridiculous because everything is fine*. But with the
proper context, we can of course say, *this is exactly as ridiculous as it needs to
be because everything is not fine*.

And yet there is a particular brand of skeptic who professes to admire some
or most of Bitcoin's design, but can't bring themselves to get fully on board
because of some pet problem Bitcoin seems not to fully solve, or some pet issue
with the way in which Bitcoin solves the problems it clearly does solve. Coppola
is very much in this camp. We would argue Peter Schiff and Mike Green are too.
All are interesting and serious people who seem to have the right attitude on
many issues Bitcoin touches, with the mysterious exception *of Bitcoin itself*. On
Bitcoin, all adopt variations of this pedantic quibbling that is superficially
sophisticated but really the most meretricious and unserious position of all
because nothing remotely practical is offered in its place. They deal with reality
not as it is but as they would like it to be. Their "solutions" are clean, slick, and
are never going to happen. Bitcoin deals with reality as it actually is. It is ugly.
And it works.

This entire line of argument will likely never go away, given it was refuted in its entirety as early as May 2011 in the now legendary *Bitcoin is Worse is Better,* by the highly respected pseudonymous cybersecurity blogger Gwern:

> The sacrifice Bitcoin makes to achieve decentralization is — however practical — a profoundly ugly one. Early reactions to Bitcoin by even friendly cryptographers [and] digital currency enthusiasts were almost uniformly extremely negative, and emphasized the (perceived) inefficiency [and] (relative to most cryptography) weak security guarantees. Critics let "perfect be the enemy of better" and did not perceive Bitcoin's potential. However, in an example of "Worse is Better," the ugly inefficient prototype of Bitcoin successfully created a secure decentralized digital currency, which can wait indefinitely for success, and this was enough to eventually lead to adoption, improvement, and growth into a secure global digital currency.[104]

Embracing this engineering ethic will immunize the curious to such inane posture talk as Nassim Taleb's unpredictable outbursts on "complex systems," "volatility," or "scale transformations," or Eric Weinstein claiming that "we need to get rid of the blockchain so that it's a locally enforced conservation law that replaces space-time with a system of computer nodes." If you want to *embed Bitcoin in a gauge theory*, Eric, go right ahead. we look forward to reading the BIP. But please *actually do it*. Don't burble Chomsky sentences in the metalanguage and expect to be taken seriously. Of colorless green ideas a decentralized currency is not made.

Bitcoin Is Venice

"Of the various centres in which republican ideas continued to be discussed and celebrated throughout the later Renaissance, the one with the most enduring commitment to the traditional values of independence and self-government was Venice. While the rest of Italy succumbed to the rule of the signori, the Venetians never relinquished their traditional liberties."
— Quentin Skinner, *The Foundations of Modern Political Thought*

We tend to find Bitcoin analogies that aren't transparently rhetorical to inevitably have some fatal flaw that ultimately makes them more confusing than they are helpful. And yet, Venice has an enigmatic appeal that we cannot bring ourselves to categorize as entirely fanciful. As a social and political order emerging from feudalism by an embrace of trade and capital formation, it is certainly instructive. But there seems to me to be more. Clearly, Bitcoin is not a *city*, but it is a system, and a symbol, in a way that transcends its instantiation as code, much as Venice transcended its islands and lagoon.

Some comparisons are cute and easy. Venice was far, far easier to defend than to attack, to the point that attack was essentially futile. Its governance model was bewilderingly opaque and constitutionally resistant to seizure. If seizure nonetheless became a realistic threat, an immune response seemed to be triggered that innovated around the danger. Was the legendary putting down of Bajamonte Tiepolo's insurrection, tipped not by the Commune's security forces but by an old woman throwing a stone from a window, a primitive *user activated soft fork*? Sure, why not. And of course, what of emerging from a dark age characterized first and foremost by monetary debasement? Pirenne's observation certainly suggests a precedent,

> If it is admitted, as it must be admitted, that the reappearance of gold coinage, with the florins of Florence and the ducats of Venice in the thirteenth century characterized the economic renaissance of Europe, the inverse is also true: the abandoning of gold coinage in the eighth century was the manifestation of a profound decline.

What of Venice's relative egalitarianism? John Julius Norwich writes in *A History of Venice* that Venice was famed,

> For a system of justice which gave impartial protection to rich and poor, aristocrat and artisan, Venetian and foreigner; for, in theory, at any rate and for the most part in practice too, every man living beneath the banner of St Mark was equal in the sight of the law.

Pirenne notes this attitude was fundamentally rooted in the necessities of commerce and hence extended beyond the city's own jurisdiction and internal affairs:

> No scruple had any weight with the Venetians. Their religion was a religion of businessmen. It mattered little to them that the Moslems were the enemies of Christ, if business with them was profitable.

Similarly, that Bitcoin is apolitical or "money for enemies" is well meme-ified at this point, but we were particularly struck by Terry Crews's rather more visceral anecdote to this effect. Crews recalled,

> I was first convinced when I was at a convention in Milan and I had fees I needed to pay, more than I could withdraw from an ATM. I had a bank wire me funds and showed up with all my paperwork and the bank manager turned me down because I was black. At that point I knew the existing financial system wasn't for me. Bitcoin doesn't know I'm black.

What of Venice's continual flouting of the proclamations of the Church, the literal counterpart to Kotkin's modern *clerisy* of elite tastemakers and thinkers of right thoughts, who already have and no doubt will continue to take, "a defiant and hostile attitude toward the commercial revival which must, from the very first, have seemed to it a thing of shame and a cause of anxiety," as Pirenne put it?

But we think the most striking comparison of all is the synthesis of disparate ideas into a financial cornerstone. Very little of commercial note was invented in medieval and Renaissance Venice — double-entry bookkeeping was likely borrowed from Genoa, having originally been imported to Italy from the Levant. The numeral system with which it is most useful is famously Indian, relayed in Arabic via Persia, the Levant, and the Maghreb; most other contributions to business administration were probably imported from Arabia and Constantinople; and the material industrial advances of the time predominantly originated in China. But Venice combined them all to perfection. Most of the outlines of modern finance were arguably present in Venice by the early fifteenth century at the latest, with very little truly *invented* since, rather than further combined, standardized, scaled, or modernized.[105] To our minds, only central banking and options have been both material and entirely novel.

Of course, technology, industry, and society have advanced immeasurably since, and yet we still live by Venetian financial customs and have no idea why. Even the word "bank," in the financial sense, originates in Venice, from the *banca* or "benches" of moneychangers by the Rialto Bridge, with Lane and Mueller pointing out that, "true banking had developed, it is now generally agreed, not from moneylending or pawnbroking, but from the manual exchange of coins." Modern banking is the legacy of a problem that technology has since solved.

The following explication of Venetian financial infrastructure around the fourteenth century from Lane's *Venice, A Maritime Republic* is remarkable in that we think it is a perfectly solid foundation for understanding the role played, *today*, by credit card networks and bank settlement schemes alike:

> The main function of a Venetian banker was not making loans but making payments on behalf of his clients. Even if a merchant had plenty of coins in his treasure chest, it was a bothersome and dangerous business to get them out every time he made a purchase, making sure each coin was genuine and in good condition. Nor did he want to go through a similar process each time he made a sale. He was happy to receive payment by being given credit on the books of a well-known banker. He could use that credit to pay for his next purchase. These credits were not transferred through writing checks, as is done today, but depended on the person who was making a payment appearing in person before the banker who sat behind a bench under the portico of a church at Rialto, with his big journal spread out in front of him. The payor orally instructed the banker to make a transfer to the account of the person being paid. The banker wrote as directed in his book, which was an official notarial record, so that there was no need of receipts. There were normally four or five such bankers with booths on the campo next to the Rialto bridge. Everyone of any consequence in business had an account so that he could make and receive payments through the banks. They were called banche di scritta or del giro because their main function was to write transfers and thus to rotate (girare) credits from one account to another at the command of the merchants.

If we add bills of exchange, credit creation, and floating the state debt, all natural extensions of the utility of these *ledgers* — and of course, if we subtract a hard reserve asset, available on-demand, that was deposited in the first place — there is not much left to account for. And note as well the seedlings of why the trust-minimizing natively digital, computational, and decentralized features of the Bitcoin for settlement and Lightning for payments dramatically improve on this setup.[106] Bitcoin may be magic internet money, but more importantly, it is money *for the internet.* Prior to 2009, you could send any information you want to anybody, anywhere in the world, instantly … *except* the most important information of all: value. Now we are all caught up.

It is often commented that Bitcoin is really more an ingenious combination of prior advances in applied cryptography than an *invention* in its own right. We are quite partial to the romantic idea that Bitcoin was discovered rather than invented. It is a foundation to scale the next great phase of economic progress.

Bitcoin is Venice.

Bitcoin Is

"Our history forbids us to be surprised that an orthodoxy of thought should become narrow, rigid, mercenary, morally corrupt, and vengeful against dissenters. This has happened over and over again. It might be thought the maturity of orthodoxy; it is what finally happens to a mind once it has consented to be orthodox. But one may be permitted a little amusement, if not surprise, that this should have befallen a modern science, which was set up, as it never tires of advertising, to pursue truth, not protect it […] If change is to come, then, it will have to come from outside. It will have to come from the margins."
—Wendell Berry, *The Unsettling of America*

Colorfully outrageous metaphors finally aside, the most remarkable fact of all remains that Bitcoin even exists. Bitcoin *is*. This is undeniable, although the reasons why can be ignored — our monetary system is optimized to strip-mine capital — and its ascent can be misunderstood — the mainstream understanding of money invalidates it by definition rather than observation.

If it seemed like a global, digital, sound, free, open source, programmable money was monetizing from absolute zero, it would seem a lot like this.

Chapter Seven

A Capital Renaissance

*A return to health and prosperity for finance,
communications, and the environment*

Is "money" a public good?

Bitcoiners may scoff at even the asking of the question and wonder if
we have been drinking the modern monopoly money Kool-Aid. Surely
money is private property? But the question is worth considering seriously
if only to answer in the firmly negative with even greater academic
precision than otherwise.

As George Selgin quipped on Twitter, in response to us noting that
the Bank of International Settlements seems to think the answer is "yes":
"The argument that money is a 'public good,' is one of many unfounded
claims made about it that serve as 'debate stoppers': by uttering those
magic words, experts hope to avoid having to otherwise defend state
money monopolies."[107]

In her classic of political philosophy, *Governing the Commons*,[108]
Elinor Ostrom gives a rigorous analysis of what she calls a *common pool
resource* and the "problem" of governing its use. To be completely clear,
we treat the following as an interesting analytical exercise and in no way
a tool for slipping a line of thinking into our discussion that is subtly
opposed to private property. Even the title of Ostrom's book is potentially
misleading in this regard; by "governing" she means something more like
"decision making with respect to" rather than "enforcing a decided-upon
rule," as the cognates of "govern" might unfortunately suggest.

This would be a particularly inapt reading given her thesis —
presented here so concisely as to absolutely not do it justice — is that
there is a vast range of common pool resource problems that are in theory,
and have in practice been, better solved without government intervention
and without even force of any kind but rather with effectively established
communities, relations, and incentives. Also, often the same class of such
problems have been made much worse with government intervention —

typically that arrogantly ignores exactly such alternative and likely already existing methods.

In fact, in the book's very last page, Ostrom laments what seems to her to be the default instinct of her academic colleagues in first, and often only, thinking of a government solution to any collective action problem. She writes,

> The models that social scientists tend to use for analyzing CPR problems have the perverse effect of supporting increased centralization of political authority. First, the individuals using CPRs are viewed as if they are capable of short-term maximization, but not of long-term reflection about joint strategies to improve joint outcomes. Second, these individuals are viewed as if they are in a trap and cannot get out without some external authority imposing a solution. Third, the institutions that individuals may have established are ignored or rejected as inefficient, without examining how these institutions may help acquire information, reduce monitoring and enforcement costs, and equitably allocate appropriation right and provision duties. Fourth, the solutions presented for "the" government to impose are themselves based on models of idealized markets or idealized states.
> We in the social sciences face as great a challenge in how to address the analysis of CPR problems as do the communities of people who struggle with ways to avoid CPR problems in their day-to-day lives.

So, with this critical clarification in mind, in what sense might money be a *common pool resource*? We would suggest in precisely the sense outlined in Chapters Four and Five, *Wittgenstein's Money* and *The Capital Strip Mine*. From Chapter Four, the social utility of money is realized not in moving on *from barter*, but in moving on *to capital*, and from Chapter Five, that capital is very much a resource that needs to be cultivated, nurtured, grown, replenished, and *not strip mined*! It is likely instructive at this point to be clearer about how *exactly* Ostrom defines a common pool resource, and how she distinguishes it from a "public good." She writes,

> The relatively high costs of physically excluding joint appropriators from the resource or from improvements made to the resource system are similar to the high costs of excluding potential beneficiaries from public goods. This shared attribute is responsible for the ever present temptation to free-ride that exists in regard to both CPRs and public goods. There is as much temptation to avoid contributing to the provision of public security or weather forecasts. Theoretical

propositions that are derived solely from the difficulty of exclusion are applicable to the provision of both CPRs and collective goods.

But one's use of a weather forecast does not subtract from the availability of that forecast to others, just as one's consumption of public security does not reduce the general level of security available in a community. "Crowding effects" and "overuse" problems are chronic in CPR situations but absent in regard to pure public goods. The subtractability of the resource units leads to the possibility of approaching the limit of the number of resource units produced by a CPR. When the CPR is a man-made structure, such as a bridge, approaching the limit of crossing units will lead to congestion. When the CPR is a biological resource, such as a fishery or a forest, approaching the limit of resource units not only may produce short-run crowding effects but also may destroy the capability of the resource itself to continue producing resource units. Even a physical resource, such as a bridge, can be destroyed by heavier use than was allowed for in its engineering specifications.

This potentially gets dangerous again in terms of the blurring of what is and is not truly and unmistakably private property. But we think that a more pragmatic analysis of "money" forces us to move beyond what we might call its "ideal qualities" — beyond *semantics therefore reality*, as per Chapter Four, *Wittgenstein's Money* — and realize that, in real life, money has always been both private property *and* affected by the "subtractive" behavior of others, free-riding in a manner that *clearly* harms the well-behaved.

Lawrence White helpfully demurred on the above to the effect that surely money *balances* are not a common pool resource given Alice cannot spend Bob's balance and vice versa, except without clear appropriation. We agree, and, in fact, think this clarification bolsters our own claim. Money balances are private property but the institution of money is a common pool resource, in arguably *exactly* the same way that a stock of fish might be a common pool resource, even though fish *fished* by fishermen have clearly become private property. We see no reason to take "depletion" only literally. We do not mean that physical coins or notes depreciate, which would ironically have the opposite effect. We mean that the *utility* of the institution depletes with inflation. And why do we care about stocks of fish and their possible depletion if not for the utility of fish? Were there not an incentive in the first place to deplete fish stocks by fishing, there would be no need to classify it as a common pool resource in need of effective governance.

What is seigniorage if not the depletion of a common pool resource by a nefarious "crowder"? What is gold mining if not a less nefarious and admittedly costly activity (so not exactly "free riding," either) but nonetheless a depletive interaction with a common pool resource? And *what is this common pool resource* if not something ultimately psychological and reliant on subjective value? Is it not an implicit consensus amongst economic actors to use the same language in their economic exchange?

As per Chapter Six, *Bitcoin Is Venice*, "Bitcoin is Logos." But really, *money is logos*. Bitcoin is just *the best* logos. It is the economic language in which it is by far the most difficult to lie. This is perhaps the cleanest and quickest way to dismiss modern monopoly money theory, albeit in a marginally cryptic and highbrow manner: The MMM theorists, and an assortment of larping "crypto-influencers," believe money is a public good, but they are mistaken; it is a common pool resource. Case closed.

Money is not the coins, or the balances, or even the UTXOs, but the consensus around economic behavior and reality these "tokens" capture. We think it is neither a philosophical stretch nor an authoritarian backdoor to say that, yes, money *literally is* a common pool resource, and that *what money is or should be* is therefore a common pool resource problem. It may be the single most important common pool resource problem; hence Bitcoin is the most important solution, and by extension the most important enabling technology for the management of a common pool resource.

This obviously distinguishes money, for example, from a far more prosaic private good like a mug. Allen using Sacha's mug clearly prevents Sacha from doing the same. The good is rivalrous. Sacha can prevent Allen from using his mug by stealing it, breaking it, etc. (in effect, incurring a *tort*). However, money occupies a nebulous middle ground between cleanly rivalrous and non-rivalrous: If Allen prints his own money, Sacha is likely none the wiser as he hasn't *stolen his coins,* and there is clearly no comparison to be made to Allen *printing Sacha's mug.* And yet Sacha's money has been affected, because it is not the token that matters, it is the consensus the tokens represent. Which is, of course, to say that money is not a private good, but a common pool resource.[109]

Why is this the case? Is there anything more we can say about money, capital, or Bitcoin that explains this connection more deeply, or is it just a coincidence? We believe the seeds of an answer have been sewn in every previous chapter. In Chapter Three, *This Is Not Capitalism*, we discussed the importance of distinguishing between stocks and flows, as much for the sake of intellectual clarity as to then more practically appreciate their interaction and application in the creation of capital.

In Chapter Four, *Wittgenstein's Money*, we stressed the importance of local, individual, actionable knowledge in forming a dynamic consensus as expressed in market prices. In Chapter Five, *The Capital Strip Mine*, we elaborated on why capital specifically — the more complex and evolved form of money that taps into larger mechanisms of social and legal consensus — is necessary to act on this information and crystallize productive capability beyond mere handiwork and barter.

In Chapter Six, *Bitcoin Is Venice*, we discussed the all-important conception of Bitcoin as a form of language. As mentioned just prior, Bitcoin is arguably (or perhaps *inarguably*) the *best* such language given it is a language in which it is nearly impossible to tell economic lies. In each case, those that were not treated with a purposefully long-term outlook were predictably subjected to disaster and disintegration.

The "answer" to the question posed is, as far as we can tell and as concisely as we can manage, that money has a unique property as a social institution — as a *common pool* resource — that may seem philosophically tantalizing in its significance. It is the maximally universal consensus required for maximally local flourishing. By mandating synchronization, it enables autonomy. By banishing uncertainty within its delineated realm, it lets uncertainty proliferate everywhere else. Moreover, it *encourages* uncertainty by offering itself up as a ballast. We do not intend to convey any kind of spiritual or religious authority, nor to be in the least sarcastic, but we must admit it is perfectly clear to us why this series of realizations could be seen to have metaphysical import.

We will leave the exploration of the potential spiritual significance of these claims to others and focus instead on the bare bones of economic localism. The heart of the claim, when stripped of emotional resonance, is that money, via capital, enables individuals to better be a part of the whole; to behave more responsibly, to contribute more effectively, and to make choices more purposefully. These cannot be effectively dictated top-down.

We think this reconciles our rejection of apparently all economic universals with our previous strong endorsement of Hernando de Soto's advocacy for coherent and consistent legal recognition of property; his goal in doing so *is to better enable capital*, but of course there is a tension. And note there may well be more than one dimension at play, given a total lack of legal property is as much a *universal* as any other.

It may be something of a fudge, but we feel that de Soto's point is far more sensibly understood as being that property rights must *universally exist*, but *not* that one scheme of property right must *itself be universal*. Property, capital, and further abstractions of economic behavior must be bottom-up phenomena — or, at the very least, if top-down they must be invisibly so and enable bottom-up shaping and utilization to the maximum possible extent. For example, it might be extraordinarily helpful for a nonlocal authority to recognize and credibly enforce property rights.[110] Lee J. Alston, Gary D. Libecap, and Robert Schneider make this point well in *Violence and the Assignment of Property Rights on Two Brazilian Frontiers*, writing,

> Title also adds value to land. Formal, state-enforced title represents the most secure form of property rights to land. Title signals government endorsement of an individual's land claim; that is, with title, ownership is enforced by the courts and the police power of the state. Under these circumstances, title provides claimants with the long-term security of ownership and collateral necessary to access formal capital markets for

land-specific investments. Formal, enforced title also reduces the private costs of defending claims, such as private marking and patrolling of claims, because the state assumes many of those responsibilities. Finally, by signaling government recognition of current land ownership, a title increases the exchange value of land by widening the market. Those buyers from more distant areas, who may have higher-valued uses for the land and access to capital markets, have the assurance that the land exchange contracts will be recognized by the courts and enforced by the state. Absent title, land exchange occurs in more narrow markets among local buyers and sellers who are similar with informal local property rights arrangements. These regional practices typically are not enforced by the courts or understood by potential buyers from more distant areas.

This may seem to constitute an endorsement of state involvement in essentially local affairs. But notice that what is being argued for is not state dictation of what is and is not a property right, but subtly and importantly different, state *recognition* of this already locally existing and locally known and understood fact: What specific person owns what specific piece of land. Moreover, the intention is precisely to disincentivize violence and incentivize capital formation, both by lowering the costs of defense.[111] Alston, Libecap, and Schneider add a few pages later,

> In general, exclusive rights to land provide the collateral necessary for farmers to access capital markets; promote land-specific investment by providing long-term security of ownership; reduce the private costs of defending the claims; and increase the exchange value of land by widening the market. When inherent land values are low and not changing rapidly on the frontier, informal tenure arrangements are appropriate, and violence is unlikely. Such arrangements are of minimal cost and serve to demarcate individual claims and to arbitrate local disputes.

Ideally, enforcement would follow in the form of credible threats of violence that add value to the landowner precisely on the basis of extending to would-be violators of this right beyond the locality. Exactly how these threats manifest is not of economic concern. The aim of all of this is, therefore, to widen the market for this capital good beyond the locality also. This is very minimally a "top-down" enterprise, and is absolutely not a high-modernist one, to once again borrow from Scott's *Seeing Like a State*.

We quote from one of the book's more vivid passages and involved and diagnostic analyses; that of the aftermath of the nineteenth century experiment in so-called "scientific forestry" in what is now Germany. What Scott is describing here is the depletion of an important source of capital due not to malice but simply incompetence, and in particular the kind of high-modernist arrogance of which the book is a scathing critique.

It is an attitude which, seemingly, tempts its proponents to think they can reorganize complex systems at will, with only macroscopic knowledge, if even that, and face no unintended consequences whatsoever — *scientism*, essentially, except as applied to fields *not quite* themselves scientific, but which rely on practical knowledge and heuristics. On so-called "scientific forestry," Scott writes,

> Only an elaborate treatise in ecology could do justice to the subject of what went wrong, but mentioning just a few of the major effects of simplification will illustrate how vital many of the major effects bracketed by scientific forestry turned out to be. German forestry's attention to formal order and ease of access for management and extraction led to the clearing of underbrush, deadfalls, and snags (standing dead trees), greatly reducing the diversity of insect, mammal, and bird populations so essential to soil-building processes. The absence of litter and woody biomass on the new forest floor is now seen as a major factor leading to thinner and less nutritious soils. Same-age, same-species forests not only created a far less diverse habitat but were also more vulnerable to massive storm-felling. The very uniformity of species and age among, say Norway spruce also provided a favorable habitat to all the "pests" which were specialized to that species. Populations of these pests built up to endemic proportions, inflicting losses in yields and large outlays for fertilizers, insecticides, fungicides, or rodenticides. Apparently the first rotation of Norway spruce had grown exceptionally well in large part because it was living off (or mining) the long-accumulated soil capital of the diverse old-growth forest that it had replaced. Once that capital was depleted, the steep decline in growth rates began.

The strip mining of capital is obvious at play and need not be belabored, but there is an even more insidious issue lurking in the background. To whatever inane extent "the economy" can be considered a noun rather than a verb, to pick up a theme first mentioned in Chapter Three, *This Is Not Capitalism*, "forests" are but a tiny, tiny part of it. And everything else is surely at least as complicated.

This hopefully gives the reader some sense of the truly profound folly of *economic planning*, as seems to have been entirely normalized under the dominant regime of political economy, per Chapter Three, *This Is Not Capitalism*, and the consequences of which were teased out in Chapter Five, *The Capital Strip Mine*. If this is what happens to but one forest under bullshit scientism, imagine such top-down management of *everything*, with multiplied irrelevant data, fresh high-minded arrogance, and greater insulation from natural negative feedback.

Money gives a universal consensus of value in part because time is universal. It may be the only such economic universal. All else is local, heuristic, practical, individual, and creative. Economics is resolutely *not a science* and anybody who claims otherwise is a charlatan.[112] One cannot run controlled experiments in economics and one cannot consistently measure outcomes of uncontrolled experiments, as discussed in the section, "Time, Energy, and the Triangle Game," of Chapter Four, *Wittgenstein's Money*.

Economics is, at best, four loosely related disciplines: applied logic, statistical analysis, social theorizing, and historical analysis. And, to be frank, the final three are variations in approach to the same core task: practical analysis of *real* economic behavior, differentiated only by the intellectual toolkit chosen. The first we might call exclusively theoretical analysis of abstract economic behavior. All are certainly worthwhile and create clearly useful knowledge if practiced rigorously and with adequate humility. But none are science. Economics makes no predictions. It might generate wisdom but it does not generate facts.

In this book we have focused mainly on alternating between applied logic and historical analysis, with what little social theorizing we offer tending to be outsourced to the likes of Ostrom and Scott. We include no statistical analysis whatsoever, not because we have anything against the practice but purely out of intellectual honesty: Neither author has relevant academic training in this area, nor did either have points that could only be made in this language.

Part of the thesis of this chapter, and in a sense the entire book, is that Bitcoin will, slowly but surely, gradually then suddenly, bring us back to an understanding and practice of economics in which the scientism just described will be acknowledged to be ludicrous, and will be impossible to enact besides. The future is bright; the future is orange.

But to look forwards, we ought to first look backwards. Some elements of Bitcoin are unprecedented, for sure. The discussion that follows on programmable money and sovereign digital identity will hopefully make that strikingly obvious and undeniable. But the ideas of sound money, low time preference, heuristics, localism, methodological individualism, and the like, are very, very old. They may be the oldest ideas of all. They are encoded in the customs of the world's oldest continuously surviving cultures; their traces are in the common law, the English language, the King James's Bible, and the works of William Shakespeare. Predicting how the very old and the very new will interact is no easy task. It is likely impossible, in fact, and we make no pretensions of being able to see the future. But hypothesizing is fun, frankly, and the more bounteous the hypothesized future the more fun the act.

Unfathomably complicated on the one hand, we see fit to characterize Bitcoin's effect with an analogy so holistic as to be glib: We stand at the precipice of a new renaissance. Time will tell if art and culture will flourish once again as we still, to this day, cherish from Florence and Venice in the late Middle Ages. But we do strongly predict what we might call a *capital renaissance*. Bitcoin will *make us* lower our time preferences. Everybody. Whether we like it or not. This will make us take capital more seriously; nurture it, replenish it, and grow it, in all its forms.

This chapter will focus on three stores of capital which we have conviction Bitcoin fixes: financial markets, the architecture of the internet, natural resources. We leave it to others to pick up the torch and tease out the consequences every which way. In fact, we encourage it; we demand it!

But the torch is not ours to give, it comes from Bitcoin itself:

Not like the brazen giant of Greek fame,
With conquering limbs astride from land to land;
Here at our sea-washed, sunset gates shall stand
A mighty woman with a torch, whose flame
Is the imprisoned lightning, and her name
Mother of Exiles. From her beacon-hand
Glows world-wide welcome; her mild eyes command
The air-bridged harbor that twin cities frame.
"Keep, ancient lands, your storied pomp!" cries she
With silent lips. "Give me your tired, your poor,
Your huddled masses yearning to breathe free,
The wretched refuse of your teeming shore.
Send these, the homeless, tempest-tost to me,
I lift my lamp beside the golden door!

This, of course, *The New Colossus* by Emma Lazarus, the sonnet written for and placed on a plaque at the base of the Statue of Liberty in New York City. Maybe it should be "the orange door." We mean no offence, moral or literary, but we believe it may be more appropriate: the requisite update for the twenty-first century. A subject for another book, perhaps, but we believe Bitcoin is possibly the most American idea since that for which Lady Liberty stands. Indeed, it *is* that for which she stands.

And just as the internet served to export the First Amendment to the entire world, more or less, contrary to the futile efforts and proclamations of local governments, we believe it is entirely reasonable to suspect that Bitcoin will export capitalism also. We of course mean the "capitalism" we have been developing and elaborating throughout this book: enforceable property rights and unencumbered trade incentivizing the nurturing, replenishment, and growth in the capital stock. And of course, as we have insisted throughout: Prices are information, trade is speech, and the capital stock is a literary corpus. Which is to say, Bitcoin *is the internet*, extended to the communication of value, furiously wrestling value back from the feudal client/server architecture of fractional reserve and central banking. The Bitcoin Protocol / Lightning Network Protocol (LNP/BP) is the peer-to-peer value protocol in the internet protocol suite.[113]

Bitcoin is liberty encoded.

Scaling In Layers

"Money will always see a multiple layered expansion as it evolves, and each layer has costs and benefits. You can mine your own gold, but this process is very expensive with a high barrier to entry. You can buy gold coins and bars easily in most parts of the world, but using them for day to day commerce is unfeasible. As a merchant, you can accept gold coins but either have to trust the purity or assay the gold yourself. Once you're using the paper certificate layers, you now are engaged in counterparty risk, but have easier capacity for transactions. Each layer serves a different function. Base layers are for final settlement, while higher layers are for facilitation of economic activity."
— Nik Bhatia, *The Time Value of Bitcoin and LNRR*

It seems a peculiarity of the modern psyche to regard the financial services industry as being at once too powerful and yet absolutely necessary. No respectable businessman or woman has not served an apprenticeship at an investment bank or, if his employers are feeling exceptionally charitable, at a management consultancy. An aspiring candidate for political office whose CV does not feature such a role would do well to surround him or herself with others whose do.

And yet the industry's influence is near-universally decried: *Main Street, not Wall Street*, is a common refrain from politicians of all stripes and all sides of all aisles, who, in some or other roundabout way, it turns out are being funded by hedge fund managers. Matt Taibbi likens Goldman Sachs to a "vampire squid wrapped around the face of humanity, relentlessly jamming its blood funnel into anything that smells like money,"[114] and this at-once hilarious, disturbing, and essentially accurate characterization is published in *Rolling Stone* magazine — later sold to Penske Media Corporation, then minority sold to Public Investment Fund of the Kingdom of Saudi Arabia, in a deal certainly advised by a fair few investment banks, very possibly including Goldman Sachs.

The conspiracy minded might have a field day with such information, but the fullest explanation is in fact rather bland, and was mostly covered in Chapter Five, *The Capital Strip Mine*. In the modern financial system, money is a bank liability. Therefore, it is impossible to do business of any kind without commercial bank involvement, and commercial banks can only exist at the discretion of a central bank. It is impossible to do *international* business without investment bank involvement, and investment banks can only exist at the discretion of the global central bank, The US Federal Reserve. As a result, there are very few such banks, their political power as allegedly *wholly* private enterprises is perhaps unrivalled in the history of capitalism — or anything that can reasonably be called "capitalism" — and their regulatory capture is complete. In fact, in obvious reference to Chapter Three, *This Is Not Capitalism*, it is probably entirely *unreasonable* to call *this* capitalism, this being the regime of central banks, investment banks, and good old regular banks so perverting the role of capital in modern economic exchange.

Economic historian Raymond de Roover coined the expression "commercial revolution" in his essay, "The Commercial Revolution of the Thirteenth Century," writing,

> By a commercial revolution I understand a complete or drastic change in the methods of doing business or in the organization of business enterprise just as an industrial revolution means a complete change in the methods of production, for example, the introduction of power-driven machinery. The commercial revolution marks the beginning of mercantile or commercial capitalism, while the industrial revolution marks the end of it.

Contrary to the fashionable championing by every tech banker and his dog of "blockchain technology," we anticipate precisely what de Roover chronicled, or as precisely as history can rhyme rather than repeat: a commercial revolution. Not a revolution in modes of production, but in business organization and finance. Saifedean Ammous is fond of saying that Bitcoin is the technology that will finally end the First World War. We might be so bold as to suggest it is the technology that will end the Industrial Revolution and bring about a second Commercial Revolution in its place. Fingers crossed we get another Renaissance as well.

In *Capitalism: History and Concepts*, N. S. B. Gras very nicely frames the delicate issue of the development of the American financial sector (with the modern metonym "Wall Street") in terms of weighing up its obvious and enormous commercial benefits on the one hand, and its obvious and enormous social costs on the other:

> Let there be no mistake about Wall Street. The investment bankers who led it were selfish and not public spirited. They were touched off by their own interests. They ignored the feelings of the public. They were negligent of petty capitalists,[115] including farmers. And, for a long time, they cared little about workers, who were regarded as articles to be bought at the market. And yet, the investment bankers, who wanted profits for the buyers of the securities which they sold, were doing much for American when they provided for the effective flow of savings into business. While emphasizing the fees from the sale of stocks and bonds and their profits from buying and selling stocks, these investment bankers were serving American even more than themselves. In ignoring

the feelings of the people they were undiplomatic, but future historians will show that they were more up to date in their business policy than the public in its emotional thinking. In ignoring petty capitalists and neglecting labor, financial capitalists proved themselves short sighted and without a political sense. In going beyond the bounds of ordinary competition in reaching out to get form one another large masses of property in a way that disturbed the smooth operation of business, especially the working of the money market, they uncovered weak links in policy just as the industrial capitalists has disclosed weaknesses in their policies. It was the financial weakness of industrial capitalists that gave to investment bankers, who represented the owners of business as against the administrators, the opportunity they seized. When Wall Street gained control, financial capitalism was born. This does not mean what has been called "security capitalism" — buying and selling securities — which has been developing since at least the fifteenth century. It does not mean simply the building up of firms with colossal assets. That is incidental, not essential. It means the influence or control of investment bankers in the interest of the owners of the securities which these bankers originate and continue to sell.

As with our previous quotation of this same essay by Gras in Chapter Six, *Bitcoin Is Venice*, we find this observation to be remarkably astute and readily transferable to our predictions of the impact of Bitcoin on financial organization. What Gras points out above is the short-term benefits to business financing of the pooling of capital for investment projects, but the long-term costs to social relations of the necessary centralization introduced by this process when carried out as vastly and quickly as happened in late nineteenth century America.

It is fashionable and easy to predict rampant decentralization on the back of hyperbitcoinization. We sympathize but disagree in part. "De-financialization" is a better meme, and a point we will return to often in this chapter and the final two that follow is a prediction not of *sweeping changes to everything*, but to gradated changes to all forms of social organization such that they return to whatever size is most natural. We predict not that *everything will be small* but rather that *not everything will be big*, will have to be big, or will aspire to be big. We will have an essentially novel form of financial capitalism that is at once industrial, informational, and global, and yet financialized and securitized at as local a level as is efficient or necessary to begin with.[116]

That said, none of this is to play down how dramatic we believe many of the changes will be. Bitcoin gives us the opportunity to replace a closed, political, analogue, client/server system with an open, apolitical, digital, peer-to-peer one. Part of the wave of superior and essentially novel competition will involve a reduction of human processes to code, and obsoleting many threats of violence with cryptography, but not all.

We caution the reader in general not to get overly excited about the prospects of "smart contracts" as somehow constituting omnipotent, floating code. Bitcoin is not a "world computer." It is a network for settling value and protecting it with adversarial, escrowed computational expense. Its computational capabilities are deliberately limited to ensure it will always perform this core task well. A two-page screed on Bitcoin magically replacing macro-bullshitters will not cut it at the big boy table. We must think more carefully and with greater technical appreciation both of the protocol and the analogue mechanics of legacy financial services.

For example, the Lightning Network may present the only feasible alternative to the "risk free rate" that is all important in contemporary finance despite emerging from economic nonsense. There will be no bitcoin lender of last resort and no return-generating enterprise perfectly free from risk. There will be nowhere to park idle bitcoin that transforms the maturity of the owned asset, contributes to capital formation, and can promise, beyond all doubt, a given safe return ... *except*, perhaps, the market clearing rate for operating Lightning channels. The Lightning Network requires sunk working capital at least as large in value as the largest expected net credit flow of those taking part. In fact, we get the impression it is often not appreciated just how expensive the opportunity costs of Lightning are, for all its benefits.

But it is a very different type of "expense" to what readers might normally understand this to mean. There is no consumption involved, and at maturity there will arguably be next-to-no *risk*, either: There will just be tied-up capital. The "expense" is purely an opportunity cost, but for would-be lenders looking for a low, but guaranteed return, sinking capital in this way benefits the entire ecosystem: Opening the channel involves a transaction fee that secures the mainchain, the payments layer is provided with extra liquidity, and the "lender" gets a modest return for routing payments. We foresee, in conclusion, that Lightning routing fees become the de facto "risk free rate."

Lightning is often lazily described as a kind of clunky workaround to the limitations of the timechain. Elizabeth Stark has vigorously rejected this notion on the technical grounds that layered architecture is simply optimal engineering.[117] Cramming all the features of Lightning, Liquid, RGB, DLCs, RSK, and so on, into the main chain is not only probably technically impossible, but in a more conceptual sense — arguably an *aesthetic sense* — is just an obviously bad idea. It would introduce unknowable attack vectors and hence holistic fragility. The naïve view is that this compounds the utility of every functionality.

The mature view is it compounds only the vulnerabilities; each functionality is primarily affected to the extent it has become more vulnerable, and utility dramatically decreases, both at the level of individual functionalities and the protocol as a whole. If TCP/IP had been configured to enable video streaming, for example, it would have broken immediately if it had ever worked at all. This is a feature, not a bug. It reflects the mindset of a prudent and humble engineer.[118]

We believe this general principle is not one of *software* engineering so much as engineering entirely in general, yet as elegantly applied to software. "This clear specialization ensures performance, reliability, and scalability of the internet," as Thibaud Maréchal puts it in "A Monetary Layer for the Internet."[119] This design principle could well be thought of as an adaptation of *federalism* from one institutional setting to another. Or, perhaps, federalism is *yet another* special case in the realm of political philosophy, government, and business administration of a still higher principle?

Back in the realm of economics, we would argue that layered *money*[120] is simply good social and institutional engineering. This might seem like an argument in favor of the Lightning Network from an oddly axiomatic basis — and almost a fatalistic one along the lines of *software eats the money*. A candidate axiom may well be Gall's law, from John Gall's *Systemantics*,

> A complex system that works is invariably found to have evolved from a simple system that worked. The inverse proposition also appears to be true: A complex system designed from scratch never works and cannot be made to work. You have to start over, beginning with a working simple system.

However, this rough idea has ample historical precedent that predates software by several centuries — probably precisely because the key insight is one of institutional design, transcending software entirely, and of which software is one special case amongst many.

As was teased in an endnote to Chapter Six, *Bitcoin Is Venice,* one of the features of the complex web of financial and banking relations in Renaissance Florence was the practice of "offsetting" — noncash and *nonbank* payments between merchants by flow of credit and debit. Richard Goldthwaite describes in *The Economy of Renaissance Florence* that "one could draw on his credit by written order for transfer to a third party, and the transfer could be passed on to a fourth party and even on to others by mere book entry." These "payment channels" were clearly private, and a final link to Lightning is to realize this assumed a kind of *going concern*. In other words, that it was worth costlessly keeping credit channels open and updating them rather than closing them at cost, which would involve settling either in bank transfer, or with true "final settlement" in specie.

While the mechanical allusion is intriguing, Goldthwaite goes on to place offsetting amid the diversity of financial customs,

> Local banks did not have a commanding position in the local credit market. On the supply side of the market, the weakness of these banks

in attracting deposits was exposed by their failure to provide an outlet for the savings that began to accumulate in the hands of artisans and shopkeepers in the second half of the fifteenth century. The depositories opened by the Innocenti, Santa Maria Nuova, and the Badia, in contrast, responded to this void in the market, signaling the new direction banking was to take in the following century. But it is when we turn to the demand side of the market that we can see banks' relative inability to attract capital. Local banks and especially pawnbrokers served the general public as sources for direct loans, but they were hardly the only conduit to credit. Direct loans were also readily available outside of banks. Evidence for loans from private persons abounds in the city's oldest notarial records [...] Moreover, debits and credits recorded in these official documents could be reassigned through another notarial act, although it is difficult to say that traffic of this kind constituted a secondary market.

Although by no means Goldthwaite's point, an obvious lesson from this historical analysis in comparing the merchant driven, hard money economic system of Renaissance Florence to the finance driven, soft money of modernity — and with an eye on a Bitcoin standard near- to medium-term future — is that financial institutions and payment methods alike will mold themselves to the heterogeneity of time preferences, commercial requirements, and interpersonal customs to be found across society.

There will not be "the bank," gatekeeper to all finance. There will be a supply and demand of capital liquid and illiquid, short term and long term, risk-seeking and risk-averse, financial and production, personal and professional, payment and settlement. Moreover, in Florence, this diversity of capital was priced and kept honest relative to the store of value of elemental gold. Gold itself was therefore disconnected from the possibility of debased coinage or even confusing alternatives for units of account. Gold was for final settlement, not for payment, credit, or capital. Of course, as effective and elegant as this system was, Bitcoin is *even better*. In this light, Lightning is not clunky or bizarre in the slightest. It is natural, complimentary, healthy, and aesthetically and institutionally sound, as will be all other successful and differentiated extensions of the base layer.

The reader may be less familiar with the concepts of "sidechains" and "discreet log contracts." Although we will not burden the reader with a full technical detailing of either, we provide the following layman's explanations. A "sidechain" is a mechanism whereby a new asset is created in a separate domain, denominated in bitcoin (or, in the more straightforward cases, meaning a kind of Bitcoin IOU), and pegged to a specific bitcoin on-chain.[121] There are various ways of implementing this idea, and various further proposals in addition to those already implemented, to which the present discussion is indifferent. All involve some semblance of trust in the operators or co-participants in the sidechain that the new asset will be allowed to be redeemed for the original bitcoin under some predetermined circumstances. Unlike Lightning, this is not cryptographically guaranteed, hence reintroduces some amount of "centralization," but the trade-off of introducing a small and well-defined level of trust is greater flexibility in manipulating the new asset in the "sidechain" environment. In any context in which trust would be absolutely necessary in the first place and the reliability of the "peg" would be the least of everybody's concerns, sidechains are potentially highly desirable upgrades on legacy systems of matching assets to owners.

Regulated securities markets are an obvious candidate to be replaced in their entirety. "Securities" are really just information. There is not a physical "thing" a security represents, no matter its form as a piece of paper or a line in a database. It is a pointer linking the legal rights to the cashflows or asset title associated with some defined fraction of a financial contract to a legal person, be it a "real" person or a corporation. One is tempted to think of it as a "rigid designator," to borrow a term of art from the philosopher Saul Kripke; in any possible world of subsequent trading and ownership, the "security" itself points to the same cash flows.[122]

There is enormous space to reduce the costly analogue complex of securities trading and reconciliation to little more than code in this manner provided the trust needed to participate in such a market is already far above the threshold to trust the sidechain peg. But the efficiency gains are just the beginning — it is programmability that really starts to get exciting. Issuers could impose a transaction royalty on their own securities so that five or ten (or *any* number) basis points of the value of each subsequent trade is routed back to the issuer. This would barely catch the eye of any serious, long-term investor, but would make most high frequency trading impossible, except in cases in which the arbitrage opportunity is so great that the issuer might even appreciate it, but would otherwise constitute a kind of tax on financial engineering.

Or the securities could mandate a lockup period: It could be programmatically impossible to sell a security less than thirty days after buying — or perhaps only ten minutes. Perhaps there is a cap on the total any one buyer can accumulate, or perhaps the transaction royalty is a function of existing holdings: No royalty if you hold over 5% (*Thank you, long-term investor, we appreciate it!*) or only a royalty if over 5% (*Hey, hey, hey! We don't like our ownership base being so concentrated!*) Perhaps you can't buy any if you hold a competitor. Perhaps the institutional ownership is limited but retail can but as much as it wants.

A discreet log contract (DLC) we likewise will not explain in all its technical glory but will summarize as a bitcoin transaction abstracted into two parts of an independently verified bet: Two parties first transfer their bitcoin to the custody of a smart contract that holds it in effective escrow until the bet-on event occurs, after which the entirety will be awarded to whoever won the bet, as determined by the agreed-upon independent adjudicator (or *process of adjudication*, which could in theory be arbitrarily complicated in order to minimize the potential for abuse).

So, in the simplest example, Sacha and Allen bet on who will win the football game tonight. They both send 1,000 satoshis to a smart contract that they have each verified to their satisfaction will pay out depending on the feed later that evening from BBC Sports. They choose BBC Sports because it seems certain BBC Sports will tell the truth about the outcome, and near-impossible it can be manipulated. When the game concludes the contract will recognize this information as it was programmed to and will pay out to the winner — that is, the contract is "smart"; BBC Sports will not take it upon themselves to adjudicate the bet, but rather the contract will be such that it will execute automatically when fed the information for which it is waiting, and there is no reason to suspect will *not* arrive.

DLCs are fascinating enough on their own as the basis of increasingly complex bets, given they too can be programmed with more or less arbitrary complexity. But we feel their real promise — at least insofar as they seem likely to impact financial services — is their combination with sidechains. This is because the on-chain bitcoin pegged to in a sidechain *can be a DLC*. This might seem like jargon salad, but the implications here are profound once appreciated. This means that, *arbitrarily complex and automatically enforced bets can be securitized.* Or, in other words, this is a mechanism for arbitrarily scalable decentralized prediction markets.

A prediction market is a market for the buying and selling of futures contracts on binary events. The market is structured such that contracts are priced between $0 and $1. A participant buys a contract on an outcome A, or its complement, ~A, for, say, $0.50, and receives $1 if outcome A occurs, or $0 if it does not. If we designate the price of a contract to be P_A, then $P_{\sim A}$ will be priced at $1-P_A$, although depending on the mechanics of the market, there may be a slight bid/ask spread to provide revenue for the exchange, or alternatively a fee to buy the contract, to preserve the balance of the contract prices.

This is very similar to how bookmakers construct their books by adjusting the odds offered to match punters' bets against one another, but there is a crucial difference here reflecting the construction of the market. The contracts exist as securities rather than isolated wagers. This allows for considerably greater liquidity, given participants need not necessarily wait until the event occurs. This liquidity in turn ought to aid price discovery, since participants with relevant insight or information can take advantage of what they deem to be temporary mispricing rather than having to lock in their bets.

Where this gets interesting is in interpreting what the prices *mean*, and therefore what a mispricing is, and what the "expectations of participants" are. The setup of prediction markets lends itself to interpreting the price as the probability of the outcome. For uncertain events for which a probability density function cannot be analytically proven to exist and which cannot be re-run a million times to derive such a function synthetically (so, most of real life) assigning a probability to a specific outcome can only meaningfully be interpreted as stating what odds you deem to constitute a fair bet. A more common and readily understandable application of assigning probabilities is to imply confidence in deviation from a base rate, but this is really a special case of the general principle just mentioned: The base rate is derived from a historic "large enough" sample for which the mean would be deemed "fair" for a random iteration. The question is whether we have relevant information leading us to believe that the non-random iteration at hand ought to deviate from the distribution mean, and hence whether "fair" odds are different from those derived from the historic data.

If you think something is 50% likely, then you think even odds are fair. In general, if you think something is p% likely, then you think odds of $(1-p)/p: 1$ are fair. This calculation can be reversed to turn typically presented bookmaker odds into probabilities, but a prediction market deliberately uses this presentation to state the prices of bets in terms of probabilities rather than odds. If you think the probability of outcome B is x% likely, and that $(1-x)/x: 1$ is, therefore, a fair bet, then a price lower than x means odds better than those you deem to be fair. They are to your advantage and should be taken. Of course, if you did take such a bet, in a prediction market as with a bookie, the result would be to push the odds on offer towards what you deem to be fair. With enough people behaving this way, the price is pushed towards what the entire sample deems to be fair, weighted by each individual's willingness to shoulder the risk implied by the mispricing.

Insofar as prediction markets have been allowed to function properly, they have been far, far superior to either "experts" or to public polls at predicting events. There are separate angles to untangle here: Why prediction markets are so accurate, and how they have tended to function in real life. Why prediction markets are better than experts is simple, and the principle is widely understood in other contexts. *The Wisdom of Crowds*, after James Surowiecki's book of the same name, is most easily conveyed as the principle that the mean of a large sample of estimates of some variable will likely be closer to the true value than the majority of the individual estimates.

The key, and indeed a necessary condition, is that the participants' estimates are independent and hence reflect a diversity of perspectives. This is the essential disqualifying factor for when crowds become exceptionally *unwise*, as in a stock market (or altcoin) bubble, for example. But if the individual estimates draw on esoteric knowledge and insights, a large enough sample will tend to produce a desirable effect. Prediction markets can only function if this is the case: if everybody believes the same thing, then nobody will take the other side of any contract. But this still doesn't answer why they are better than polls. Prediction markets can be thought of as *weighted polls*, where the weighting reflect sincere belief, as captured by willingness to risk loss on an incorrect prediction.

More simply we might say, *willingness to bet*. This has two mutually enhancing effects. The first was articulated most fully by Friedrich Hayek in addressing the socialist calculation problem, building on the earlier work primarily of Ludwig von Mises, by describing markets as aggregation mechanisms for widely dispersed knowledge. The possibility of profit entices those with unusual knowledge to engage in the market, hence moving prices in the direction that best reflects reality, despite the fact that no single person or even large subgroup of people have or could possibly have the relevant knowledge in its entirety.

The counterpoint to the possibility of profit is the possibility of loss, which is equally valuable. As profit rewards and pulls in those with knowledge, loss punishes and pushes out those without knowledge. This is particularly valuable in the case of predictions as we want to weed out the pernicious cases of participants who have no idea what they are talking about. Such people may submit bullshit estimates for reasons other than contributing to correct prediction: professional prestige, for example, or misguided institutional architectures that pressure participants to make meaningless predictions they would rather not. *A bet is a tax on bullshit*, goes the saying originating with economist Alex Tabarrok.

Gambling is clearly betting at scale, but so are derivatives and insurance. Although these products vary dramatically in terms of incentives and social characteristics of average participants, and so on, they are all really just bets. We suspect it is not commonly realized or thought about this way, but all forms of betting rely on network effects in that building a book requires (*means* to some extent) depth and liquidity in a market that is matched off at scale by a bookmaker (or market-maker or insurer) and presented to the customer as simply a "product" concocted by the central entity, rather than the real raw ingredients.

We predict DLCs securitized on sidechains consolidate these three functionalities and provide a better service to users. And not just a *cheaper* service, but again, as with regulated securities trading, a *better*, newer, previously impossible service also. The reason is essentially that there are significant value-based frictions to realizing network effects in all three far, far greater than currently exist, and that cannot be realized via a central party.

It is only currently possible to buy a future on an event if the event is known to be of such wide interest that a deep and liquid market can be confidently predicted to exist. This is because the bookmaker must set the initial odds and risk loss as a covering counterparty. They may be wildly off the mark in the initial period before liquidity coming in starts to move the odds. If you can virtually guarantee liquidity then this is less of an issue. So, sports and politics are fairly safe to make markets in.

There is also an interesting exception to this general rule: Highly esoteric events can give rise to markets for futures but usually only if the buyer or seller of the future is very well capitalized. This presents two ways to overcome the risk to the bookmaker, broadly speaking: stake collateral or pay a fee. So, this might be a gambling addict pledging his car to a gangster to get in on a dog fight, or it might be a retainer paid by a wacko hedge fund to hold a credit default swap with an investment bank. Presently, the undercapitalized can only buy futures in markets that are strongly suspected in advance to be highly deep and liquid.

Prediction markets as securitized DLCs remove the counterparty risk to the bookmaker because there is no bookmaker in the first place: This role is automated. The only analogue is whoever facilitates the on-chain contract and the sidechain issuance, but this is more of a temporary technical and financing role that doesn't require taking either side of the bet, hence doesn't limit the size of the bet, either.

What this means is that there are no restrictions on what kinds of futures markets can exist. The relatively undercapitalized can make and participate in any and every kind of market. On the one hand this means that insurance, derivatives and gambling can all be done slightly more efficiently. But on the other hand, we can now have futures contracts on anything at all!

Perhaps an Uber driver realizes they make three times as much on days it rains and wants to hedge against it being sunny for too long. Maybe a surf instructor has exactly the opposite problem and happily sells the future to the Uber driver buyer. Maybe you work in real estate in London as well as having a mortgage on your house there, and so in a sense are massively overleveraged to the London real estate market. If something happens to the industry, your career will tank in perfect correlation to your home equity. Maybe you want to hedge that away, or maybe you explicitly want exposure to London real estate instead, for whatever reason. Maybe you are an investor in Tanzania and want to hedge your exposure to Indonesian and Peruvian investments. A bank might do this for you, but for an enormous fee that is only beneficial to, again, the already very well capitalized.

And, in fact, the space is evolving so fast that we are rushing to cite evolving applications as this book goes to print. But it is looking likely that it will be possible to link DLCs to Lightning also (excitingly, in a taproot-native manner, for the technically inclined) so as to issue Lightning-native assets with interestingly different properties to sidechain tokens. Again, avoiding the technical weeds, the most tantalizing proposition seems to us to be Lightning stablecoins, less so because they are intrinsically worthwhile or interesting and more because they suggest an immediate and enormous opportunity: to obsolete credit card networks, issuing and acquiring banks, and replacing the expensive legacy system of "payment by credit relay" with fiat-denominated and fiat-backed free and instant value transfer.

It seems straightforward to us that not only will this work, but that it will dominate, and that it will provide a technical and financial onramp for users for when fiat-denominated assets are no longer desirable in the first place, and plain-old bitcoin on Lightning can be used instead. But the interim of taking out tens of billions of dollars of rent-seeking cost from a system that is being replicated in the course of being replaced will be fun to watch.

The Merchant Strikes Back

"No intelligent student of modern events can possibly have overlooked
the vast change which the last fifty years has wrought on the
enhancement of the influence of finance as a social factor
overshadowing all other contemporaneous forces, with the exception of
religion and love. Contemplating the ceaseless and irresistible advance
of the financial power, and the simultaneous weakening of those
authorities which base their claims on political predominance, tradition,
custom, precedent convention, expediency, and the cognate origins, the
philosophic watchman could hardly avoid reflecting that finance must
increase, while these must decrease."

— Ellis Powell, *The Evolution of the Money Market 1385–1915*

Technological wizardry entirely aside, by far the biggest change to the
financial services industry will be entirely prosaic and understandable to those
literate in neither software nor finance. That "money" will once again "store
value," and almost certainly gently appreciate with the sustainable return on
aggregate production capital, will mean that an enormous amount of
contemporary financial intermediation will simply be unnecessary. It won't be
replaced by code — it will simply disappear. Its political clout will collapse as
it will have nothing illicit left to offer — or to bribe. The centralization of
finance, or, equivalently yet more provocatively, the financialization of
everything, may seem to some to now be so thorough and permeative as to be
everything, everywhere, *everywhen*. As Ben Hunt teases, *this is water*. [123]

But it needn't be. Much of the *unwinding* of financialization is
straightforward enough to imagine. Antal Fekete writes, in the provocative essay
"Whither Gold?" of the consequences of moving off the gold standard and onto
a fully fiat monetary system,

> That we have lost the facility to reduce the world's total indebtedness
> without resorting to default or monetary depreciation becomes clear at
> once if we consider the fact that a debt of x dollars can no longer be
> liquidated. If it is paid off by a check, the debt is merely transferred to
> the bank on which the check is drawn. The situation is no better if it is
> paid off by handling over x dollars in Federal Reserve notes, ostensibly
> the ultimate means of payment. In this case the debt is transferred to the
> U.S. Treasury, the ultimate guarantor of these liabilities. But substituting
> one debtor for another is not the same as liquidating the debt. The very
> notion of "debt maturity" has lost all reasonable meaning previously
> attached to it. at maturity the creditor is coerced into extending his
> original credit plus accrued interest in the form of new credits, usually

on inferior terms. It is true that the option to consume his savings remains open to him — but is it not a strange monetary system, to say the least, which forces the savers to consume their savings whenever they are dissatisfied with the quality of available debt instruments, or with the terms on which they are offered?

It is simple enough to predict that the perversities Fekete bemoans will evaporate. Savers will never be tempted to consume their savings, and in fact, "their savings" will exist in a natural state entirely outside of "finance." There is no point in trusting a depository institution and implicitly taking on its liabilities when the natural state of Bitcoin is that of perfectly safe rest.

"Debt maturity" will *regain* reasonable meaning, and debt will be priced accurately relative to equity given there will be no coercion at maturity beyond that implied in a contractual obligation *to pay*. That savings and debt need not be directed via banks at all, and that, relatedly, we can expect there to be no artificially lowered cost of capital on account of cozying up to the financial and political elite, straightforwardly implies a dramatic redistribution and re-localization of financing power. The default will be to invest locally rather than globally, with only the option of centralized, and publicly listed securitization rather than the need or the expectation. While pooling capital at a far larger scale will still be possible, there is little reason to suspect it will be preferable.[124]

The precedent here is clear, and we think can be seen as an optimistic counterpoint to Joel Kotkin's *The Rise of Neo-Feudalism*. We expect Robert S. Lopez's account from *The Commercial Revolution of the Middle Ages, 950–1350*, to be closely reflected from this starting point on:

> The early Middle Ages promoted salve artisans to serf status and occasionally paid lip service to the moral nobility of labor — were not St. Joseph and all the Apostles laborers? — but offered no fresh opportunities for industrial development. From the tenth century on, however, the rise of the merchant class brought forth a new source of potential support. As middlemen between supply and demand, merchants had a personal stake in the expansion of both; they had capital, extended credit, and promoted their business through market research. No unsurmountable prejudice separated them from craftsmen: many if not all of them originally came from the same social background, and the struggle for urban emancipation from feudal control supplied a common cause.

And yet, for all these subtle economic and financial adaptations, it is possible, if not likely, that the re-decentralization of finance and *de-financialization of everything*[125] will have even more profound *social effects* that we can only begin to imagine. "What if securities ownership was more widely and directly distributed?" is practically a mechanical question in contrast to the spiritual weight of "what if finance and financialized patterns of thought cease to be dominant cultural forces?" In *The Culture of Narcissism,* Christopher Lasch writes of the profoundly damaging psychological effects[126] of the dissolution of the Protestant work ethic as a motivating force in American life. All the more powerful and telling of Lasch in no way intending to make a point about economics, he writes,

> In an age of diminishing expectations, the Protestant virtues no longer excite enthusiasm. Inflation erodes investments and savings. Advertising undermines the horror of indebtedness, exhorting the consumer to buy now and pay later. As the future becomes menacing and uncertain, only fools put off until tomorrow the fun they can have today. A profound shift in our sense of time has transformed work habits, values, and the definition of success. Self-preservation has replaced self-improvement as the goal of earthly existence. In a lawless, violent, and unpredictable society, in which the normal conditions of everyday life come to resemble those formerly confined to the underworld, men live by their wits. They hope not so much to prosper as simply to survive, although survival itself increasingly demands a large income. In earlier times, the self-made man took pride in his judgment of character and probity; today he anxiously scans the faces of his fellows not so as to evaluate their credit but in order to gauge their susceptibility to his blandishments.

There is an astonishing overlap with what we *know* is caused by degenerate fiat money and what Lasch highlights *as partial causes* of a narcissistic breakdown in traditionally prudent rules of thumb for economic behavior. Is it fair to predict, therefore, that a reversal of these causes might make us *less* narcissistic? This certainly seems reasonable insofar as it might mean that a more natural trustingness ought to equate to less defensive selfishness — less *living by our wits.* The Protestant work ethic is easily caricatured as egocentric, and probably rightly if taken to an extreme, as Lasch sardonically emphasizes from time to time. But we would do well to remember that its flourishing — arguably even its stable existence — depends on a backdrop of trust. Economic capital cannot exist without social capital, and yet, as Lasch shows, the strip mining of economic capital seems to have a reflexively destructive influence on the social fabric.

In *The Organization Man,* William Whyte takes more direct aim at the economic roots of changes in the popular ethic. Whyte picks up on much the same desperation and decay as Lasch[127] but argues for a kind of tragic logical inevitability: The more successful raw individualism is in creating endlessly proliferating capitalism, the bigger will become capitalistic institutions and the stronger will be their social influence that is by nature antithetical to the small and the heterodox. Contrary to the naïve conception of Corporate America as a bastion of individualism, Whyte argues it is more like a petri dish for risk aversion, cowardice and collectivist sentiment. He writes of the historical transition,

> By the time of the First World War the Protestant Ethic had taken a shellacking from which it would not recover; rugged individualism and hard work had done wonders for the people to whom God in his infinite wisdom, as one put it, had given control of society. But it hadn't done so well for everyone else and now they, as well as the intellectuals, were all too aware of the fact.
>
> The ground, in short, was ready, and though the conservative opinion that drew the fire of the rebels seemed entrenched, the basic temper of the country was so inclined in the other direction that emphasis on the social became the dominant current of U.S. thought. In a great outburst of curiosity, people became fascinated with the discovering of all the environmental pressures on the individual that previous philosophies had denied. As with Freud's discoveries, the findings of such inquiries were deeply disillusioning at first, but with characteristic exuberance Americans found a rainbow. Man might not be perfectible after all, but there was another dream and now at last I seemed practical: the perfectibility of society.

Admittedly ironic as Whyte writes it, this is *high-modernism* par excellence. Whyte also makes a prescient observation, for having been astute in the fifties but obvious and widely resented as a social tragedy of financialization and corporate bigness today. He notes that, at large enough corporations, the executives effectively cease to be members of the community of the workforce of the corporation in any meaningful sense, and are probably more accurately classed as financiers. [128] He describes the shift as follows:

> The difference can be described as that between the Protestant Ethic and the Social Ethic. In one type of program we will see that the primary emphasis is on work and competition; in the other, on managing others' work and on co-operation. [129]

Lo and behold, senior corporate managers are far more likely to have an MBA than to have worked an entry level job in the industry in which they now manage. They personify *"big city capitalism,"* as Whyte derides it, and if your city isn't big enough — for few are — they tend to radiate that they are from somewhere else and are likely going somewhere else as well. Wherever they are from, they are homogeneously at home in and only in *the big city*, which is to say they aren't really from anywhere at all.

We jest, of course, in our caricature, but that these people have scrambled as close to the fiat spigot of artificial money as possible gives them immense control over society's common pool of capital and hence immense cultural power to boot. It is worth seriously contemplating what example they set and what trickles down to the merely medium cities and below. It is even worth contemplating what that kind of unchecked power can do to a person's character and intellect.

The intellectual appeal of finance is that it provides a totalizing vision and toolkit. Absent Whyte's sarcasm, contemporary finance truly is high-modernism par excellence. Once a budding financier masters the basics, he can explain absolutely everything from chemical manufacturing to logistics to software-as-a-service to real estate to government debt to *money*.[130] The same language, mental models, patterns of thought, and so on, can be gleefully recycled time after time in remaking the world as they see fit.

At some or other level of suitable abstraction, everything becomes understandable as a combination of long or short exposure, volatility, diversification, leverage, cash flows, securitization, or whatever else. Since their domain is *everything,* they have no domain. There is simply no other explanation for the seemingly never-ending corporate fascination with *Blockchain, Not Bitcoin* — a string of words that literally has no meaning; a Chomsky slogan, were there such a thing, given it is not quite a full sentence. There is no content in this expression it is possible to actually *believe*, and so it works as a kind of anti-secret handshake, whereby the technically incompetent and intellectually unsophisticated yet desperate to be thought of as competent and sophisticated make themselves known.[131]

But they don't really *know* anything, or *understand* anything, besides the meta-game of management, which is, of course, a euphemism for social manipulation rather than productive contribution. Recall Whyte above: Managers used to be trained to work and learn to manage. By his time, the transition was already underway towards being trained to manage and literally not knowing how to work. By now that transition seems well and truly complete.

So, what then are the social consequences? In the aptly titled *The Culture of The New Capitalism*, Richard Sennett observes that an obvious consequence of this organizational framework of prioritizing management rather than competence is a disorienting mix of constant change in roles and responsibilities yet indifference to the quality or even the completion of the alleged purpose of the previous change. He provides the following enigmatic critique:

> An organization in which the contents are constantly shifting requires the mobile capacity to solve problems; getting deeply involved in any one problem would be dysfunctional, since projects end as abruptly as they begin. The problem analyzer who can move on, whose product is possibility, seems more attuned to the instabilities which rule the global marketplace. The social skill required by a flexible organization is the ability to work well with others in short-lived teams, others you won't have time to know well. Whenever the team dissolves and you enter a new group, the problem you have to solve is getting down to business as quickly as possible with these new teammates. "I can work with anyone"

is the social formula for potential ability. It won't matter who the other person is; in fast-changing firms it can't matter. Your skill lies in cooperating, whatever the circumstances.

These qualities of the ideal self are a source of anxiety because disempowering to the mass of workers. As we have seen, in the workplace they produce social deficits of loyalty and informal trust, they erode the value of accumulated experience. To which we should now add the hollowing out of ability.

A key aspect of craftsmanship is learning how to get something right. Trial and error occurs in improving even seemingly routine tasks; the worker has to be free to make mistakes, then go over the work again and again. Whatever a person's innate abilities, that is, skill develops only in stages, in fits and starts — in music, for instance, even the child prodigy will become a mature artist only by occasionally getting things wrong and learning from mistakes. In a speeded-up institution, however, time-intensive learning becomes difficult. The pressures to produce results quickly are too intense; as in educational testing, so in the workplace time-anxiety causes people to skim rather than to dwell. Such hollowing out of ability compounds the organizations' tendency to discount past achievement in looking toward the future.

Mastery and competence are dramatically devalued at the expense of what Sennett calls "cooperation," presumably unintentionally echoing Whyte's far more blatant derision in using this word, but which we are happy to characterize more bluntly as *manipulation*. Moreover, notice a clear, if somewhat abstracted, analogue to the toxic effects of leverage: There is no space — no *time* — to experiment or to discover. Things need to be done effectively and immediately because everybody's roles — *locations* even — are due to be changed at a deadline well before what would be required to really *learn*; to *understand*. Sennett elaborates on the kind of person all this benefits, hence who tends to climb the corporate ladder, hence who wields cultural power both by example and by resource:

> Only a certain kind of human being can prosper in unstable, fragmentary social conditions. This ideal man or woman has to address three challenges.
> The first concerns time: how to manage short-term relationships, and oneself, while migrating from task to task, job to job, place to place. If institutions no longer provide a long-term frame, the individual may have to improvise his or her life-narrative, or even do without any sustained sense of self.
> The second challenge concerns talent: how to develop new skills, how to mine potential abilities, as reality's demands shift. Practically, in the modern economy, the shelf life of many skills is short; in technology

and the sciences, as in advanced forms of manufacturing, workers now need to retrain on average every eight to twelve years. Talent is also a matter of culture. The emerging social order militates against the ideal of craftsmanship, that is, learning to do just one thing really well; such commitment can often prove economically destructive. In place of craftsmanship, modern culture advances an idea of meritocracy which celebrates potential ability rather than past achievement.

The third challenge follows from this. It concerns surrender; that is, how to let go of the past. The head of a dynamic company recently asserted that no one owns their place in her organization, that past service in particular earns no employee a guaranteed place. How could one respond to that assertion positively? A peculiar trait of the personality is needed to do so, one which discounts the experiences a human being has already had. This trait of personality resembles more the consumer ever avid for new things, discarding old if perfectly serviceable goods, rather than the owner who jealously guards what he or she already possesses.

Once again, Sennett strives to maintain an air of calm disinterest and anthropologically motivated curiosity, whereas we are minded immediately to scorn and disgust. If Sennett is correct, this is horrific.

Those who succeed in a financialized society are those, without a sense of place or of self,

- who would rather consume than own;
- to whom "potential," whatever they convince themselves that means, trumps competence;
- who disdain craftsmanship;
- who have convinced themselves they can learn things on the fly — or that their *ability* to learn things ought to trump whatever they or others have actually learned;
- who have no attachment to time, place, circumstance, company;
- whose motivation is never to *make anything around them better*, but to make themselves an ideal candidate for promotion and hence for the accrual of yet more money, power, and cultural cachet;
- who proudly call themselves "global citizens";
- who believe this transparently nonsense elocution has grave moral import and who deploy it primarily to bridge the cognitive dissonance that would otherwise be triggered by culturally colonialist political activism;
- who couldn't tell you the primary languages of Afghanistan, the national dish of Cameroon, or the year of Chilean Independence because they aren't from *everywhere*, or even from anywhere, hence they know nothing besides the arduous and unending ritual of convincing fellow know-nothings they know everything.

In short, then, narcissists, who are overwhelmingly likely to gradually remake the institutions in which their narcissism grants them success in their own narcissistic image.

Lasch concludes his book with a grave warning against allowing the cultural power of the constitutionally narcissistic to go unchecked, ending on a call to arms, of sorts. He writes,

It is true that a professional elite of doctors, psychiatrists, social scientists, technicians, welfare workers, and civil servants now plays a leading part in the administration of the state and of the "knowledge industry." But the state and the knowledge industry overlap at so many points with the business corporation (which has increasingly concerned itself with every phase of culture), and the new professionals share so many characteristics with the mangers of industry, that the professional elite must be regarded not an independent class but as a branch of modern management. [...] Professionals, [Daniel Moynihan] observes, have a vested interest in discontent, because discontented people turn to professional services for relief. But the same principle underlies all of modern capitalism, which continually tries to create new demands and new discontents that can be assuaged only by the consumption of commodities. Moynihan, aware of this connection, tries to present the professional as the successor to the capitalist. The ideology of "compassion," he says, serves the class interest of the "post-industrial surplus of functionaries who, in the manner of industrialists who earlier turned to advertising, induce demand for their own products.
Professional self-aggrandizement, however, grew up side by side with the advertising industry and must be seen as another phase of the same process, the transition from competitive capitalism to monopoly capitalism. The same historical development that turned the citizen into a client transformed the worker from a producer into a consumer. Thus, the medical and psychiatric assault on the family as a technologically backward sector went hand in hand with the advertising industry's drive to convince people that store-bought goods are superior to homemade goods. Both the growth of management and the proliferation of professions represent new forms of capitalist control, which first established themselves in the factory and then spread throughout society. The struggle against bureaucracy therefore requires a struggle against capitalism itself. Ordinary citizens cannot resist professional dominance without also asserting control over production and over the technical knowledge on which modern production rests.[132] [...] In order to break the existing pattern of dependence and put an end to the erosion of competence, citizens will have to take the solution of their problems into their own hands. They will have to create their own "communities

of competence." Only then will the productive capacities of modern capitalism, together with the scientific knowledge that now serves it, come to serve the interests of humanity instead.

Between Sennett's measured discomfort at the social ramifications of the "new capitalism" and Lasch's blistering assault on the homogenously banal financial and managerial elite at its helm, we find all the seeds of a positive reversal: We stand to reclaim local and democratic control over ownership of capital, of production and of technical knowledge; to strive for craftsmanship, competence, and independence, not surrender; to be first and foremost producers, not consumers and clients; and to rid ourselves of a surplus of ignorant meta-thinkers. In short, we stand to *de-financialize*.

What do we stand to gain? As these parasitic, rent seeking intermediaries whittle away,[133] should institutions want to save, be they pension funds, charities, endowments, corporate treasurers, insurance floats (or what is left after securitized DLCs are done with them), they need not engage in leveraged speculation. They need *never* engage in the scourge of "passive investment," nor accidentally pool the leverage of governance that is legally and fiduciarily due to their beneficiaries into a glaring political attack vector for degenerate fiat activists to infiltrate and co-opt. They need only stack sats — something they can do with no bankers, brokers, or asset managers, and that will be commonplace among teenagers, if not even younger children.

And, of course, this presents an *even greater social benefit*. Finance as it exists today is a chokepoint for extra-legal and supra-democratic political attack, in the sense of activists pushing high-modernist agendas via the absolute practical necessity for corporations to have at least a commercial bank, if not access to capital markets. The looming threat of regulators, goliath capital "allocators," or even individual banks cutting off corporations from the ability to finance themselves — with artificially cheap, politically preferential capital or otherwise — is why multinational corporations virtue signal for LGBTQ+ rights in the United Kingdom but dare not do so in Saudi Arabia, and for Black Lives Matter in the United States but conveniently ignore slave labor and genocide in China.

The customer base of Nike, McDonald's, or whoever, and the beneficiaries of assets managed by BlackRock, or whoever else, may or may not care about these causes. But this doesn't matter: This is not a clumsy attempt at marketing. Or rather, it *is*, but the customer is the tax-collecting state, the operationally necessary rent-seeking banking cartel, and the social caste of narcissists that populate both ranks, rotating amongst roles, and from which the decision makers wish not to be excommunicated. It is very much *not* individual consumers or savers.

This is perhaps the cleanest way of describing how the merchant strikes back. Much of her financial necessities and actions will be entirely within her own control. She will return to a state of having only one customer: the customer.

A Free and Open Internet

"There is nothing wrong with wanting pay for work, or seeking to maximize one's income, as long as one does not use means that are destructive. But the means customary in the field of software today are based on destruction."
— Richard Stallman, *Free Software, Free Society*

After "big banks," our feeling is the next most ominous corporate presence in the public imagination is that of "big tech."[134] The political influence of the investment banks is simply too intertwined with the continued functioning of fiat money for the average public intellectual, otherwise quite upset by corporate power, to even articulate the damage done by their very existence. On the other hand, it has become rather fashionable lately to call for the breakup of "big tech," whether coming from Senator Elizabeth Warren[135] or Facebook co-founder Chris Hughes. Hughes made an unfortunately pompous pitch in a May 2019 *New York Times* editorial, *It's Time to Break Up Facebook*, writing,

America was built on the idea that power should not be concentrated in any one person, because we are all fallible. That's why the founders created a system of checks and balances. They didn't need to foresee the rise of Facebook to understand the threat that gargantuan companies would pose to democracy. Jefferson and Madison were voracious readers of Adam Smith, who believed that monopolies prevent the competition that spurs innovation and leads to economic growth.

But crudely applying antitrust, as Warren and Hughes in essence are suggesting, will not work. Warren and Hughes grudgingly acknowledge that "Big Tech" doesn't fail the standard antitrust test of abusing their market positions to gouge consumers on price, but instead that their market shares give consumers little choice but to sign up to more stealthily abusive practices. "It is not actually free," Hughes tells us, "and it certainly isn't harmless." But the two seem to believe that Facebook, Google, and others succumb to temptation to inflict such harm solely *because* they are big. Hence, make them smaller! Break them up! It doesn't appear to have seriously occurred to either that they are big *because* they inflict such harm.

Facebook and Google are not Standard Oil and AT&T. They operate business models whose network effects tend towards monopoly due to continuous redeployment of increasing returns to scale. Users pay not with money but with data, which Facebook and Google then turn into productive capital that creates products for another group entirely. The quality of the service to the users — the unknowing and hence unrewarded capital providers — scales quadratically with the size of the network and so, in combination with being free in monetary terms, this means that any serious attempt to compete would require monumentally more capital than could ever generate a worthwhile return. The proper regulatory approach is not to cut off the heads of these hydras one at a time, but to acknowledge that these are fundamentally new economic entities.

Artificial intelligence makes this all the more imperative. By this buzzword of all buzzwords, we do not mean "magic we cannot explain"; we mean the honing of proprietary corporate algorithms on enormous complexes of unwittingly generated data to identify patterns no human could; identifications that will be re-applied to dynamic pricing decisions in order to make what will surely be called "efficiency gains."

This would be all fine and dandy, as opposed to highly ethically suspect, if the contributors of the data had any idea of their own involvement, either in contribution or the eventual gaining of efficiency. Information that only previously existed transiently and socially is now being turned into a kind of productive capital that can only have value in massive aggregations. This is why those who generate the data are happy to do so for free, for it is of no monetary value to them, and is why those who will derive any productive value from it will only be the already very well capitalized.

This is an unflattering but perfectly accurate description of the business models of Facebook and Google. They stalk you wherever you go on the web, wherever you bring your smartphone, and wherever you interact in any way with one of their "trusted partners." This is all in an effort to manipulate your sensory environment to slip in as many ads as possible. This is so effective that they buy data from outside their platforms to supplement the potency of their manipulation.

They are the largest surveillance organizations in the history of the world. It is certainly worth mentioning both the astonishing technical achievements that the likes of Facebook and Google represent, and also that their free-to-use model has the effect of amortizing the distribution of premium Western digital infrastructure to the entire world. Such outcomes are certainly laudable, but we wonder to what extent their users really understand the balance of incentives and manipulation involved. As Jaron Lanier writes in *Who Owns the Future?*

> The problem is broad and we are all part of it. Individuals of high or low station are not reasonably able to avoid playing along in an immediately compelling system, even if that system is destroying itself in the big picture. Who wouldn't want to get a quick online ego boost, or accept an insanely great deal on an online coupon, or insanely easy home mortgage financing? These might seem like unrelated temptations, but they reveal themselves to be similar once you think about information systems in terms of information, instead of imposing outdated categories on them.

In each case, someone is practically blackmailed by the distortions of playing the pawn in someone else's network. It's a weird kind of stealth blackmail because if you look at what's in front of you, the deal looks sweet, but you don't see all that should be in front of you.

Since Lanier wrote this in 2013, the image of the likes of Facebook and Google in the consciousness of Western elites seems to have severely soured, following privacy scandals, accusations of election interference, tax evasion, and more. But the direction taken makes us uneasy. The moniker "big tech" seems intended to evoke "big oil" or "big banks" and the attendant regulatory issues with which we are all familiar.[136]

In the intervening time, "Big Tech" has gone from fantastic growth and novelty to enormous profits and market capitalizations, lending justification to this change in attitude. But this diverts attention from the real problem — a genuinely new problem — to one that is simply older, more familiar, and more popular. The problem is not with capitalism *in general*, as we have gone to lengths to demonstrate in previous chapters; it is with the very particular challenges that unprecedented appropriation of data and autonomy over the internet pose to how we have come to think about capitalism in the first place. Lanier explains,

> "Disruption" by the use of digital network technology undermines the very idea of markets and capitalism. Instead of economics being about a bunch of players with unique propositions in a market, we devolve toward a small number of spying operations in omniscient positions, which means that eventually markets of all kinds will shrink.

Lanier is a highly heterodox thinker, and it is unfortunate that this position is not widely held, or even widely understood. As if praising capitalism wasn't bad enough optics for thinkers of right thoughts, the problem Lanier identifies is with the way we have decided to build the technology on which we now rely. This might seem innocuous. If we build a dangerous bridge, we knock it down and build a safe one. Can we rebuild the internet? Yes and no.

In *To Save Everything, Click Here*, Evgeny Morozov brilliantly critiques the surprisingly commonplace notion that "the internet" is a kind of sacred ideal of social organization whose progress only a philistine would consider slowing. Morozov shows up one technology "thinker" after another as pretending to technological sophistication but in reality, advocating anti-humanism. The internet — entirely a creation of human beings — is so glorious, he mocks, that humans should take heed and reorganize themselves to best imitate and serve it.

Warren and Hughes both succumb to this way of thinking. Clearly desperate not to be cast aside as luddites, although both are in their own peculiar ways, they caveat their agendas with refrains in blind veneration of "technology" in the total abstract; technology without humans, yet that no intelligent human could possibly oppose. Warren claims her real motivation is to, "*ensure that the next generation of technology innovation is as vibrant as the last.*" Hughes claims that, "even after a breakup, Facebook would be a hugely profitable business with billions to invest in new technologies — and a more competitive market would only encourage those investments."

If the problem isn't capitalism itself then it is the insufficient working of capitalism due to insufficient state intervention. The problem is never technology, for technology is a jealous God. It is certainly never that certain technologies fare better in a culture of irresponsibility, high time preference, and latent anti-humanism. The culture- and value-agnostic attitude is akin to growing several bacteria in a petri dish, returning to find that one had grown to exhaust the available resources and starved the rest to death, and concluding that the problem was this particular unfortunate outcome rather than the nature of bacteria. Best to cut them all down to size and try again.

What if we built the internet badly? What if Facebook and Google are not perversions of the high-bandwidth digital milieu, but are its logical endpoint? What if we spoiled our opportunity for digital ecological diversity and instead optimized for maximizing flows in the guise of "growth," only later realizing that carnivorous bacteria can grow awfully fast, provided there are fewer tangible stocks to consume in doing so?

The internet as we know it was built for reasons that were neither good nor evil, but practical. It is an engineering project with trade-offs, not an ethereal force of pure social progress, as Morozov might put it. Richard Stallman, the vociferous founding father of the free software movement, is perhaps best known outside hackerdom for coining the expression "free as in freedom, not as in beer," to crisply capture what it was his movement held dear: not costs but values.

For reasons that are inextricably linked to free and open-source software, and to which we will return below, this captures the fundamental trade-off of the internet quite nicely. It is free as in beer, not as in freedom, when really it should be free as in freedom, not as in beer.

Free as in Beer

"Perhaps we can't imagine life after 'the Internet' because we don't think that 'the Internet' is going anywhere. If the public debate is any indication, the finality of 'the Internet' — the belief that it's the ultimate technology and the ultimate network — has been widely accepted. It's Silicon Valley's own version of the end of history: just as capitalism-driven liberal democracy in Francis Fukuyama's controversial account remains the only game in town, so does the capitalism-driven 'Internet.' It, the logic goes, is a precious gift from the gods that humanity should never abandon or tinker with. Thus, while 'the Internet' might disrupt everything, it itself should never be disrupted. It's here to stay — and we'd better work around it, discover its real nature, accept its features as given, learn its lessons, and refurbish our world accordingly. If it sounds like a religion, it's because it is."
— Evgeny Morozov, *To Save Everything, Click Here*

The internet is free as in beer. If you want to ping packets around the network layer, nothing can stop you. Ping away. The rest of the worldwide network of networks will happily oblige. TCP/IP, the protocol suite that facilitates the limitless pinging of packets, is open and permissionless — in fact almost radically so. Anybody can send anything if they know how to. Lawrence Lessig crisply captured the primary consequence of this in his *Code 2.0*,

This minimalism in the Internet's design was not an accident. it reflects a decision about how best to design a network to perform a wide range over very different functions. Rather than build into this network a complex set of functionality thought to be needed by every single applications, this network philosophy pushes complexity to the edge of the network — the applications that run on the network, rather than the networks' core. The core is kept as simple as possible. Thus if authentication about who is using the network is necessary, that functionality should be performed by an application connected to the network, not by the network itself. Or if content needs to be encrypted, that functionality should be performed by an application connected to the network, not by the network itself.

This feature of the internet is widely understood and celebrated, and, in fairness, we think deserves an exemption from Morozov's critique. It is celebrated because some of its consequences are truly fantastic. Most of all a kind of imbued humility about what will come next that is encouraged and not constrained by the vision of the original engineers. Hence, we have a whole range of protocols that operate on top of TCP/IP, from those powering email, the web, and file transfer, and a whole range of applications that operate on top of *these*, all the way up to Facebook and Google; not because the designers of TCP/IP said these ideas were good ones, but because they didn't say they weren't, which is a vastly more expansive grant. This is Gall's law once again.

But it represents a trade-off, because if something is free, it is difficult if not impossible to discern the kind of meaningful economic information that one might from a price in a market, amongst the more subtle of which is that the willingness to pay a price indicates a sincere belief and an honest commitment. There are still costs to insincere or dishonest behavior that will simply be dispersed throughout the network, rather than borne by the perpetrator.

We might wonder if dishonest actors can be identified and punished? This presumes a kind of "network layer identity," which might theoretically be desirable, but sadly is impractical. Identification presumes the ability to differentiate between different flows of information on the network. The only way to do so given what TCP/IP transfers is the source IP address, which is physically determined. There are many reasons this may not be ideal as a means of identification for honest actors. Anonymity may be desired, and IP addresses could be deanonymized. It may be desired to utilize the same identity from different physical locations; by a different person on the move; or by more than one person; or any number of other reasons.

It is also not an ideal way to identify dishonest actors, who can spin up new IP addresses, or route their traffic through any number of trusted ones. Besides this, there is, in theory, no way to differentiate the source, given any supposedly identifying information can be spoofed for free, without committing to indicating sincerity or honesty by paying an economic price. Hence, there is no way to create identities native to the network layer that can develop reputation. As Lessig identified, the necessary complexity of authenticating identity is pushed to the application layer. At the network layer, all alleged identities are treated as equal, and have equal opportunity to misbehave. All this inevitably influences how the network can feasibly be used, and what can feasibly be built on top of it, given the costs of misbehavior are borne by all.

Imagine an alternate model of consuming services over the internet. Imagine it is not the case that the likes of Facebook, Google, Twitter, and whoever else, operate enormous servers that authenticate our identities on our behalf, and with which we interact only as clients and volunteer the data necessary to run the applications for free. Imagine instead that we ran our own servers, hosting our own data, to which these services connected through APIs on the basis of our (somehow possible) network layer identities. Twitter could show your photos to your followers, and Facebook could show your private messages to your friends, but only because you allow them to and can remove this access with the click of a button.

Furthermore, they couldn't ban you. They would just be protocols, and couldn't influence your behavior any more than "email" can ban you. Nor could they give access to your data to anybody other than the identities you specify, any more than "email" can secretly send your emails to somebody other than the desired recipient. As these analogies reveal, even calling them "them" seems like a kind of category error. This model of the internet would treat everybody as roughly equal nodes, which, bizarrely, is how it is usually currently disingenuously described. The Jedi mind trick here is that all nodes are roughly equal in terms of relaying encrypted data, but not at all in terms of controlling it. When looking at the far more important factor of control of information rather than temporary possession in transit, the internet looks a lot more like television than most of us care to admit; a few central hubs broadcast everything to everyone. Even more weirdly on the internet, the "everything" is mostly data *about you*, that you gave these hubs for free.

It is important to understand why the fantasy described above didn't come to pass. That network layer pings are free means that running your own server which welcomes API calls from the entire world is intractable for almost everybody. A dishonest actor could either choke the bandwidth of, or, more perilously, expose weak security in, just about any personal server in the world. Only the extremely well resourced could prevent this, which is in fact exactly what happens in the less fantastical reality that has developed.[137] The network effects that Facebook and Google enjoy exist *because* such services can only be reliably provided at the scale that follows bacteria-like growth by first and foremost centralizing and monetizing user data.

Furthermore, they retain user lock-in by providing applications for identity that port across other web services, many of which are simply sucked into or replicated within their own walled gardens for simplicity's sake. If you try to move any of the content outside the walled garden, say to combine with services elsewhere on the web, even if the users give you permission to do so with content that is allegedly *theirs*, Facebook will sue you out of existence. This is not to say that Facebook is perfect at network security, but it is probably better than you are, and it is definitely better than you and a billion others each running one one-billionth of Facebook. And so, in theory it costs you nothing to interact with the internet, but the consequences of this very fact make it practically impossible to do many of the things which would otherwise be desirable. Free as in beer, but not as in freedom.

And yet, obviously, we *can* use the internet for a great deal of desirable things (it's not all bad!). It would be worth our while probing on what can be done peer-to-peer, what requires corporate intermediation, and why. One of the great triumphs of the internet is the free and open-source movement, very loosely the idea that software can and should be presented in a way that its users can not only understand it but can change it, and can resubmit their changes back to the community. Collaborative development — creation of communal capital — is possible at scales and complexities almost certainly never before seen, and which clearly rely on the internet for coordination. *The Cathedral and the Bazaar*, by Eric Raymond, is considered one of the foundational expositions of the movement. In the introduction, Raymond writes,

> Open source represents some revolutionary concepts being thrown at an industry that thought it had all of its fundamental structures worked out. It gives customers control over the technologies they use, instead of enabling the vendors to control their customers through restricting access to the code behind the technologies. Supplying open-source tools to the market will require new business models. But by delivering unique benefits to the market, those companies that develop the business models will be very successful competing with companies that attempt to retain control over their customers.

But we know this didn't quite work out in many cases. Facebook, for example, gives no control whatsoever to customers by *completely* restricting access to its code. That's kind of the whole point. And yet that code is primarily built on what is called a "LAMP" stack — arguably the archetypal web services software architecture. meaning the service uses

- a *Linux* kernel to run
- an *Apache* web server, reading from and writing to
- a *MySQL* database, to run applications written in
- the *PHP* programming language.

Linux, the operating system kernel, is probably the most famous free and open-source project out there. Apache too is open source, and powers an estimated 35% of the web's top one million sites, as are MySQL and PHP, whose general usage is more difficult to measure as they have purposes beyond facilitating websites.

So, why can so much of Facebook be open source but not Facebook itself? Why can't we cut out the final rent-seeking layer and have a "FLAMP" stack instead? While Linux, Apache, MySQL, and PHP are applications that it may be in one's interest to tinker with, what Facebook *the application* provides cannot work in this way: It mimics a protocol in that it facilitates real-time data exchange between its users. Using Facebook in complete isolation is basically meaningless. As a kind of intermediated pseudo-protocol, it is effectively a single application running simultaneously for every user. If it is indeed to function as a "social network," there can only be one version. Protocols need consensus.

There are free and open-source protocols, to be sure. In fact, the Internet Protocol suite[138] are all free and open source. However, to return to Lessig, these are minimalistic and push complexity to the edge of the network. Few can be described as "applications," and those that can are extremely simple. None are expected to add "new features" with any regularity whatsoever. They are explicitly intended to be building blocks for further applications, and so necessarily tolerate network congestion as a trade-off to remain open. This minimalism aids consensus formation.

Notice that for a potentially complex pseudo-protocol, management by a centralized private party elegantly solves many of the problems raised thus far. Identity can be centrally issued and authenticated. The complexity of the application can be arbitrarily high without incurring trade-offs in consensus, as users are merely clients. The application can be updated arbitrarily often and quickly for the same reason.

Congestion by dishonest actors can be punished based on their issued identities. Although by no means guaranteed from the outset, this will all be extremely difficult to unseat once popular given the network effects implicit in a protocol, or pseudo-protocol. This gives an incentive not only to try, but to devote significant resources to trying, given the potentially asymmetric payoff of future economic exploitation of the user base of the pseudo-protocol that simply doesn't exist for a free and open-source alternative. Facebook is inevitable.

Free as in Freedom

"Perhaps in the end the open-source culture will triumph not because cooperation is morally right or software 'hoarding' is morally wrong ... but simply because the closed-source world cannot win an evolutionary arms race with open-source communities that can put orders of magnitude more skilled time into a problem."
— Eric Raymond, *The Cathedral and the Bazaar*

What can be done peer-to-peer and what requires client/server corporate intermediation? What makes consensus either easily achieved or not required; what does not require digital identity; and what does not suffer from the absence of economic incentives due to a fundamental lack of scarcity, can be peer-to-peer. Anything else may be possible, but will be very difficult, and will likely be rapidly outspent and defeated by a private, centralized competitor.

Scarcity, consensus, and identity are closely related. In the absence of scarcity, consensus is simply not required. But where scarcity exists, value exists, where value exists, markets exist, and market prices are a kind of consensus. What's more, they are no mere vote, but a consensus reflecting sincere and honest belief. Identity also requires consensus, as it is no good if Alice and Bob disagree about who exactly Carol is. If the means of establishing identity are not scarce, then anybody can plausibly claim to be anybody else and the necessary consensus fails. But if a scarce and nonfungible asset can be used as an identifier, then consensus follows immediately.

The foundational trade-off of the internet was to cast scarcity, consensus, and identity aside in favor of freedom and openness. Where scarcity, consensus, and identity have might have proved useful, private, centralized pseudo-protocol managers have lodged themselves within the ostensibly peer-to-peer network as increasingly unavoidable gatekeepers. The merits of this trade-off are looking more and more suspect, as the theoretical freedom and openness that paved the way for the gatekeepers seems now to be causing the erosion of real openness and real freedom. We do not need total scarcity, total consensus, and comprehensive identification, but we do need balance. Thankfully, we can very likely get it.

What we describe as a "trade-off" is really an ahistorical dramatization. Prior to the release of the Bitcoin codebase in January 2009, there was no known way to make data scarce. But today this is very well understood. Monetary discussion entirely aside, the Bitcoin timechain is the first ever instance of completely distributed trustless consensus. What's more, it is a free and open-source, permissionless protocol. It can be built on top of by developers looking to harness digital scarcity, digital consensus, or digital identity. Even aside from its profound monetary and financial implications, we do not think it is an exaggeration in the slightest to suggest that, on a long-enough time horizon, the internet will be rearchitected around Bitcoin.

Several large and well-liked companies have cracked how to avoid funding their consumer internet services via surveillance: Netflix and Spotify decided to opt instead for the ancient and oft-forgotten model of: *You give us money; we'll give you stuff.* These are anomalies in the pantheon of consumer tech giants. You couldn't start a similar company this way today. You'd be laughed out the VC office: *Pay for it? Are you kidding? Nobody pays for anything!*

Without too much indulgence on why these companies have been successful, the obvious one-word answer would be: *streaming.* They invented, or at least perfected, *commercial* streaming which, given what we are now used to with the internet, seems obviously superior as a way to consume content. But this simple analysis obscures part of the problem. Prior to Bitcoin (prior to *Lightning*, really), payments had relatively high fixed costs, especially for small ticket size or low margin items, and especially for both. This is why cafés are often resistant to accept credit cards and almost never accept American Express.

The alternative to Spotify used to be that you pay for each song one at a time in iTunes, at an annoyingly high price, because Apple still had to be able to process the payment. Or you just stream it illegally, which is very, very naughty, and your humble authors certainly never did. With movies, illegal streaming was the *only* real alternative. And yet, fascinatingly, it was also clearly a better experience than buying or renting, even aside from the desirable cost of "free."

One interesting effect of this is that BitTorrent usage is substantially down from ten years ago. BitTorrent is an amazing technical achievement that also happens to be completely illegal.[139] Regardless, BitTorrent's legacy has been to drag record labels and film studios kicking and screaming into the twenty-first century. Napster tried to do this as a company and was sued out of existence, so instead the cypherpunks regrouped and made the exact same idea free and open source. And there is an obvious moral here too for PayPal versus Bitcoin. It is no coincidence that most of the *PayPal Mafia* are table-bangingly pro-Bitcoin. At least PayPal wasn't sued out of existence, but it came close and clearly didn't achieve what they originally intended.

What Netflix and Spotify both did was dress up this obviously better consumer experience with an interface and a proposition that was (1) legal and (2) *worth paying for in big chunks.* And we all did.

But … now we actually *can pay* in little chunks. Your humble authors have personally paid on the order of $0.03 for coffee, and even that was really just a gimmick as the coffee may as well have been free, but it could easily have been $0.003, $0.003c, or $0.000000003c. If you can pay $0.0003c online with next to no fees, why not pay $0.0003c *per second* to stream music? If you listen to Spotify three hours a day, that would come out at around $10 per month. And why stop at music and movies? Why not podcasts, too? Why not absolutely any kind of content at all: live streaming, writing, gaming, messaging … in fact, why even call it "content"? Content is a category of human understanding but the computer doesn't care. Why not price *data* in sats per second? What kind of problems would that solve?

And we can go *even further*! There may be circumstances in which the mental accounting of constant microflows presents too much of a psychological burden for consumers, or perhaps too uncertain a cash flow stream for creators, or both. There is a compelling alternative in this case because the *hodler*, even in *hodling — precisely in hodling!* — still has a valuable resource they can trade: Lightning liquidity.[140]

Consider the following: The way a consumer pays for content is to provably stake their bitcoin in a Lightning channel programmed to direct its fees to the content creator. This is a win-win, *particularly* pre-hyperbitcoinization, because the consumer's behavior is economically identical to hodling, but the producer still gets paid. Moreover, there is no custodial risk as would necessarily exist for an equivalent arrangement in fiat, and the arrangement can be near-costlessly closed at the consumer's discretion. Programmable money gonna be programmed!

This represents a far fairer and more philosophically aligned content monetization model than the current mode of online advertising *and potentially even than* Lightning micropayments. What is being exchanged here is very clearly time for time. Time is money, as they say, and "cost" is only meaningful with respect to alternative opportunities for expenditure *of time or money.*

In this setup, the consumer locks up their money for a period of time, such that they have definitely chosen among options and are consuming one specific thing. And during that time — until the consumer decides an alternative option is superior — the producer has a right to the economic fruits of this money.

It's beautiful. Recall Jaron Lanier's worry quoted above that "instead of economics being about a bunch of players with unique propositions in a market, we devolve toward a small number of spying operations in omniscient positions, which means that eventually markets of all kinds will shrink." We have just substituted markets back in for spying. Bitcoin fixes this with proof of stake.

The more one explores these options, the more tempted one is to throw one's hands up in the air and say something like, "the application space of software is any coherent thought, Bitcoin is software money, and people are unboundedly creative, therefore anything and everything will eventually exist and there's no point in even trying to predict it. Just *buidl.*" And while neither of the authors are software engineers by trade, we wholeheartedly encourage such a response to this passage. It's time to *buidl.*

In short, anything that would ideally require consensus or digital identity, or suffers from the absence of economic incentives due to a fundamental lack of scarcity, and hence could not previously be peer-to-peer … can now be peer-to-peer. Social media can be self-hosted and require micropayments for interaction to dispel spam or Distributed Denial of Service attacks. It could conceivably be integrated with content to allow fans to pay creators directly without a centralized pseudo-protocol taking a rent-seeking cut — be it a social media platform, a payments processor, or whoever else. We could perhaps go even further still and abstract the very idea of self-sovereign identities, embracing Bitcoin private keys in a manner agnostic to the protocols they plug into.

API calls can likewise monetize from day zero without worrying about the fixed cost of resisting Denial of Service attacks, or equivalently as a way to bid up access to rate limit available resource that is being accessed legitimately but is nonetheless fixed. Even something like a *distributed cloud* is not that difficult to imagine when you start to work out the technicalities. Storage can be leased out on the basis of continuous streaming of proof of continued hosting and accessibility both for streaming of payment in return and at penalty of financial loss if conditions are not fulfilled. The era of payment streaming is well and truly here, and the era of Google and Facebook is well and truly over.

Both the clever staking hack just mentioned and regular, direct micropayments offer a subtler benefit than alluded to so far that arguably is also, *fairer and more philosophically aligned advertising*, but in a social sense rather than a technical or financial sense. Currently, the customers of content creators are not consumers but advertisers, and the customers of advertisers are consumers. We have covered the technical and financial benefits of removing these middlemen, but there is also the social benefit of removing an attack vector for censorship.

It may not be in an advertiser's strictly *economic* interest to de-platform (by omission) a content creator — especially if the content is popular and provably monetizable. But this may be outweighed if the content is also politically inconvenient such that advertisers can appease the politically powerful by preventing its monetization, hence its distribution, and likely also its creation. While strictly speaking it is the internet platforms who are the "servers" in this client/server model, removing the social influence of enabling advertisers moves us to a more obviously healthy peer-to-peer model.

Dhruv Bansal captured the general theme powering these examples by observing that, "*distributed systems create better outcomes (by incentivizing instead of coercing), fairer interactions, and more robust systems.*"[141] Or, in other words, fairer and more philosophically aligned *everything*. It's not just applications: It's *infrastructure*. It's not just that Visa and Mastercard enable micropayments to let you route around Facebook and Twitter or Spotify and Netflix — it's that Visa and Mastercard themselves become distributed. Everybody runs one one-billionth of Visa and gets one one-billionth of the (astronomically lower) fees. Bansal further disputes the contemporary faddish notion that the way to extend the utility of the technical breakthrough of Bitcoin to *applications* is to build and launch *more blockchains* and issue *more tokens,* that "[t]he thing we need to export from bitcoin is its market — the idea that we can build an open, distributed market that anybody can join. That's the part we need to lift: not 'the blockchain'."[142]

Bitcoin introduces incentives to a space where they were sorely lacking, and hence can likely form a robust base for near-enough every internet-based distributed system to be built from this point forward. Bansal's framing above is invaluable in suggesting that "growing Bitcoin" does not just mean *getting more people to buy it* (although that certainly wouldn't hurt) but rather, *getting more projects to tap into its utility as a marketplace*. This is, of course, a variation of *number of people go up*, because the result (possibly very near term) will almost certainly be "apps" built on "the Bitcoin stack" whose end users are indifferent to or even ignorant of the fact they are using Bitcoin.

And so, in pushing out the logic of what can and cannot be better incentivized, it becomes increasingly clear that, ultimately due to the fundamentality of money, Lightning is much more than an online switchboard for micropayments: It is a data network turbocharged by economic incentives as a primitive. By the time this book goes to press, Lightning will, for example, almost certainly be the largest onion-routed network in the work, overtaking TOR (*the* onion router, ironically enough).

TOR itself is a fascinating technical project but it has largely petered out, at least in terms of its user growth. The reason why is entirely straightforward when contrasted with Lightning: Operators of Lightning nodes are incentivized; operators of TOR nodes are not. There is only risk and no reward to running a TOR exit node, whereas there are theoretically unboundedly many reasons to run a Lightning node given the network's extensibility to *even higher layer* applications tapping into the same incentive structure.

By the time it ossifies, Lightning may very well be seen far more as a foundational building block for internet architecture than just as money. Admittedly more semantic and rhetorical than substantive, we think it is helpful to divorce Bitcoin and Lightning on the basis that Bitcoin *is money*, while Lightning is *the interface between money and data*. It seems to us a poetic disservice to Lightning to refer to it as merely a "second layer," that "fixes some quirk in Bitcoin," technically true as this may be.

Functional sidechains are likewise not mere "extensions" of Bitcoin but could perhaps equally be stylized as *the interface between money and capital*. Hence the potential interoperation of Lightning and Liquid or RSK, for example, allows capital to seamlessly interface with the architecture of the internet, via a robust peg to a global, digital, sound, free- and open-source, programmable money. It is difficult to overstate the profoundly novel implications of these technical achievements — not to mention many not covered, and many that have likely not yet been invented, given Bitcoin is a perfectly open network, with the building blocks of programmability that compound day by day, month by month, year by year.

And of course, this is all rooted in Bitcoin itself, as will be every other "higher layer" to subsequently emerge. In this same talk, Bansal introduces an incredibly powerful explanatory tool we encourage readers to grasp, if not master.[143] We will summarize it here, but of course we highly recommend just watching his talk: *Mining is two coupled markets for settlement and security*; transaction fees are users' bids for settlement rights; and the mempool is the miners' ask for ordering transactions by offered fees. Similarly, hashes are miners' bids for the right to add the next block, and the difficulty adjustment is the users' asks for how much security they desire to be expensed. In this sense, Bitcoin itself can be understood as achieving its function and utility *as money* by acting as a completely distributed interface between energy, time, and data. Mining and transacting are a market that incentivizes the creation of a record of *truth*, extensible to other applications on account of its global accessibility and programmability, and robust on account of its distributed nature. Bansal concludes,

> The important thing to recognize is it is not "the blockchain" that is making all of this work. It's the idea that every aspect of this market is distributed. The order pool is distributed, order matching is distributed, and market making is distributed. This is very, very powerful and Bitcoin is the first thing to ever work this way. This is the part of Bitcoin we need to export to other layers.

All the architectures described in this section — and those previous on finance also — are case studies in Gall's law, once again: Complex systems that work invariably evolve from simpler systems that worked, while systems built to be complex from scratch will fail. Rate-limiting payment streaming API calls are complex; sidechain-securitized DLCs are complex; but Bitcoin is simple. Bitcoin worked first before these more complex layers were even conceived of, never mind implemented. Bitcoin's design is very much in the spirit of the lower internet protocols on which it runs. As Lessig would say, it, *"pushes complexity to the edge of the network — the applications that run on the network, rather than the networks' core. The core is kept as simple as possible."*

Many of the problems we are proposing Bitcoin "solves" were arguably caused by the inability to capture digital scarcity within the internet protocol suite. But complaining about this is clearly foolish and anachronistic. It was *not known how to* attain digital scarcity prior to Bitcoin. Trying to bundle scarcity into the suite would certainly have not succeeded, and would probably have broken something else besides.

With an appropriately low time preference, Bitcoin can be seen as a natural extension of this protocol suite. It *is* a fundamental internet protocol. Likewise, it was *not known how to* attain payment streaming prior to Lightning, and bundling this feature into Bitcoin would certainly have failed, and would probably have broken the whole thing. With an appropriately low time preference, it seems highly unlikely that any other so-called blockchain will still exist a hundred years from now. But it is near certain that Bitcoin will. It will have become an integral part of the infrastructure of the internet. Arguably, it already has.

Power and Waste

"If society is a contract, it is not a contract between the living only, but a contract that includes the dead, the living and the unborn — in short, not a contract at all, but a relation of trusteeship, in which the living have charge of assets inherited from the dead which they in turn must pass on to those unborn. Simply to waste in the lifetime of a nation's temporary tenants, the capital accumulated over centuries, is to breach the trust on which future generations depend. And of course, this is exactly the complaint, made in other terms, by environmentalists in our time — that we are destroying an asset that we hold in trust for future generations, and violating a fundamental duty of justice in doing so."
— Roger Scruton, *Green Philosophy*

Bitcoin mining consumes only the cheapest energy in the world. Furthermore, it directly incentivizes the discovery of cheaper and cheaper energy like nothing else in the history of capitalism, by monetizing *this very fact* nearly directly. It has recently become popular to espouse that wind and solar have the lowest levelized cost of energy for new projects, and the progress of their deflationary cost curves with increases in cumulative production suggest the costs could go much lower still.[144]

Of course, this cannot be read as necessarily implying that *all generation* will be wind or solar, or even all new projects, or frankly even *most* new projects, at any particular point in the future as the very metric *levelized cost* has the potential to be highly misleading if presented in isolation and without reference to geography, reliability, maintenance, expected uptime, necessary additional infrastructure and i*ts feasibility and cost*, and so on and so forth.

Costs measured entirely as averages are no consolation when the wind stops blowing, the sun stops shining, and the power goes out entirely lest we fire up a coal plant at utterly exorbitant cost — as precisely just happened in the United Kingdom around the time of writing the final draft of this book.[145] But at a minimum, it ought not to be controversial to say that renewable generation is likely to *increase* dramatically from this point, and that a great deal of it will be enabled by Bitcoin.

As bitcoin mining is unusually sensitive — reactive, even — to the cost of the energy it consumes, this means it is overwhelmingly likely that Bitcoin will be the cleanest *consumer* of energy in the world before too long, entirely as a side effect of its brilliant design and not at all because it is conscious of its environmental impact. By the time this book goes to print, this could well already be true. Bitcoin embodies efficiency and sustainability in the abstract, with little care or concern for practical instantiations. This particular instantiation is neither special nor surprising.

Lest we risk being misunderstood, we should be absolutely clear upfront that energy consumption is synonymous with human flourishing, probably more so than any other single economic indicator. Vaclav Smil puts it bluntly in *World History of Energy*, "improving the quality of life has been the principal benefit of this quest for higher energy use that has brought about increased food harvests, greater accumulation of personal possessions, abundance of educational and leisure opportunities, and vastly enhanced personal mobility."[146]

And this is not even to mention the clear correlation with dramatic improvement in factors further removed from purely economic success and related more obviously to well-being in general, such as access to sanitation, life expectancy, infant mortality, the fruits of directing surplus economic energy towards research into science and medicine and, arguably coming full circle, into more efficient harnessing of energy — the ability, say, to harness natural gas rather than coal.

We must be sure also to credit the role of human ingenuity in harnessing energy — in *ever having harnessed energy* — rather than risk portraying humanity's exponential advance in as predetermined or historicist. Lynn White writes in *Medieval Technology and Social Change*,

> The later Middle Ages, that is roughly from A.D. 1000 to the close of the fifteenth century, is the period of decisive development in the history of the effort to use the forces of nature mechanically for human purposes. What had been, up to that time, an empirical groping, was converted with increasing rapidity into a conscious and widespread programme designed to harness and direct the energies observable around us. The labour-saving power technology which has been one of the distinctive characteristics of the Occident in modern times depends not only upon a medieval mutation in men's attitudes towards the exploitation of nature but also, to a great extent, upon specific medieval achievements.

We echo also the comments of Carlo Cipolla in stressing the difference in impact between the Commercial Revolution and the Industrial Revolution. Early capitalism may have worked out a blueprint for how to scale productive enterprise, but it was not until the explosion of harnessing of mechanical power many centuries later that these insights really came to fruition. Cipolla writes in *The Economic History of World Population*,

> The enthusiasm and skill displayed by medievalists in describing merchants, bankers, textile manufacturers, and town-life mostly had the effect of concealing from the average cultivated person — and often from the medievalists themselves — that even the most highly developed European societies of the Middle Ages remained fundamentally agrarian. The fraction of the active population and resources engaged in trade and manufacture was small, most of the trade

itself was connected with agricultural products, the famous merchants and bankers were generally part-time landlords … and finally … by far the greatest part of the energy used was actually derived from agriculture.

The Agricultural Revolution of the eighth millennium B.C. and the Industrial Revolution of the eighteenth century A.D., on the other hand, created deep breaches in the continuity of the historical process.[147]

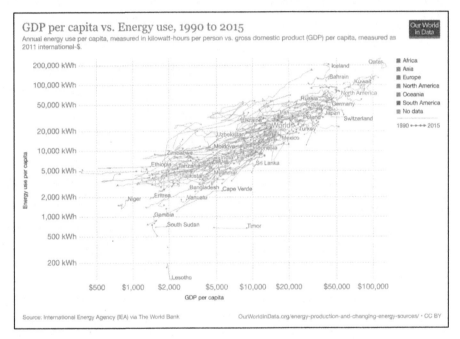

Figure 5. Energy use and GDP.

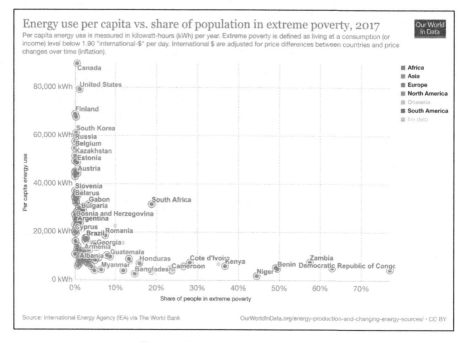

Figure 6: Energy use and extreme poverty.

Figures 5 and 6 clearly demonstrate the correlation between human flourishing and energy use, charting per capita energy use against per capita GDP and the share of population in extreme poverty. If human flourishing is something we care about, we should celebrate energy generation costs falling and competition for energy consumption on the free market alike. Bitcoin catalyzes and accelerates both. We may still be inclined to balance this concern against mindfulness of the environmental externalities of the source of energy generation, as opposed to consumption. If this is the case, then we have even less choice about supporting Bitcoin's development.

"The cheapest option for power generation" is by definition any that is free, in the sense that generated energy would otherwise be wasted, and intermittent sources of power such as wind and solar face a permanent load balancing problem given the sources of their generation is inherently unpredictable and will never match up perfectly, or even nearly, with grid demand.

Adding a bitcoin mining rig to a renewables project provides a permanent buyer of otherwise wasted electricity, lowering the volatility of cash flows of renewables projects, which in turn lowers their cost of capital, ensures more get financed and on better terms, and drives down the deflation curve even faster given Wright's Law indicates a strong and almost certainly causal link between the rate of exponential cost declines and the pace of cumulative production increases. Bitcoin will be the greatest catalyst to renewables adoption in the history of the industry. The authors are professionally aware of numerous vast projects underway to this exact effect, and, once again, this may be entirely well known and appreciated by the time the reader has arrived at this material.

The case for natural gas flaring is even more stark: Methane leakage is a natural part of the process of extracting and transporting natural gas and is a far more potent greenhouse gas than carbon dioxide. Prior to Bitcoin, this problem had no economical solution. Bitcoin mining puts this otherwise wasted energy to work in a way that is not only profitable, given the source is properly contextualized as "free" for the same reasons as wind and solar excess detailed above, but is clearly and indisputably environmentally friendly. This statistic will certainly be out of date by the time of publication and forever after, but at the time of writing, global methane flaring alone consumes around twenty times the energy of the existing bitcoin mining outlay.

Or, put more suggestively, Bitcoin can be twenty times more secure — or as secure at twenty times the capitalization — purely by humanity collectively being less interested in virtue signaling and more serious about doing something to protect the environment. Natural gas bitcoin mining may be the single most environmentally friendly activity in the world (if working from admittedly dubious definitions) because it is profiting from directly reducing emissions, and without subsidies. If you claim to care about the environment *at all* you must support Bitcoin. There is no alternative to reducing this category of emissions, which we know for a fact given literally none exist or ever have. So-called environmentalists have no choice. They are either Bitcoiners, ignorant, or liars. Equivalently, anybody who does not support Bitcoin by definition is not a serious environmentalist.

Extending the Grid

"Many Bitcoin defenders make the mistake of attempting to compare the amount of energy consumption taking place in the banking system to bitcoin's energy consumption, in an attempt to argue bitcoin consumes less energy. I do not find this comparison accurate, because as discussed in my book, I do not think bitcoin replaces banking, or the functions of banking. It rather replaces central banking, being a primitive and barbarian edifice, consume nowhere near as much energy as bitcoin in the same way outhouse cleaners consume less energy than a sewage system, or horses consume less energy than cars. That did not stop cars from displacing horses, and our quality of life has not suffered from all the extra energy we have 'wasted' on cars instead of riding horses."
— Saifedean Ammous, *Bitcoin Mining: Energy and Security* [148]

All this said, the discussion so far has been essentially trivial and as much a test of politically motivated disingenuousness as it is a topic of worthwhile intellectual interest. We are minded to agree wholeheartedly with Saifedean Ammous as quoted just above.

We should not make our support of Bitcoin contingent on so-called "environmentalist" talking points that *are themselves contingent* and may change in the future, particularly given the spectacularly awful record so-called "environmentalists" have with respect to the single cause they claim to favor. Doing so diminishes the seriousness of our support for Bitcoin *and, perversely*, for the environment. The idea that energy consumption is de facto bad, either for the environment or in general, is imbecilic and profoundly anti-human, and should not be accepted as an axiom of our support for Bitcoin, or any other technology that indisputably benefits humanity.

Bitcoin does not only benefit the environment *specifically* because of a handful of contingently economical use cases related to renewable energy; Bitcoin benefits the environment because it encourages long-termism and proper cultivation and preservation of capital. Renewable energy integration is one consequence. We hope it will be permanent, in the sense that it would be remarkable if Bitcoin could *make* renewables *actually* sustainable, but we must honestly recognize that it may be transient, yet that there will be many, many more wonderful consequences. The appropriate way to conceive of Bitcoin's relationship to the environment is in how the changes it will incentivize in economic activity and industrial organization at large will likely lead to massive reductions in pollution and waste. A society operating on a Bitcoin standard will be unimaginably more *sustainable* than anything we are used to in the late twentieth and early twenty-first century, to repurpose a word beloved of the habitually politically disingenuous. That is, to use this word *correctly*.

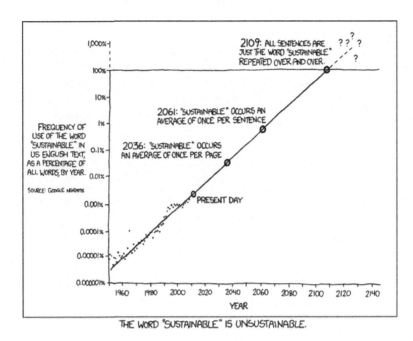

THE WORD "SUSTAINABLE" IS UNSUSTAINABLE.

Figure 7. Credit to Randall Munroe, available at https://xkcd.com/1007/.

We think the best way to ease into the realization of how dramatically Bitcoin will alter the global energy market is simply a cold, hard look at prices. Pure-profit bitcoin mining needs to operate in the range of energy costs of 2–5 ¢/kWh, whereas the standard for residential consumption in the developed world is more in the range of 15-30 ¢/kWh, and for industrial use much more varied depending on the end use, but something like 40 ¢/kWh may be typical.[149]

This also lets us handily dispel another fearmongering classic: Bitcoin mining will *never* siphon away power that would otherwise go to some other activity deemed entirely subjectively by objectors to be "more worthwhile" because anything anybody deems even remotely worthwhile will outbid miners. This is an amusing consequence of Bitcoin being *extremely efficient*. It is far more efficient than any alternative use, hence will ubiquitously be outbid for the same resources.[150] Bitcoin creates a globally uniform incentive to develop sources of energy that are as cheap and as sustainable as possible. We have already covered the likely impact on intermittent renewables, but the implications will go far, far beyond this.

In our view, everything discussed so far is a special case of a profound general shift that Bitcoin is slowly but surely bringing to global energy markets: It allows the physical infrastructure for transporting either generated electricity or energy dense fuels to be extended over the internet. It augments a physical network with a digital one.[151]

This might seem *so general* and *so abstract* as to be vacuous but what we mean by this is simple and precise. Prior to Bitcoin, generated energy, or energy dense fuels extracted but not immediately transformed into electrical power, could only be as economical as the market for their clearing allowed.[152] This originally meant storage and transportation costs, but the landscape was radically altered by the build-out of electricity grids in the late nineteenth and early twentieth century.

"The grid" — as a kind of metonym referring to the institution and the social behavior it engenders rather than specifically the physical infrastructure — has what we might call "pooling effects." Whereas a "network effect" increases the utility of a service to its users at above the rate of addition of new users because it matters to users who else is also a user, a "pooling effect" would capture a similar extra-linear increase in utility that is brought about by the simple fact of *there being more users* improving the service, irrespective of who they are.

Insurance has pooling effects. Allen doesn't care if Sacha is also insured for either of our sakes, but the dispersion of risk benefits the insurance provider, enabling it to offer us both a policy in the first place. In a sense, this is true of any market, however complicated its construction. Market depth has impersonal social utility via *social scalability*.[153]

The same goes for "the grid." The more generators and consumers of electricity enter into the same market, the better the prices and reliability for all. It is rare that either a buyer cannot buy from or a seller cannot sell to "the grid" in relatively developed economies because the utility operator handles the load balancing, the network maintenance, the backup generation, and so on and so forth, much as an insurer diversifies its exposure, spreads its liability duration, arranges reinsurance, etc.

But not all is puppy dogs and rainbows. There are trade-offs to this setup that, admittedly, are anachronistic complaints prior to Bitcoin. First of all, electricity is not the only form of energy. It is just by far the most useful and standardized for the majority of human applications of mechanical power. Yet everybody is familiar with the example of gasoline in cars, as an alternative, or natural gas for heating homes and cooking.

Unlike oil and natural gas, electricity does not exist for capture in "natural form"; it is the product of having already generated energy that is intended to be consumed. And so, the preponderance of "the grid" means that raw fuel of any kind must either be physically transported to an economical generation site, or the transmission infrastructure must be built out to the natural generation site.[154]

Oil, and its many derivatives, is possibly the only exception to how prohibitively costly this can conceivably become, largely because, among all fuel sources, oil is unique in having an enormous and homogeneous end-market in vehicles that *does not*, at some eventual point, require transformation into electrical energy. This is easy enough to tell by the fact that the price of oil — prior to subsidies, taxation, or other forms of market interference — varies little from one place in the world to just about any other. In fact, it may be the only industrial commodity with this property, to this extent.[155] In other words, the infrastructure to efficiently remove as many costs as possible already exists at massive scale and is minimally dependent on either "the grid" or the opportunity cost presented by the use case of converting oil derivatives into electricity. Oil is likely unaffected by Bitcoin.

But all other sources of energy generation rely in part on "the grid" — not locally and heterogeneously, necessarily, but in an aggregate sense, because of the efficient market clearing it offers, and hence their infrastructure is mostly locally optimized for grid integration — which is really to say it cannot ever be fully *local*.[156]

Bitcoin fixes this: This is no longer necessary, because Bitcoin is digital infrastructure that can be built out to natural generation sites at comparatively minuscule cost, and mining offers a clearing price for energy that requires no transmission costs.[157] It is our prediction that the mechanism just outlined will start to greatly reduce the financing costs and operational complexities of nuclear, hydroelectric, and geothermal power in the near future. Once again, for reasons to which Bitcoin and Bitcoiners are likely entirely indifferent, *honest* environmentalists have no choice but to support Bitcoin.

The environmental benefits of these generation methods are hopefully obvious, but in particular consider the proposition of each growing in use *without requiring* transmission infrastructure. They could be anywhere. They could even catalyze new norms and heuristics of geographic population predicated on cheap energy rather than without consideration of energy cost at all, and hence, by definition, on wasteful energy.

We can pair this insight with an observation from Chapter Six, *Bitcoin Is Venice*, that one of the silver linings of the 2020 lockdowns will likely turn out to be the widespread realization that a great deal of knowledge work can be done from basically anywhere. Consider also that most major global population centers such as Tokyo or Los Angeles were founded prior to their being reached by the Industrial Revolution and hence with pre-fossil fuels sources of power and transportation in mind. We jested much earlier in this chapter that Bitcoin will finally end not only the First World War, but the Industrial Revolution also, and bring about a Commercial Revolution in its place. Here we see another avenue by which this might be said to come true: Urbanization will finally catch up with the product of the Industrial Revolution, rather than being locked into anxiously divergent co-dependency.

The geography of most modern urbanization can ultimately be traced back to navigable waterways and deep harbors, followed by hundreds or even thousands of years of network effects pertaining to industry (i.e., progressive integration of labor and capital) and the iteratively compounding Pareto distributions that naturally follow. Water transport is a relevant concern to economic activity in the twenty-first century, but *only just*. That *all urban development* has been locked into path dependency on an economic concern now millennia out-of-date is surely a cause of unimaginable waste and inefficiency. Bitcoin mining provides the first ever realistic alternative incentive structure for development, predicated precisely on minimizing waste. This all strongly leads us to conclude the inevitability of dramatic long-term changes in patterns of human habitation.[158]

Contrast this vision with the tragic reality today in many developing countries, such as the Democratic Republic of the Congo, a country of 90 million in which close to 90% do not have access to electricity. Instead, much of the largely rural population relies on charcoal to cook its food. This has to be procured by cutting down trees — devastating one of the world's largest rainforests and centers of biodiversity — and burning the wood, which in turn creates tragic indoor air pollution, a problem that leads to the deaths of millions of children each year. This situation shows no signs of changing given the inordinate expense of financing grid construction to these populations, which have very little ability to create capital, partly as a result of centuries of exploitation, colonialism, violence, and dictatorship. Zooming out, some 600 million people in sub-Saharan Africa still lack access to electricity, for similar reasons.

Bitcoin mining presents a potential solution, wherein foreign or domestic investors could finance hydro projects in the Congo River basin. Traditionally, such projects might hope to attract investment for capital expenses, but not operational expenses, and often fall into disuse or disrepair. For example, several dams built in the past five years in the Virunga Park region were not able to utilize the entirety of their energy output, because of the time and resources it would take to connect up the customers and local population.

However, bitcoin mining can provide immediate revenue, and this capital can be used to progressively build out the grid. Since these new customers will pay more than bitcoin miners, over time, bitcoin mining will be phased out, with miners moving elsewhere in search of profits. In a similar vein, bitcoin mining could also feasibly help usher in a new age of nuclear energy, as the operators of plants with a fixed output now no longer need to worry about the inefficiency of wasted power production. Instead, this is a feature, with overbuilt power being able to be directed towards the digital extension of the grid.

If countries like the DRC can harness their stranded energy assets, then they can create new centers of economic activity, reduce poverty, and end dependence on imported oil and costly indebtedness to such organizations as the IMF. The latter presents an intriguing future where developing countries, instead of having little economic or political choice but to entangle themselves with the IMF to finance modernization efforts, can sell bitcoin bonds on the open market, on the promise of verifiable but not-yet-monetized renewable energy resources. As of summer 2021, El Salvador is already doing so, raising more than $400 million in "volcano bonds." When one considers again the scale of unharnessed renewable energy sources in the developing world, this process could be a game changer in reducing dependence on the West.

And, of course, we might also hope that the simple push to restart such intense engineering projects at a greater scale than seen previously — wherever and for whatever reason this happens to be — will itself catalyze the kind of cost declines under cumulative production increases a la Wright's Law we have already seen with wind and solar — this time around with fundamentally *better* sources of energy generation and sounder economics devoid of political interference.

Sustaining the Unsustainable

"The concentration of the farmland into larger and larger holdings and fewer and fewer hands — with the consequent increase of overhead, debt, and dependence on machines — is thus a matter of complex significance, and its agricultural significance cannot be disentangled from its cultural significance. It *forces* a profound revolution in the farmer's mind: once his investment in land and machines is large enough, he must forsake the values of husbandry and assume those of finance and technology.

"Thenceforth his thinking is not determined by agricultural responsibility, but by financial accountability and the capacity of his machines. Where his money comes from becomes less important to him than where it is going. He is caught up in the drift of energy and interest away from the land. Production begins to override maintenance. The economy of money has infiltrated and subverted the economies of nature, energy, and the human spirit. The man himself has become a consumptive machine."

— Wendell Berry, *The Unsettling of America*

The reader may understandably have been put off by our treatment so far in the past few sections of "the environment" as if a purely financial matter.[159] While we rather have little choice, given we are committed to discussing the relationship between stocks of capital — the environment, in this case, finance and communications infrastructure above — and *capitalism*, we do appreciate the inherent crassness of the approach, necessary or not.

The perception of crassness is not merely aesthetic, and in fact follows from the motivating factor for this entire chapter: Humans respond to economic incentives whether they want to or not. If *our* treatment of "the environment" has been crass, that is because human interaction with the environment under degenerate fiat "capitalism" *is crass*. We would certainly like our discussion to be humbler and more reverential, but that would require a compelling reason to believe that contemporary capitalism itself can adopt a suitable reverence and humility. To zoom out even further, then, the thesis of the entire book is that it can: Bitcoin fixes this.

But we can be much more specific about *why this is the case*, rather than outsourcing our analysis to the connotations alone of words like "local," "reverent," "humble," and so on and so forth. We can once again adopt the terminology of *time preference*, and we can even quantify our analysis in the simple terms of *discount rates*. Tarek El Diwany provides precisely such an analysis in *The Problem with Interest*, writing,

Imagine a farmer who wishes to buy a plot of land and farm it. His purchase and operating costs are to be financed entirely on borrowed funds. The land is capable of supporting a highly intensive technique which is forecast to produce £150 per year of net profit for fifteen years, and which results in the land's desertification. An alternative production technique produces only £100 per year of net profit but allows the land to regenerate and maintain its productive potential indefinitely.

Discounted cash flow analysis allows the modern farmer to compare these two sets of cash-flows and select the most profitable [...] it is the farming approach that provides the highest total present value that is then recommended [...] With interest rates at 5% the highest present value (£2,000) resides in the low intensity farming approach, whilst with rates at 10% the highest present value (£1,140.91) resides in the high intensity option.

The incentive towards intensive farming, and thus desertification, increases as the interest rate increases. This unfortunate result is entirely due to the familiar way in which the discounting process progressively reduces the present value of the land's output in future years toward zero. £100 of net profit earned in year fifty has a present value of approximately £0.85 if the interest rate is 10% per year.

No wonder then that the analyst who relies on discounted cash-flow analysis has little care for what the land can produce in year fifty. Whether the land at that time is desertified or not is of little relevance, since its contribution to present value is negligible.

Lest we confuse the reader, we repeat our warning as originally stated in Chapter Five, *The Capital Strip Mine*,

Of course, we must not confuse the nominal interest rates forced upon economic actors by artificial debt creation with real time preference. A low rate on a manipulated market reflects neither an abundance of available funds for investment nor creates that which it is pretending to be. Or, perhaps more provocatively: An interest rate should be a discount rate; it should reflect the balance of time and opportunity cost. But high time preference incentives create high discount rates, which viciously recreate high time preference incentives in the form of short-term investment horizons. Low interest rates do not solve what is essentially a character flaw, and in fact they exacerbate it by providing the unknowingly flawed not only with no negative feedback that might be of character-building value, but also with an abundance of artificially cheap capital to waste on their high time preference nonsense.

El Diwany has just shown us such a vicious circle: If a farmer starts off with a short-term outlook for any reason at all, he will likely finance and operate his farm in such a way his high-time preference infects everything his operation touches — even non-economic factors such as his own ethics, psychology, and philosophy of life.

That El Diwany does not make this precise distinction[160] gives us an opportunity to explain precisely why dictating artificially low interest rates does not solve this problem and in fact exacerbates it. It is not the number that matters but the attitude the number reflects and from which it emerges: that of a high time preference, or, as cheekily alluded to above, a character flaw.

Artificially low interest rates will catalyze artificially high debt financing, which creates exactly the same problem, albeit for slightly different reasons. The levered farmer may well *need* to produce £150 of profit a year because the interest on his debt financing has squeezed his operation past the point at which £100 of pre-interest earnings is sustainable. This rhetorical slight ought to be lingered on for longer because it captures a profoundly tragic irony:

Fiat money so perverts incentives that it makes the sustainable unsustainable.

"Local," "reverent," and "humble" are not just buzzwords under such a degenerate financial regime. The farmer who *needs to produce now* because of a globally decreed artificially low interest rate is already eschewing the local and will have a hard time revering nature, the environment, his stock of natural capital, or however else we might be minded to characterize such things. This is no mere hypothetical, as the following extract from *The Future of the Great Plains*, the report of the Great Plains Committee of the US House of Representatives in 1936 following the ecological disaster of the dust bowl, makes painfully clear,

> The First World War and the following inflation pushed the price of wheat to new levels and caused a remarkable extension of the area planted to this crop. When the price collapsed during the post-war period Great Plains farmers continued to plant large wheat acreages in a desperate endeavor to get money with which to pay debt charges, taxes, and other unavoidable expenses. They had no choice in the matter. Without money they could not remain solvent or continue to farm. Yet to get money they were obliged to extend farming practices which were collectively ruinous.

Furthermore, recall our abstract definition of "leverage" in Chapter Three, *This Is Not Capitalism*, as "*induced vulnerability to shocks in exchange for a magnified gain in their absence*": This implies a lack of humility. In the real world, outside the models of degenerate fiat economists, there are always shocks. Leaving money on the table by foregoing leverage and maintaining an equity buffer to absorb an unforeseeable shock is a form of humility. Maximizing one's long-term vulnerability in exchange for magnified short-term gains is usually either arrogant, stupid, or both.

Foreshadowing Chapter Nine, *Global Money, Local Freedom*, such a choice also limits or even removes the ability to acquire knowledge and competence. Knowledge and competence are arguably the theoretical and practical sides of the same coin: the hard-won product of experience and discovery. Contrary to high-modernist arrogance, in any practical setting in which they are worthwhile in the first place, they cannot be deduced or made to pop out of a model, but must be arrived at by experimentation — at least *originally*. And once arrived at, they exist as a form of capital we would do well to at least nurture, if not eventually replenish with education and grow by *more experimentation.*

Entrepreneurship is one such form of experimentation, as we covered in Chapter Four, *Wittgenstein's Money*, but it is one kind among many.[161] Experimentation *requires* room for failure, since the nature of a worthwhile experiment is that we cannot know its outcome, or else we wouldn't bother running it in the first place.[162] As covered also in Chapter Five, *The Capital Strip Mine,* leverage eliminates room for failure, meaning it removes the opportunity to experiment and, in turn, the possibility of incrementally acquiring knowledge and competence. Leverage and short-termism literally make us stupid.

The inverse is also true. We wouldn't go as far as to say that equity finance and long-term thinking is itself necessary and sufficient for achieving reverence, humility, applied intelligence, and personal nirvana. But removing potentially overwhelming incentives towards irreverence and arrogance certainly doesn't hurt the cause.

Furthermore, ensuring that such irreverent, arrogant stupidity is forced to reckon with its own inevitable consequences rather than enjoy the coerced charity of socialized losses and involuntarily taxed bailouts won't hurt either. This hints at what is likely the simplest practical path to "localism": not some elaborate social scheme, just the removal of artificial disincentives towards a state that would otherwise be natural, and the removal of artificial incentives towards its unnatural antipode.

This is more or less the argument of Roger Scruton in positioning environmentalism as a deservedly (politically) conservative cause. He writes in *Green Philosophy*,

> For the conservative, politics concerns the maintenance and repair of homeostatic systems — systems that correct themselves in response to destabilizing change. Markets are homeostatic systems; so too are traditions, customs and the common law; so too are families, and the "civil associations" that make up the stuff of a free society. Conservatives are interested in markets, and prefer market forces to government action wherever the two are rivals. But this is not because of some quasi-religious belief in the market as the ideal form of social order or the sole solution to social and political problems; still less is it because of some cut of homo economicus and the "rational self-interest" that supposedly governs him. It is rather because conservatives look to

markets as self-correcting social systems, which can confront and overcome shocks from outside, and in normal cases adjust to the needs and motives of their members.

Later in the same chapter, however, Scruton helpfully walks back this position to one of admirable nuance:

This is not to say that the big NGOs are always wrong in their campaigns or that multinational companies always behave responsibly. On the contrary, Greenpeace and Friend of the Earth have drawn attention to real abuses, and used their high profile to good effect in educating the public. As companies get bigger, developing the capacity to move from jurisdiction to jurisdiction, evading their liabilities in each, so does their accountability dwindle. Shareholders rarely ask questions, and certainly not about the environmental consequences of actions that are bringing them a return on their investment. It is one of the weaknesses in the conservative position, as this has expressed itself in America, that its reasonable enthusiasm for free enterprise is seldom tempered by any recognition that free enterprise among citizens of a single nation state is very different from free enterprise conducted by a multinational company, in places to which the company and its shareholders have no civic tie. It is this carelessness towards "other places" that underlies environmental catastrophes like BP's oil-rig spill in the Gulf of Mexico, or the "slash and burn" cropping by multinational agribusinesses in the Amazon rainforest.

Precisely the environmental damage Scruton highlights evidences that the incentives in question are far from abstract, and the drive to reckless extraction unrelenting. El Diwany's farmer may have been hypothetical but exactly the mechanics of incentives for nurture versus extraction described, rooted ultimately in time preference but distorted by finance, has caused nothing short of an ecological disaster in the past fifty to sixty years or so in the form of widespread soil erosion.

Soil and Yield

"The first agricultural communities reached Europe's doorstep in southern Bulgaria around 5300 BC. At first farmers grew wheat and barley in small fields surrounding a few timber-framed buildings. Agricultural expansion into marginal land lasted about two thousand years before the agricultural potential of the region was fully exploited and persistent cultivation began to exhaust the soil. With no evidence of a climate shift, local populations grew and then declined as agricultural settlement swept through the area. Evidence for extensive late Neolithic soil erosion shows that agriculture spread from small areas of arable soils on the valley bottoms into highly erodible forest soils on steeper slopes. Eventually, the landscape filled in with small communities of several hundred people farming the area within about a mile of their village.

In these first European communities, population rose slowly before a rapid decline that emptied settlements out for five hundred to a thousand years, until the first traces of Bronze Age cultures then appeared. This pattern suggests a fundamental model of agricultural development in which prosperity increases the capacity of the land to support people, allowing the population to expand to use the available land. Then, having eroded soils from marginal land, the population contracts rapidly before soil rebuilds in a period of low population density."

— David Montgomery, *Dirt: The Erosion of Civilizations*

We find soil erosion to be the perfect example of an environmental issue for our purposes for a number of reasons: It is caused locally and can only be fixed locally, even though the consequences are global; it is *entirely obviously* a problem of time preference which results from an obsession with maximizing flows rather than nurturing, replenishing, and growing stocks; but most of all, it does not seem to us to be commonly appreciated or even understood to be a problem. In fact, many of its consequences are celebrated.

Hence, it is, to our minds, a more worthwhile problem to discuss in the context of *being a problem*, because contemporary society has been propagandized to not take it seriously, if it is even noticed at all. We think, therefore, that the terms of the following discussion can effectively be airdropped into any number of better-known and more widely appreciated environmental debates — emissions, pollution, deforestation, biodiversity loss, etc. — but that in doing so its effect, its *sting*, will be lessened ever-so-slightly. Soil erosion is our exemplar of high-time preference society strip mining environmental capital.[163]

Much like our commentary in Chapter Two, *The Complex Markets Hypothesis*, comparing Andrew Jackson and the Bank of the United States nearly two hundred years ago to Tarek El Diwany and the Bank of England barely ten, soil erosion is by no means a temporally or geographically isolated phenomenon. Its specter has haunted every civilization in recorded history.

In *Rome's Fall Reconsidered*, Vladimir Simkhovitch[164] writes, first of all somewhat tongue-in-cheek,

> What is the cause of this this moral corruption and degeneration of which all Roman writers of the period complain?
>
> In that very same ode Horace tells us why he takes so desperate a view of things. The great deeds of the Romans were the deeds of a sturdy farmer race [...] and these farmers' sons existed no longer. If they could not maintain themselves on their farms, still worse were the chances for a respectable existence in Rome; there they lost what little they have and became demoralized, dependent paupers.

Later, Simkhovitch more seriously identifies,

> The process of concentration followed many parallel routes. Indebtedness was undoubtedly the greatest factor in abolishing small holdings. Unproductivity of agriculture naturally led to cattle-ranches which required much larger holdings. Wealthy men acquired and accumulated vast domains rather for the pleasure of possession than as a paying investment. But the process of deterioration went on, and legislative interferences could neither stop the robbing of the soil nor the depreciation of land values.

And finally, to link culture, finance, and soil fertility so as to come full circle, Simkhovitch asks,

> Why then did the Roman farmers fail to improve their methods of agriculture even when pressed by necessity to do so, even when threatened with extermination? It was easier said than done. Behind our abstract agricultural reflections are concrete individual farms [...] the owners of the rundown farms are impoverished, and when a farmer is economically sinking, he is not in a position to improve his land.
>
> Only one with sufficient resources can improve his land. By improving land, we add to our capital, while by robbing land we add immediately to our income; in doing so, however, we diminish out of all proportion our capital as farmers, the productive value of our farm land. The individual farmer can therefore improve his land only when in an economically strong position. A farmer who is failing to make a living on his farm is more likely to exploit his farm to the utmost; and when there is no room for further exploitation, he is likely to meet the deficit by borrowing, and thus pledging the future productivity of his farm.

Such is the process that as a rule leads to his losing possession of his homestead and his fields, and to his complete proletarisation.

Montgomery likewise is not describing a purely historical curiosity, but rather a permanent feature of the struggle to sustain civilization, as dire an issue today as it has ever been in the past. He warns,

> Across the planet, moderate to extreme soil erosion has degraded 1.2 billion hectares of agricultural land since 1945 — an area the size of China and India combined. One estimate places the amount of agricultural and used and abandoned in the past fifty years as equal to the amount farmed today. The United Nations estimates that 38 percent of global cropland has been seriously degraded since the Second World War. Each year farms around the world lose 75 billion metric tons of soil. A 1995 review of the global effects of soil erosion reported the loss of twelve million hectares of arable land each year to soil erosion and land degradation. This would mean that the annual loss of arable land is almost 1 percent of the total available. Clearly this is no sustainable.
>
> Globally, average cropland erosion of ten to a hundred tons per hectare per year removes soil about ten to a hundred times faster than it forms. So far in the agricultural era, nearly a third of the world' potentially farmable land has been lost to erosion, most of it in the past forty years. In the late 1980s a Dutch-led assessment of global soil erosion found that almost 2 billion hectares of former agricultural lands could no longer support crops. That much land could feed billions of people. We are running out of dirt we cannot afford to lose.

Montgomery makes the connection here to the ultimate utility of healthy soil: feeding people. Global soil erosion threatens humanity's collective ability to adequately feed itself: a dramatically necessary precondition of any other kinds of capital accumulation. Practitioners of hyper-degenerate *hyper-fiat* "yield farming" on so-called "cryptocurrencies" are living off the surplus of real yield a real farmer somewhere has harvested.

And yet the results of inadequate care for the capital stock of arable land go well beyond the sheer quantity of calorific output. There are problems in terms of *quality* potentially much deeper still. The levels of Glyphosate, the chief ingredient in the most widely used herbicide in the US, Roundup, in the breast milk of American women has been found to be around a thousand times the level allowed in European drinking water.[165]

Glyphosate also impedes absorption and translocation of calcium, magnesium,[166] and selenium[167] in soil, and overexposure is thought to be a leading cause of the recent unprecedented prevalence of celiac disease, breast, thyroid, liver, kidney, and pancreatic cancer, and myeloid leukemia. In 2015, the International Agency for Research on Cancer classified Glyphosate as "probably carcinogenic to humans." In an article titled, "Dirt Poor: Have Fruits and

Vegetables Become Less Nutritious?" and even more tellingly subtitled, "Because of soil depletion, crops grown decades ago were much richer in vitamins and minerals than the varieties most of us get today," *Scientific American* reports on a landmark study by Donald Davis from the University of Texas with the startling summary that Davis's team,

> Studied U.S. Department of Agriculture nutritional data from 1950 and 1999 for 43 different vegetables and fruits, finding "reliable declines" in the amount of protein, calcium, phosphorous, iron, riboflavin (vitamin B2) and vitamin C over the past half century. Davis and his colleagues chalk up this declining nutritional content to the preponderance of agricultural practices designed to improve traits (size, growth rate, pest resistance) other than nutrition.[168]

We are not only strip mining the land; we are strip mining human health.

The reader may well be wondering if this is all a hobby horse of the authors and be unsure where this is all going and what — if anything — it has to do with *capital* or *capitalism*. Just in case this is so, we repeat one of the first quoted extracts of the entire book which the reader may have forgotten by now; from Henri Pirenne's *Medieval Cities*:

> Lombardy, where from Venice on the east and Pisa and Genoa on the west all the commercial movements of the Mediterranean flowed and were blended into one, flourished with an extraordinary exuberance. On the wonderful plain cities bloomed with the same vigor as the harvests. The fertility of the soil made possible for them an unlimited expansion, and at the same time the ease of obtaining markets favored both the importation of raw materials and the exportation of manufactured products. There, commerce gave rise to industry, and as it developed, Bergamo, Cremona, Lodi, Verona, and all the old towns, all the old Roman municipia, took on new life, far more vigorous than that which had animated them in antiquity.

Soil was not sufficient to the Renaissance, but it was necessary, for the very simple reason that it underpins all capital formation. It is literally *the original capital* that must be nurtured, replenished, and grown in order to sustain capital formation of any other kind.

Henry Kissinger is known for the rather menacing aphorism, "who controls the food supply controls the people; who controls the energy can control continents; who controls money can control the world." We have covered how Bitcoin completely re-localizes the money, and goes to great lengths, if not *total*, to re-localize the energy, but the food supply is worth digging into a little further.

The food supply is the yield of the carrying capacity of arable land. This is why soil erosion matters, and matters greatly. It may often take the form of literal strip mining, but arguably more importantly it is *capital* strip mining. Entirely aside from it being a barely well-known or publicized problem, this is why we consider it to be the perfect example of environmental capital that ought to be nurtured, replenished, and grown, yet is not: Unlike biodiversity loss, for example, soil erosion is a distinctly human and communal problem.

As belabored in Chapter Five, *The Capital Strip Mine*, soil *literally is* capital. It has a carrying capacity and a yield that has human utility. This is by no means to dismiss biodiversity loss, carbon emissions, or other forms of environmental damage, and we absolutely insist that virtually every such problem is ultimately caused by short-termism and selfishness or stupidity in general, but more specifically that all are motivated by degenerate fiat finance and money. However, we make no apologies whatsoever for placing human beings above all other life forms and ecosystems, for two exceedingly simple reasons, one philosophical and one practical.

Philosophically, only humans *care*. Only humans *can* go out their way to protect other life forms. Many contemporary environmental activists,[169] as opposed to *real* environmentalists or what might be more easily understood and appreciated by the label *conservationists*, would do well to remember that "the environment" is not a benign spirit of peace and harmony. In moral terms it very nearly *pure evil*. Everything in "the environment," including the environment itself, is either indifferent to your pain and suffering and willing to take advantage of it, or is actively trying to kill you.

Like Bitcoin, it doesn't care, but unlike Bitcoin, that apathy is reflected in unrelenting violence. Humans and humans alone *care* and self-regulate their capacity for violence and use their surplus time and energy above subsistence to attempt to protect and conserve the environment that is constantly trying to kill them. Humans alone have advanced to *civilization*, or, personal sacrifice and interpersonal compromise in the pursuit of the fruits of voluntary cooperation rather than immediate-term selfish violence. While many plants and animals might appear to plan and act for the future, only humans have a time preference that they arrive at *intellectually* rather than merely instinctively. And, of course, in the *very, very, very* long run — the kind of time horizons over which Bitcoin makes one think and take seriously — life on earth will eventually be annihilated if humans cannot develop the technological means of grafting it onto an extra-terrestrial ecosystem.

Practically, the only rational hope for protecting non-human life forms and ecosystems is to first and foremost prevent human suffering. Desperate, suffering, and mal-incentivized humans will inevitably destroy things. They will consume capital — and more. They will consume resources that do not even have an economic carrying capacity in the first place, do not constitute capital, and hence do not damage human relations but damage *only* the environment. They will cause biodiversity loss, for example, without a second thought. As we will argue later in this chapter and return to at the start of Chapter Nine, *Global Money, Local Freedom*, indisputably the most environmentally damaging governments have been communist — an ideology hardly known for its valuing of capital or its propensity to avoid suffering, desperation, and mal-incentivization amongst the governed. Not just to avoid the never-ending disaster of communism, but to protect the environment from *any* form of collective human endeavor, the incentives must be fixed.

This all sheds high-modernist efforts to "protect" the environment by arrogantly engineering it beyond belief or recognition in a particularly hilarious light. There are too many examples to list anywhere near exhaustively, but let us consider just a few, from a range of times and places. As highlighted above, *Seeing Like a State* begins with an extensive analysis of German "scientific" forestry in the early nineteenth century: The attempt to use "science" to "manage" forests and optimize the output of timber, with repeated scare quotes because, of course, it was anything but scientific, and the forests were not managed so much as destroyed. We won't quote what runs for twenty or so pages, and in fact the quote much earlier in this chapter is perfectly applicable here, but we will offer a shorter, pithier summary of the fallout instead:

> A new term, Waldsterben (forest death), entered the German vocabulary to describe the worst cases. An exceptionally complex process involving soil building, nutrient uptake, and symbiotic relations among fungi, insects, mammals, and flora — which were, and still are, not entirely understood — was apparently disrupted, with serious consequences. Most of these consequences can be traced to the radical simplicity of the scientific forest.

Or consider Allan Savory's frustration at the modern treatment of livestock: Both what bovine animals are and are not used for in modern agriculture, writing in *Holistic Management*,

> No other aspect of Holistic Management has caused such controversy as the suggested se of animal impact has. That trampling by livestock damages both plants and soils is a deeply held belief throughout the world [...] Some range scientists have for years rejected the one idea that has more promise of solving the riddle of desertification than any other. Meanwhile, they have supported the development of machines of extraordinary size and cost to break soil crusts and disturb vegetation through mechanical impact toward the same end. Because we have now lost most of the large herding wildlife species, and the predators that induced their movement, we are left only with livestock in most instances to stimulate that role, which we do by bunching them (there is no need to panic or stampede them), using herding or fencing, and planning their moves. There is no other tool than animal impact, I believe, that can do more to regenerate the world's damaged soils and reverse desertification.

Unfortunately, livestock — cattle and goats in particular — are generally seen as an enemy of the land and wildlife, rather than its savior. Recent concern over the methane released by ruminating cattle has reinforced this view. Yet, as far as we know, all ruminants — buffalo, bison, antelope, sheep, goats, pronghorn, deer, giraffe, and the like — produce methane as a by-product of rumination. Moreover, atmospheric methane levels did not increase between 1999 and 2008, even though livestock numbers increased seventy percent over the same period.

Savory later adds,

One of the greatest immediate benefits from animal impact can be seen in the restoration and maintenance of brittle environment water catchments, which store not only more water but also more carbon. While partial or total rest can sustain soil cover in the perennially moist nonbrittle environments, no technology exists that could replace animal impact on all the ranches, farms, pastoral lands, national parks, and forests that cover the bulk of most brittle environments, where either form of rest is so damaging to soil cover.

Those who remain opposed to livestock — and they are many, including scientists, environmental groups, vegetarians, governments, and international development agencies, remain unaware of the fact that no form of technology, nor burning, nor resting land can effectively address the desertification occurring in the world's grasslands while feeding people at the same time.

Or consider, finally, the modern fad of "fake meat." A means of *feeding people* that many, if not all, of the groups cited above by Savory would likely heartily endorse over the evils of traditional agriculture; truly astonishing in social-historical terms; verging on a Poe's law violation of the most risibly ignorant, arrogant, high-modernist imposition on local knowledge; not justified on the basis of an unobtrusive personal commitment to vegetarianism or as a protest against factory farming, to be clear — both perfectly reasonable causes — but rather as a mandated prescription for *everybody, everywhere* to Save The World from an apocalypse of cow farts.

As if Savory wouldn't laugh (or possibly cry) at the absurdity of condemning the environmental impact of an animal uniquely suited to regenerating "the environment" following its destruction by humans, there is an added layer of comical hubris in that meat-alternatives unequivocally require intense monocropping that accelerates soil erosion. This is degenerate fiat environmentalism in a nutshell: Passionately proposing what it fails to recognize is the cause of the problem and opposing its only realistic solution. Beyond meat indeed, and beyond civilization also.

Culture and Agriculture

"The wealth that ultimately sustains any nation or community is derived from green plants growing on regenerating soil, a fact that even the most sophisticated conventional financial planning methods do not take into account."
— Allan Savory, *Holistic Management*

We do not throw around the word "civilization" lightly. This profound ignorance of what agriculture *is* and *is for* touches on a seminal feature of its link to civilization. Much as we cannot have liquid derivatives markets without the foundation of real productive capital, we cannot have culture without agriculture. Arguably we can't even have productive capital, hence liquid derivatives markets depend on the soil also. Savory laments this loss of foundational knowledge in hyperspecialized, degenerate fiat modernity.

The root of the essentially communitarian trade-offs of all capital, be it liquid derivatives markets, culture, or whatever, is in the trade-offs inherent in adopting agriculture in the first place. Montgomery captures this well,

> For over 99 percent of the last two million years, our ancestors lived off the land in small, mobile groups. While certain foods were likely to be in short supply at times, it appears that some food was available virtually all the time. Typically, hunting and gathering societies considered food to belong to all, readily shared what they had, and did not store or hoard — egalitarian behavior indicating that shortages were rare. If more food was needed, more was found. There was plenty of time to look. Anthropologists generally contend that most hunting and gathering societies had relatively large amounts of leisure time, a problem few of us are plagued with today.
>
> Farming's limitation to floodplains established an annual rhythm, to early agricultural civilization. A poor harvest meant death for many and hunger for most. Though most of us in developed countries are no longer as directly dependent on good weather, we are still vulnerable to the slowly accumulating effects of soil degradation that set the stage for the decline of once-great societies as populations grew to exceed the productive capacity of floodplains and agriculture spread to the surrounding slopes, initiating cycles of soil mining that undermined civilization after civilization.

The overbearing interference of fiat money has drowned out the local signal of received wisdom with malign incentives driving degenerate modern culture towards the delusion that it can have the benefits of both the hunter-gatherer lifestyle and agricultural civilization, and the costs of neither. Which is to say we want the product of a fully built civilization but not the work of building and maintaining it in the first place. We want to be able to live moment to moment, carefree, conflict-free, trade-off-free, like nomadic hunter-gatherers for whom "time" means next to nothing. We don't want to have to think long-term to make interpersonal compromises or personal sacrifices. But, of course, we do want medicine, plumbing, literature, and leisure. We want air conditioning and TikTok and soy chai lattes. We just want to consume these things without having first produced them.[170]

But we cannot. We have to make a choice. If we continue to strip mine every source of capital from which every consumable good emerges — tangible, cultural, spiritual, whatever — this choice will be made for us. Civilization will collapse. We will be the farmer who ate all the seed rather than planting even a little; the agricultural society who maximized flow instead of stock and stumbled into desertification when the stocks ran dry.

It is a peculiarly modern fantasy that civilization makes life easier: That it frees us from the shackles of a state of natural oppression and allows us all to find and to be our true selves. This is juvenile quackery. Civilization certainly makes life *better*, but earned at the cost of *hard work*. Civilization *is proof of work*. Civilization is the choice, *as a community of individuals opting into voluntary cooperation* to defer gratification: to invest rather than to consume. Individuals are perfectly free to opt *out of* these hard choices by returning to a pre-civilizational state, but it would be preferable to all if, in doing so, they had the decency to in fact remove themselves from civilization rather than skimming its consumable surplus while contributing nothing to its maintenance. There is nothing *easier* than gayly wandering in the wild and wondering whether one's imminent death will come at the hands of illness, starvation, predation, or some even funnier, more easily preventable affliction.

We *need* to start thinking long term. Bitcoin fixes this. Bitcoin will *make us* think long-term, whether we want to or not. Those who selfishly refuse to will go bankrupt only locally. They will be systemically unimportant. Their childishness will be met only with finally being treated like children: *We don't hit each other, do we? That's right, we don't! Now use your words like a big boy.* Those who ignore this sage advice will strip mine away only their own capital. They will get sick, starve, or be eaten by a bear of entirely their own character-flawed making. The prudent, the responsible, and the mature will thrive.

Besides the likely benefits to preservation and stewardship of environmental capital that will clearly be directly attributable to Bitcoin, there is a more broadly obvious source of optimism. By far the greatest source of environmental destruction in the at-all-recent past has been big government, big business, and, worst of all, the two acting in tandem.

Although this is a slightly facetious framing, we like that it elides association with any contemporary political position or controversy. We furiously resist being painted with the asinine branding of either "left" or "right," and have avoided any such branding seeming a natural or accurate one by going out of our way to insult the shibboleths of both.

The reader may recall endnote 6 from Chapter Two, *The Complex Markets Hypothesis*, in which we praised the committed liberal Matt McManus. Even if he would, we won't say "leftist" as we don't feel this does his thought and work justice, but we will make the following observation of the gravity of Bitcoin's likely impact for respectable thinkers who *would* self-identify as either *of the left* or *of the right* or, perhaps more charitably, as *liberals* or as *conservatives*. Liberals will likely struggle with the unprecedented extent to which Bitcoin undermines state authority, and conservatives will likely struggle with the equally unprecedented extent to which Bitcoin drives rapid change in social relations.

We say neither from a position of political preference. Rather, we are mindful of Hume's *is/ought*: We are not saying this is a *good* or a *just* thing, necessarily, we are just saying it is going to happen, and all our notions of the good and the just, regardless of their potentially political motivations, will just have to deal with this. Reactionary objections will, as always, make a mockery of the left/right borderline nonsense split, very much in the spirit analyzed by Virginia Postrel's wonderful, *The Future and Its Enemies*. We might easily and naturally adopt Postrel's rhetoric to say, *Bitcoin is the future, and it will make enemies of all political stripes.*

The thesis underlying the facetiously presented claim just above is more or less that the fiat monetary system encourages artificial *bigness* of all kinds — all manner of toxic bloat that would not be sustainable if not also protected from legitimate feedback or internalization of true costs.

"Big government" is a slur, admittedly. We mean something a little more specific than how such a slur might be read, and will only make the point here in reference to environmental issues before tackling it in much more detail in the final two chapters. We mean government that is so big as to escape responsibility and accountability. If a government is responsible for everything then it is responsible for nothing, and if everybody is accountable only to the government then the government is accountable to nobody. As Ostrom, Scott, Jacobs, and Hayek would forcefully argue, this is a recipe for widespread yet heterogeneous *local* disaster. Ironically it is specifically a recipe for no responsibility and no accountability — in every area touched, but most certainly including natural resources.

The environmental record of the Soviet Union, for example, is nothing short of catastrophic. Readers may be unaware that the Aral Sea, once the fourth largest lake in the world, literally disappeared under the USSR's incompetent industrial policy. Once providing 20% of the USSR's fish stock and employing forty thousand people in fishing alone, never mind other supporting and supported industries, the total lack of accountability and responsibility inherent in such a totalitarian model led to thinking it was a good idea to divert most of the rivers feeding the lake to irrigation projects which, unsurprisingly, also failed.

But we need not resort to the specter of communism as we risk misleading the reader into thinking the problem with bigness lies with incompetently managed large-scale projects, and totalitarianism, no less. This can be true, but far more insidious is the prevention of small-scale projects that would otherwise have been perfectly competent. An EU directive mandating abattoirs could not operate without a qualified vet — without which British abattoirs had been quite alright for literally thousands of years — led to the closure of most small abattoirs which could not afford such a superfluity. This then directly exacerbated — and could reasonably be said to have *caused* — the foot-and-mouth outbreak in 2001 given most cattle then had to travel hundreds of miles across the country to the closest brilliantly regulated abattoir.

Rather than a local problem, dealt with by local people with local knowledge, the outbreak became a national disaster. There are, clearly, uncountably many such examples to choose from but we will cease at this amusing juxtaposition, lest the entire book become about regulatory incompetence, rather than Bitcoin, which will fix it.

"Big business," too, is something of a slur. It might seem to run contrary to a reading of our tone of "market absolutism." But this is a grave philosophical error, and a remarkably modern and lazy one at that.[171] Although still tragically impoverished, it might nonetheless be reasonable to characterize the authors as "freedom absolutists," "responsibility absolutists," or ideally both given each can only be coherently understood in light of the other. But it is a peculiarly modern cluelessness to equate these positions with "market absolutism." Roger Scruton put it wonderfully,

> It is not as though the complaints from the left against the petroleum companies, the agribusinesses, the producers of GM crops, the developers, the supermarkets and the airlines were all based on fabrications, or as if these businesses can be run just as they are without any lasting environmental damage. In fact, the greatest weakness of the position that John Gray describes as "neo-liberalism" — the ideological summoning of the market, as the sole remedy to all social and economic problems — is the refusal to make the distinction, apparent to all reasonable people, between big business and little business. When businesses are big enough they can cushion themselves against the negative side effects of their activity, and proceed as if all objections could be overcome by a consultant in "Corporate Social Responsibility," without any change in the way things are done.

It is perhaps not so much "bigness" that is in itself a problem, but the kind of bigness to which Scruton alludes that only can only come into existence and be sustained in the first place by a government equally big, equally unsustainable, and equally as disinterested in allowing decentralized feedback mechanisms to take their toll.

As was detailed in Chapter Six, *Bitcoin Is Venice*, government that big — and, in particular, that indiscriminately wasteful and destructive on account of its bigness — will not survive a Bitcoin standard. Bitcoin *is* the negative feedback that forces it to reckon with its own unsustainability. As Ostrom, Scott, and Scruton would have recommended all along, government and business alike will be forced to become far more local, contextual, knowledgeable, and competent.

Culture and Capital

"What has not been often said, because it did not need to be said until fairly recent times, is that the responsible consumer must also be in some way a producer. Out of his own resources and skills, he must be equal to some of his own needs. The household that prepares its own meals in its own kitchen with some intelligent regard for nutritional value, and thus depends on the grocer only for selected raw materials, exercises an influence on the food industry that reaches from the store all the way back to the seedsman. The household that produces some or all of its own food will have a proportionally greater influence. The household that can provide some of its own pleasures will not be helplessly dependent on the entertainment industry, will influence it by not being helplessly dependent on it, and will not support it thoughtlessly out of boredom."
— Wendell Berry, *The Unsettling of America*

In this chapter, we have provided considerable analysis of financial and communications infrastructure, as well as natural resources: Three distinct domains of physical capital that we anticipate will come to be greatly impacted by Bitcoin's accelerating adoption. Although clearly relying on Bitcoin's value, and not to detract from the importance of continued (likely inevitable) monetization, but we cannot help but feel that each of these three have an additional aesthetic appeal in that they rely on tapping into essentially novel properties of Bitcoin *as technology*, rather than relying only on its appreciation. Programmable securities, money streaming, and a global buyer of energy of last resort are tremendously exciting. Their growing promise is evidence that Bitcoin is, "not just a digital rock," to cite an expression frequently utilized by Elizabeth Stark.

All this said, we are keen to emphasize that Bitcoin is *not just* a technology. Far more important than Bitcoin potentially leading to a change in the architecture of the internet, for example — interesting solely on account of being new and representing change — is why this change will be valued by its users, and what kind of behavior it will incentivize and reward. Which is to say that it is far more interesting to us as *capital* than as *technology*, and its creators and users far more important in our minds as *capitalists* than as *technologists*.

This all reflects more deeply that "capitalism" is a philosophy of human interaction and cooperation as relates to creating common pool resources of economic potential energy. It not just a way of doing business — or, at least, it ought not to be when implemented properly, and not in degenerate, fiat form. Its tenets follow from balancing personal responsibility and initiative with the net benefits of communitarian compromise and fostering the long-termism required for both to be borne out and flourish. Wendell Berry's discerning observation above comes from an essay within *The Unsettling of America* titled, *The Ecological Crisis is a Crisis of Culture*. Capitalism is ultimately a product of culture, and the strip mining of capital in any form is always, in part, a cultural crisis.

David Montgomery reflects on Berry's philosophical legacy in the final few pages of *Dirt*, stressing the connection between hard economic reality and the ideals that guide its creation. Berry, writes Montgomery,

> Argues that economies can be based on either industrial or agrarian ideals, and that an agrarian society need not be a subsistence society lacking technological sophistication and material well-being. He sees industrial societies as based on the production and use of products, whether fundamental to survival (food) or manufactured along with the desire for it (pop tarts). In contrast, an agrarian economy is based on local adaptation of economic activity to the capacity of the land to sustain such activity. Not surprisingly, Berry likes to talk about the difference between good farming and the most profitable farming. Still, he points out that everybody need not be a farmer in an agrarian society, nor need industrial production be limited to the bare necessities. The distinction in Berry's view is that agriculture and manufacturing in an agrarian society would be tailored to the local landscape. While it is difficult to reconcile current trends with this vision for an agrarian economy, a reoriented capitalism is not unimaginable. After all, today's quasi-sovereign global corporations were inconceivable just a few centuries ago.

We propose that substituting "agrarian" for "capitalist" and "industrial" for "fiat" changes next to nothing in this extract, except, interestingly, the focus. Neither Montgomery nor Berry are Bitcoiners (to our knowledge, at least!) and so their inclination is to paint this degenerate mode of capitalism as, ultimately, the economic result of a form of cultural self-affliction. Our only dissent may possibly be to insist on probing further and pinpointing the causality at play as a vicious circle. Cultural flaws lead to defective capitalism: industrial, extractive, consumerist, and toxically big, rather than agrarian, replenishing, capitalist, and local. In a word, *fiat* ... but defective capitalism leads in turn to defective culture and, given long enough to play out, feeds on itself.

In the following, penultimate, chapter, we will consider the impact of the degenerate fiat influences of short-termism, myopia, arrogance, irreverence, and selfishness on stocks of capital far more abstract than the more clearly *physical* domains discussed here. Furthermore, the domains of social, urban, and cultural capital will be far more questionably "private" than these clearly economic and rivalrous stocks of capital, are more obviously common pool resources to a greater or lesser extent, and on this account may even have more in common with money itself.

And of course, we will ponder the role Bitcoin may come to play in removing distortion from information flows that inform their governance and constitution, restoring truth, and enabling these stocks of capital also to be nurtured, replenished, and grown.

Chapter Eight

These Were Capitalists

Social, urban, and cultural capital; their communitarian essence and their unlikely champions

Following Hernando de Soto, we see capital as "economic potential energy"; a stock of crystallized and stored time; the memory of experimentation and discovery; a tool allowing us to not need to work completely from scratch, and shared in a common language to spare us equally from isolation. As de Soto explains in *The Mystery of Capital*:

> To unravel the mystery of capital, we have to go back to the seminal meaning of the word. In medieval Latin, "capital" appears to have denoted head of cattle or other livestock, which have always been important sources of wealth beyond the basic meat they provide. Livestock are low-maintenance possessions; they are mobile and can be moved away from danger; they are also easy to count and measure. But most important, from livestock you can obtain additional wealth, or surplus value, by setting in motion other industries, including milk, hides, wool, meat, and fuel. Livestock also have the useful attribute of being able to reproduce themselves. Thus the term "capital" begins to do two jobs simultaneously, capturing the physical dimension of assets (livestock) as well as their potential to generate surplus value. From the barnyard, it was only a short step to the desks of the inventors of economics, who generally defined "capital" as that part of a country's assets that initiates surplus production and increases productivity.

Capital is whatever can be transformed or used to produce goods that satisfy human wants. It can be stored, deployed, and accumulated, because it is *productive*. But as discussed in Chapter Four, *Wittgenstein's Money*, it follows also that capital is, like value, entirely *subjective*. We call capital that which we use in the process of creating a good. Milk may be the good which will satisfy our want for a beverage, but it can also be the capital which we can use to produce a cake which will satisfy our hunger. Capital is thus an abstract idea we superimpose on reality to describe things which have subjectively useful potential energy. De Soto writes,

Capital is born by representing in writing — in a title, a security, a contract, and in other such records — the most economically and socially useful qualities about the asset as opposed to the visually more striking aspects of the asset. This is where potential value is first described and registered. The moment you focus your attention on the title of a house, for example, and not on the house itself, you have automatically stepped from the material world into the conceptual universe where capital lives. You are reading a representation that focuses your attention on the economic potential of the house by filtering out all the confusing lights and shadows of its physical aspects and its local surroundings. Formal property forces you to think about the house as an economic and social concept. It invites you to go beyond viewing the house as mere shelter — and thus a dead asset — and to see it as live capital.

Our imagination and recognition of objects, concepts, or associations *as capital* makes them such. To see is to create. At the core of forming and accumulating capital is our ability to mutually recognize and agree on its existence and to record it such that there is an accessible consensus for consultation and resolution of dispute. Absent functional registries — or even the voluntarist recognition and respect for what *would be* in a registry — we fail to benefit from the productive accumulation of land or property because we fail to initially will capital into abstract existence.

In Chapter Seven, *A Capital Renaissance*, we predicted Bitcoin's likely near-term impact on stocks of capital across finance, communications, and energy. But we anticipate its influence will extend much further than just these areas of essentially physical infrastructure. In fact, we anticipate it will extend well past what might most easily be referred to as *economics* and into social affairs also.

This is a far more speculative proposition. Most of what we analyzed in the previous chapter we are familiar with as it is starting to happen: It is really just than a question of understanding technology and extrapolating the implications of its logic. Our argument requires little more than assuming that people will be motivated to seek out economic efficiencies.

But there is surely at least a little more to it than this. "Seek out economic efficiencies" is ill-defined, and we have argued at length, and at too many points throughout the book to now recite, that "efficiency" defined too narrowly and over too short a period of time is a false idol. It breeds arrogance, fragility, and, ultimately, destruction. Arguably even referring to "economic" efficiencies — as if the purely "economic" can be reductively isolated for controlled analysis — is deeply misleading. Following from remarks in earlier chapters but in particular in endnotes towards the beginning of Chapter Two, *The Complex Markets Hypothesis*, and Chapter Three, *This Is Not Capitalism*, in which we listed our primarily influences from the economic literature, we rather suspect the probably widely held impression that there *even can be* the exclusively "economic" is rather the fault of contemporary academic economics and its historical legacy.

In his presidential address at the first annual meeting of the Economic History Association, *The Tasks of Economic History*, economic historian Edwin Gay drew attention to "the beginnings of [his] discipline in order to emphasize how the subsequent shift in its development has made us economic historians instead of historical economists." He traces the emergence of economic history as a distinct discipline to a reaction against what he calls "*the tendency to abstract theorizing*" originating in nineteenth-century Germany that was not present in the work of economists even a generation earlier, when economics itself was still young, observing that, "There had been in the writings of Adam Smith and Malthus and of some of their Scotch and German predecessors much incidental use of economic history and of observation of contemporary economic life."

We would certainly like to think we have tried to ground our analysis as much as possible in both history and contemporary observation, and have done our best to give the abstract theory of contemporary academic economics a bad name, particularly when clearly historically and practically illiterate or, arguably worse, ambivalent! Gay goes on,

> Karl Knies, one of the profoundest of the critics, not only maintained the principle of historical relativity against the "absolutism of theory," but also insisted upon the continuity of historical development and the interaction of all manifestations of the human spirit, economic, legal, political, social and religious, during each period of history. In man's physical environment, he held, in the sphere of laws to which the growing economy must be adapted; but in the successive economic activities and institutions there are such differences as well as likenesses that only analogies may be discovered, not the working of laws [...]
>
> [...] While strongly emphasizing the role of the state and the community, and the immensely strong social disposition of man that originates and maintains those institutions, Knies especially inveighed against the defective psychology of those economists who based their entire deductive system upon the operation of one compelling motive, that of "desire for wealth," "hope of gain," or self-interest. Like the other historical economists, he demanded that whole complex of motives and interests, varying among themselves in intensity at different occasions and times should always be taken into account by the investigator of any form of human behavior.

N. S. B. Gras makes a similarly holistic and humanistic observation, more specifically of the individual capitalist in *Capitalism: History and Concepts*, writing,

> The essential element of capital is something produced and then saved, not used up. Into this saving of goods to constitute capital, there goes

necessarily a large amount of what is found in administration — planning, forbearance, and management. Business administration, like political administration, is made up of policy formulation, management, and control. In reality, capitalism is basically psychological. It is production in a certain way with a certain objective.

That capitalism is basically psychological, as Gras suggests, ought to have some transferrable bearing on every area of human endeavor. We can use this insight to grasp at the same material and the same frustration as Gay (and implicitly Knies, also) but run the thinking in the opposite direction: Not that the "economic" must be treated as, in part, legal, political, and social and religious, but that the legal, political, and social and religious could be treated as, in part, economic. Our own argument extends that of Gras — that the lessons of *real* capitalism can be applied wherever *something is produced and then saved, not used up.*

In this chapter we will expand on three distinct but interwoven forms of capital: social, urban, and cultural. We are not arguing for putting a monetary value on all aspects of our lives, by any means. We are rather proposing that the memory of experimentation and discovery, tools allowing us to not need to work completely from scratch, and common languages to spare us equally from isolation, all go well beyond the merely and exclusively economic.

And yet at the same time, money almost always has a role to play. As explained in Chapter Four, *Wittgenstein's Money,* money is the right to time, whilst capital is time that has been crystallized towards a specific end. But no matter how illiquid, how abstract, and how removed from its financial aspect capital has become, money will always be bidding for time and directing time to one end rather than another. The nurture, replenishment, and maintenance of all capital cannot avoid being affected by the contemporary state of money. Our hope is that as money evolves towards the censorship-resistant, integrity-assured, sound, and free and open-source, that healthy financial capital accumulation hastens and its methods radiate out to other more abstract forms of capital. We discussed the former in Chapter Seven, *A Capital Renaissance,* and will discuss the latter in this chapter.

We grant that this hypothesis is on the more speculative end, which is why we will repeatedly turn to history as a guide rather than theory, exclusively. We provide examples that might inspire the future.

Let us take the simple example of office space. It has often morphed to emulate the dominant technology of the age. In the early twentieth century, the industrial factory drove aggregate productive economic activity. The hierarchical structure that benefited factories was transcribed into rigid bureaucracies. Now that software has begun eating the world, you hear insurance companies talk of open-plan office and flat hierarchies. Dominant ideas spread.

Saifedean Ammous has, on several occasions, spoken about the impact of soft and hard money on time preference and how that core monetary instinct can spread to other behaviors like choosing what to eat, how to build, and what art and culture to value — what to *consume,* in ever more abstract and yet vital forms than the merely economic. A society using soft money is subconsciously infused with the realization that value melts and must be spent quickly. It will favor immediacy, sacrificing the future in search for gratification now. Another way of putting it would be that low stock-to-flow money focuses people's attention on flow.

From its inception, the euro's operating philosophy was to predictably lose 2% of its purchasing value annually. That's it. That's its objective. Damn the stock. Focus on the flow. Eventually, you get politicians and economists excitedly measuring GDP (i.e., the temporary flow created by the wealth) and GDP growth (i.e., the temporary change of the temporary flow created by the wealth), which we merrily debunked in Chapter Three, *This Is Not Capitalism.* If your core social institution teaches you that capital stocks lose value fast, farmers stop thinking about how best to preserve the richness of the soil and wonder instead how many bushels of wheat they can grow per acre this season and possibly next. Musicians stop coveting a legacy of contribution beyond their death and are forced to focus instead on how many albums they can sell, and how short they can get away with making their songs to game the per-track monetization of music streaming platforms.

Under a monetary system both sound and open, a new set of ideas could spread. We might once again learn to understand social systems as complex and organic structures that produce desirable emergent properties as a result of decentralized decision-making. The result probably won't look neat and orderly. It won't look "efficient." But it would be resilient and effective. It will get the job done and be adaptable enough to solve whatever new problems are yet to arise. It will do so by seeking and responding to feedback incessantly. It won't work off a single masterplan, but rather by multitude of experiments and discoveries. Those who accumulate capital under this framework *are capitalists.* They are individual actors in a broader network that look to increase its productive capacity through personal initiative.

Since under real capitalism, as we define it, healthy productive systems are expected to maintain or appreciate in value over time, the default assumption is conservation and the goal is accumulation. This naturally brings about a lower time preference as we believe whatever we contribute to a capital pool will reward us in the future. And, of course, in complete opposition to the interlocking vicious circles of debt, short-termism, exploitation, and fragility described throughout the book, but especially in Chapter Five, *The Capital Strip Mine,* and Chapter Seven, *A Capital Renaissance,* here we would expect a virtuous circle. Widespread low time preference contributes to the nurture, replenishment, and growth of capital stocks.

Price deflation can, after all, be conceived of as the reward we reap from providing a depth of liquidity to a store of value which innovators can redeploy in tackling fundamental uncertainty with judgment and skill. When innovators increase the quantity or quality of economic output and trade the surplus on a sound and open monetary network, everybody benefits. Everybody owned some share of all "coins," and the value traded on the network has increased. We win. And interestingly we start to grasp that there are such second-order benefits from participating in a growing network. Ultimately, we shift our attention away from the current flow of that network and towards its stock, instead.

This is straightforward for economic stocks. In this chapter we do our best to extend Gras's reasoning to many more abstract areas than the merely economic in which, *something is being produced and then saved, not used up*. We will likewise endeavor to emulate Gay; to remain mindful of, "the interaction of all manifestations of the human spirit, economic, legal, political, social and religious, during each period of history."

Across the areas of social, urban, and cultural capital, we will attempt to analyze the effects of an appreciation for nurturing, replenishing, and growing these stocks; how time can be crystallized, the memory of experimentation and discovery preserved, and an organic language allowed to evolve, all in a peer-to-peer network of voluntary cooperation.

We will praise a handful of individuals who championed this cause across each domain and were active in fighting against some or other high-modernist, client/server modeled, centrally conceived and decreed imposition of capital strip mining. These individuals may not have thought of themselves this way, and furthermore it may read as odd or out of place, but in standing against the destruction of memory and for the creation of capital, these were capitalists.

Ties That Bind

"It is easier to build strong children than to repair broken men."
— Frederick Douglass

The first direct use of the phrase "social capital" has been attributed to Lyda Judson Hanifan in his 1916 essay, "The Rural School Community Center":

> In the use of the phrase social capital, I make no reference to the usual acceptation of the term capital, except in a figurative sense. I do not refer to real estate, or to personal property or to cold cash, but rather to that in life which tends to make these tangible substances count for most in the daily lives of a people, namely, goodwill, fellowship, mutual sympathy and social intercourse among a group of individuals and families who make up a social unit [...] If he may come into contact with his neighbor, and they with other neighbors, there will be an accumulation of social capital, which may immediately satisfy his social needs and which may bear a social potentiality sufficient to the substantial improvement of living conditions in the whole community.

Social capital is the productive potential of social networks to create value. It emerges from trust and the willingness to cooperate. We would argue that it is, alongside environmental capital, a prerequisite for all other forms of capital accumulation. We can scarcely imagine much accumulation occurring in a world where atomized individuals never meet nor cooperate, nor where all interaction is coerced. Cooperation is a form of consensus; it is an interpersonal compromise and personal sacrifice directed towards a positive sum game of a resultingly multiplied stock of productive capital. Neither isolation nor coercion, but cooperation alone creates sustained compounding across time and space. Not to mention it is concordant with human nature. Humans are social beings, but are not homogeneous.

We might imagine a spectrum of human interaction along which interpersonal compromise and personal sacrifice increases from none all the way to total. At the middle is a communitarian sweet spot. Individuals interact rather than ignore one another, but they do so only voluntarily. This is essentially the textbook definition of "anarchy" — in the political sense rather than vernacular English in which it rather more unfortunately connotes something like "chaos." It is a cultural perversion of the normalization of toxic fiat bigness and forsaking responsibility that this is deemed in any way "extreme." In our conception and framing, this is not at all an extreme but very much a delicate balance. The true "extremes" are violence or no interaction at all.[172]

We suspect the popular confusion on this point once again originates in contemporary academic economics, or at least in its recent historical roots. That individuals "*seek to maximize their utility*," or even describing cooperation in general or capital accumulation as applied to economics as a "*positive sum game*" without inquiring as to the causal process that generates any sum, positive or otherwise, is foolish in the extreme. It is simply unrealistic. It is ignoring if not rejecting Gay's insistence "that whole complex of motives and interests, varying among themselves in intensity at different occasions and times should always be taken into account by the investigator of any form of human behavior."

Cooperation is necessarily sacrifice for the very simple reason that people are different. They have different experiences and they want different things, not only of the available scarce resources but, even more irreconcilably, *of each other*. Cooperation over a period of time greater than *this very moment* likely requires a promise, which is a sacrifice of that agent's own future wants and preferences, which by then may have changed.

In economics, the positive sum is merely a potential. Recall our rigorous and avowedly methodologically individualist walkthrough of capital formation in Chapter Four, *Wittgenstein's Money*: Savings become "investment" by wrestling with uncertainty and seeking to create productive capacity with the potential to increase the capital stock, and ideally eventually reward the original contribution of the saver. That a "return" is generated at all indicates a "positive sum," but note two points: Returns are never guaranteed as all economic activity is fundamentally uncertain, and savers hoping for a return must turn their liquid money over to an entrepreneur. The act of transforming liquid, fungible money into illiquid, nonfungible capital is anti-entropic.

The entrepreneur *does work* in suffusing money with her creativity and agency to transform disorder into order. But she does so *specifically* and *locally*. She has a purpose and a goal in mind. One can save in general but one cannot invest in general. One must invest *in something*. Hence one must make a decision amongst unboundedly many options — a decision that by definition would not have been taken by those others whose cooperation is required because, if they had arrived at the same choice, they would have made it on their own.

Navigating uncertainty *requires* cooperation, respect, and trust, and, as explained in Chapter Four, *Wittgenstein's Money*, and elaborated upon in Chapter Five, *The Capital Strip Mine*, the fundamental uncertainty of economics comes about in the first place due to the individual making the purposeful decision to engage in a network whose aggregate of knowledge, time, and energy is well beyond what she could ever bring to bear herself. She joins knowing she will have to bid her time and energy — or her *stored time and energy* — against others for the same scarce resources as others, but that there will *probably* be a positive sum, and it will *probably* be shared fairly should cooperation remain honest and trustworthy.

But, as advertised, we would argue this reasoning around social dynamics goes well beyond economics. An important step towards this realization may be that there is nothing intrinsically selfish about a desire to participate in a positive-sum game. The motivation of the agents *may be selfish*, but it may not. If so, this need not be read in a derogatory sense as "uncaring of others." Maybe it should be read that way, or maybe it simply means: *apathetic to others and solely interested in oneself.*

But maybe the agents are not motivated by "selfishness," in whole or even in part. Maybe the growth in capital stocks is deemed by its contributors as a good in and of itself. Or perhaps it is specifically a *social good*, part and parcel with the sacrifice and compromise that led to its creation. We are very much not claiming to know. In fact, we are claiming *not to know*, because this is unknowable. The idea that it can be derived from axioms, as the degenerate fiat economist would try to, is farcical. Human beings are not algorithms; their capacity for creativity, intuition, morality, and the recognition of the value of minds beyond their own cannot be modeled — except poorly and by a charlatan.

In *On Human Conduct*, Michael Oakeshott drives this point home entirely without reference to economic activity, writing,

> Of course, what is true of an agent's diagnosis of his situation is true also of his response to it. his act is ineluctably his own and its outcome will unavoidably be himself in a new situation, but it does not follow that what he intends, the meaning of his action, must be a self-gratification. For to act is to choose, and where there is choice there may be decision to perform an action whose meaning is the imagined and wished-for satisfaction of wants which are not the agent's own but those of another. And it is in virtue of his character as a reflective consciousness, and not because his "will" is "free" or because of his "sympathy" for others, that an agent is not bound to care only for his own interests. Agents are related to one another in terms of understandings, not neuro-physiological organizations or of suppositious gregarious "instincts"; they may care for one another because they can think of one another. The myth of the necessarily egocentric agent is a denial of agency.

"Private property" is a form of personal sacrifice and interpersonal compromise from which we might reasonably claim economic activity stems, in the sense that scarcity necessitates restraint and invites cooperation. But we would argue — and we expect Oakeshott would whole-heartedly agree — that this is simply a special case of respecting the agency of others in a far more holistic and spiritual sense. We do not restrain from theft or destruction because these are wrongs against property, nor do we avoid breaching contracts because doing so is to slight the paper on which the contract is written or the language in which it is spoken. Nor are we exclusively motivated by our own longer-term selfishness that aspires to an intact reputation — some may be all of the time, and all may be some of the time, but as Oakeshott argues, to propose this as a universal motivation is essentially to deny agency, to say we would all lie, cheat, and steal, all of the time, if only we knew for sure we would get away with it.

Rather, we restrain from theft, destruction, and breach of contract because we respect the agency of others. It is this very act of respect that creates worthwhile trust because it is offered with nothing expected in return. It is a good, in and of itself. It is both a moral good and an economic good — which might seem callous, but we believe is as concise and as helpful a definition of "social capital" as can be found. It immediately resolves an apparent contradiction between the private and the public: Nobody *owns* society, so how can one contribute "capital" in at all an analogous manner to the economic activity described in depth thus far? What could it even conceivably mean to be a "social capitalist"?

We think it is perfectly reasonable, if a little abstract, to think of "society" — or perhaps a little more precisely, the trust on which a well-functioning society operates — as a kind of common pool resource, just as we argued of *money* in Chapter Seven, *A Capital Renaissance*. Society is a network of which one is a part. And, of course, there is a clear relation: Trust is only necessary due to uncertainty, and money is a social institution whose function is to allow individuals to wrestle with uncertainty effectively, *and socially*. Our argument is very simply — and hopefully uncontroversially — that money does not solve all social problems. In particular, given *money is not capital*, there are forms of capital whose nurture, replenishment, and growth requires more than money, or perhaps do not require money at all. Social capital is one such.

Social capitalists are individuals whose actions encourage the accumulation of trust in social networks to which they belong. This may take the form of proposing improvements or amendments to (non-monetary and non-economic) social practices that other network participants are free to adopt or ignore. Or it may simply arise from consistently and visibly demonstrating trustworthiness that others are inspired to emulate, hence reproduce, hence help to grow. It might be thought that a dictator could build social capital by mandating that institutions under his command operate both more trustworthily themselves, and promote trustworthiness in general.

But we would argue this is insufficient; it is too far along the spectrum of personal sacrifice and interpersonal compromise and is ultimately tyranny, no matter how superficially pleasant the result. As with "anarchy" above, we mean the word "tyranny" in the political science sense of "absolute coercive power," rather than the vernacular English of something along the lines of: *cruel, unreasonable, and oppressive government*. The latter may very well also be the case, and, if anything, the force of our argument in this section rests on distinguishing the two: The latter is *overwhelmingly likely to eventually result* from the former. Absolute coercive power does not allow for social capital to develop naturally, and is likely, if not certain, to eventually destroy whatever social capital it originally encountered. A dictator may be a social planner —

and may even be a highly competent and effective social planner, in the short run — but he is not a social capitalist.

Throughout history, humans' ability to create social capital has always been linked to de Soto's understanding of capital as fundamentally being an idea: a layer of abstract consensus by which humans subjectively contextualize objective reality. As Yuval Harari explains in his bestseller *Sapiens*:

> Fiction has enabled us not merely to imagine things, but to do so collectively. We can weave common myths such as the biblical creation story, the Dreamtime myths of Aboriginal Australians, and the nationalist myths of modern states. Such myths give Sapiens the unprecedented ability to cooperate flexibly in large numbers. Ants and bees can also work together in huge numbers, but they do so in a very rigid manner and only with closer relatives. Wolves and chimpanzees cooperate far more flexibly than ants, but they can do so only with small numbers of other individuals that they know intimately. Sapiens can cooperate in extremely flexible ways with countless numbers of strangers. That's why Sapiens rule the world, whereas ants eat our leftovers and chimps are locked up in zoos and research laboratories.

The first social capitalists willed the idea of a tribe into existence by articulating a representative symbol of the reality of natural affinities and kin selection, just like a lawyer creates physical capital by registering a property in a registry. Once the tribe, as a concept, was born, it existed in people's minds and could be nurtured, replenished, and grown. It became possible to give your extra fish to someone you didn't know well because you understood it built out trust in the network. You may have stood to benefit from it in the future, or you may have valued the trust as a good in and of itself. Neanderthals, who were considerably more matter-of-fact guys and gals, limited their groups to close relatives, stopping capital compounding in its tracks.[173]

This gradual capital accumulation continued for thousands of years until specialization, trade, and the emergence of money. This all highlights the intellectual poverty of the overly economic approach to capital. A factory may be the first example that springs to mind, or perhaps a derivatives market, but all is rooted in *land* and in *trust*. We might even say that *money* is actually a highly specific form of capital that functions as an institutional technology to solve for the emergent problem of the social scalability of trade, to once again cite Nick Szabo's excellent, *Money, Blockchains, and Social Scalability*. In a nod to Carl Menger who explored the origins of money as an historical social phenomenon, Harari echoes this, writing,

> Trade may seem a very pragmatic activity, one that needs no fictive basis. Yet the fact is that no animal other than Sapiens engages in trade, and all the Sapiens trade networks about which we have detailed

evidence were based on fictions. Trade cannot exist without trust, and it is very difficult to trust strangers.

Over millennia, we see two forces in constant dialogue molding human societies, which we might think to characterize as *bottom-up* and *top-down*.[174] The bottom-up pressure is that of belonging. It is a sense of being a part of a larger group. It lives in Men's hearts. The top-down force is violence, often wielded by an ambitious conqueror. We propose the image of a *dialogue* because the sustained violence of a state can be thought to create a nation and the emotional power of a nation can be imagined to birth a state.

After the agricultural revolution, we find human societies in large settled tribes called city-states. As Ernest Renan argues in his essay, "What is a Nation?" Tribes like Athens or Sparta were an "extension of the family," where, "all citizens were related to a certain degree." These were prototypical bottom-up social networks. The bootstrapping of social capital by which they came into being was largely peer-to-peer. Their founders were social capitalists. Contrast this to the Roman Empire.

Again, Renan explains, it was "first formed by violence, then maintained by interest." It is the imposition of one city-state's will on "this large gathering of cities, of entirely different provinces." It was top-down: It was a server dictating to clients. Even though it led to a flourishing of (economically) capitalist trade around the Mediterranean, it was not sustained by social capitalists. The network was not grown organically by its members. While *Pax Romana* was appreciated by many, it remained imposed by fiat and from a central point of failure. All roads lead to Rome, they said. So, what if Rome fell? So would the entire network. Top-down institutions depend on a constant projection of strength. Ironically, this is precisely what makes them brittle. They depend on a high flow, eventually depleting their own stocks in the process.

Bottom-up institutions however grow by enriching their stock. It is a slower, more tentative process. It builds over a far longer time horizon. But once built, they last. Their energy is potential. They are capital. An obvious contrast to the institution of the Roman Empire is Christianity, both in terms of contemporary coexistence and relationship and historical legacy — possibly even *irony*. Renan writes, "Christianity, with its universal and absolute character, works more effectively in that same direction."

As Christianity spread in its early years, and as with the growth of many religions, it tended to form a relatively homogeneous dimension of belief and interaction rooted in its core tenets. While its adherents may have been of different ethnicities, involved in different social structures and economic networks, Christianity nonetheless provided a common language or protocol that if facilitated cooperation. Even if the initial proselytizing is violent, religious beliefs eventually embed themselves in values, forming a consensus, enabling easier cooperation, and spreading over time and space. It is no coincidence, but is rather more likely a kind of reproductively beneficial mutation, that every major religion of which we are aware explicitly preaches humility and restraint.

Our praise elsewhere in the book of the principles of Islamic finance picks up on what is arguably an epistemic version of this basic behavioral tenet. Excessive interest-bearing debt is neither humble nor restrained; it is avaricious. It preys on the weak and plays with the fire of fundamental economic uncertainty. We have presented this view elsewhere as a truism of healthy economic activity, but in keeping with the theme of this chapter, it is every bit as much a moral, spiritual, and religious truth as an economic one.

Furthermore, these traits are not arrived at from a calculus, nor from their purely aesthetic appeal. Their value is practical, and it seems overwhelmingly likely to us — if probably historically unknowable — that those cultures that embodied these virtues practically thrived on account of them, and spread the virtues practically on account of their thriving. With the growing strength of their stock over longer and longer periods, so grew their ability to repurpose useful flows, but the stock was always the point.

Recall from Chapter Four, *Wittgenstein's Money*, that the *meaning* of profit is greater enabled investment: This applies just as well to social capital, if not with even greater importance. Those cultures that instead promoted short-termism and flow maximization depleted their social and environmental capital, eroded away the trust of their citizens and the health of their soil, and went extinct — exactly as our degenerate fiat society now risks. Hence, in an ironic if predictable twist, Christian love preaching that "[t]here is neither Jew nor Gentile, neither slave nor free, nor is there male and female, for you are all one in Christ Jesus,"[175] proved more scalable and durable than Roman force. A messy peer-to-peer Christian network fed mostly by the bottom-up adoption of ideas outlived the client-server model of a centrally-planned Roman Empire.

This makes for an interesting contrast to the more mature state — we might say more the *oppressive* state — of Christianity as caricatured in *The Grand Inquisitor*, the story within a story, told by Ivan to his brother Alyosha in Fyodor Dostoyevsky's masterpiece, *The Brothers Karamazov*. We will assume some familiarity so as not to retell the entirety of what is widely deemed to be one of the most brilliant passages in world literature. Within the story (within the story!) The Grand Inquisitor can be thought of as tempting Christ with a malicious perversion of the logic just outlined. The Inquisitor puts it to Christ that human beings cannot handle freedom, scoffing,

> Instead of taking over men's freedom, you increased it still more for them! Did you forget that peace and even death are dearer to man than free choice in the knowledge of good and evil? There is nothing more seductive for man than the freedom of his conscience, but there is nothing more tormenting either. And so, instead of a firm foundation for appeasing human conscience once and for all, you chose everything that was unusual, enigmatic, and indefinite, you chose everything that was

beyond men's strength, and thereby acted as if you did not love them at all — and who did this? He who came to give his life for them! Instead of taking over men's freedom, you increased it and forever burdened the kingdom of the human soul with its torments. You desired the free love of man, that he should follow you freely, seduced and captivated by you. Instead of the firm ancient law, man had henceforth to decide for himself, with a free heart, what is good and what is evil, having only your image before him as a guide — but did it not occur to you that he would eventually reject and dispute even your image and your truth if he was oppressed by so terrible a burden as freedom of choice?

He then argues precisely that the Christianity *of Christ*, and of Christ's gift of freedom, *could not scale* on its own and required the promotion of a centralized institution that, in turn, demanded subjugation, arguing,

And so, turmoil, confusion, and unhappiness—these are the present lot of mankind, after you suffered so much for their freedom! Your great prophet tells in a vision and an allegory that he saw all those who took part in the first resurrection and that they were twelve thousand from each tribe. But even if there were so many, they, too, were not like men, as it were, but gods. They endured your cross, they endured scores of years of hungry and naked wilderness, eating locusts and roots, and of course you can point with pride to these children of freedom, of free love, of free and magnificent sacrifice in your name. But remember that there were only several thousand of them, and they were gods. What of the rest? Is it the fault of the rest of feeble mankind that they could not endure what the mighty endured? Is it the fault of the weak soul that it is unable to contain such terrible gifts? Can it be that you indeed came only to the chosen ones and for the chosen ones? But if so, there is a mystery here, and we cannot understand it. And if it is a mystery, then we, too, had the right to preach mystery and to teach them that it is not the free choice of the heart that matters, and not love, but the mystery, which they must blindly obey, even setting aside their own conscience. And so, we did. We corrected your deed and based it on miracle, mystery, and authority. And mankind rejoiced that they were once more led like sheep, and that at last such a terrible gift, which had brought them so much suffering, had been taken from their hearts. Tell me, were we right in teaching and doing so? Have we not, indeed, loved mankind, in so humbly recognizing their impotence, in so lovingly alleviating their burden and allowing their feeble nature even to sin, with our permission? Why have you come to interfere with us now?

The inquisitor's torment is the classic emotional manipulation of totalitarianism: To present what we have described as a spectrum of sacrifice and compromise as, in fact, a binary; the danger of total isolation, total selfishness, total freedom, and totally distributed and spontaneous organization is *so great*, and the damage to society from allowing even its possibility *so extreme*, the argument goes, that we must opt for total centralization instead.

Totalitarians tend not to use the word "tyranny" even though that is exactly what they mean, and they tend to avoid or even to outright lie about the unfortunate reality that the only way to achieve this is with violence. They claim they are engaged in science, yet even their moral — or *immoral* — propositions can transparently be shown to be nothing of the sort. Furthermore, anybody who opposes the centralized, client/server, top-down, pseudoscientific scheme of the would-be tyrant is not to be entertained but must be suspected of, and vilified for, only the most egregious selfishness and anti-social tendencies, if not also stupidity in the face of rejecting Science™.

The totalitarian habitually distracts from the false premise at the root of his actually logical case with irrelevant emotional bargains, haphazardly employing shame, guilt, fear, anger, envy, pride, and temptation. He only speaks of virtue while only exploiting vice, and ensuring the pull of sin is kept front of mind in those being manipulated. He is, in short, devilish.

Personal Sacrifice and Interpersonal Compromise

"The scientific elite is not supposed to give orders. Yet there runs through all of them a clear notion that questions of policy can be made somewhat nonpartisan by the application of science. There seems little recognition that the contributions of social science to policy-making can never go beyond staff work. Policy can never be scientific, and any social scientist who has risen to an administrative position has learned this quickly enough. Opinion, values, and debate are the heart of policy, and while fact can narrow down the realm of debate, it can do no more. "And what a terrible world it would be! Hell is no less hell for being antiseptic. In the 1984 of Big Brother, one would at least know who the enemy was — a bunch of bad men who wanted power because they liked power. But in the other kind of 1984 one would be disarmed for not knowing who the enemy was, and when a day of reckoning came the people on the other side of the table wouldn't be Big Brother's bad henchmen; they would be a mild-looking group of therapists who, like the Grand Inquisitor, would be doing what they did to help you."
— William H. Whyte, *The Organization Man*

In *The Organization Man,* William Whyte makes the case that the bigness of the American corporation[176] creates all manner of subtle erosion of individualism and communitarianism alike, and instils a kind of pseudo-social isolation. One consequence is the rise of scientism, as described above, and ending on the startling invocation of Dostoyevsky.[177]

While the inquisitor's telling of Christianity is obviously false as a historical assessment, Dostoyevsky is cunning in making sure to have the inquisitor reveal himself and his philosophy to be *explicitly* anti-human. The inquisitor mocks Christ's reverence for mankind, and even admits that what the Church ought to aspire to is a tyrannical regime purporting to represent God, but operated according to the principles of the Devil. In what is probably the extract's most oft-cited moment, Christ, who has said nothing throughout as he is berated by the inquisitor, kisses him on the lips. We would, in general, recommend exactly this treatment for any interactions with an aspiring totalitarian: Do not accept their premises, do not argue, and do not engage, because the offer of engagement is in fundamentally bad faith. It is not a conversation but an attempt to manipulate; you will get nowhere besides being deliberately confused, guilted, and shamed. It is as likely as anything that the purpose of the exchange is not even to convince you of anything but to make an example of dissenters for whatever audience has been assembled.[178] What you should do is what Dostoyevsky has Christ do: Demonstrate only that you recognize and value their agency as fellow human beings, then leave.

The totalitarian position may well be conceived as the point of the false binary of compromise and sacrifice such that neither *voice* nor *exit* are allowed, to borrow terms from Albert Hirschman's classic of political economy, *Exit, Voice, and Loyalty*. As concisely as possible, and certainly to not do justice to a nuanced argument and fascinating book, Hirschman roughly means by "voice" something akin to "politics": expression of opinion, debate, lobbying, and social maneuvering as a decision-making procedure. By "exit" he simply means *leaving*, removing oneself from the organization in question which, depending on the type of organization in the first place may mean physically relocating or just rescinding membership. Of organizations that disallow either, Hirschman offers the following:

> There are probably no organizations that are wholly immune to either exit or voice on the part of their members. The ones that have been listed [in a table on the same page], in their intended structure, make no explicit or implicit allowance for either mechanism. Exit is here considered as treason and voice as mutiny. Such organizations are likely to be less viable, in the long run, than the others; exit and voice being illegal and severely penalized, they will be engaged in only when deterioration has reached so advanced a stage that recovery is no longer either possible or desirable. Moreover, at this stage, voice and exit will be undertaken with such strength that their effect will be destructive rather than reformist.

We think Hirschman's explanation here can readily be understood as implying that a totalitarian state will tend towards making bottom-up capital formation or accumulation impossible, be it economic, social, or otherwise, spurring depreciation, and inducing an accelerated final collapse.

Importantly, it is much easier to destroy capital than to create it. Indeed, it is arguably much easier to destroy *anything* than to create it. Commitment to the project of civilization requires the restraint from the sheer thrill of destruction due to an intellectually, morally, and spiritually-motivated recognition of its costs: Not just that something or other has been destroyed, but that the act of destruction makes is significantly less likely anything like it will ever be created again.

We have previously explained de Soto's core thesis in *The Mystery of Capital* that "free trade" cannot be imposed by fiat in an otherwise unfree society and be expected to produce economic miracles overnight. What is needed is functioning institutions of capital, which in turn, as described, require trust. Likewise, trust itself takes time to grow. It cannot be willed into existence by decree any more than yelling at a flower will make it blossom any faster. We would argue that even seemingly "economic" capitalism must be sense checked against the requisite social roots. In *The Shock Doctrine*, Naomi Klein criticizes the blatant sham of post-communist corruption in newly "capitalist" Russia, noting,

Several of Yeltsin's ministers transferred large sums of public money, which should have gone into the national bank or treasury, into private banks that had been hastily incorporated by oligarchs. The state then contracted with the same banks to run the privatization auctions for the oil fields and mines. The banks ran the auctions, but they also bid in them — and sure enough, the oligarch-owned banks decided to make themselves the proud new owners of the previously public assets.

And there is nothing particularly special about Russia. Practically identical accounts could be given of fellow former Warsaw Pact nations such as Ukraine, Belarus, Bulgaria, Macedonia, Romania, and Albania, now routinely cited as, collectively, by far the most corrupt nations in Europe, trailing only Russia as the undisputed and runaway leader. What is more interesting amongst formerly communist nations is arguably which *do not suffer* rampant corruption. The obvious examples are Lithuania, Latvia, Estonia, and Poland, all of which are fascinating on account of their well-documented *resistance* to the capital-destructive force of communism.

The modern history of Eastern Europe is clearly an enormous topic in its own right to which we cannot do justice here. But the reader is encouraged to contemplate that likely the simplest explanation — while not at all exhaustive — of why the latterly listed nations fared so differently to their peers — both under communism and after — is that they each had a far deeper stock of social capital in the form of disparate cultural identity, religion, or both. Unlike their unfortunate neighbors, the populations of these nations were committed to nurturing and replenishing (if not quite growing) these stocks even and especially under active oppression and likely further penalty if caught. In the more unfortunate cases listed above, whatever social capital existed prior to communist annexation was decimated and has not returned, the void filled instead by mafiosi.

If less intrinsically violent, at-root similar follies are so commonplace in the West that we likely no longer pay much attention. Legal scholar and prolific political blogger Glenn Reynolds made the following astute observation in a 2010 post:[179]

> The government decides to try to increase the middle class by subsidizing things that middle class people have: If middle-class people go to college and own homes, then surely if more people go to college and own homes, we'll have more middle-class people. But homeownership and college aren't causes of middle-class status, they're markers for possessing the kinds of traits — self-discipline, the ability to defer gratification, etc. — that let you enter, and stay, in the middle class. Subsidizing the markers doesn't produce the traits; if anything, it undermines them.

What Reynolds identifies here is the effect of a top-down decree to skip to the reward of the nurture, replenishment, and growth of social capital. Tragically, the effect is to undermine the process of ever hoping to generate this reward in a bottom-up manner — which is, of course, to say, *sustainably*. There is surely an uncomfortable similarity to the Russian corruption outlined by Klein. Indeed, this represents a kind of moral rather than legal or economic corruption; it is a high-modernist scheme to *pretend* to possess social capital. As Scott would say, to make it *visually resemble* what a stock of social capital would probably look like, rather than functionally. It derives from aesthetic knowledge, not practical. Practically, it will be little more than a cargo cult. When the unexplained, unexamined, and misunderstood support for the scheme dries up, it will collapse.

Aleksandr Solzhenitsyn famously wrote that, "the line dividing god and evil cuts through the heart of every human being." It may sound trite but it demands emphasis in understanding how what we call social capital can even exist in the first place: Human beings are intrinsically neither good nor bad. They have free will and they respond to incentives. Just as with humility and restraint, every major religion preaches a variation of this fundamental tenet, and with strikingly good reason.

The most tragically simple way to make a human being behave selfishly is to destroy their incentives *not to be selfish in the first place.* And the simplest way to do *this* is to manipulate their environment and circumstances such that they can or must only think over short periods of time and without reference to the people and institutions that comprise their actual surroundings.

An obvious conception of what it means to *have a low time preference* is precisely to think beyond not just the current moment, but to think beyond oneself, to care about forms of gratification beyond the immediate and the biological, and that are rooted in an embrace of community and the fundamental compromise it entails. This is precisely the invitation of Abrahamic religion calling for charity and rejecting interest.

Abstaining from, for example, sex, drugs, alcohol, and the like, and committing one's time towards the more intangible and the more abstract, *makes one vulnerable*, because while the experience of a flow can be captured in the past and never taken away, stocks point to the potential of the future, and hence can always be destroyed. The very existence of stocks of any kind and of any value embodies restraint; restraint implies selflessness and humility; and selflessness and humility are the essence of low time preference.

In contrast to the degenerate fiat trope of *homo economicus,* it is natural for human beings to want to help one another, but only *provided* they are first assured of their own safety and sustenance. We can call this "selfishness" if we want to, but doing so is hardly helpful — it is biological reality. It was a trope in the Soviet Union that the women who worked in grocers and food facilities would go to work skinny and leave work fat, by stuffing their clothes with whatever they could get their hands on, lest they and their families starve on government rations.

The tragic irony of the totalitarian deceit is that the epidemic of widespread and unchecked selfishness against which the lying totalitarian proselytizes is unlikely to exist in any circumstances other than the deprivation caused by totalitarianism itself. Wealth comes from capital. The destruction of capital, whether from total coercion or total isolation, will lead to poverty one way or another.

It is only when personal sacrifice and interpersonal compromise are pushed so far as cooperation remains voluntary and consensus remains honest; when society is structured neither as atomized individuals nor as homogenized tyranny, but as bottom-up, dynamic community; when the state cedes authority and autonomy to organic and voluntary social institutions, that fruitful capital formation will take place, and from which prosperity has a chance of following.

Thomas Paine may well have put all this best in any written English, opening his polemical masterpiece *Common Sense* with the proclamation,

> Some writers have so confounded society with government, as to leave little or no distinction between them; whereas they are not only different, but have different origins. Society is produced by our wants, and government by our wickedness; the former promotes our happiness positively by uniting our affections, the latter negatively by restraining our vices. The one encourages intercourse, the other creates distinctions. The first a patron, the last a punisher.
>
> Society in every state is a blessing, but government even in its best state is but a necessary evil; in its worst state an intolerable one; for when we suffer, or are exposed to the same miseries by a government, which we might expect in a country without government, our calamity is heightened by reflecting that we furnish the means by which we suffer. Government, like dress, is the badge of lost innocence; the palaces of kings are built on the ruins of the bowers of paradise. For were the impulses of conscience clear, uniform, and irresistibly obeyed, man would need no other lawgiver; but that not being the case, he finds it necessary to surrender up a part of his property to furnish means for the protection of the rest; and this he is induced to do by the same prudence which in every other case advises him out of two evils to choose the least. Wherefore, security being the true design and end of government, it unanswerably follows that whatever form thereof appears most likely to ensure it to us, with the least expense and greatest benefit, is preferable to all others.

The state may plan, but the nation builds. People form a nation. Rulers form a state. The nation is common but private. It is a network owned and controlled in constituent parts by individuals, resting on the consensual adoption of values. We turn one final time to Renan for a moving description of the nation:

A nation is a soul, a spiritual principle. Two things which, properly speaking, are really one and the same constitute this soul, this spiritual principle. One is the past, the other is the present. One is the possession in common of a rich legacy of memories; the other is present consent, the desire to live together, the desire to continue to invest in the heritage that we have jointly received. Messieurs, man does not improvise. The nation, like the individual, is the outcome of a long past of efforts, sacrifices, and devotions. Of all cults, that of the ancestors is the most legitimate: our ancestors have made us what we are. A heroic past with great men and glory (I mean true glory) is the social capital upon which the national idea rests. These are the essential conditions of being a people: having common glories in the past and a will to continue them in the present; having made great things together and wishing to make them again. One loves in proportion to the sacrifices that one has committed and the troubles that one has suffered. One loves the house that one has built and that one passes on. The Spartan chant, "We are what you were; we will be what you are," is, in its simplicity, the abridged hymn of every fatherland.

Those individual social capitalists who nurture, replenish, and grow social networks by nourishing them with acts and ideas that other participants choose to adopt are the heroes that feed our collective imagination. These contributions sustain communities, tribes, cities, and, ultimately, nations so that they can foster trust within themselves, can communicate, and can cooperate.

A King Among Us

"Injustice anywhere is a threat to justice everywhere. We are caught in an inescapable network of mutuality, tie in a single garment of destiny. Whatever affects one directly, affects all indirectly."
— Martin Luther King Jr., *Letter from Birmingham Jail*

It is difficult to think of a greater hero in this respect than the Reverend Martin Luther King Jr., or a greater contributor to advocacy for the fostering of trust in a community or a nation, given few examples so clearly illustrate the willful destruction of social connections as segregation. By cordoning black Americans from all others, the United States for nearly a hundred years following the abolition of slavery still sustained two separate and unequal social networks. "Unequal" because the value of networks grows at a rate proportional to the value of its accumulated stock, social, economic or otherwise. Since black Americans were only ever around 10% of the population, and controlled a minuscule proportion of the total economic productive and financial capital, their capital stock was relegated to a much smaller network that was furthermore *kept poor* through coercion.[180]

In addition to this obvious *moral* tragedy and injustice, it is worth noting that the two disconnected networks were hence less valuable than an integrated network would have been. The extreme difficulty in generating bottom-up social capital caused racial tension and animosity, while top-down racist policymaking hindered the organic development of social capital by nipping interactions in the bud. King experienced this reality first-hand:

> From the age of three I had a white playmate who was about my age. We always felt free to play our childhood games together. He did not live in our community, but he was usually around every day; his father owned a store across the street from our home. At the age of six we both entered school — separate schools, of course. I remember how our friendship began to break as soon as we entered school; this was not my desire but his.[181]

King also added,

> If it had been possible to give Negro children the same number of schools proportionately and the same type of buildings as white children, the Negro children would have still confronted inequality in the sense that they would not have had the opportunity of communicating with all children. [...] The doctrine of separate but equal can never be.[182]

There was little "goodwill, fellowship, mutual sympathy and social interaction" as Hanifan described it. Individual initiative was often aborted by social pressures. This is the milieu King was reared in and sought to change. His life's work would be to mend the social fracture that had plagued America since its birth. In true capitalist fashion, his action was bottom-up and only political in the sense that by mobilizing thousands and convincing millions his message reached the capital's marble halls. King would almost certainly not have described himself this way, once saying, "I do recall, when I was about five years of age, how I questioned my parents about people standing in breadlines. I can see the effects of this early childhood experience on my present anticapitalistic feelings."[183]

But again, we attribute this to the effect on the public consciousness of the perverse success of the legacy of contemporary academic economics, combined, of course, with the casual tolerance of blatant institutional racism simultaneously present and normalized in the governing class. By his *"anticapitalistic feelings,"* King clearly means the atrocious combination of top-down economic planning, state sanctioned racism, and high time-preference atomic individualism altogether slapped with the label "capitalism," although we would argue it was nothing of the kind.

Years before King's *March on Washington*, it was through local and often economic pressures that he won his first victories. The Montgomery bus boycott used the immediacy of marketplace feedback to demonstrate to operators that segregation was unacceptable to its customers. During the Birmingham Campaign, pressure was put on segregated businesses to serve people equally irrespective of the color of their skin. King and the broader Civil Rights movement understood that boycotts created an immediate feedback loop that reverberated up the social and economic power structures. Money incentivized people to change and cooperate. It forced a reckoning with what consensuses were and were acceptable: What interpersonal compromise and personal sacrifice was just, as opposed to tyrannical.

At the core of King's message stood Christian love, asking the oppressed to see their oppressors as brothers in Christ and collectively turn the other cheek. Instead of violence begetting more violence, the Civil Rights movement respected the most fundamental expression of the agency of others: their thoughts. Change would not be imposed on the reluctant. It would first be realized in hearts and in minds, changed by action. Every black person walking to work instead of taking a segregated bus or ordering food in a segregated diner contributed to healing the racial divide. King's method of nonviolent resistance built local, then national support. Far beyond "raising awareness," the movement changed people's opinions and, in doing so, built social capital. The focus was on humanizing the oppressed and planting a seed of empathy in the oppressor — a tactic entirely deliberately adapted from the abolitionist movement over a hundred years earlier. King opposed both racists, who wanted to keep people apart, and black separatists, who looked to only to build social capital within their community. King's third way was reconciliation. It went against the natural survival instinct of fighting fire with fire. He fought destruction with creation; he called for true pacifism:

> True pacifism is [...] a courageous confrontation of evil by the power of love, in the faith that it is better to be the recipient of violence than the inflictor of it, since the latter only multiplies the existence of violence and bitterness in the universe, while the former may develop a sense of shame in the opponent, and thereby bring about a transformation and change of heart.[184]

Further, King explained:

> Our ultimate aim was not to defeat or humiliate the white man but to win his friendship and understanding. We had a moral obligation to remind him that segregation is wrong. We protested with the ultimate aim of being reconciled with our white Brothers.[185]

The Reverend Martin Luther King Jr. never failed to remind Americans of their shared experience. His was a revolutionary message similar to that of the Founding Fathers. It did not call on ethereal and new ideas born from the minds of intellectuals and decreed from on high. It was anchored in old traditions and beliefs. The Founders appealed to God's natural law and rights earned from the King. Martin appealed to the founding American promise:

> So even though we face the difficulties of today and tomorrow, I still have a dream. It is a dream deeply rooted in the American dream. I have a dream that one day this nation will rise up and live out the true meaning of its creed: We hold these truths to be self-evident, that all men are created equal.

We have quoted extensively in this section. Perhaps because our words feel meek in comparison to King's. We will close with his words, one last time, on the very essence of social capital, for King himself was undoubtedly a great social capitalist. In the end, it all comes down to understanding the other as like ourselves: not identical, nor incompatible. Similar but different. Fellow humans, with different experiences, different knowledge, and different but worthwhile agency. In a word, as peers:

> One day a man came to Jesus and he wanted to raise some questions about some vital matters of life. At points he wanted to trick Jesus, and show him that he knew a little more than Jesus knew and throw him off base. Now that question could have easily ended up in a philosophical and theological debate. But Jesus immediately pulled that question from midair and placed it on a dangerous curve between Jerusalem and Jericho. And he talked about a certain man who fell among thieves. You remember that a Levite and a priest passed by on the other side — they didn't stop to help him. Finally, a man of another race came by. He got

down from his beast, decided not to be compassionate by proxy. But he got down with him, administered first aid, and helped the man in need. Jesus ends up saying this was the good man, this was the great man, because he had the capacity to project the "I" into the "thou" and to be concerned about his brother.

Building for People

"If you say: 'Well, look, you're a feeling type, and I'm a thinking type, so let's not discuss that because we are always going to be on different sides,' then it removes from this discussion what I feel to be the absolute heart and soul of the matter when it comes to buildings. Now I don't want to deny at all what you are saying about personalities. But I really cannot conceive of a properly formed attitude towards buildings, as an artist or a builder, or in any way, if it doesn't ultimately confront the fact that buildings work in the realm of feeling. So when you say, 'Look you're that type, and I'm this type, and let's agree not to talk with one another about that fact,' what's the implication? Is the implication that you think that feeling is not related to buildings?"
— Christopher Alexander, *Contrasting Concepts of Harmony in Architecture*, debate with Peter Eisenman[186]

In 1947, the United Kingdom passed the Town and Country Planning Act. *Building permits* gave way to *planning permits*. Land ownership no longer conferred development rights. Local planning authorities became arbiters with a grand vision. That year, the United Kingdom stopped building and started planning.

Individuals building with a human perspective were replaced by civil servants planning from a bird's eye view. Two years later in the United States, the Housing Act was passed and, as Robert Caro puts it in *The Power Broker*, "For the first time in America, the government was given the right to seize an individual's property not for its own use but for reassignment to another individual for his use and profit."

The individual, thought to be driven by a selfish profit motive, was to give way to the enlightened central planner thought to be motivated only selflessly to maximize welfare. Private property rights were relegated to a second-tier concern. By centralizing power, the UK government also invited lobbying both from corporations which could mold rules to their advantage and individuals who could impinge on other's rights with *Not in my Backyard* (NIMBY) campaigns to stop, for example, farmers from properly developing their land.

The shift to architectural central planning (among many other equally awful varieties) after the Second World War was precipitated by three major developments: the spread of mass manufacturing, the rise of the automobile, and the success of exactly this mode of planning during the war.[187] Taken together, these forces remolded man's relationship with urban space. The automobile blurred the landscape into a green haze onto which we did not mind imposing industrial-scale monotony. Developments became grand affairs that fit in an even grander vision. The aesthetic dreams of intellectuals replaced the varied tastes of people.

Today, only one in three new homes in America is "self-built" by individuals. In the United Kingdom, the figure is an abysmal one in ten. A regulatory thicket makes it prohibitively difficult and costly for individuals to build. Large developers with glossy brochures have replaced individuals with a sketch of their "dream home." Housing thus first and foremost became a proposal on a planner's desk or sales on a developer's profit and loss statement. It became a flow. It no was longer conceived and built by people who saw their home as an asset they would own for decades, and which might remain in their family for centuries.

Roger Scruton captures this tragedy beautifully, arguing in his documentary, *Why Beauty Matters*, that "architecture that doesn't respect the past is not respecting the present, because it is not respecting people's primary need from architecture, which is to build a long-standing home."

The issue with modern housing isn't necessarily that it is built *by corporations*. After all, so are our phones and cars. The issue is that alignment is poor. Of course, perfect alignment of interest between companies and their customers never exists, no matter how free or how regulated a given market is. But we would argue some social structures and institutions certainly create more or less alignment.[188] One might think that a real estate agent is aligned with the seller. They are paid on commission and benefit from a higher price.

But we're forgetting one thing: time. Waiting another week for an offer $10,000 higher would only get the agent a few hundred dollars more. This is time that could be better spent on another sale. For the agent, each sale is a flow of which they receive a cut. For the seller, the sale is the liquidation of a stock the value of which they would ideally maximize. These are propositions that put very different values on *time*. The entity focused on flow is looking at immediate profit. The owner of a stock puts a high value on the future.

Similarly, when individuals build homes, they build a stock that they will likely hold for decades. Developers have an entirely different perspective. If something breaks when the home is twenty years old and the warranty is long expired, that is not their problem.

Figures 8 and 9: Cookie-cutter corporate developer builds, up close and birds-eye view (Images from Google Maps).

This difference in perspective can matter a great deal to the experience of living in a home or a place. This is not so just because something might break years down the line, but because the feeling of *being at home* itself may be fundamentally broken by the misalignment of incentives in crafting the original design. Once again reflecting de Soto's insight that *capital* is essentially a shared experience and the product of collective imagination, Ann Sussman and Justin B. Hollander insist on the importance of "narrative" to urban design in *Cognitive Architecture*,[189] writing,

> Imagining scenarios or stories and not actually acting on them is a significant attribute of the human narrative capacity. The term for this behavior is "decoupling" or "the separation of mental action from physical action." Biologists once again consider it highly advantageous. Decoupling allows us to imagine multiple narratives without "engaging the motor apparatus"; its existence has a huge role in allowing us to lead rich and diverse lives. Decoupling permits the creation of imaginative work which makes possible the foundation for the arts.
>
> Why does this matter for architecture or planning? It suggests one more way people consistently look for orientation and connections to their environment. Much as we seek out faces from infancy on, we look for ways to make attachments and derive meaning from our physical surroundings. Every plan and urban design has the potential to acknowledge and respond to this trait in some way or another, or as is frequently the case in built environments today, ignore it. One could make the argument that it is the inherent lack of a narrative quality in many of the post-war American suburbs, (as opposed to the earlier nineteenth-century street-car versions) that gives these areas their feelings of placelessness and anomie.

As captured by Sussman and Hollander, the history of the built environment in the twentieth century mirrors the path of money. Politicians want to keep housing "affordable," like central bankers want to keep prices "stable." Supply of both housing and money are centrally dictated as exemplified by the UK government's annual housing construction targets (i.e., a flow).[190] And naturally the whole affair is subsidized by self-referentially mispriced toxic loans, courtesy of commercial fractional reserve banks "guaranteed" by a central bank.

Control of the urban form is an ancient struggle. The Romans operated a centralized Empire. This is made clear from the cities and settlements they left behind. Military rationality was imposed on the land. Communal buildings and spaces occupied prominent central locations and were surrounded by orderly grids, as shown in the figures below. Following the Empire's collapse, property rights were *de facto* decentralized as the central government weakened. The result was local urban capitalists reappropriating their cities bit by bit. Some streets remained, although a little less straight. Blocks split. And new public spaces formed from communal compromises. Piazza Navona, one of Rome's top tourist attractions, follows the outline of an old stadium, as shown in Figure 10.

Figure 10. The City Shaped by Spiro Kostof.

Medieval post-Roman jumble proved more resilient than Ancient Roman rationality and efficiency. While a central vision can optimize for some variables, it struggles to cope with dynamism and complexity. Which is, of course, to say that it struggles with the growth of capital in all its forms. The result is efficient but brittle. Over the long-term, uncertainty forces adaptation and selects for successful small-scale experiments. This method of building dominates our history as Charles Marohn explains in *Strong Towns*:

> When we ponder the layout of ancient cities, we must acknowledge that they are the by-product of thousands of years of human tinkering. People came together in villages and tried different living arrangements. What worked, they copied and expanded. What didn't work, they discarded. That is, if those experiments hadn't already killed or disbanded them.
> The traditional way of building — the way they would have all intuitively understood as the only proper way to do things — used individual action to maximize the collective value of the place.

Beyond the aesthetic concerns, Marohn also explains that planners, unlike individual builders, cannot make financially viable cities. Large developments come with complex economic interdependencies that no simple model can capture. Just as planned economies suffer from an inability to tap into distributed knowledge, planned cities ignore the reality on the ground. Political expediency also biases planners towards "growth" at all cost (i.e., not real growth but mere *increase*). Marohn said:

> Each iteration of new growth creates enormous future liabilities for local communities, a promise that the quickly denuding tax base is unable to meet. Not only did these new areas need police and fire protection, street lights, libraries, and parks, but all those miles of roads, streets, sidewalks, curbs, and pipe; all those pipes, pumps, valves, meters,

culvert, and bridges would eventually need to be fixed and replaced. At the local level, we traded our long-term stability for near-term growth.

Under a healthy trial-and-error system, individual investors would add to private capital and pay taxes from its collective profits to finance common public infrastructure. But the great planning experiment since the Second World War wanted nothing to do with that. Decades on, it is interesting to see how planned towns have fared. In a 2002 report, the UK government noted the following:

> While many New Towns have been economically successful, most now are experiencing major problems. Their design is inappropriate to the 21st Century. Their infrastructure is ageing at the same rate and many have social and economic problems. Many are small local authorities which do not have the capacity to resolve their problems.

The first sentence of the quote above is pure gold. Never mind their objective failure in every other respect, they have been *economically* successful! There was "growth"! Look at all these people. Unfortunately, the towns are financially unviable. They are ugly and they were narrowly designed with the car in mind. Unplanned towns centuries older are proving more resilient and adaptable.

Under a social system respecting bottom-up organization, the easiest things to build are the smallest, such as a family home. They require little money, time, or coordination. Such structures receive instant feedback. There is no bailout. Large communal projects, on the other hand, are much more difficult endeavors to see through as they require political support. We might think to characterize the support as flowing from the governance principles of the common pool resource of the social capital of those affected — and even the cultural and aesthetic capital they may wish to preserve. Individuals, mindful of their strong property rights, will need to come to consensus. The need to sacrifice and compromise will be greater all around.

In a top-down system, the opposite is true. Building a home on a plot of land you own becomes more complicated than a developer building 500 "units" on a field or the government expropriating land to make room for a highway. Meanwhile, the central authority is shielded from knowing whether or not any given experiment has worked, for two reasons.

First, there is no perfect counterfactual to compare against. How much better would a street of unique homes be to one where they all looked the same? We cannot know for sure even though surveys show an overwhelming majority of Brits would rather live in old rather than new-build homes. Second, even if the experiment receives significant negative feedback, the government can simply decree and force adoption. Bailing out bankrupt developments or stopping individuals from building profitably alike kill any potential for fulfilled experimentation and discovery of social truths.

James Scott highlights this fundamental dichotomy in *Seeing Like a State,* lamenting the influence of the patron saint of top-down architecture and urban planning, Le Corbusier. Scott seems to see Le Corbusier's crime as more than just the disaster of his own architectural output and that he inspired, but in more psychological and even philosophical terms as deriving from a kind of despicable and solipsistic anti-humanism. As Oakeshott might have complained, Le Corbusier seemed to lack any respect for others' agency. Scott writes,

> Believing that his revolutionary urban planning expressed universal scientific truths, Le Corbusier naturally assumed that the public, once they understood this logic, would embrace his plan. The original manifesto of CIAM[191] called for primary school students to be taught the elementary principles of scientific housing: the importance of sunlight and fresh air to health; the rudiments of electricity, heat, lighting, and sound; the right principles of furniture design; and so on. These were matters of science, not of taste; instruction would create, in time, a clientele worthy of the scientific architect. Whereas the scientific forester could, as it were, go right to work on the forest and shape it to his plan, the scientific architect was obliged to first train a new clientele that would "freely" choose the urban life that Le Corbusier had planned for them.
>
> Any architect, I imagine, supposes that the dwellings she designs will contribute to her clients' happiness rather than to their misery. The difference lies in how the architect understands happiness. For Le Corbusier, "human happiness already exists expressed in terms of numbers, of mathematics, of properly calculated designs, plans in which the cities can already be seen." He was certain, at least rhetorically, that since his city was the rational expression of a machine-age consciousness, modern man would embrace it whole-heartedly.

Scott's critique of this flavor of high-modernism as applied specifically to urban planning leans heavily on the life and work of Jane Jacobs. Scott praises Jacobs's far superior attentiveness to precisely the agency Le Corbusier anti-humanly denies and rejects, as revealed in her appreciation of different forms of *order*, writing,

> A fundamental mistake that urban planners made, Jacobs claims, was to infer functional order from the duplication and regimentation of building forms: that is, from purely visual order. Most complex systems, on the contrary, do not. Display a surface regularity; their order must be sought at a deeper level [...]
>
> [...] At this level one could say that Jacobs was a "functionalist," a word whose use was banned in Le Corbusier's studio. She asked, "What function does this structure serve, and how well does it serve it?" The "order" of a thing is determined by the purpose it serves, not by a purely aesthetic view of its surface order. Le Corbusier, by contrast, seemed to have firmly believed that the most efficient forms would always have a

classical clarity and order. The physical environments Le Corbusier designed and build had, as did Brasília, an overall harmony and simplicity of form. For the most part, however, they failed in important ways as places where people would want to live and work.

An Immense Laboratory of Trial and Error

"You can draw any kind of picture you want on a clean slate and indulge your every whim in the wilderness in laying out a New Delhi, Canberra, or Brasilia, but when you operate in an overbuilt metropolis, you have to hack your way with a meat ax."
— Robert Moses, quoted in Robert Caro, *The Power Broker*

As wonderful a contrast as can be drawn between Jacobs and Le Corbusier, there perhaps exists no ideological clash in urban planning as emblematic as that pitting Jacobs against Robert Moses in New York City in the 1950s and 1960s. Jacobs championed localism. She was a resident of Greenwich Village who opposed the sweeping changes she experienced as a result of the Housing Act of 1949. Her methods, like those of King, were distinctly and unmistakably bottom-up. She organized neighborhood and citizen campaigns to redress the imbalance of the Housing Act by giving a voice to people whose property rights she felt had been weakened. Through her writings, she further spread awareness of her struggle and ideas. Her 1961 book *The Death and Life of Great American Cities* remains a classic of urban planning. What power she had was entirely organic. It came from people willingly listening to her and agreeing with what she said.

Opposite Jacobs, Moses was almost a caricature of centralized, coercive, and unaccountable power. He was a New York City public official, never elected, wielding enough power through the government departments he controlled to worry mayors and even the President of the United States of America. His departments could raise their own funds, giving Moses the ability to ignore criticism and, crucially, to deny the possibility of feedback. He planned, and decreed, from his ivory tower on Randall's Island between Manhattan and Long Island, because he knew best. As Robert Caro recalled in *The Power Broker*,

> Moses said that he was the antithesis of the politician. He never let political considerations influence any aspect of his projects — not the location of a highway or housing project nor the award of a contract or an insurance commission, he said. He would never compromise, he said. He never had and he never would.
> He was America's greatest road builder, the influential single architect of the system over which rolled the wheels of America's cars. And there was, in this fact, an irony. For, except for a few driving lessons he took in 1926, Robert Moses never drove a car in his life.

Jacobs and Moses may be the single best anthropomorphized embodiment of the conceptual conflict in the characteristics of social processes to which we have been drawing attention throughout the entire book, respectively: bottom-up versus top-down, process versus equilibrium, organic versus synthetic, dynamic versus static, experimentation versus modelling, discovery versus decree, evolution versus design; even, if somewhat anachronistically, peer-to-peer versus client/server.

From Jacobs's perspective, cities were, "an immense laboratory of trial and error." She saw planners as people who, "have ignored the study of success and failure in real life [...] and are guided instead by principles derived from the behaviour and appearance of towns." Their enduring conflict is practically ontological. Jacobs looks as what a city *is*. Moses dreams what a city *ought to be*. Jacobs accepts the irreducible complexity and uncertainty of the built environment. Moses viewed the problem as a complicated puzzle with clear solutions. As Jacobs said,

> Simple needs of automobiles are more easily understood and satisfied than the complex needs of cities, and a growing number of planners and designers have come to believe that if they can only solve the problems of traffic, they will thereby have solved the major problem of cities.

What planners get in the end, she argued, was a "[d]ishonest mask of pretended order, achieved by ignoring or suppressing the real order that is struggling to exist and to be served."

Scott praises and elaborates on this tendency in Jacobs's thought, arguing,

> Jacobs has a kind of informed respect for the novel forms of social order that emerge in many city neighborhoods. This respect is reflected in her attention to the mundane but meaningful human connections in a functioning neighborhood. While recognizing that no urban neighborhood can ever be, or should be, static, she stresses the minimal degree of continuity, social networks, and "street-terms" acquaintanceship required to knit together an urban locality. "If self-government in the place is to work," she muses, "underlying any float of population must be a continuity of people who have forged neighborhood networks. These networks are a city's irreplaceable social capital." […] It follows from this vantage point that even in the case of slums, Jacobs was implacably opposed to the wholesale slum-clearance projects that were so much in vogue when she was writing. The slum might not have much social capital, but what it did have was something to build on, not destroy. What keeps Jacobs from becoming a Burkean conservative, celebrating whatever history has thrown up, is her emphasis on change, renewal, and invention. To try to arrest this change (although one might try to modestly influence it) would be not only unwise but futile.

Jacobs described Ebenezer Howard, one of the founding figures of modern planning, as follows:

He conceived of good planning as a series of static acts; in each case the plan must anticipate all that is needed and be protected, after it is built, against any but the most minor subsequent changes. He conceived of planning also as essentially paternalistic, if not authoritarian. He was uninterested in the aspects of the city which could not be abstracted to serve his utopia.

As a kind of Devil's Advocate in defense of planners, let us offer that it is true valuable communal projects like highways or even parks will always face opposition. Some people will be negatively affected and will oppose any change. But we would argue that the reason people can block developments through NIMBY actions is because property rights were weakened and centralized in the first place. If a communal project would indeed add value to a community, that community would be in a position to offer to pay those affected so that they willingly cede their land for development.

The problem comes when such bottom-up feedback mechanisms are short-circuited. By taking only a top-down view, Jacobs said, paternalists "want to make impossibly profound changes, and they choose impossibly superficial means for doing so." This is the real problem. At first glance, we might think Moses too was a capitalist. He built lots, after all. But that is not enough. Without a proper feedback mechanism, he was flying blind. His methods clearly did not mobilize private initiative. The result, Robert Caro explains, was that,

> He had built more housing than any public official in history, but the city was starved for housing, more starved, if possible, than when he had started building, and the people who lived in that housing hated it — hated it, James Baldwin could write, "almost as much as the policemen, and this is saying a great deal." He had built great monuments and great parks, but people were afraid to travel to or walk around them.

Jacobs is understandably even less charitable in her assessment, writing in *Dark Age Ahead*,

> Robert Moses, the nearest thing to a dictator with which New York and New Jersey have ever been afflicted (so far), thought of himself as a master builder, and his much diminished corps of admirers still nostalgically recall him as that; but he was a master obliterator. If he had had his way, which he did not because of successful community opposition, one of Manhattan's most vibrant, diverse, and economically productive neighbourhoods, SoHo, would have been sacrificed to an expressway.

Accumulating capital of any variety is nigh impossible without small experiments feeding information back into an adaptable system. Jacobs appreciated the importance of the capital stock. She welcomed organic small-scale change but she rejected abrupt change imposed from outside. "Whenever the capital is lost, from whatever cause, the income from it disappears, never to return until and unless new capital is slowly and chancily accumulated," she said, clearly marking herself as a conscientious urban capitalist — that is, a nurturer and replenisher of urban capital — and of the most remarkable of recent times, at that.

A Quest for Social Truth

"Turn off 'Wet Ass Pussy' and turn on a Bitcoin podcast."
— Marty Bent, *Tales from the Crypt*

Culture is a common frame of reference. It is a corpus of symbols used to communicate. Culture is language, or the sounds and images we attach to ideas. It is stories with their archetypes embodying the codes and mores of encouraged and reprimanded behavior. But it is equally how we respond to these ideas and behaviors. In consuming culture, we create it, too. Culture is a web of metaphors, which we use to filter the raw information of the world into a distillation of the communal relevance of individual yet shared experience. "Metaphors make connections which are not contained in the fabric of reality but created by our own associative powers," Scruton argued. So, just like Hernando de Soto's physical capital, culture too is the product of our imagination.

Art is part of culture, and we might define art as the imaginative expression and communication of communal symbols and metaphors as sounds, shapes, or symbols. But the symbols and metaphors *must* be communal. Art that appeals only to its creator is objectively bad art, and a culture that celebrates bad art is an objectively bad culture, one unable to convey worthwhile imagination or to effectively communicate.

The creation of *good art* is necessarily mindful of interpersonal compromise and personal sacrifice because it is a quest for social truth. It speaks to the human condition, not the artist's condition. And yet it must be individual. It cannot be imposed or dictated because such a candidate "art" could not possibly be authentic. Art speaks to the shared experience of individuals compromising for mutual benefit, neither isolated nor oppressed.

As a form of capital, and, more specifically, a form of *language*, solipsistic art is gibberish, and totalitarian art is a social lie. Great art — *beautiful* art — emerges only from the delicate equilibrium of patient and respectful sacrifice, of a cultural commitment to the importance of capital stocks.

The value of art cannot be entirely "subjective" since it draws meaning from a common pool of shared reference and understanding. We see the accumulation of cultural capital as adding richness and depth to a people's common symbols and metaphors. We can conceivably deplete the cultural stock in obvious ways such as by literally, physically destroying works of art. But we can do so subtly also by elevating irony and derision beyond their station.

There is clear value in irony. In fact, *ironically*, appreciating its utility requires appreciating the objectivity of the value of art in the first place: Irony chides arts that has failed in its quest for truth, beauty, or goodness and provides a negative counterweight in support of communal standards. But to value irony as an end in and of itself is immature and toxic. Irony and derision can only exist in reference to that which they tear down.

Perversely, irony relies on some remains of cultural capital in order to coherently express its destructive message. If elevated beyond commentary and analysis to its own pedestal of artistic value, its essence become desacralization and the making trite of deep truths we might prefer to respect and conserve. George Steiner wonders aloud in, *In Bluebeard's Castle*, if a stock of social and cultural capital can become so dense and complex that the natural urge to irony can become overwhelming, asking,

> Is it reasonable to suppose that every high civilization will develop implosive stresses and impulses towards self-destruction? Does so delicately balanced, simultaneously dynamic and confined an aggregate as a complex culture tend, necessarily, towards a state of instability and, finally, of conflagration? The model would be that of a star which, after attaining a critical mass, a critical equation of energy exchanges between internal structure and radiant surface, will collapse inward, flaring out, at the moment of destruction, with just that magnitude of visible brilliance which we associate with great cultures in their terminal phase. Is the phenomenology of ennui and of a longing for violent dissolution a constant in the history of social and intellectual forms once they have passed a certain threshold of complication?

We would argue that the impression created by much of so-called "modern art" can be understood as the sort of joy one gets watching valuable things burn — a literal *conflagration*. It is the struggle of culture's *terminal phase*, with nothing left to say and no will to say it. A painting going up in flames undeniably possesses a violent, dangerous, uncomfortable beauty, but it requires there first *be a painting*. The more beautiful the painting, the more terrifying this catharsis.

On the other hand, modern art itself being set on fire is little more than a relief. The destruction of value through derision surely provides a transient joy. We laugh as a urinal is displayed next to real works of art.[192] But eventually we are left with nothing sacred, nothing we can take seriously. It all becomes a self-referential circle jerk of irony descending slowly into total relativism without an anchor; nothing *to which to be* relative; without a meaning; without a social truth in sight. Just incoherent jokes everybody nervously pretends to understand. "Breathe, breathe in the air. Don't be afraid to care," we hear on the opening song of Pink Floyd's magisterial *The Dark Side of the Moon*. A parent gives their newborn the first lesson in life: Live and care for something.

This, of course, is not an appeal for only art that makes us unequivocally happy, or that does not challenge us or cause us discomfort. If taken seriously the results of such a proposal would be utterly banal, while the alternative, if properly executed, is at least briefly funny. It is rather an appeal for art that is mindful of its cultural context, rather than that which takes an ignorance, a rejection, or even a mockery of context as its defining trait and the zenith of value to which it appeals. That something might "make you think" is the archetypal excuse of an objectively bad artist who has nothing to say in the first place and certainly nothing worth making you think *about*.

Good artists draw on what came before them, and contribute to it, manipulate it, challenge it, even. They suffer from what the literary critic Harold Bloom calls *the anxiety of influence*, the title of his first book.[193] Bloom believes artists are often moved to create due to the impression of beauty triggered in them by other, necessarily prior, great works, but they then struggle to act on this inspiration with genuine originality rather than with an output that is merely derivative of their own inspiration.[194]

This is sacrifice and compromise personified: One can always create something trivially original on the grounds of trivial individualism. The challenge is to create something meaningful *to others* and true to oneself that manages to say something new, or at least newly, to infuse just enough individual creative spark as to manipulate the common pool of symbols and metaphors into a novel combination. This is indescribably difficult, if not effectively impossible for most, and its achievement is the epitome of artistic talent.

Great art exists, and can only exist, as part of a corpus — with a defined place and role in a stock of cultural capital. Its honest creation requires at once an individualism and yet a submission to something greater than oneself. Steiner again wonders in, *In Bluebeard's Castle,* how best to analyze this characteristic, and if "religious" is quite right as a designation. It is an astute question given the etymology of "religion" in Medieval French and Latin as originally possessing not such an institutional meaning as we are used to, but a more transcendental notion of reverence and conscientiousness. Steiner writes,

> To argue for order and classical values on a purely immanent, secular basis is, finally implausible. In stressing this point Eliot is justified, and the Notes towards the Definition of Culture remain valid. But if the core of a theory of culture is "religious," that term ought not to be taken, as it so largely was by Eliot, in a particular sectarian sense. If only because of its highly ambiguous implication in the holocaust, Christianity cannot serve as the focus of a redefinition of culture, and Eliot's nostalgia for Christian discipline is now the most vulnerable aspect of his argument. I mean "religious" in a particular and more ancient sense. What is central to a true culture is a certain view of the relations between time and individual death.
>
> The thrust of will which engenders art and disinterested thought, the engaged response which alone can ensure its transmission to other human beings, to the future, are rooted in a gamble on transcendence. The writer or thinker means the words of the poem, the sinews of the argument, the personae of the drama, to outlast his own life, to take on

the mystery of autonomous presence and presentness. The sculptor commits to the stone the vitalities against and across time which will soon drain from his own living hand, art and mind address those who are not yet, even at the risk, deliberately incurred, of being unnoticed by the living.

Great art refers backwards and yet at once calls forwards. Bad art is a flow — transiently unimportant to either the past or the future — and "modern art" is evidently *so anxious* of its influence that it gives up and pretends it has none. But this means it is about nothing. It is a joke whose punchline must be told in a language that nobody speaks.

The canon — the stock of cultural capital — must be nurtured and replenished if it has any hope of growing — by which we can only mean incremental adventurous contributions which, if they are to be taken seriously or are to take themselves seriously, are surely anxious of their influence. Bloom writes in his later, *The Anatomy of Influence*,

> I happily plead guilty also to charges that I am an "incessant canonizer." There can be no living literary tradition without secular canonization, and judgments of literary value have no significance if not rendered explicit. Yet aesthetic evaluation has been viewed with suspicion by academic critics since at least the early part of the twentieth century. The New Critics deemed it too messy an undertaking for the professional scholar-critic [...] But the New Cynicism's roots in the social sciences have produced a more clinical posture still. To speak of the art of literature is viewed as a breach of professional responsibility. Any literary academic who issues a judgment of aesthetic value — better, worse than, equal to — risks being summarily dismissed as a rank amateur. Thus, the literary professoriate censures what common sense affirms and even its most hardened members acknowledge at least in private: there is such a thing as great literature, and it is both possible and important to name it.

The fashionable duplicity of his colleagues which Bloom here conveys as flippant humor has a dark parallel in Czesław Miłosz's masterpiece of psychological and political insight, *The Captive Mind*. A then-recent defector from communist Poland, Miłosz detailed with satirical genius the mental gymnastics in which soviet intellectuals engaged to try to outwardly justify what they clearly knew to be propagandistic lies. Miłosz labeled this act, *ketman*, after the apparently similar practice in nineteenth century Persia, as (questionably) reported by Arthur de Gobineau,[195] by which nearly every outwardly practicing Muslim concealed their disbelief in its strictest of tenets. The goal of this charade — far more so in Poland than in Persia — was to avoid plausible accusations of "wrongthink" — to borrow an apt Orwellian-ism — while attempting to retain some semblance of artistic credibility.

Clearly the latter failed also and produced the opposite extreme of the solipsistic extremity of "modern art": not art of *and only of* the individual, but art denying and only denying the individual. Art communicating symbols and metaphors of high-modernist, politically convenient, violently imposed central decree — *not* the symbols and metaphors of a common pool of cultural relevance but *despite* such a pool and *against* such a pool. In short, not a social truth but a social lie. Miłosz pillories those doomed to fail at producing true art under such conditions and details the techniques used even by the audience of such "art," who must also pretend to appreciate it if they wish to be otherwise left alone — precisely the behavior Solzhenitsyn raged against some twenty years later in, *Live Not by Lies*, published the last day before his exile from the USSR.

None of this is to say that great art cannot be cynical, or even profoundly sorrowful or tragic. Roger Scruton poignantly argues in his documentary, *Why Beauty Matters*, that

> The great artists of the past were aware that human life is full of chaos and suffering. But they had a remedy for this, and the name of that remedy was "beauty." The beautiful work of art brings consolation in sorrow and affirmation in joy. It shows human life to be worthwhile.

And later adds,

> Of course, this habit of dwelling on the distressing side of human life isn't new. From the beginning of our civilization, it has been one of the tasks of art to take what is most painful in the human condition and to redeem it in a work of beauty.

But it is to say that, no matter the depths of melancholy plumbed, the goal of great art is to celebrate the human, be it finding humor in absurdity, pathos in injustice, or inspiration in the overcoming of evil. Solzhenitsyn, a truly great artist, often captured all three simultaneously, for example satirizing Bloom's traditional opponents better than Bloom ever did himself, writing in *The First Circle* of the schoolgirl Clara, that "[t]heir teacher had advised them not to read Tolstoy's novels, because they were very long and would only confuse the clear ideas which they had learned from reading critical studies about him."

As much as we heartily endorse anti-communist political dissidence,[196] surely the epitome of art in the twentieth century as melancholic yet celebratory, and anxiously influenced yet daringly original, was the flood of innovation from the African American community in the United States. This explosion of form advanced from ragtime and blues, through jazz, and, with the latter infusion of gospel music, ended up directly influencing near enough every genre of popular music of the last fifty to one hundred years, from bebop to soul to funk to rhythm and blues to hip hop and rap.

Of course, this canon created such a rich stock of musical symbology and meaning as to seed a lineage of successful genres not even traditionally associated with the same original cultural and ethnic community, such as country music and rock and roll. Jazz in particular is rightly heralded not only as *by far* the greatest American contribution to art, but we would argue further is perhaps one of only two entirely original breakthroughs in artistic form achieved globally in the twentieth century, along with film.

Jazz exemplifies cultural merit. It is a synthesis between common codes and individual freedom. It is based on rhythms and progressions that allow musicians who have never met to play together, and yet its very essence is improvisation. It encourages and rewards spontaneous creativity. It is made anew every night. The beauty of jazz exists in a subtle balance between the communal and the personal. As Wynton Marsalis, the first ever jazz musician to win the Pulitzer Prize, says,

> The music helps you to develop individuality but it also teaches how to place your individuality in the context of service of a group of equally empowered individuals [...] jazz music is about dialogue [...] not only you get to play in solo but you have to know how to listen and be cool and accompany.

Jazz mirrored the country in which it was born, and more closely still the communities in which it was born: Common principles coordinating a complex and dynamic sea of improvisation that nobody could control. It was rooted in community but gave full exposure to its individual voices. Its origins in nineteenth century New Orleans present a literary, if nonetheless obvious, interpretation of its own form: It is a protest by a disparate collection of oppressed minorities against a form imposed on them. And yet the protest is not an outright rejection, but an audacious improvement. Marsalis tells journalist Jonathan Capehart in an appearance on his *Cape Up* podcast,

> The music was born in a time of segregation and prejudice and injustice, and the musicians were always engaged in a battle to bring the nation to its creed. The first public integration in the twentieth century was on a jazz band stand: Benny Goodman. The musicians were integrated long before the public and the culture was.[197]

Ted Gioia places roots of jazz's inherent cultural dynamism even earlier, writing in, *The History of Jazz,*

> The traces of the early Moorish incursion [into medieval Western Europe] may have laid the groundwork for the blossoming of African-American jazz more than a millennium later. Can it be mere coincidence that this same commingling of Spanish, French, and African influences was present in New Orleans at the birth of jazz? Perhaps because of this marked Moorish legacy, Latin cultures have always seemed receptive to fresh influences from Africa. Indeed, in the area of music alone, the number of successful African and Latin hybrids (including salsa,

calypso, samba, and cumbia, to name only a few) is so great that one can only speculate that these two cultures retain a residual magnetic attraction, a lingering affinity due to this original cross-fertilization.

The mantle of the genre of cultural content most clearly associated with the African American community in the US, once held by jazz, seems today to have been passed to rap and hip hop. The appreciation of canon, of context, of straining to balance individuality with community, and of celebrating improvisation within a recognizable form lends itself to an equally worthwhile rejection of the so-called "conservative" culture war talking point of rap and hip hop as "not real music." Of course, this view is hollow reactionism and aesthetic illiteracy.

Not only should it be obvious that, in theory, rap provides a unique medium for the development and expression of artistic talent with characteristics irreplicable by any other genre. But in practice, too, these self-professed "conservatives" would struggle to find as well told a story as Public Enemy's *Black Steel In The Hour Of Chaos*, Eve's *Love Is Blind*, Eminem's *Stan*, or Aesop Rock's *No Regrets*; as potent and varied a lyricist as RZA, Busdriver, Kendrick Lamar, Jedi Mind Tricks, The CunninLynguists, or Chance, The Rapper;[198] or, to pick an exemplar of inspired creativity across numerous dimensions, a track so brimming not only with raw musicality but canonical *anxiety of influence,* contextual awareness and self-awareness, and wit, as Jay-Z's "Death of Auto-Tune." They would surely struggle to find as lucid an affirmation of the merits of Scott's mētis as Dr Dre's opening to the N.W.A. classic, *Straight Outta Compton*: "You are now about to witness the strength of street knowledge."

The half-baked critique suffers from the assumption that codified knowledge is absolute in itself and sufficient for cultural appreciation. Neither are so. As with fighting, business, social relations, and urban living, art needs experimentation and discovery. These faux-sophisticated critics exhibit what Virginia Postrel would call a fear of *dynamism.* [199] They are stasists: They peddle the convenient excuse of wanting to protect the old as grounds to reject the new, and in doing so they forfeit the ability to create or to recognize creation. They fight against what they see as extremist individualism from a perspective of equally extremist collectivism — that of having decided for all what is and is not art from political principles rather than truly aesthetic ones. They manifest an alternating reading of *anxiety of influence*, albeit ironically and unintentionally.

We are rather more partial to the esoteric take of venture capitalist Ben Horowitz[200] (whose job is pretty much to *be open minded*) that rap is inherently capitalistic, and amongst contemporary popular music is, moreover, uniquely so. Well-known for starting his blog posts with rap lyrics he hopes will more powerfully convey the message he is trying to instill in the entrepreneurs whom he is counselling, Horowitz told Bloomberg News that hip hop "is the music of entrepreneurship. It is pro-aspirational. It is pro-becoming the man as opposed to railing against the man. If you meet anybody in hip hop, they think of themselves and talk about themselves as an entrepreneur."[201] In a widely admired post from 2014, *The Legend of the Blind MC*, addressing the source of his fascination with the genre, Horowitz writes,

> I was in New York City in 1986 and there was an explosion of a new kind of music called Hip Hop. It was unlike any other kind of music because the rappers were celebrating having nothing while aspiring to have everything. The songs were about growing up in the housing projects, surviving in the streets, and how great it was and how great they would become. At the time, Rock n' Roll was about rejecting the world, but Hip Hop was about embracing it with all of its flaws.[202]

Rap and hip hop done well is life-affirming. It is contextual; it relies on a common pool of cultural symbolism and metaphor. It calls backwards and forwards, ever anxious of its influence. It is the projection of individual experience into the social realm, grasping for novelty and canonical contribution. It is a celebration of human potential laced with caution for the temptation of human flaws. Which is all to say it is, of course, art.

Of course, none of this is to say that all rap and hip hop is *good* art. In fact, it is precisely to set up that such an argument would be ridiculous. Moreover, it would be infantilizing and insulting to the rappers and hip hop artists who are — objectively — very good. Bad art is just as likely to be found in rap or hip hop, as in pop, country, dance music, or for that matter, film, prose, or poetry.[203] In fact, Marsalis is well known for his furious and consistent critique of rap and hip hop as culturally degrading. Although careful never to be misunderstood as sweepingly criticizing *all such artists*, nor the artfulness of the form itself as opposed to specific instances, Marsalis is nonetheless unapologetic in his lament of their gross cultural influence, notoriously telling Capehart on the same podcast cited above that,

> I started saying in 1985 that I don't think we should have a music talking about n***ers and bitches and hoes. It had no impact. I've said it. I've repeated it. I still repeat it. To me that's more damaging than a statue of Robert E. Lee.

This sentiment is curiously echoed by Anthony, the character played by Chris Bridges, better known as the rapper Ludacris, in the 2004 movie, *Crash* — albeit with a tinge of paranoia that magnifies its humor but sadly lessens its impact.

Anthony chides his friend Peter, played by Larenz Tate, who turns on a hip hop station on the radio while the two are driving, "Nah, nah, you wanna listen to music of the oppressor, you go right ahead, man."

Peter responds incredulously, "How in the lunacy of your mind is hip hop music of the oppressor?"

Anthony sardonically quips, "Listen to it, man. N***er this, n***er that. You think white people go around calling each other honkies all day? 'Hey honky, how's business?', 'Great, cracker, we're diversifying!'" Before calmly continuing, as Peter sings a spoof racist country song over Anthony's monologue:

> You have absolutely no idea where hip hop music comes from, do you? You see, back in the sixties, we had smart, articulate Black men, like Huey Newton, Bobby Seale, Eldridge Cleaver, Fred Hampton. These people were speaking out and people were listening! And then the FBI said, "Oh no, we can't have that! I know! Let's give the niggers this music by a bunch of mumbling idiots, and sooner or later they'll all copy it and nobody will be able to understand a fucking word they say." End of problem.

The conspiratorial overtones somewhat soften the seriousness of this otherwise impassioned and incisive analysis. It seems not to have occurred to Anthony never to suspect conspiracy as an explanation when incompetence works just as well, if not better.[204]

Mumbling idiocy is not art, in whatever genre one might encounter it. It is more likely transient indulgence entirely without literary merit than it is at all mindful of its contribution to a stock of literature. Yet the brand of mumbling idiocy to be found in some contemporary rap and hip hop is particularly interesting because its defense by self-proclaimed cultural custodians may be the most obvious, cynical, and decadent display of *ketman* in all of degenerate fiat culture. It naturally invites a cultural analysis that has little to do with the content itself, hence is barely a critique of its creators, but instead of their disingenuous celebration — an inquiry not into primary cultural content, but into how our reaction to such content itself becomes culture.

Nowhere can so clearly be evidenced *living by lies* as the exalted defense of *any* rap or hip hop — no matter how stupid, offensive, or banal — from the self-proclaimed custodians of culture in modern America. And in fact, the more stupid, offensive, and banal, the better, provided its object of commentary is essentially *itself*. Provided the content is suitably narcissistic. There is hardly a better way to oppressively alienate the consumers of would-be culture than to bombard them with obnoxious, self-indulgent non-content. Marsalis deplores the vulgarity of "*n***ers and bitches and hoes*" with good reason: It is everywhere. It pins the cultural consumer in a desperate void of isolated meaninglessness. As if meaninglessness was not isolation enough on its own, for what is *meaning* if not a (re)discovered social truth that can, by definition, be shared?

This was the primary essence of what Martin Luther King Jr. criticized when he said he wasn't a capitalist — although, again, we suggest "consumerism" is a more apt description of what King abhorred.

Marsalis makes a fascinating point in the same interview cited above, that normalized consumerism and neglect of, or even *forgetting*, art that has nothing immediate to sell, has made it both subversive yet near practically impossible to create art that honestly conveys a moral statement. He says, "You have to figure out how to make your statement be a product. So, if you say 'don't kill people,' you have to kill people. If you say 'I don't like pornography' you gotta show pornography. So, it's difficult to come together and be for real because things are products first."

Capehart asks if this cheapens the message, and Marsalis replies, "Very strongly, yes, it cheapens it. It's like, you can join this church but you don't have to read the book. 'Now let me stand up here in front of y'all and I'mma show you what I don't want you to do!'"

Custodial Degeneracy

"So in our timidity, let us each make a choice: whether to remain consciously a servant of falsehood (of course, it is not out of inclination but to feed one's family that one raises one's children in the spirit of lies), or to shrug off the lies and become an honest man worthy of respect from one's children and contemporaries."
— Aleksandr Solzhenitsyn, *Live Not by Lies*

We believe the source of this custodial degeneracy clearly stems from exactly the frequent and practically lifelong object of Bloom's ire within the literary establishment, but which has since seeped into degenerate fiat culture at large. The short answer is, *political power* — an assault on Marsalis's powerful affirmation that, "I think people's lives are too serious to waste on the party line." But the long answer is worth exploring. Bloom told the *New York Times* in 2011,

> I had so deep a revulsion, as I still do, against what was happening in the academies of supposedly higher education, from pretty much 1969, 1970 on, that eventually it drove me out of teaching graduate students; it drove me out of the English department at Yale; I became a department of one. I don't want to take part in this madness in which sexual orientation, ethnic identity, skin pigmentation, gender, origin of one sort or another, is deemed to be the most crucial element in apprehending a poet, or a playwright, or a story writer, or a novelist, or even an essayist.[205]

There are two similarities across the quite different critiques of Miłosz, Solzhenitsyn, Bloom, and Marsalis to which we would draw special attention: All inveigh against the nonsensical yet fashionable idea that the *topic* of a piece of cultural content can be grounds alone for judging its merit — rather than *its merit* — and the infuriating inanity of publicly pretending otherwise for fear of being misinterpreted as possessing insufficient ideological support for the politically correct view of whatever *that topic* happens to be.

In this case, the pretenders are readily understood as utilizing the taboo of race as a shield to promote a solipsistic and vapid turn in culture at large. This in turn exacerbates the toxicity of the taboo, making social and cultural relations all the more fragile and individuals all the more segregated, and intensifies the pretenders' ability to continue to wreak cultural havoc for ultimately political gain.

Today we rarely hear the likes of "Across 110th Street," Bobby Womack's impassioned tirade against the depravity of exactly such tragically racialized havoc:

Hey Brother, there's a better way out

Snorting that coke, shooting that dope, man, you're copping out
Take my advice, it's either live or die
You got to be strong if you want to survive

Instead, the culture is flooded with all manner of mumbling idiocy, in many cases barely distinguishable from an audiobook of a pornographic screenplay (to pick another vexatious sub-category among many to racialism). The custodians of culture will naturally hail such content as "empowering," "inspiring," and "important," because it is scandalous, *because it is about sex*, and sex is Important with a capital "I" — irrespective of how awful is the work itself, calling neither backwards nor forwards but merely outwards, loudly.

Of course, in being awful, it will be nowhere near as interestingly, *substantively* scandalous as the likes of Virginia Woolf, Carol Ann Duffy, or Kim Addonizio, but the custodians likely no longer know who these dangerous, *difficult* women are. In her essay, *The Language of Sex,* Marilyn Simon writes,

> There are a number of prominent tenets that characterize current values surrounding sex and sexuality. The overarching one is, of course, a belief that we are freer, wiser, and more ethical with regards to human sexuality than any civilization prior to us. This is our "pride." And while it is self-evidently true that official political and institutional systems have become much more open and accepting of sexual orientations, this does not mean that the past was as monolithically repressive as we like to assume. All one has to do is read the Marquis de Sade, or Dostoevsky, or Christopher Marlowe, or Chaucer, to say nothing of the exploits of Roman antiquity, to know that even the most unconventional, "non-binary" sexual appetites have been abundant for many, many centuries. Yet because contemporary notions of sexual liberty require a repressive past from which we have freed ourselves, our ethics of sexual freedom engender feelings of arrogance and superiority, which are hardly ethical attitudes to hold, to a historical inheritance that we neither know nor understand.[206]

Knowing and understanding nothing of that which they custody, the custodians will likely instead wax lyrical about carrying on the legacy of the likes of Lil' Kim, Adina Howard, and Faith Evans, because the content of all is *about the same thing*. It might be legitimately offensive if it weren't so pathetic — *and obviously fake*.

The urge to community — or, to put it more suggestively, *to intercourse* — neither to isolation nor dependence, but to *culture*; will always re-emerge. The question is not "if" but only, "how easily?", "how healthily?", and "how well?" It may be apt to ask as well, how much damage has and can still be done suppressing it? How much violence? And how much damage will the violence will leave in its wake? How much is the tedium of unending scandal really worth?

Roger Scruton takes particular issue with the emptiness of scandal for scandal's sake, observing in *Why Beauty Matters*, "What is shocking first-time round is boring and vacuous when repeated. This makes art into an elaborate joke, though one that, by now, has ceased to be funny." He adds, "Yet, the critics go on endorsing it, afraid to say that the emperor has no clothes," as clear a plain English explanation of Miłosz's *ketman* as we could ask for. No doubt "the critics" practice *aesthetic ketman* in the well-secured privacy of their own homes; that is, secretly indulging in art they know really is beautiful but which they cannot admit in public.

Scruton opens, *Why Beauty Matters*, saying,

> At any time between 1750 and 1930 if you had asked educated people to describe the aim of poetry, art, or music, they would have replied "beauty." And if you had asked for the point of that, you would have learned that beauty is a value — as important as truth and goodness. Then in the twentieth century, beauty stopped being important. Art increasingly aimed to disturb and to break moral taboos. It was not beauty, but originality, however achieved, and at whatever moral cost, that won the prizes. Not only has art made a cult of ugliness; architecture too has become soulless and sterile. But it is not just our physical surroundings that have become ugly. Our language, our music, and our manners are increasingly raucous, self-centred and offensive, as if beauty and good taste had no real place in our lives. One word is written large on all these ugly things, and that word is "me." My profits, my desires, my pleasures.

Scruton critiques that such immediate satisfactions as profits, desires, and pleasures have come to be valued more highly than the intangibility of beauty itself, later adding, that, "beauty is assailed in two directions: by the cult of ugliness in the arts, and by the cult of utility in everyday life." There is clear utility in immediate satisfaction, but there is questionably little *value*. Scruton details the wave of modernist architecture that swept across Britain in the sixties and seventies, the promoters of which proudly championed its *function* rather than its *form*, much of which has since fallen into disuse and dereliction. Standing in front of what appears to be an abandoned functionalist office block in his hometown of Reading, Scruton chides: "This building is boarded up because nobody has a use for it. Nobody has a use for it because nobody wants to be in it. Nobody wants to be in it because the thing is so damned ugly."

An obsession with utility is high time preference and selfishness incarnate. It is a maximization of flow and a rejection of stock. It is a worship of consumption yet a disregard for investment. Scruton captures the essential long-termism of a proper appreciation of beauty wonderfully: "Put usefulness first and you lose it. Put beauty first and what you do will be useful forever."

And so, to provocatively encapsulate Scruton's, Bloom's, Marsalis', and Anthony's points alike, we might ask: *What the f*** happened in 1971?*[207] We would argue that what Scruton, Bloom, Marsalis, and Bridges's character are all picking up on, in their own ways, is the turn to the elevation of derision and immediacy, no longer as a force of balance and maintenance of standards, but as an ideal of merit: the transition to valuing not the difficulty of quality but the ease of shock. It takes no literacy to be shocked. Shock may be *useful* for politics or for commerce, but does nothing for the spirit. It is manipulative, not additive. It is selfish, not selfless. It is transactional, not transcendent. It drags us down rather than lifting us up. Shock is a flow, and an entirely empty flow at that. Nothing is left behind. Nothing is learned. Nothing of value is created and, arguably, the prospect of value itself is slighted.

1971 is, naturally, a tease on our part. We believe that these trends are not random and do not change with the winds, but are rooted in the interrelation of capital of all kinds, no matter how superficially heterogeneous. This is not to say that the connection is so simple as that money has ruined art, and that disingenuous promoters of garbage are all in on the same material bribe. But in a sense, they *are in* on the same *spiritual* bribe. Their conditions are such that *they cannot care about the long-term* and they cannot care about value to a wider community. They *have to* obsess over flows and they have to obsess over self-preservation within a socio-economic system that rewards politics rather than merit, acquiescence rather than honesty, and utility rather than beauty. This is why *topics* matter but content does not. Art, like business, is subsumed into politics.

Cultural content becomes bullshit in and of itself, little more than a commercial for the degenerate fiat regime, with all the crassness that a "commercial" typically provides. Its consumers are at once oppressed by its awfulness and alone in their inability to resist. And they are just that: no longer an *audience* but *consumers*. They consume these flows even though neither they nor anybody else are savers or investors in the culture from which the flows are strip mined. In a clarifying essay published on Facebook following his controversial podcast appearance mentioned above, Marsalis pinpointed this exact issue as a central cause of the degeneracy to which he objects, writing,[208]

> A number of (NOT ALL) hip hop musicians have gone on record saying that the marketplace and the industry encourages them to make their material more commercial by adding violent and profanity laced, materialistic and over-the-top stereotypical images and concepts to their work.

Never mind Wordsworth's warning, "Getting and spending, we lay waste our powers." What could Wordsworth possibly have to say about our complicated modern world?

A Cultural Renaissance

"There is nothing new except what has been forgotten."
— Marie Antoinette

We think there is merit, therefore, in looking to history to explore the landscape of capital of all forms in a time and place in which investment was taken seriously — not just as a financial exercise, but as the natural result of spiritual and communal health. In both the flourishing of artistic output and the embrace of the Commercial Revolution on which this output rested, Renaissance Florence is an ideal candidate, as Scruton would likely have appreciated.

Commerce laid at the heart of Florence's rise out of the Middle Ages, and the city's mock republican institutions granted it relative stability, a necessary precondition to capital accumulation. Although property rights were not beyond the meddling of the richest families going after their rivals, as a whole, the Florentine system provided merchants with protection from each other at home and from others abroad. In stark contrast with its medieval history, Florence had come to be ruled by a class of people interested in commercial profits rather than land conquest. Force would serve commerce by safeguarding property, ensuring contracts, and keeping trade routes open. Gone were the days of aristocratic families feuding for the control of arable land. The symbol of this new system was Florentine currency, the florin. As Paul Strathern explains,

> Florence's banking supremacy, and the trustworthiness of its bankers, led to the city's currency becoming an institution. As early as 1252 Florence had issued the fiorino d'oro, containing fifty-four grains of gold, which became known as the florin. Owing to its unchanging gold content (a rarity in coins of the period), and its use by Florentine bankers, the florin became accepted during the fourteenth century as a standard currency throughout Europe.

Goldthwaite pinpoints the interrelation of the beautiful architecture, cultural flourishing, and economic success, writing in *The Economy of Renaissance Florence,*

> The best evidence for the success of the economy, however, is its physical manifestations at the time, and these are as dramatic as such things can be. In 1252 Florence struck its first gold florin, and by the end of the century the florin was the universal money in international commercial and financial markets throughout western Europe. [...] In 1296 a new cathedral was projected, and when, after two subsequent decisions to increase its size, it was dedicated on the completion of its great copula in 1436, it was the largest cathedral, and perhaps the largest

church of any kind, in Europe. In 1299 work began on the city's great public hall, which has been called one of the most original buildings in medieval Italy. The standard international money of the time, one of the largest sets of walls of any European city, what was to become the largest cathedral in Christendom, and a massive and original seat of government were not insignificant indicators of the success of the Florentine economy at the time when both Dante and Giotto were on the scene.

From this growth in commerce arose banks. Merchants trading goods across Europe were in control of evermore assets. In exactly the sense described by de Soto, the legal framework upheld by the Florentines — and such fellow northern Italian merchant city states as Venice, Pisa, Genoa, and Siena — allowed mere assets to be put to work as *capital*. Banking families like the Medici often started in a trade, like wool, and provided competing merchants with working capital. Banking was therefore not a purely financial business. It remained firmly rooted in enterprise. Florentine bankers were first and foremost merchants who understood what it took to run a business.

Among the great banking families of late medieval and Renaissance Florence and even perhaps Italy, none shine so bright as the Medici. And yet, the three great Florentine families of the 14th century, the Acciaiuoli, Bardi, and Peruzzi once controlled more extensive and richer banks than the Medici ever did. Neither were the Medici particularly innovative bankers. According to Strathern, the Medici were in fact conservative in their enterprise:

Giovanni di Bicci was a cautious man and preferred to consolidate. This was a trait he shared with his predecessor as head of the Medici clan, his distant relative Vieri, and he certainly passed it on to his son; as bankers, the Medici made their money through caution and efficiency, rather than innovation. Contrary to banking lore, they did not invent the bill of exchange, though they may have had a hand in the invention of the holding company; their success was based almost exclusively on the use of tried-and-trusted techniques pioneered by others. The Medici Bank never underwent rapid expansion, and even at its height was not as extensive as any of the three great Florentine banks of the previous century.

And yet, financial success or innovation is not why the Medici name echoed through the centuries. The Medici were successful bankers, of course. They made a fortune from the European wool trade, with branches as far from home as London and Bruges. Their control over both the Papal accounts and the alum trade, which had been monopolized by Rome, provided reliable profits shielded from competition. But the Medici legend was born from investing not in banking or even in commerce but in intangible cultural projects that would yield impossible-to-measure returns. Through patronage, the Medici would allocate capital, accumulated through meticulous and conservative banking activities, to ventures of which no accountant could make sense. And yet, the value the Medici created outlasts all that of the more financially successful Italian families.

Because Florentine bankers could rely on hard money to make sensible investments, they understood the simple truth behind accumulation of wealth. Their incentives were very simply not to maximize flow. We would argue that it is this deep intuitive understanding of wealth that led merchants, especially the Medici, to accumulate cultural capital through spending on the arts and sciences. In fact, as Strathern writes, the Medici invested in cultural capital because it was the hardest asset they knew:

> It had only been in his later years that Giovanni di Bicci had begun to understand that there was more to life than banking and its attendant risks. Money could be turned into the permanence of art by patronage, and in the exercise of this patronage one gained access to another world of timeless values, which appeared free from the corruption of the religious authorities, or the devious politics of power and banking.

The Medici banked their financial capital into cultural capital that would outlive them all in *beauty* that remains useful centuries after any transiently commercial utility expired. As Cosimo de' Medici said: "I know the ways of Florence, within fifty years we Medici will have been exiled, but my buildings will remain." In a way, Cosimo was too optimistic. The Medici were exiled within thirty years. But the buildings do remain, along with the Medici name. Brunelleschi's dome, which tops Florence cathedral, or artists like Michelangelo and Leonardo da Vinci were at the very center of the Renaissance, which spread from Florence throughout Europe and then the world. All owe a debt of gratitude to the Medici.

Robert S. Lopez characterizes this outstanding social and cultural effect that spread forth from Florence and Venice in the final few paragraphs of *The Commercial Revolution of the Middle Ages, 950–1350,* writing,

> No doubt there were many people who complained that alien moneylenders came "with nothing but a pen and an inkpot" to write down the advances made out to kings or peasants in the form of simple vouchers, and in return for such scribblings eventually carried off the material wealth of the land. But the merchants also wrote books in large number. It is no small token of their ascendancy in the thirteenth and early fourteenth century that the most widely copied and read book was that of Marco Polo, where practical information on markets interlards the romance of travel, and that the greatest poem of the entire Middle Ages was written by a registered if not very active member of the Florentine guild of spice-sellers, Dante Alighieri. The merchants also

built town halls, arsenals, hospitals, and cathedrals. When the Great Plague struck, Siena had just begun work on an extension of her enchanting Duomo, so that it would outdo the cathedral of her neighbors and commercial rivals in Florence.

Beyond Medici generosity was a deep understanding of investing. Despite cultural benefits not being as cleanly measurable as financial returns, bankers like Cosimo de' Medici knew how to get the best out of capricious artists. According to Strathern, "Cosimo may have been conservative in his banking practice, and may have consciously conducted himself in a modest and retiring fashion, yet surprisingly he was capable of tolerating the most extravagant behaviour amongst his protégés."

As Cosimo himself once said: "One must treat these people of extraordinary genius as if they were celestial spirits, not as if they are beasts of burden." The risk profile of cultural investment is rather more reminiscent of venture capital than it is the relatively stolid project of merchant banking: Many will fail, but some might succeed beyond your wildest expectations. Embracing the asymmetry of outcomes is key to success.

It is by allying both conservative lending with supportive patronage that the Medici managed to accumulate first financial and then cultural capital like few before or since. For that reason, the three great Medici — Giovanni di Bicci, Cosimo de' Medici and Lorenzo the Magnificent — stand as exemplar cultural capitalists, the first two being also shrewd financial capitalists. They mobilized private capital to foster an environment of exceptional cultural creativity. Strathern encapsulates perfectly the Medici genius:

> The new art may have required science, but it also required money, and this was largely provided by Cosimo, who according to one admiring historian "appeared determined to transform medieval Florence into an entirely new Renaissance city". This was hardly an exaggeration, for Cosimo funded the construction, or renovation, of buildings ranging from palaces to libraries, churches to monasteries. When his grandson Lorzen the Magnificent examined the books many years later he was flabbergasted at the amounts that Cosimo had sunk into these schemes; the accounts would reveal that between 1434 and 1471 a staggering 663,755 gold florins had been spent. [...] Such a sum is difficult to put into context; suffice to say that just over a century beforehand the entire assets of the great Peruzzi Bank at its height, accumulated in branches all over western Europe and ranging beyond to Cyprus and Beirut, were the equivalent of 103,000 gold florins.
>
> Yet such munificence was always built on a foundation of solid banking practice. An examination of the Medici Bank records shows that while it made use of the most efficient financial instruments available, it was in no way innovative in its practices; it was if anything highly

conservative compared with other similar institutions. Neither Giovanni di Bicci nor Cosimo de' Medici introduced any novel methods or ways of doing business, their practice being based entirely on the efficient and prudent use of proven methods pioneered by others.

Pacienza y Fe

"Dying is easy, young man. Living is harder."
— George Washington in *Hamilton: An American Musical*

It may seem odd to argue for the health of a renaissance society as compared to the relative poverty of our own, especially in light of some of the figures given in Chapter Seven, *A Capital Renaissance*, detailing improvements in just about every sensible metric of human flourishing in line with increased harnessing of energy following the Industrial Revolution. But our assessment of health and poverty is really more about attitude than outcome.

We cannot help the size of the stock we inherit from our forebears; we can only decide what to do with it and how to aim to pass it on in turn. The imperative *to decide* is rooted across all stocks of capital in the scarcity of time and energy and so our attitude towards scarcity itself is at the root of what will become of economic, social, and cultural capital alike. The degenerate fiat attitude has been to optimize for efficiency, and the results on all forms of capital have been nothing short of catastrophic.

Jane Jacobs forcefully makes this point in the ominously titled, *Dark Age Ahead*, writing,

> Perhaps the greatest folly possible for a culture is to try to pass itself on by using principles of efficiency. When a culture is rich enough and inherently complex enough to afford redundancy of nurturers, but eliminates them as an extravagance or loses their cultural services through heedlessness of what is being lost, the consequence is self-inflicted cultural genocide. Then watch the vicious spirals go into action.

The nervous celebration of politically correct mumbling idiocy is but one consequence of the cultural genocide of which Jacobs warned. It is a consequence of impatience and resentment, and of a rejection of the principles the Medici embraced, that the creation of cultural capital is the soundest investment of all. For what is its "return"? What is its "risk profile"? Finding and funding a Brunelleschi might be a one in a thousand or one in a million shot.

It may take decades to pay off as the talent is cultivated to the point of the possibility of conceivable repayment of the principal, should such a dubious calculation even be deemed worthwhile. Shock, on the other hand, is instant and guaranteed. Any talentless hack can shock an audience expecting merit by aggressively failing to produce any. And what of the character traits instilled by such relentless, resentful, impatient, disingenuous, living-by-lies garbage? What can we expect to be the consequences of abandoning the difficulty of the search for social truth for the ease of oppressive isolation? What of the consequences for mental health? Will we produce strong men and women, able to face the fundamental uncertainty of life armed with the ability to generate practical knowledge? Will we produce robust communities and civic spirit? Will we produce truth, goodness, or beauty? Will we produce *knowledge*?

No, we will not.

We will produce narcissists; easily manipulated by greed and fear, prone to solipsism, irrationality, dependence, fragility, and panic, whose incentives are so warped as to make duplicitous selfishness a necessity of social navigation and survival; optimized for strip mining capital and not much else; who will turn around and march through institutions nominally dedicated to the nurture, replenishment, and growth of some or other form of capital, hijacking and repurposing them into broadcasters of narcissism. In *The Culture of Narcissism*, Christopher Lasch predicted as much,

> Institutions of cultural transmission (school, church, family), which might have been expected to counter the narcissistic trend of our culture, have instead been shaped in its image, while a growing body of progressive theory justifies this capitulation on the ground that such institutions best serve society when they provide a mirror reflection of it. The downward drift of public education accordingly continues: the steady dilution of intellectual standards in the name of relevance and other progressive slogans; the abandonment of foreign languages; the abandonment of history in favor of "social problems"; and a general retreat from intellectual discipline of any kind, often necessitated by the need for more rudimentary forms of discipline in order to maintain minimal standards of safety.

Rejection of great art and literature — whether on the grounds of "bourgeois sentimentality" in one era, fashionably ironic cynicism in another, "irrelevance" and the favoring of "social problems" in another still — is hardly different to confiscation of physical capital: It severs a tie with the past and makes us unable to learn from the cumulative experience of our communities. It renders us simultaneously dependent and alone. The real tragedy of the political appropriation of productive capital is not so much the violence of the theft, but the aborted yield that might have flowed from the asset because control is transferred to those who have no idea what they are doing. They lack the knowledge and competence to even replenish the capital, never mind to continue to harvest its output.

This separation of control and knowledge; the destruction of patiently stored time; the disbarment of the will to risk and to sacrifice in order to build, will cause a harrowing parallel to a collapsing debt spiral: a collapsing spiral of the knowledge of *how to do things*. We will need to rediscover them. Doing so will not be pleasant.

The same will go for literature and art: We will end up with a culture that simply, tragically *doesn't know anything*. Yet, composed of human beings as it is, it will still face every need that literature and art fulfill, and so it will have to improvise impoverished simulacra in lieu of the real thing. In one of the most striking moments in Scruton's *Why Beauty Matters*, he interviews Alexander Stoddart, the celebrated sculptor whose monuments of such Scottish intellectual giants as David Hume, Adam Smith, William Playfair, and James Clerk Maxwell beautifully adorn the streets of Edinburgh. Stoddart describes,

> Many students come to me from sculpture departments — secretly of course — because they don't want to tell their tutors that they've come to truck with the enemy. And they say, "I tried to make a model figure, and I modeled it in clay, and then the tutor came up and told me to cut it in half and dump some diarrhea on top of it, and that will make it interesting.

Scruton concurs, "It's what I feel about the kind of standardized desecration that passes for art these days — it actually is a kind of immorality because it is an attempt to obliterate meaning from the human form." And Stoddart fiercely fires back, "Well, it's an attempt to obliterate *knowledge*."

The production of culture that results will be predictably immature and shallow because we have made ourselves unconscious of history and have severed the link to what has already been learned. In the podcast cited above, Marsalis answers Jonathan Capehart's question as to whether it is fair to call him a "race man" as well as a "Jazz man" by saying, "Yeah, it's fair." Capehart asks him to "define it," and Marsalis responds,

> I think it's a person who has pride in whatever their subculture or subgroup is, in this case Black American. It doesn't mean you're against other people but you're conscious of the history of your subculture and you embrace it, you believe it, and you don't mind speaking on it.

We believe Lin-Manuel Miranda to be a contemporary master of a proud and celebratory embrace of subcultural ethnicity and, resultingly, an art that straddles the isolation of feigning color blindness and the oppression of imposing racialism. His work is outstanding cultural capitalism. His best-known musical, *Hamilton*, draws on and reimagines the common founding myth using the newer language of hip hop and newer reality of American ethnic diversity. The result is a truly inclusive piece of art that invites all to join and provides a new lens of understanding. It is challenging but respectful. It is intimately aware of its canon

— not only literary but social and cultural — yet it finds a novel combination of expression, so original and powerful as to extend the canon's meaning.

In the Heights goes even further in its implicit celebration of Americana and may well be the most subtly yet unabashedly pro-American work of art of which we are aware. The musical, also recently adapted into a film, blends a celebration of Dominican and more broadly Latin-American culture with acute commentary on racial grievances, and yet entirely eschews resentment and segregation. The message is unequivocally that the infusion into the mainstream of Latin-American culture improves American culture as a whole *for everybody*. Echoing Martin Luther King Jr., the more positively and organically this happens, the better. Central imposition on the grounds of resentment will in turn cause only equal and opposite resentment, and besides is insulting to the intrinsic merits of the culture being championed. The journey of several characters is marked by the transition in their cultural self-identification from bitterness and opposition to confidence and celebration; we might say, from derision to creation.

In the Heights goes to pains to testify that *this* culture (for all culture is local and specific) is, at its social and spiritual core, as American as they come. It is rooted in hard work and sacrifice, embrace of opportunity, and love for community and respect for its culture and its *literature*. The matriarch Abuela Claudia's beautiful solo song, *Pacienza y fe,* embodies the ethic of the musical: Patience and faith. Long-termism, commitment, and a rejection of cynicism. Conscientiousness, reverence, and responsibility. There is surely no more intimate and committed an integration than the naming of one's child after an element of the host society — no less an element integral to the experience *of immigration*, as main character *Usnavi* is, named after his parents' misreading of a US Navy ship they passed as they first arrived in America.[209] Playing on "power" as in either electricity or societal influence, Usnavi encourages his community members during a power cut,

> All right we're powerless, so light up a candle.
> There's nothin' goin' on here that we can't handle.

We could hardly come up with a better slogan of localism, experimentation, and bottom-up social coordination if we tried. *In The Heights* is *good*. It is artistically good, but more importantly it is morally good. Lin-Manuel Miranda is amongst the greatest cultural capitalists of our time.

Chapter Nine

Global Money, Local Freedom
Competence, authority, and how to fix the world

In *Dark Age Ahead*, Jane Jacobs makes a compelling case for the inextricable interrelationship between bottom-up social, urban, and cultural capital, more traditionally conceived economic productivity and financial capital, *and* the knowledge and competence of governmental bodies claiming top-down authority over the communities that collectively create such capital stocks. Charting the Commercial Revolution in Europe as originating first and foremost with Venice's contact with the far more economically and culturally advanced cities of the Middle East and Asia, she writes,

> Disadvantaged in almost every way thought they were, the early medieval cities typically benefited from subsidiarity and fiscal accountability.
> Subsidiarity is the principle that government works best — most responsibly and responsively — when it is closest to the people it serves and the needs it addresses. Fiscal Accountability is the principle that institutions collecting and disbursing taxes work most responsibly when they are transparent to those providing the money.
> The cities of the Roman Empire had lost these advantages in the desperate years before the collapse, when the imperial treasury extorted from them as much as it could and disbursed the money for schemes and needs according to its own, frequently crazed, priorities. The early medieval cities regained the two principles slowly, in various ways. Some, like London, received royal charters authorizing them to farm (that is, collect) their own taxes. Others, like Hamburg and cities of the Low Countries and northern France, gained subsidiarity and fiscal accountability through the efforts of merchants and citizens united by common interests and then, increasingly, by custom. Many others, like Venice itself, Florence, Bologna, and Genoa, achieved subsidiarity and fiscal accountability as by-products of their own sovereignty as city-states.
> Both principles are important, but the need for subsidiarity has become especially acute [...] Yet both subsidiarity and fiscal accountability of public money have almost disappeared from the modern world, as if a

cycle is returning to the Roman imperium, rather than to principles that Western culture long after Rome's failure.

Steven Epstein is even more specific in his highlighting of the Genoese's appreciation of bottom-up governance to cultural and economic thriving as early as the eleventh and twelfth centuries, writing in *Genoa and The Genoese, 958– 1528*,

> [I]t must be remembered that medieval Genoa was an independent state whose leaders were solving the problems of self-government largely through trial and error. Several important features of the early commune merit comment. Above all, the sworn association represented a local effort at self-help to establish a regime with moral as well as legal authority. The oath helped to accomplish this by giving the commune a quasi-religious sanction, but all the specific rules described here should be seen as attempts to empower the commune and not just by instilling fear in the people. Instead, the powerful Genoese, as well as some in the second rank, chose a system that allowed a number of residents to participate.

It is all well and good championing localism as obviously good, globalism as obviously bad, Bitcoin as obviously good and contrary to globalism, and hence Bitcoin as a natural complement to localism. It may even be tempting to read the Jacobs quote and think it amusingly obvious, if anachronistic, that what she is really pointing out is the downstream flaws of degenerate fiat money and the absence of Bitcoin. But we should be clear that our argument is stronger even than this: Bitcoin will *cause* localism. There will be no other choice. The causal process we anticipate is worth further explanation.

That is not to say that Bitcoin will lead us to a pacifist utopia in which any attempt at violence suffers metaphysical intervention by the spirit of Satoshi. That money can grant power is clear enough as there will always be a clearing price for violent thuggery. Lysander Spooner put it typically dryly in, *No Treason*:

> So these villains, who call themselves governments, well understand that their power rests primarily upon money. With money they can hire soldiers and with soldiers extort money. And, when their authority is denied, the first use they always make of money, is to hire soldiers to kill or subdue all who refuse them more money.

Indeed. But what will distinguish a Bitcoin standard from Spooner's Civil War and Reconstruction-era United States, Hayek's Pax Americana, The

Venetian Republic, The Roman Empire, or any other period and polity besides, is that for the first time in history, power will *not* grant money.

There are two reasons to believe this. The first is the essence of the section, "Bitcoin is Ariadne," in Chapter Six, *Bitcoin Is Venice*: Bitcoin simply cannot be seized by any force less severe than torture, and even then, it is possible — and will surely become widespread for any value worth protecting — to render even torture obsolete. If you want bitcoin, you will have to offer something deemed more valuable to its holder.

The second is subtler, and we believe is not widely understood. A distinguishing feature of Bitcoin is that it is the first ever truly stateless money. Contrary to some naïve Bitcoiner and even gold-bug talking points, gold has constituted the base for specie throughout history, but has never acted fully and wholly as money. This historical observation provides an amusing afterthought to the satirically presented in Chapter Four, *Wittgenstein's Money*. In medieval and renaissance Venice or Florence, for example, the alleged three roles of money — store of value, medium of exchange, and unit of account — were each fulfilled by different objects or concepts: Elemental gold was the store of value (sometimes silver or bullion), bank transfer via attested ledger alteration (tellingly called *ghost money* in Florence[210]) was by far the most common medium of exchange for transactions above the petty, and the polity-prescribed (that is, *government*) denominations of coinage via the mint were the units of account. The opening of Chapter Four is once again disproven … by reality.

The reader might object that this itself is irrelevant semantics that allows us to escape the primacy and importance of gold and *the gold standard*. Quite the contrary. Elemental gold has a cost. Nearly all human civilization across the world and throughout history independently arrived at the utility of elemental gold as a store of value because, of the options, it has the highest cost, hence the lowest inflation and the greatest monetary utility.[211]

Elemental gold approximates what Nick Szabo called *unforgeable costliness*. Brilliantly anticipating contemporary pushback against "wasteful" Bitcoin mining, in *Shelling Out*, Szabo explains,

> At first, the production of a commodity simply because it is costly seems quite wasteful. However, the unforgeably costly commodity repeatedly adds value by enabling beneficial wealth transfers. More of the cost is recouped every time a transaction is made possible or made less expensive. The cost, initially a complete waste, is amortized over many transactions. The monetary value of precious metals is based on this principle.

Even though the typical government monopoly on violence naturally included a monopoly on the right to mint coins,[212] it did not extend to a right to escape economic reality. Debased coins would be valued abroad precisely in line with their debasement: That is to say, not by their government-insisted fake unit of account but their true store of value. Foreign exchange markets kept government mints (relatively) honest given economic feedback from seigniorage allowed only the smallest windows of temporary benefit prior to longer term and more extreme damage.

Even when backed with such military might as were the Roman, Spanish, or British empires, for example, that we might think could overrule economic feedback essentially emanating from decentralized trade webs that could simply be co-opted, the essential cost of elemental gold still forced itself to be felt. Organized violence at such a scale *has a cost*. The greater the scale, the greater the cost, and in fact, the greater the incentive to *maintain* a gold standard effectively than to attempt to subvert it. While not a singularly causal factor, it is certainly not a coincidence that the three great empires just cited all collapsed more or less in line with the value of their currencies.

The fiat era created a dramatic historical anomaly. For the first time in recorded history, the cost of creating new money *literally was zero*. This has had profound effects on political economy. While money can always buy power, power could now buy money, and without economic calculation. There is no cost too great to seizing power, and next to no incentive not to give it a shot, because *any costs* can later be paid back, and then some.

This, we believe, is the root cause of the cult of toxic bigness first described in Chapter Seven, *A Capital Renaissance*, and bemoaned throughout Chapter Eight, *These Were Capitalists*, as well in terms of its effect on more intangible capital stocks. Rather than a naturally homeostatic process of increased size leading to inefficiency, in the fiat era, the bigger you are — either as a business or a government — the more powerful you become, hence, entirely perversely, the more efficient you become. Of course, the less efficient everybody else becomes because they are transparently being stolen from: This is the political source of what was described as *strip mining* in Chapter Five, *The Capital Strip Mine*. The more communal capital is consumed, the more energy the capital consumer can direct towards seizing power and paying back himself but likely nobody else.

Bitcoin fixes this. And in a remarkably simple way, it undoes everything just described. It returns a cost to money — a higher one even than gold — and makes toxic bigness unsustainable. Hence, Bitcoin isn't so much explicitly a pro-localist tool. If anything, the reality is even more profound: Localism *itself* is natural, healthy, sustainable, and right. Bitcoin is a pro-reality tool. Bitcoin destroys the historically anomalous countervailing force and, in doing so, is set to let localism happen without having a particular bias of its own beyond the far more abstract concerns for sustainability, efficiency, accountability, and truth — all natural bedfellows to localism.

One way to conceive of the tragedy of modernity, and its impact on the strip mining of social, urban, and cultural capital is perhaps that narcissism is artificially subsidized. Through subsidy it is normalized, and through normality it becomes a part of the culture itself, and encourages its own championing and reproduction. From an artificial inception, it takes root and sustains itself as it drags the culture down. Again, Christopher Lasch points a way out the nightmarish labyrinth:

> In a dying culture, narcissism appears to embody — in the guise of personal "growth" and "awareness" — the highest attainment of spiritual enlightenment. The custodians of culture hope, at bottom, merely to survive its collapse. The will to build a better society, however, survives, along with traditions of localism, self-help, and community action that only need the vision of a new society, a decent society, to give them vigor. The moral discipline formerly associated with the work ethic still retains a value independent of the role it once played in the defense of property rights. That discipline — indispensable to the task of building a new order — endures most of all in those who knew the old order only as a broken promise, yet who took the promise more seriously than those who merely took it for granted.

In this chapter, we take the promise seriously and pose the question we will address. With less of a focus on individual actors and communities under voluntary association, and less of a concern for if and how they choose to create capital, we focus on the governing bodies that have nominal authority over this behavior and ask, very simply, what becomes of them under a Bitcoin standard? What, if anything, will the new order look like, and how will it be built?

The Separation of Money and State

"I don't believe we shall ever have a good money again before we take the thing out of the hands of government. That is, we can't take them violently out of the hands of government, all we can do is by some sly roundabout way introduce something they can't stop."
— Friedrich Hayek

It has been a standard refrain of economists since at least the time of Adam Smith, and arguably earlier still, back to Turgot and the Salamanca School, that deeper and more complex economic integration ought to lead to peace, since war would needlessly destroy these benefits.

This analysis strikes us as naïve given it ignores entirely an important *opportunity cost*, that of the potential economic gains and losses of warfare and oppression. Or, more generally and across all scales: the political economy of violence. Deeper and more complex economic relationships seem likely to create capital that is not only more productive but more massive, more industrial, and more vulnerable. There is a calculus of *returns to violence* at play that lacks a clear resolution without much more case-by-case context. Michelle Garfinkel and Stergios Skaperdas put it amusingly in *Conflict and Appropriation as Economic Activities,*

> The source of the surprise, at least from the point of view of most economists, is simply the failure of apparently rational individuals to engage in mutually advantageous trade spontaneously. In the absence of external or internal restraints, however, an individual with easy access to a pistol might find it more convenient to take what he wants from others outright by threatening to use force than to obtain what he wants through peaceful trade. As a general rule, resources can be used not only for production but also for appropriative purposes such as theft as warfare. Individuals and groups can either produce and thus create wealth or seize the wealth created by others.

Bitcoin is a resource: Can it be used not only for production but also for appropriative purposes? In Chapter Six, *Bitcoin Is Venice,* in the section, "Bitcoin Is Ariadne," we answered firmly in the negative: No, Bitcoin may be the most peaceful technology ever invented. One conception of Bitcoin's role in the sense of a kind of grand narrative might be that it *completes the industrial revolution.* Relying as it does on the global communications infrastructure that is itself one of the great achievements of the capital formation following advances in scientific and technical knowledge, consider Carlo Cipolla's framing of the social impact of the Industrial Revolution, in, *The Economic History of World Population*:

> Hitherto, all societies that have been industrialized seem to have experienced an almost total disappearance of the recurrent peaks of the death rate. The reasons are manifold. New scientific knowledge about plants and livestock, extraordinary improvements in transportation, progress in medicine and sanitation — all have allowed men to cope with famines and epidemic diseases. Two of the three main causes of the peaks have been brought under control. Unfortunately, one cannot say the same of the third cause, war. The technical progress that has enabled man to control famines and epidemics has increased his destructive efficiency in warfare. This is not the proper place to speculate about the future. But one cannot help thinking that unless industrial societies learn to control war (and for the moment there is no evidence that they are moving in this direction) they may again experience demographic catastrophes — possibly of suicidal magnitude.

This book is an enormous speculation about the future, and hence we are perfectly comfortable suggesting that maybe — just maybe — Bitcoin helps fix this. Of course, Bitcoin can be used to pay mercenaries, assassins, or even investment bankers, so we reiterate it does not usher in a pacifist utopia by default. Power is real. Violence is real. Jack Hirshleifer cautions in *Economic Behavior in Adversity*,

> The institutions of property and law, and the peaceful process of exchange, are highly beneficial aspects of human life. But the economist's inquiries should not be limited to such "nice" behaviors and interactions. Struggle, imposing costs on others, and downright violence are crucial phenomena of the world as we know it. Nor is the opposition between the "nice" and the "not nice" by any means total. Law and property, and thus the possibilities of peaceful exchange, can only persist where individuals are ultimately willing to use violence in their defense.

Bitcoin does not fix the line between good and evil in every human heart. But in light of Hirshleifer's astute identification of the necessity of violence, or credible threats of violence, as a defensive measure as well as an offensive one, it is reasonable to surmise that Bitcoin may start to fix many incentives to behave violently. This is because of its intriguing profile as a technology. It is almost certainly impossibly costly to attack Bitcoin itself, as opposed to the human beings who use it, and trivially costless to defend it. The only way to seize properly stored bitcoin is through torture. Bitcoin that is stored not just properly but *very well* can likely not be seized at all. It has to be volunteered up, meaning the would-be torturer has to offer something of value in exchange.

Bitcoin strongly incentivizes individuals to eschew violence in their dealings with one another. But what of institutions?

Scaling the Sovereign Individual

"Life is to be lived, not controlled; and humanity is won by continuing
to play in the face of certain defeat."
— Ralph Ellison, *Invisible Man*

As returned to several times throughout the book, in particular in Chapter
Seven, *A Capital Renaissance*, and Chapter Eight, *These Were Capitalists*,
capital is a social institution. "Individual capital" can only really mean money
nobody else uses or a tool nobody else wants. In the remainder of this chapter,
we will try to extend our reasoning so as to analyze how to scale up Bitcoin's
novel profile of returns to violence from individuals to institutions.

Admitting that some or other enterprise must exist socially immediately
invites questions of hierarchy and power. And the concepts of both hierarchy
and power invite further considerations of knowledge and competence. Who in
the hierarchy has power? What power do they have? How competently can they
exercise this power? What knowledge do they have and how does this affect
their competence? How do the answers influence the decisions they are
authorized to make? Does there exist feedback between any of the inputs and
outputs of the processes involved?

We will not pretend to have solved this problem completely, for all social
circumstances, and for all time. But we will shortly present a simplistic model
of the likely interactions between different positions in a hierarchy, given their
levels of knowledge and competence, and their authority to make decisions, and
their likelihood to obey decisions handed down.

On this last point, to be sure to avoid naivety, we assume it is clear that
"decision making authority" is ultimately backed with credible threats of
violence, however far removed from the communication experienced by the
agents.[213] We use the terms "local" and "global" throughout, and while this may
be close to literally true in some cases, we stress it is only the relative positioning
that matters: Local agents are governed by global agents, and are closer to the
"facts on the ground," so to speak. But a global agent in one relationship may be
a local agent in another, relative to a global agent by whom they are in turn
governed.

Finally, we admit upfront that our model is unavoidably partisan (we
suspected our conclusion in advance and hence can only be so honest in its
presentation); the repeated citing of Elinor Ostrom, James Scott, Jane Jacobs,
Wendell Berry, Hernando de Soto, Tarek El Diwany, and Friedrich Hayek
throughout not only the book but, in particular, Chapters Seven and Eight, gives
a strong indication of the direction of our argument.

If the intersection of the theses of the aforementioned thinkers can be boiled
down to a single proposition it is likely that: *knowledge and competence are only*

ever local. There are meaningful categories of universals in mathematics and physics, but not in any remotely social affairs. Humans create universals across disciplines so as to comprehend and communicate, but, as the linguistic philosopher Alfred Korzybski is well known for saying, *the map is not the territory*. More bluntly, "social science" is not science! Michael Oakeshott put it appropriately scathingly in *On Human Conduct*, writing,[214]

> Projects of other kinds, purporting to endow the understanding of human conduct with superior "scientific" quality have supervened to distract and to corrupt this genuine but modest enterprise. In the commonest and least equivocal of these "sociological" projects the identity to be investigated is said to be a "society": that is, an alleged totality of human relationships. But whether it is because of a palpable difficulty of representing such a totality as itself human beings associated in terms of a specifiable procedure or practice, or because to regard it as a practice and not as a process seems to be no better than an apology for the absence of a "scientific" understanding, a "society" is identified as a "system." It is recognized as a process to be understood in terms of its regularities or its causal conditions, and not as a procedure whose postulates are reflective intelligence, contingent beliefs, and acknowledgements of authority or utility. Accordingly, this "system" is said to have a "structure" which contains and displays functional relationships between its parts or properties. And change in this structure (so called "social change") is understood to be a process analogous to the metabolic or evolutionary change of biological organisms. What are called "cultures" are said to "evolve" and to survive in a process of "natural selection"; that is, by proving themselves to eb "adaptively superior innovatory ways of surviving." Or "social change" is understood in terms borrowed from entropy. In the more naïve versions of this "sociological" understanding of human conduct the so-called "law-like relations between the component of social systems" are merely correlations of characteristics. In the more sophisticated versions, the explanatory "laws" are the alleged psychological or bio-evolutionary "laws" or causal conditions said to be postulated in the correlations of characteristics. But however this may be, and whether or not a "general sociological theory" is made to emerge from this engagement to understand "social processes," it is remote from anything recognizable as an engagement to theorize human conduct. Theorems about the so-called "behaviour of social systems," or about the behaviour of their alleged components, can be represented as theorems about the actions and utterances of human beings only in a masquerade of categories.

Paul Graham gives a more socially motivated explanation of essentially the same issue in the essay, *Hackers and Painters,* and with a potent punchline:

Everyone in the sciences secretly believes that mathematicians are smarter than they are. I think mathematicians also believe this. At any rate, the result is that scientists tend to make their work look as mathematical as possible. In a field like physics, this probably doesn't do much harm, but the further you get from the natural sciences, the more of a problem it becomes.
A page of formulas just looks so impressive (Tip: for extra impressiveness, use Greek variables.) And so there is a great temptation to work on problems you can treat formally, rather than problems that are, say, important.

The greatest possible extent to which either knowledge and competence can be meaningfully claimed to be *global* is that the global agent in question has as undistorted lines of communication as possible to local knowledge and competence, *in every locality over which it has nominal authority*. And even then, as Oakeshott would likely strenuously insist, any attempt to *theorize* on that basis — any belief that the information presented can be condensed to the deduction of prior, simpler, knowable axioms — is charlatanism. The more mathematical, which is to say, *by necessity universal*, the more inadvertently transparent his charlatanism will be. As Scott would say, it is *high-modernist arrogance*, and as Graham would say, this arrogance evidences and emphasizes the essential unimportance of the speaker and his project.

To whatever extent it is believed to be necessary or is attempted,[215] this process will nonetheless undoubtedly destroy knowledge and competence. It cannot help but introduce interference into an otherwise useful informational signal.

Knowledge, Competence, and Authority

"One also needs to ask why those institutions that could have prevented the bubbles have singularly failed to do so, although they had been given unusually strong powers with little accountability to democratic institutions" the central banks. They cannot feign ignorance: apart from employing the largest number of economists of any institution and spending vast resources on 'research' (none of it on the taboo topic of credit creation), I have also contacted many central banks and finance ministries and have in the past twenty years published many articles based on my credit model, warning of pending crises (such as today's UK banking collapse) and indicating that bubbles and subsequent collapses could easily be prevented by monitoring and restricting speculative (non-GDP) credit creation. Central banks — and governments for that matter — were not interested. It is thus suggestive that the very independence and lack of accountability of central banks has been a factor in allowing the creation of credit bubbles and the propagation of the current crisis."
— Richard Werner, *Understanding the Credit Crisis*

We propose the *Farrington-Meyers Law of Institutional Dynamics*: Knowledge and competence only flow up, and ignorance and incompetence only flow down. Global ignorance and incompetence will lead to local ignorance and incompetence, while local knowledge and competence might lead to global knowledge and competence.

Notice the latter implications are not exhaustive: On the one hand, local agents can be ignorant and incompetent, and global agents can be knowledgeable and competent. The former is contained and the latter is delicate. It seems to us there could be some sort of hand-wavy minimax principle at play here: Global knowledge and competence is likely to be the minimum of the local knowledge and competence it governs, while local ignorance and incompetence is likely to be the maximum of global ignorance and incompetence which governs it — *all crucially contingent* on the strength of information flow up and authority flow down.

So as not to fall into precisely Oakeshott's ire above, we will leave this as is rather than work into a *theory of social everything*, mindful that what this means in practice will surely vary from one circumstance to another, and in any *real situation* will feature many more variables than we have outlined. Just to really hammer this home, most of these variables will likely be unmeasurable or in principle unknowable, or it may not even make theoretical sense to conceive of them as "variables" given this is resolutely *not science* but social conjecture. We stress once more this is a tongue-in-cheek, hand-wavy model aimed at convincing the reader with reasonable coherence and consistency that there might be some sliver of truth to the tongue-in-cheek, hand-wavy claim that Bitcoin fixes everything; but not that this claim absolutely is true and we can prove it with Science™.

Our thinking derives in part from the following incisive passage in *Seeing Like a State*, in which James Scott first outlines the broad strokes of his critique of high-modernism:

> Designed or planned social order is necessarily schematic; it always ignores essential features of any real, functioning social order. This truth is best illustrated in a work-to-rule strike, which turns on the fact that any production process depends on a host of informal practices and improvisations that could never be codified. By merely following the rules meticulously, the workforce can virtually halt production. In the same fashion, the simplified rules animating plans for, say, a city, a village, or a collective farm were inadequate as a set of instructions for creating a functioning social order. The formal scheme was parasitic on informal processes that, alone, it could not create or maintain. To the degree that the formal scheme made no allowance for these processes or actually suppressed them, it failed both its intended beneficiaries and ultimately its designers as well.

Scott's framing makes it clear that this dynamic is not necessarily nefarious — although it may be — nor the result of individual failings — although again the individuals may be highly flawed — but rather emerges as a feature of hierarchical design and imposition itself. Planners need not be ignorant or incompetent to be *made relatively more* ignorant and incompetent by their distance from that which they plan and their insistence on arrogant rejection of feedback on their plans.

And so, the question remains: Relative to whatever arrangements of *designed or planned social order*, what effect will Bitcoin have? Our thesis is straightforward and follows not only from the preamble in this section or chapter, but arguably from the threads embarked upon across the book:

In Chapter One, *Wrestling with the Truth*, we introduced practical knowledge as the often-superior alternative to aesthetic and codified knowledge, which between them form the basis of high-modernist arrogance.

In Chapter Two, *The Complex Markets Hypothesis*, we argued that contemporary academic economics provides a standardized analysis of financial markets that is essentially high-modernist in motivation. Given markets are the epitome of practical and *unplanned* social order, the results are predictably awful, and we endeavor to provide an alternative analysis that assumes this complex order emerges from local knowledge and competence.

In Chapter Three, *This Is Not Capitalism,* we argued that, under the dominant regime of political economy, price signals are not being allowed to communicate the compression of accurate information about economic reality.

In Chapter Four, *Wittgenstein's Money*, we demonstrated that arguably the most important feature of functioning money *is to provide global signal* to guide necessarily local economic decision making.

In Chapter Five, *The Capital Strip Mine*, we traced the effect of this signal to money's most important enablement — capital — and deduced the likely consequences of this overwhelming interference on capital formation, as well as how this reflexively loops back to cause even more problems for money itself.

In Chapter Six, *Bitcoin Is Venice*, in the section, "Bitcoin Is Ariadne," we covered that Bitcoin is inherently peaceful technology incalculably easier to defend than to attack, and also that, as software, it is highly mobile as capital — arguably it possesses the maximum *possible* mobility. In the section, "Bitcoin Is Halal," we argued that Bitcoin will promote a system of capital formation that is fundamentally sustainable, for which we have the blueprint already, and for which the shenanigans of *The Capital Strip Mine* will happily be impossible to recreate. In "Bitcoin Is Gravity," we argued that capital will irresistibly be attracted into Bitcoin's orbit, advancing its mission by co-opting its adopters' incentives to its own ends. In "Bitcoin Is Logos" and "Bitcoin Is Techne," we argued that Bitcoin is in fact best understood as an informational signal for capital formation and, more importantly, works *at all*, not just as an idea but as a technology.

In Chapter Seven, *A Capital Renaissance*, we argued that Bitcoin at least provides necessary means — if insufficient in isolation — for a range of categories of tangible capital to become more locally competent and knowledgeable. Ideally this will lead to a stronger upwards signal if not overpowered by countervailing authority.

In Chapter Eight, *These Were Capitalists*, we argued that a range of categories of necessarily more intangible capital can only blossom when rooted in local knowledge and competence and are likely to suffer under especially arrogant global agents intent on imposing downward flowing authority, of which we gave some historical examples. This fits nicely with the argument developed just above in this section, but we will conclude by tying up the final loose end: What happens to the power of this authority under a Bitcoin standard?

We are relatively confident it will diminish. Perhaps not everywhere, and perhaps not all at once, but on average, and over the very long run, we believe incompetence and ignorance will no longer flow downwards with anything like the kind of power we have become used to and localism really will thrive. Localism will thrive not because it gives us warm, fuzzy feelings and "just works better if left alone," or some such similar sentiment, but far, far more importantly — and of arguably historical importance — the overwhelming interference in its working broadcast by global authorities will finally come to an end. It *will be left alone*. Perhaps not absolutely, but much more so than currently.

We see three clear reasons to believe this shift is likely:

1. Bitcoin increases the costs of global violence against local agents;
2. Bitcoin decreases the costs of local defense against the violence of global agents; and,
3. Bitcoin allows capital to become far more mobile than ever before,[216] which is really a way of saying that the first two points are even truer, for a new and different reason.

Altogether, this strongly suggests that Bitcoin will bring about dramatically lower returns to violence for institutions as well as individuals, as just about every input to the returns equation has changed favorably. We will discuss each in order.

The Shifting Returns to Violence

"A shepherd has a great deal of leisure; a husbandman, in the rude state of husbandry, has some; an artificer or manufacturer has none at all. The first may, without any loss, employ a great deal of his time in martial exercises; the second may employ some part of it; but the last cannot employ a single hour in them without some loss, and his attention to his own interest naturally leads him to neglect them altogether. These improvements in husbandry too, which the progress of arts and manufactures necessarily introduces, leave the husbandman as little leisure as the artificer. Military exercises come to be as much neglected by the inhabitants of the country as by those of the town, and the great body of the people becomes altogether unwarlike. That wealth, at the same time, which always follows the improvements of agriculture and manufactures, and which in reality is no more than the accumulated produce of those improvements, provokes the invasion of all their neighbours. An industrious, and upon that account a wealthy nation, is of all nations the most likely to be attacked; and unless the state takes some new measures for the public defence, the natural habits of the people render them altogether incapable of defending themselves."
— Adam Smith, *The Wealth of Nations*

Bitcoin raises the cost to attack. This is true in the trivial sense that SHA256 almost certainly cannot be broken with less than the total energy available in the universe. But it is true in what we might call a more holistic sense as well. As discussed in the conclusion of Chapter Eight, *These Were* Capitalists, Bitcoin provides the much-needed negative feedback to defang toxic bigness and force the artificially big to reckon with their own unsustainability. Under the dominant regime of political economy, the monetary cost of exerting authority backed by violence is effectively zero. The true costs are borne invisibly in the misallocation and consumption of social capital.

The welfare/warfare state literally prints money to fund its asinine and locally destructive high-modernist schemes. The cost is borne by the schemes' victims, as a kind of nonobvious stealth tax in addition to the more obvious senses in which they are victimized by authoritative interference in locally generated economic signal resulting in accidental consumption of local capital. Bitcoin fixes this, because Bitcoin thwarts toxic bigness and reverses the exponential positive feedback loop of power accrual with externalized costs. It internalizes the externalities and forces a reckoning. While the microphone of fiat generates a compounding cacophony of louder and louder noise, Bitcoin unplugs the speaker and lets us listen for a signal.

Bitcoin lowers the cost to defend. This, too, is true in the trivial sense of hash outputs and public key signatures being effectively free to verify, and properly secured bitcoin being both easy to set up and nearly impossible to attack thereafter. But, again, the implications run deeper.

An obvious criticism of this line of argument might be that it is naïve about the true extent to which *software is eating the world*. Sure, more and more economic value is becoming encoded in software, but almost all of it will only ever exist as production capital. In fact, this was cited in Chapter Six, *Bitcoin Is Venice*, as precisely an advantage! We claimed it

> created the independent skilled-laborer-cum-entrepreneur as a class of economic agent whose capacity for capital creation is human, not financial.

Of course, this does not mean all capital, value, culture, and life will move to the cloud.

We anticipated this criticism by also arguing,

> Physical capital still matters, clearly. So does cultural capital. These are so obvious as to be weird to need to point out. But those in a position to extract protection rents on physical capital, likely with the allure of cultural capital, will need to adjust to this new reality. Sticks are out, carrots are in. What are you gonna do about it? Build a wall? Good luck with that.

As per this articulation, we have only really stated that the costs to attack have been raised. The obvious concern, and cause for accusations of naïveté, is that most physical capital of worthwhile value is relatively immobile, if not *entirely*. Frederic Lane sets the stage nicely, writing in *Force and Enterprise in Oceanic Commerce*,

> I think it may be accepted as a general proposition that every economic enterprise needs protection against the destruction or seizure of its capital and the disruption of its labor force. In creating protection under a system of law, governments imposed practices concerning the appropriation of land, labor, and others goods. Establishing these practices was part of the process of organizing production. If production, such as the growing of sugar cane or the mining of silver, was done by organizations separate from government, then the situation could be described by saying that the government created conditions favorable to the development of business enterprise.

But if, as we predict, such conditions are natural in and of themselves; if protection of production itself is unnecessary or is even meaningless — how does a government "protect" or "enforce" an on-chain smart contract? — we leave it to the reader to ponder what exactly of value is being provided to producers, especially given how mobile capital will likely also become …

Bitcoin makes capital more mobile. Of course, if all else fails — if the attackers have deep pockets and no economic sense, perhaps a penchant for violence for the emotional thrill rather than any aspirations of wealth — then you can just run away. This may mean leaving physical capital behind, but we suspect increasingly it will not. We sowed the seeds across many points of Chapter Seven, A *Capital Renaissance*, to now sensibly suggest that a great deal of capital will likely become more mobile, on the basis of the internet (admittedly metaphorically) digitally extending its previously solely physical utility.

In *Exit, Voice, and Loyalty*, Hirschman compares the norm in academic economics to find "voice"[217] to be somehow primitive or vulgar to an apparent symmetry in academic political science in which "exit" is equally horrid. In a sense, this implicitly touches on the same criticism of reductivism criticized by Edwin Gay in the first section of the previous chapter, that, when viewed appropriately holistically, the more naturally political concept of voice has obvious relevance in economics, and vice versa with exit in politics. Regardless, Hirschman writes,

> The economist is by no means alone in having a blindspot, a "trained incapacity" (as Veblen called it) for perceiving the usefulness of [voice]. In fact, in the political realm, exit has fared much worse than has voice in the realm of economics. Rather than as merely ineffective or "cumbrous," exit has often been branded as criminal, for it has been labelled desertion, defection, and treason.

We agree this seems to be a strange concept for many contemporary thinkers, but the logic is entirely natural and arguably compelling. Davidson and Rees-Mogg cut through this outmoded thinking in *The Sovereign Individual*, with respect to taxation, never mind more nefarious or destructive modes of appropriation,

> Those with the earning ability and capital to meet the competitive challenges of the Information Age will be able to locate anywhere and do business anywhere. With a choice of domiciles, only the most patriotic or stupid will continue to reside in high-tax countries.

Hirschman, however, does have an appropriately holistic outlook, and places the urge to *exit* not just outside of economics alone, but firmly within the cultural, spiritual, and historical context of the United States of America, writing,

> This preference for the neatness of exit over the messiness and heartbreak of voice has then "persisted throughout our national history." The exit from Europe could be re-enacted within the United States by the progressive settlement of the frontier, which Frederick Jackson Turner characterized as the "gate of escape from the bondage of the past." Even though the opportunity to "go West" may have been more

myth than reality for large population groups in the eastern section of the country, the myth itself was of the greatest importance for it provided everyone with a paradigm of problem-solving. Even after the closing of the frontier, the very vastness of the country combined with easy transportation make it far more possible for Americans than for most other people to think about solving their problems through "physical flight"' than either through resignation or through ameliorating and fighting in situ the particular conditions into which one has been "thrown." The curious conformism of Americans, noted by observers ever since Tocqueville, may also be explained in this fashion. Why raise your voice in contradiction and get yourself into trouble as long as you can always remove yourself entirely from any given environment should it become too unpleasant?

That this spirit lives on even though the frontier is long closed has led many to feel that there is perhaps no America for Americans. Curiously conformist in their anti-conformism, we predict many Americans will take up the challenge of new and emerging nations to which they can exit and relive this foundational myth. As we will get to several sections down, we predict it will become common for American States to fashion themselves as independent enough of the nation at large[218] to be viable such targets for immigrants.

We do caution, however, that it seems unlikely exit will be a panacea. This will only be true in some cases, in some industries, with some technologies. But the extent to which it *is true* and to which this reasoning does apply will be fascinating to watch unfold.

We offer three musings to conclude this section: Linking *returns to violence* back to Scott's pathology of high-modernism; an observation on the possible historical contingency of a model of *returns to violence* that we feel is typically taken for granted, and; a musing on what rapidly decreasing returns to violence means for the political process.

On high-modernism. The reader may have wondered, much in line with the quote from Garfinkel and Skaperdas in the introductory section to this chapter, whether or not this entire way of conceiving of the economics of violence is unfortunately taboo, and as a result is not widely discussed or appreciated?[219] In the same essay, *Conflict and Appropriation as Economic Activities*, Garfinkel and Skaperdas make the following fascinating point:

> Can the activities of the Bihari landowners, the police, the French farmers, the British coalminers, and the possible responses of other constituencies be exempt from study by economists? Going through an economics principles text or scanning the literature of the past century would suggest a positive answer. But surely this answer must not have been the result of a perception that conflict and appropriation have no relevance for economic welfare. Rather the absence of conflict and

appropriation in mainstream economic writing appears to have its origins in late nineteenth-century Britain — starting with the marginalists and culminating in Marshall — with the purpose of making political economy analytically more tractable in accordance with a principle of division of labor in the social sciences. Tractability in the field of "political economy" was conveniently achieved by ignoring anything that smacked of politics, including conflict. To make the transformed discipline more respectable in the scientific circles of their time and to signify the break with the past, these gentlemen gave it a new name: economics.

If we recall Scott's general criticism of high-modernism that it attempts to make *legible* what in reality has no decipherable form,[220] it makes sense to us without torturing the connection too much that this is exactly what has happened in the economic literature. Unlike investment, cash flows, or population, and the like — that is to say, unlike *stocks and flows* — violence is nearly impossible to quantify. This is surely only exacerbated by it being a taboo, hence the standard approach seems to have been to ignore it. Or, if addressed at all, to do so entirely unrealistically and call it *uneconomical* or *irrational*, as if *returns to violence* are zero by definition for any society civilized enough to be worth the economists' attention.

On historical contingency. There may be a subtle and not-widely-addressed feature of capital that depends on the contingent interplay of returns to violence and the stage of a society's economic development. If the costs to attack are relatively low and the costs to defend relatively high, all no matter the size and mobility of the capital, is there not a perverse incentive to invest in capital that is as massive and immobile as possible? Or rather, in the absence of natural incentives for capital to be small and mobile, may one as well create it as enormously as possible, if there are in fact other benefits to doing so?

Might this be as totally straightforward as locally increasing returns to scale? That is, a la Adam Smith, division of labor in a factory is economical. But it assumes and clearly requires a factory. If no matter what capital you locally create it will be subject to the same irresistible level of downward flowing incompetence and ignorance, then you may as well build a factory.

This tentative conclusion can likely be scaled beyond individual enterprises to nations also — or, if the reader prefers, *sovereign corporations*, whatever that comes to mean. For all our championing of "localism," the reader may have noticed our simplistic and deliberately tongue-in-cheek model still assumes that some or other "global" authority still at least exists, however relatively defined and however minimal its power. But is that necessarily the case? We suspect probably not. There will certainly be *more sovereigns*, and *more local sovereigns*, very likely in the form of *more and more local nation states*. Leopold

Kohr recalls in the Preface to the 1986 paperback edition of his *The Breakdown of Nations*,[221]

> One of the few ever to embrace the idea of division without reservations was an Italian lady from Siena. As a wartime refugee from Mussolini who had fled to London, she understood perhaps better than most that the vast unity of states imparted vastness also to the reach of terrorism and persecution. She alone seemed genuinely delighted at the prospect of a return to an Augustan world of small states. Clapping her hands, she exclaimed: "What a blessing! Imagine, you would have to flee a distance of only fifteen or twenty miles to reach the safety of exile."

This may seem radical but it has such clear historical precedent that we would argue it is mundane. We do not just mean that, *in the past there were more nations, and that seems more likely to us to happen again than for there to now be even fewer.* We mean that, when this was true, it was true *for the same reasons* as we are now about to experience. In *Anarchy and its Breakdown*, Jack Hirshleifer writes,

> In the early fifteenth century, the introduction of cannon made it possible to batter down old-style walls, ending a long historical period of indecisive siege warfare. A major consequence was a sharp reduction in the number of independent principalities in western Europe [...] actually, this technological predominance of the offence was temporary, being shortly reversed by improvements in the art of fortification. But the economic effect remained much the same, because their enormous cost put modern fortifications beyond the reach of smaller political units.

To very mildly adapt Hirshleifer's terminology to our own: A shift in technology caused the costs of attack to fall and the costs of defense to rise. Even though production capital at the time was typically more mobile than today, we here face a slightly different issue given we are talking about polities, not individuals. It is very, very difficult for a "state" to "move". It may well have been practically meaningless since the first permanent settlements of human populations at the dawn of the agricultural revolution.

This historical period, while not unique in this respect, is fascinating on account of it requiring the *inauguration of property rights*. Not the enforcement of property rights, the protection of property, the transfer of title, or the collateralization of title so as to create capital ... the *creation of the rights* in the first place, ex nihilo, so all these activities might follow. The classical reference in the course of such argumentation is, of course, John Locke's *Second Treatise on Government*, and while we have a great deal of sympathy for the idea of *mixing one's labor with the land*,[222] our concern here is not theoretical but historical. We are not asking how this *should* happen, or *should have happened*; we are asking how it *did* happen and how it *does* happen. Very much in keeping with our focus on realism and violence rather than abstraction and morality, in *Might Makes Rights: A Theory of the Formation and Initial Distribution of Property* Rights, John Umbeck frames the problem as follows:

> In the most general sense, ownership rights are "the expectations a person has that his decision about the uses of certain resources will be effective."[223] Interpreted in this manner, ownership can emerge from a variety of circumstances. For example, a person may acquire a right in coconuts simple because he is the only one who can climb a tree. Similarly, an individual may have rights to fish because he alone knows where to catch them. Or, a pretty woman may have the rights to a seat on a crowded bus because she is pretty. Notice, however, that even in these cases the individuals can be deprived of their rights by other individuals. Non-tree climbers can cut the coconut tree down, the fisherman can be continually watched and followed until his private fishing post is discovered, and the pretty woman can be thrown from her bus seat or made physically unattractive. in other words, ownership rights to property can exist only as long as other people agree to respect them or as long as the owner can forcefully exclude those who do not agree.
>
> If the individuals agree to respect each other's ownership rights, they may do so either implicitly, in which case they are usually called customs or traditions, or explicitly through contract, in which case they are called laws or rules. Included in the former group would be such things as not "cutting in" to a line of waiting people or asking if a seat is already taken in a theatre. Casual empiricism suggests that the rights to a relatively valuable resource are usually assigned explicitly through contract and not left to custom.[224] It is the contractually agreed upon distribution of newly formed rights that this paper is trying to explain.
>
> However, even if all individuals enter into an explicit agreement to assign and respect each other's ownership rights, some force or threat of force will still be required. This follows from the postulate of individual maximization. If one can violate the terms of the agreement and deprive another of his assigned rights he will do so if the gains exceed the costs. Therefore, the contracting group must agree to impose costs upon anyone who would take someone else's property. This will involve the forceful exclusion of would-be violators. *Ultimately all ownership rights are based on the abilities of individuals, or groups of individuals, to forcefully maintain exclusivity.*[225]

As mentioned in Chapter One, *Wrestling with the Truth*, but alluded to throughout the book, the final, emphasized claim is no longer true given the existence of Bitcoin. This is precisely the near-miracle Bitcoin represents, property that can be defended without violence or even the threat of violence, given it is infinitely costly to attack.

Regardless, this is hardly a fair criticism of Umbeck, whose essay we approvingly quote was written in 1981. After an interesting theoretical discussion, to which the above quote serves as an introduction, Umbeck turns his attention to the California gold rush of 1848 and, to quote part of the title of the paper, *the formation and initial distribution of property rights* in this period. Umbeck provides the following concise summary:

> Immediately following the discovery, the first miners worked independently of one another. They would and live in small groups, but the actual mining was done on an individual basis. These first miners found gold bearing land to exist over an area three hundred miles long and one hundred miles wide along the western foothills of the Sierra mountains. Throughout 1848, with the relatively abundant gold land and the relatively small number of miners, there were no indications that anyone explicitly claimed exclusive rights to the particular piece of land. Most of the miners carried guns, yet the reports of violence during the early period are remarkably scarce. Apparently, it was less costly to move to new land than to fight.
>
> With the huge population increase of 1849, gold land became relatively scarce and the potential for conflict increased. However, instead of violence, the miners chose to enter into explicit contractual arrangements with all those present at a particular gold deposit. In these contracts, it was provided that each individual was to get a parcel of land of specified size. As long as the miner worked this parcel, called a "claim," at stipulated intervals, he had exclusive rights to the land and all the gold contained.

In the *Illustrated History of Plumas, Lassen and Sierra Counties, California*, Farriss and Smith elaborate,

> The first workers on the bar had taken up claims of a generous size, and soon the whole bar was occupied. The region was full of miners and they came pouring down upon the river, attracted by the reports of a rich strike, until their tents and campfires presented the appearance of a vast army. Those without claims far exceeded in number the fortunate ones. A miners' meeting was called to make laws. Majority ruled in a mining camp in those days, and it was voted to cut down the size of claims to forty feet. The claim owners were powerless to resist, but had to admit to the fiat of the majority. The miners were then registered in the order of the date of their arrival upon the bar, and in that order were allowed to select claims until all were taken. Even then there was a great crowd of disappointed ones.

William Bonner and Pierre Lemieux comment on this precise extract from Farriss and Smith in *The Idea of America*,

> Notice that the majority always prevailed at the miner's meetings. I have copies of nearly 200 original contracts formed by miners to assign exclusive land rights. In every case, the provisions of the contracts were determined through majority-rule vote. Of course, in the absence of any agreement, violence would be the allocator, and, if we assume that the miners were about equal in their abilities to shoot each other, the majority would always decide an outcome. Notice, also, that preference in claim section was given to those who were first to arrive in the district.

This is all notable for our purposes for several interrelated reasons. First, although violence and credible threats of violence were always possible in the background, and did occasionally materialize, both peace and capital formation followed from spontaneous social organization.[226] The motivation was maybe not quite so noble as *inherent human goodness* as we previously suggested, but is surely at least economically rational in a communitarian rather than individualist sense. The individual returns to violence for starting a gun fight and stealing some gold were likely attractive, but the returns to economic cooperation were more attractive still.

Second, the multiple references above to "majority rule" imply credible threats of violence. Voting is something of a shortcut to figure out what the results of violence would be so as not to need to be resorted to. Bitcoin, on the other hand, cannot be interacted with this way. You either play by the nonviolent rules or you don't play at all. But given Bitcoin is well on track to become the global reserve currency and likely the backing of every currency in the world (if not *just* the only currency in the world) what this really means is: You play by the non-violent rules or forego economic exchange. No stuff for you!

Finally, this period might seem remote to our own experiences of law and economics. While the technology, the demographics, and the details of capital formation and economic exchange are all difficult to relate to, we would argue the situation is strikingly similar in one crucial respect: We, too, are operating on a frontier. Not a geographic frontier, as were the forty-niners, but something of an economic frontier — possibly a *conceptual frontier.* We have never before had a digital bearer asset, nor an asset of any kind with trivial costs to defend and practically infinite costs to attack. This moment is at least as historically relevant as the settling of the American West. Likely more so.

On the political process. Rapidly falling returns to violence simply makes politics less interesting. There will be next to no opportunity for intelligent sociopaths to game the political process and the idea of "political entrepreneurship" will become increasingly vacuous. Should governments as we know them still exist, and, for the sake of argument, should they remain large, they will almost surely at least become a lot more *boring*. They will just administrate.

They will operate in the background to keep administration ticking over. However big they manage to get (and to whoever's annoyance!) may be in a peculiar sense justified on the basis it will only be possible in the first place if they are governing their polities exceptionally well. Recall from Chapter Seven, A *Capital Renaissance*, Bitcoin forces any and all institutions to reckon with the consequences of toxic and unsustainable bigness. Hence bigness will only be possible if healthy and sustainable.

This is a rather dry and mechanical reading, but we believe there are likely to be softer, more intangible, and frankly more pleasant and civilized benefits also. The *Wealth of Nations* quote at the head of this section is interesting in that Smith seems to take several aspects of martial costs for granted, that (1) the costs of attack and defense are fixed, meaning the calculus this suggests results in, (2) "the state" needing to take "new measures for the public defense," or else, (3) "the natural habits of the people render them altogether incapable of defending themselves."

We know point (1) is false, and (2) is possible but by no means necessary, and would probably require substantially more circumstantial information to decide rather than being deducible in principle, as per the discussion a few paragraphs up. But (3) may be the most interesting. We have covered already that "the people" almost certainly *will be capable* of defending themselves. But this raises an immediate question of what they will do instead? If there is no honey pot of "new measures for the public defense" worth devoting energy to seizing, and also therefore no need to worry that somebody else will seize it if they do not, what will they spend their time and energy doing?

We have one pretty generic idea, which is that whatever people get up to, they will be more open to negotiation, cooperation or, as a last resort, arbitration, given the *previous* last resort of credible threats of irresistible state-level violence will be nowhere near as compelling — if compelling at all. This was precisely the lesson of Umbeck's analysis quoted above. Roughly similar circumstances in nineteenth-century California created roughly similar outcomes to what we predict; the profile of returns to violence encouraged a kind of communitarianism and spontaneous social contracting. There was no overwhelming state force to rely on to enforce contracts in the first place, but there was a clear economic benefit to cooperation in place of violence.

Perhaps also it isn't too much to hope that pandering to power becomes at worst pointless and at best frowned upon as barbaric; and equally that public figures who resolutely stick to their morals will be respected rather than chastised as extremists. Be they business leaders, intellectuals, elected officials, or whoever, we may graduate to a far better class of public figure than we are used to today who no longer constantly scampers around currying favor with elites and visibly keeping abreast of moral fashions, but who just does their job and otherwise keeps their mouth shut. If there is no power to tap into in the first place then it may not be too much to hope for that they will concentrate their efforts on their actual jobs instead.

Beyond this we have no idea, but we also do not think the answer matters. Whatever it is, it will likely be good! It will be productive! Its utility will not be backed or validated by credible threats of violence but by profit and returns in the market or by communal acceptance and support. We readily and happily admit this is intangible to the point of outright fluff, but so what? What is the point of contemplating and analyzing the political economy of violence if not to learn how best to create space for the intangibly *nonviolent*? What is this entire line of questioning if not a way of asking, at the societal level: *Why can't we have nice things*? Or, perhaps, in anticipation of a Bitcoin standard: *When **can** we have nice things, and how nice will they be, exactly?*

The Sovereign Community

"If the American people ever allow [private] banks to control the issue of their currency, first by inflation, then by deflation, the banks and corporations that will grow up around them will deprive the people of all property until their children wake up homeless on the continent their Fathers conquered [...] I believe that banking institutions are more dangerous to our liberties than standing armies [...] The issuing power should be taken from the banks and restored to the people, to whom it properly belongs."
— Thomas Jefferson

In Chapter Seven, A *Capital Renaissance*, we characterized the likely *general way in which* Bitcoin fixes finance, communications, and our relationship with the environment as being that Bitcoin makes access to and control over these capital stocks more decentralized. In Chapter Eight, *These Were Capitalists*, we also detailed successes in more abstract cases of "capital." The primary effect, in the former *was* and the latter *probably will be*, to remove single points of failure and the heightened risk of failure at these points brought about by excessive leverage that wouldn't exist if it weren't for distorted flows of knowledge and competence as conveyed in prices, language, and culture.

So, as a tangible example following from Chapter Seven, A *Capital Renaissance*: The Lightning Network performs a similar role to the card networks, but is nearly impossible to meaningfully "attack" as a peer-to-peer network rather than a client/server model, the "servers" of which are a handful of multi-national, multi-centi-billion-dollar companies with data centers, regulators, CEOs and their friends and families ... in other words, attack vectors galore. Likewise, Bitcoin creates an incentive to extend "the grid" digitally rather than physically. This obviously introduces a number of fascinating binaries worthy of comparison, but consider one not yet mentioned: known versus anonymous.

A miner can *connect to the network* while under a waterfall, in a sunlit desert, or on a geothermal spring, or anywhere at all they can transport a diesel generator, without anybody anywhere in the world knowing their identity, their location, their hardware ... anything at all really besides that they proved their work and that they are entitled to and receive the block subsidy and the transaction fees. Now we have peer-to-peer energy as opposed to the gigantic server of "the grid" and the helpless clients of "pretty much everybody who wants reliable electrical power."

As an intangible example following from Chapter Eight, These *Were Capitalists*, consider that the very prediction just outlined of economic dependence being gradually pared back and eventually removed will in turn remove the primary incentive for *everything to be political*. The politicization of everything rests on grudging compliance, and people tend to comply out of fear that the resources on which they depend will be withdrawn for insufficient ideological support. If it is possible to live independently of centralized leverage over material well-being there is no reason whatsoever to heed unrelenting panic porn and comply with the continued descent into a panopticon of social credit; which is to say, the incessant strip mining of social and cultural capital.

With true self-sovereignty and independence, there will be no need for *ketman* — we can heed Solzhenitsyn's advice rather than Miłosz's, and live no longer by lies. Independent of ever-invasive corruption, we will finally be free to do so; to no longer host an economic, social, and cultural cancer, but to carve it out and let it expire. We find a guilty, sadistic pleasure in the realization that those who have the most power over others to lose due to the ripples of Bitcoin's pressure on political economy are also those so ideologically compromised as to be the very last people to understand Bitcoin itself, if they ever do.

Once the reader grasps the rough mental model here of the obvious benefits of peer-to-peer networks over client/server models, it is not difficult to extrapolate. Nor is it difficult to ensure such extrapolation can be kept realistic rather than utopian simply by accurately referring to Bitcoin's astonishing and novel technical properties. To repeat Kissinger's aphorism first quoted in Chapter Seven, A *Capital Renaissance*, "who controls the food supply controls the people; who controls the energy can control continents; who controls money can control the world."[227] We are on the cusp of a brave new world in which nobody controls the money, hence the energy, hence the food supply. What happens to control of the people, the continents, and the world, remains to be seen.

To keep up the theme of resilience, but to move even further way from the idea of "the sovereign individual," we would further argue Bitcoin provides less powerful states with a means to resist and escape predation and exploitation. Probably the most obvious example, and in a sense the one that ultimately underpins the rest as far as *money* goes, is the important role played in US dollar hegemony by OPEC pricing, which we cited already in Chapter Five, *The Capital Strip Mine*. We assume this is relatively well known and well understood and so offer two completely different flavors of example, both of which have recently been explored in great depth by Alex Gladstein of the Human Rights Foundation.

In his essay *Fighting Monetary Colonialism with Open-Source Code*,[228] and drawing extensively on *Africa's Last Colonial Currency* by Fanny Pigeaud, Ngongo Sylla, and Thomas Fazi, Gladstein investigates the history and ongoing reality of the French colonial CFA franc system. In fifteen sub-Saharan African nations, across more than 180 million inhabitants in an area two-thirds the size of India, citizens of countries ranging from Senegal to Gabon use the CFA franc instead of a national currency. The currency — launched at the end of the colonial period in the 1940s — has been gradually debased by more than 99% against the French franc, or what is now the Euro. The latest major devaluation was in 1994, when half of the purchasing power of the CFA franc was destroyed in an attempt to boost the competitiveness of CFA nation exports. Since colonial times the French state has used the CFA system to cheaply harvest resources ranging from uranium to tin to lumber from CFA nations at below market prices, often selling finished goods back to those very same CFA nations at above market prices. The French state has a de facto first right of refusal on exports coming from CFA nations, as well as construction and service contract imports. The CFA nations are prevented from building their stocks of productive capital, and end up exporting raw goods, unable to develop manufacturing bases. This parasitic relationship has helped finance and subsidize the French welfare state over the past seven decades, and has given it a huge captive market for goods that it would have trouble selling elsewhere. Historically, CFA nations had to keep as much as 100%, and only recently 50%, of their reserves in Paris with French banks. CFA nations may have won their independence in the 1960s, but remain financially dependent on France.

Political leaders who threatened to disrupt the CFA system were dispatched with violence, or were left by the French to fend for themselves against violent insurgencies. The economic histories of Burkina Faso, Togo, Guinea, and Mali are especially vivid in this regard. Today, the French state is introducing some reforms to some CFA nations, but they are considered surface-level by many observers. Going back decades, the French government has propped up a variety of odious dictators to keep the CFA system in place. With the exception of Senegal, none of the 15 CFA countries have experienced meaningful democratization, and countries like Guinea Bissau, Chad, Niger, and Benin remain some of the poorest on earth. Here, the French continue to operate a capital strip mine on par with the most striking colonial operations of the past. And, given President Emmanuel Macron's plans for French expansion in Africa in coming decades, it is unlikely that the French will agree to a reduction in control in this matter.

What choice do CFA citizens have? They can seek political change through rebellion or revolution, but it is unclear if independent states with their own currencies will fare that much better. Yes, countries like Ghana with independent monetary policies have fared demonstrably better than CFA nations, but Nigeria, with price inflation at a mere 15%, is a low bar for success. Hyperinflation would be a constant and fatal threat to any new currency. At the national level, there simply isn't much hope for a better currency. And so, many CFA citizens are now opting into Bitcoin. Though their per-capita use lags behind Anglophone countries like Ghana and Nigeria, some countries like Togo are now in the top ten in terms of peer-to-peer cryptocurrency volume as noted by Chainalysis's 2021 Global Crypto Adoption Index,[229] adjusted for population and internet penetration. If the regime won't change, and the old colonial powers won't leave, at least citizens can opt for a currency that they control. This is why activists like Farida Nabourema from Togo and Fodé Diop from Senegal call Bitcoin the currency of decolonization.

This hope is echoed by some in Palestine, as well. The Palestinian political struggle is well known throughout their world, but their economic struggle is barely discussed, yet equally severe if not worse in terms of human impact. Gladstein explores this crisis in his essay, "Can Bitcoin Be Palestine's Currency of Freedom?"[230] in which he reveals how the capital stock of citizens in the West Bank and Gaza Strip has been relentlessly eroded over decades of Israeli colonial policy. After twenty years of Israeli occupation, these trends were clear in 1987, as Sara Roy's article, "The Gaza Strip: A Case of Economic De-Development," makes clear, that the Palestinian economy was becoming completely dependent on Israel for jobs and imports, and unable to build up a manufacturing or agrarian base. Over time, farmers and builders in Palestine were priced out by subsidized Israeli goods, and were forced to give up their economic productivity and independence for higher-paying jobs in Israel. Statistics show, for example, despite a rising Palestinian population, a decline in agricultural jobs between the 1960s and 1990s. These trends were amplified after the Paris Protocol of 1994, an overlooked but hugely influential economic document signed by the newly-minted Palestinian Authority, which granted Israel near-total control over the Palestinian economy, made the Shekel legal tender in the West Bank and Gaza, gave it control over exports and imports, and discretion over labor policy and remittance flows.

Over the past twenty-five years, these trends have become even more severe, especially in Gaza, where Israeli (and Egyptian) restrictions after the 2000 Intifada and 2006 electoral victory of Hamas in addition to consistent bombings and embargoes have completely collapsed economic activity. The situation on the ground in Gaza is shocking, with 50% unemployment and virtually all of the productive capital destroyed. Even in the West Bank, individuals have no access to the kind of fintech or investing options that citizens of Israel enjoy, and continue to have to use an effectively foreign and imposed currency while living under the enormous corruption and bureaucratic waste of Fatah and Mahmoud Abbas, a nepotistic and increasingly authoritarian ruler. Some Palestinians are peacefully protesting through the use of Bitcoin, which they view as a way to gain independence from Israel, in the spirit of the first intifada. That late 1980s movement, which was largely successful in making the occupation expensive and costly for Israel (previous to it, Israel had profited from the occupation), was aimed towards achieving self-sovereignty through agriculture and reducing dependency on the Israeli economy. These goals of resistance, however, are impossible if Palestinians still have to use the shekel. With Bitcoin, they have access to a global, digital, sound, open-source, programmable money, in which no party is privileged, nor can interfere.

One could well argue that injustices of international relations prevail all over the world, and even tease that "world peace" is perhaps too grand an aspiration if not an indication of unseriousness on account of being as much a traditional punchline as a serious aim. We do not think this hunch at all diminishes the hope Bitcoin may provide to the people of West Africa and Palestine, but as a final example distinctly above the level of the individual, we would highlight adversarial subdivisions within federal or quasi-federal states. For much the same reasons as may allow the likes of Mali to get out from under the yoke of France, and Palestine from Israel, so too will Catalonia and the Basque Country have an extra-legal means to defy Spain, the regions of the Po Valley to defy Italy, and Texas, Wyoming, and Florida to defy the US Federal Government, should they choose to exploit it.

The latter seem already to be very much on this path and we do not think it will be long at all before they will be in a financial position to turn down Federal "aid" and hence be unthreatenable when they then decide to extract themselves and their citizens from the hooks of the US Federal Government. We feel this path is worth highlighting as being of subtle geopolitical importance, and which should not be ignored or brushed aside under the false binary of only "the individual" on the one hand and "the state" on the other. We must ask, *which state*? After all, states have rivalries, incentives, and hierarchies as well and there is no reason to believe that Bitcoin cannot be useful, in remarkably similar ways as already discussed for individuals, based only on *relative* power and locality.

Moreover, states have rivalries, incentives, and hierarchies also with corporations as well as other states — what we might call non-sovereign corporations as opposed to sovereign corporations — presumably under the protection of a sovereign corporation far more powerful than themselves. As can be gleaned from numerous quoted extracts primarily in Chapter Seven, *A Capital Renaissance*, it is a common trope for environmentalists to bemoan that western corporations engaged in pollution, extraction, etc. are often as powerful or conceivably *even more powerful* (certainly better capitalized) than the developing economies bearing the brunt of their waste and destruction. The potential for sustainability and self-sufficiency offered by Bitcoin may come to provide a means and a hope for states to extricate themselves from the likes of multinational energy and finance companies which can rightfully be said to operate on a neo-colonial basis: not only strip mining the literal, *natural* resources of poorer nations and preventing the bootstrapping of their own capital stocks, but imposing alien cultural values on the populace via the leverage of financial control — typically whatever direction the winds of moral fashion happen to be blowing that week in London, New York, and Washington D.C.

Furthermore, we expect Bitcoin to reinvigorate pro-democracy movements worldwide for three simple and related reasons. Democracy as an intellectual concept seems to us to be given zealous and therefore unthinking and undue support amongst thinkers of right thoughts in the West, 99% of whom are likely entirely unaware of the serious arguments against their essentially religious view, or frankly have ever even thought about it beyond a form of religious affirmation.

However, we have some hope that inviolably sound money may be a missing piece for the serious pro-democracy camp. A crude characterization of the typical objection is that democracy seemingly inevitably tends towards short-termism in general, and impatient consumption of what has not yet been produced in particular.[231] And, as above, the historically unprecedented power granted along these lines by the mechanics of fiat money makes the temptation to subsume capital stocks under the power of the state simply irresistible. So irresistible, we believe, that this degenerate cultural and political force pulls every otherwise *civil* dispute into its gravitational orbit. Any and every private disagreement is escalated to the level of politics, meaning everything becomes political; everybody has their pet political cause for which they fight for state preference, and the social fabric by which disputes are resolved and individuals learn responsibility and compromise itself begins to dissolve. Bizarrely, then, the extreme of collectivism itself causes an entwined extreme of individualism somehow even more perverse.

But does it not follow that removing the real root of this problem ought also to remove this temptation? Without a money that has this specific flaw of costless creation and control, but is furthermore designed such that even much milder violations of long-termism and capital formation such as unbacked debt become extremely problematic, might we be in a position to reject toxic collectivism *and* toxic individualism in one fell swoop, and return to healthy, voluntarist, communitarian balance? We are open to this being a naïve view, but there are further supportive and interrelated reasons to potentially find it compelling.

Second, Bitcoin is fast becoming a single voter issue that is potentially historically unprecedented. "Freedom" is almost never a practical political position in a democracy, no matter its apparent popularity, for two basic reasons: It negates the very purpose of the politician proposing it and hence makes no *political* sense.[232] But also, the more uniformly entrenched and accepted are individually bought preferences from the state, the more "freedom" will come to have some minor benefit to everybody but some major cost, also to everybody. Everybody's major cost will be different, but nonetheless the grounds for opposition will be clear and compelling. It is impossible — arguably *dangerous* — to try to coordinate an escape from this communal trap because any defector from a mutiny stands to acquire the state preferences of the left-behind mutineers.

Bitcoin, on the other hand, is not a negative issue, but an entirely positive one. It is a civil rights movement that applies to absolutely everybody *except* those already entrenched in finance and politics, and which effectively bribes them to become and stay a part of it. An individual need not be *against* a litany of petty infringements too numerous to keep track of or even count. She need only support Bitcoin, which will itself obsolete these infringements. Politicians in democracies will not be able to muddy the waters on a handful of pettily tyrannical positions about which nobody cares in particular — besides, of course, their donors, who care deeply about keeping freedom at bay on those specific issues and no others; if they come out against Bitcoin, they mark themselves as explicitly anti-freedom and will be the object of relentless, *global* ridicule and attack.

Many will nonetheless try; we suspect the more technologically and mathematically illiterate who not only have not spent time understanding Bitcoin, are not used to spending any time understanding any technology, but who have only ever lived in a degenerate fiat world in which outcomes are dictated by power, consequences for capital and civilization be damned. This is potentially a potent force for freedom, prosperity, and human flourishing that mechanically depends on the democratic process.

Christopher Lasch wrote in *The Culture of Narcissism*,

> Modern bureaucracy has undermined earlier traditions of local action, the revival and extension of which holds out the only hope that a decent society will emerge from the wreckage of capitalism. The inadequacy of solutions dictated from above now forces people to invent solutions from below. Disenchantment with governmental bureaucracies has begun to extend to corporate bureaucracies as well — the real centers of power in contemporary society. In small towns and crowded urban neighborhoods, even in suburbs, men and women have initiated modest experiments in cooperation, designed to defend their rights against the corporations and the state. The "flight from politics," as it appears to the managerial and political elite, may signify the citizen's growing unwillingness to take part in the political system as a consumer of prefabricated spectacles. It may signify, in other words, not a retreat from politics at all but the beginnings of a general political revolt.

Published in 1979, this was certainly premature and possibly overly hopeful and naïve. Lasch possibly foresaw a cyclic rebound from the desolation of narcissism he diagnosed? We cannot know for sure, but, as argued in Chapter Seven, *A Capital Renaissance*, and again in Chapter Eight, *These Were Capitalists,* we think it reasonable to ascribe Lasch's concerns, at least in part, to precisely the breakdown in social and cultural capital we believe has resulted from degenerate fiat capitalism. We think his comments above can be read as an excellent explanation of a pro-freedom and essentially local and distributed democratic momentum building around Bitcoin.

Third and finally, we think, as opposed to the questionable merits of "national democracy" on display around the world, that local democracy might actually *just work*, if those contributing are properly incentivized; or, as we might think is a more appropriate assessment, if they are *no longer improperly disincentivized.* It might result in truly effective governance. As Prince Hans-Adam II of Lichtenstein writes in *The State in the Third Millennium*, "Perhaps for the first time, there is the possibility of turning states into peaceful service companies, which will, not only service oligarchs and monarchs, elected or not."

Knowledge and competence are necessarily local, and we believe it stands to reason that a localized democracy, while not necessarily perfect, will at least be relatively far more likely to embody and reflect these virtues, absent the distortion of signal provided by hierarchies premeditated on previously increasing returns to scale of violence. The combination of more localized, knowledgeable, and competent democratic government with a passionate and potentially near-universal pro-freedom single issue constituency, and inviolably sound money which in turn mandates low time preference, we find to be tantalizing.

Richard Sennett teases this very question in *The Culture of the New Capitalism*, which as a whole could easily be thought of as a demurely caustic critique of the artificial bigness and short-termism of degenerate fiat capitalism, although Sennett himself would surely avoid such brash language. He writes,

> Absurd as it may seem, we might refine the question about economics and politics to this: do people shop for politicians the way they shop at Wal-Mart? That is, has the centralized grip of political organizations grown greater at the expense of local, mediating party politics? Has the merchandising of political leaders come to resemble that of selling soap, as instantly recognizable brands which the political consumer chooses off the shelf?

> If we answer yes to all of the above, the crux of politics becomes marketing, which seems bad for political life. The very idea of democracy requires mediation and face-to-face discussion; it requires deliberation rather than packaging. Following this train of thought, we would observe with dismay that all the seductive tricks of advertising are now deployed to market the personalities and ideas of politicians; more finely, just as advertising seldom makes things difficult for the customer, so the politician makes him or herself easy to buy.

There is certainly something poetic in the idea that buyable politicians are ultimately a product of the qualities of money itself, and that fixing the money will limit the set of what can in fact be bought.

A low time preference society will make sacrifices for the future, and, having mutually invested in the future, will be more likely to band together to protect this investment. This is practically tautologically valid. In *Governing the Commons,* Ostrom makes the general point that effectively *governed* common pool resources tend to respect custom and compromise. In other words, they tend to embody *localism*, since such governance mechanisms literally cannot scale beyond communities that actually know one another, and whose competence derives from familiarity and experience; what Scott called mētis: practical knowledge as opposed to theoretical.

This idea is likely true at the level even below what we just described as the "social" — perhaps the *personal* or even *psychological*. Localities small enough to make for custom and compromise that enabled effective governance of common pool resources will make their constituents feel like they have a more personal connection with the governors and a more meaningful stake in the outcome of effective governance. Kohr gives an impassioned plea to this end,

> The small state is by nature internally democratic. In it the individual can never be outranked impressively by the power of government whose strength is limited by the smallness of the body from which it is derived. He must recognize the authority of the state, of course, but always as what it is. This is why in a small state he will never be floored by the glamour of government. He is physically too close to forget the purpose of its existence: that it is here to serve him, the individual, and has no other function whatever. The rulers of a small state, if they can be called that, are the citizen's neighbours. Since he knows them closely, they will never be able to hide themselves in mysterious shrouds under whose cover they might take on the dim and aloof appearance of supermen. Even where government rests in the hands of an absolute prince, the citizen will have no difficulty in asserting his will, if the state is small. Whatever his official designation, he will never be a subject. The gap between him and government is so narrow, and the political forces are in so fluctuating and mobile a balance, that he is always able either to span the gap with a determined leap, or to move through the governmental orbit himself. This is, for instance, the case in San Marino where they choose two consuls every six months with the result that practically every citizen functions at some time during his life as his country's chief of state. Since the citizen is always strong, governmental power is always weak and can, therefore, easily be wrested from those holding it. And this, too, is an essential requirement of a democracy.

We think it is reasonable to run Ostrom's argument in the other direction: In a world of prevalent and undisturbed localism, common pool resources are overwhelmingly likely to be much more effectively governed.[233] Arguably the most critical aspect of their governance is mindfulness of stocks and flows such that they are at least preserved, and then and only then, grown sustainably for the future. In other words, that they are *resilient*.

And surely there is a virtuous circle, or ought to be? Surely the presence of well governed common pool resources encourages long-termism, which encourages the appreciation of stocks of wealth rather than their strip mining, which encourages the development of practical skills to nurture such stocks, and the respect and admiration of the practically skilled in the popular imagination? If so, we can only hope that this shift comes at the expense of those respected and admired notionally for mastery of impractically specialized theory, but really, when it comes down to it, for their success at navigating the world of degenerate fiat power, entirely despite possessing any real knowledge or competence. Savory expresses essentially this worry about the current state of governance — who it tends to attract and how they tend to behave — writing in *Holistic Management*,

> Tragically, we are now less aware of our dependence on a well-functioning ecosystem than we were in earlier, less sophisticated, eras. Economists now have more leverage in the U.S. government than the farmers who formed it ever did. Accountants and lawyers serve as the chief advisers to the business world in which some corporations now wield larger budgets and more influence than many national governments. To be the specialists they are, most economists, accountants, and lawyers have considerable training in the narrow confines of their professions but less of an education in the broader sense, with some exceptions — ecological economists being one. As a consequence, most of these specialists exhibit little knowledge of the natural wealth that ultimately sustains nations, the quantity and quality of which is determined by how well our ecosystem functions.

Let us hope that the functioning of our ecosystem, the knowledge of natural wealth, and *an education in the broader sense* become valued once again. Or, at least, that their continual devaluation over the degenerate fiat era be allowed to reverse and return to their natural state.

Fiat Delenda Est

"A purely peer-to-peer version of electronic cash would allow online payments to be sent directly from one party to another without going through a financial institution. Digital signatures provide part of the solution, but the main benefits are lost if a trusted third party is still required to prevent double-spending."
— Satoshi Nakamoto, *The Bitcoin White Paper*

We have done our best to limit ourselves to the study of "capitalism," and although our treatment has indulged in a variety of disciplines, the core subject matter remains essentially an economic and political phenomenon. Besides the occasional rhetorical flourish, we don't believe we have strayed too far afield. But the *Renaissance* is not remembered as something so dry as an "economic and political event." We collectively conceive of it as a blossoming of literature, philosophy, art, and culture. This is what life is really about, or certainly ought to be. The Renaissance was undoubtedly *enabled* by the nurture, replenishment, and growth of capital, but only as a kind of technical prologue: An introduction to set the stage for the main event.

And so, we hope of Bitcoin. We hope that one day it will go unnoticed as a second Renaissance flourishes all around us. We hope it *just works*, such that we can all focus on what is more important in life than the plumbing of economic exchange. Ideally, infrastructure would *just work*, and we would not spend our time analyzing capital, but creating it. This is the real goal; Bitcoin, a tool, is just the first step.

As for the authors, we hope we have at least done a decent job explaining how and why we took that first step. The section, the chapter, the book— it is all a roundabout of saying:

Fix the money, fix the world.

Endnotes

[1] We see no reason to believe either of these quotes represent out-and-out lies, to be clear. What is truly bizarre, yet absolutely worth understanding, is that they seem perfectly sincere. The circumstances, the incentives, and the ideology behind both seem to lead their speakers to believe these really are desirable outcomes. It is not that they are *corrupt*, so much as they are *corrupted*. As much as anything else, this book explores *why*.

[2] David Deutsch makes a similar point in the first few pages of *The Fabric of Reality*. He asks the reader to ponder the possible utility of "an ultra-high-technology 'oracle' which can predict the outcome of any possible experiment, but provides no explanations," concluding that, "but its usefulness would always depend on people's ability to solve scientific problems in just the way they have to now, namely by devising explanatory theories. It would not even replace all experimentation, because its ability to predict the outcome of a particular experiment would in practice depend on how easy it was to describe the experiment accurately enough for the oracle to give a useful answer, compared with doing the experiment in reality. After all, the oracle would have to have some sort of 'user interface'. Perhaps a description of the experiment would have to be entered into it, in some standard language. In that language, some experiments would he harder to specify than others. In practice, for many experiments the specification would be too complex to be entered. Thus the oracle would have the same general advantages and disadvantages as any other source of experimental data, and it would be useful only in cases were consulting it happened to be more convenient than using other sources. To put that another way: there already is one such oracle out there, namely the physical world."

[3] Both descend from *judo*. Jigoro truly was special.

[4] By "modern academic economics," throughout the book, we do not pretend our target is a monolithic school of thought but rather a patchwork of many. The historical development of each took its own path, but, today, none seem to disagree with one another on theoretical issues of substance. Also, any aspiring academic economist would do well to slot into at least one (ex-Bitcoin fixing this, of course). Rather than explain this every time, we will continue to say "modern academic economics," (or if the mood takes us, "degenerate fiat economics") by either of which we mean something like the following: In macroeconomics, the combination of *general equilibrium theory* is traced from Léon Walras's contribution to the *marginal revolution* through Marshall and Robinson to Arrow and Debreu. Keynesianism, originating with Keynes obviously, but contemporarily and primarily as pseudo-mathematically bastardized by Hicks in the United Kingdom via Oxford and Cambridge and Samuelson in the United States via Massachusetts Institute of Technology, and now deployed as, more or less, *for all x, if x, then boost aggregate demand with central bank intervention*; and Friedman's monetarism; in microeconomics, the dominant "neoclassical" school, traceable from Walras and Jevons's marginalism through Pareto, Pigou, Marshall, Hicks, and Sraffa

(amongst many others), and most recently repackaged and ossified in the overtly financial framing of the Chicago School. *Behavioral Economics* is usually thrown in here and there to paper over obvious explanatory gaps with the endlessly reusable *deus ex machina* of "if the model doesn't work, it's probably because people are stupid. The model is fine. The model is always fine." If we don't use either of the two expressions just mentioned but instead say "economics" with no qualifiers, the reader is free to assume we mean something legitimate, as will hopefully be clear in context.

We will go into this in more detail later on, but our thinking is derived from, essentially, *every other school*: Classical, Austrian (i.e., the intellectual legacy of Menger's superior contribution to the *marginal revolution*), Complexity, Post-Keynesian, New Institutional, German historical, Ergodicity, Marxist, Islamic, and thinkers too heterodox to assign a "school" at all; not to mention study of fields other than academic economics and our real-life experience of running businesses and operating professionally in capital markets.

To foreshadow a line of inquiry we save for Chapter Seven, *A Capital Renaissance*, consider the following essentially correct observation from *Dirt: The Erosion of Civilizations* by David Montgomery: "Almost unquestioningly accepted in Western societies, classical economics distilled from Smith's views, as well as variants like Keynesian economics, neglect the fundamental problem of resource depletion. They share the false assumption that the value of finite resources is equal to the cost of using them, extracting them, or replacing them with other resources. This problem is central to soil exhaustion and erosion, given the long time required to rebuild soil and the lack of any viable substitute for healthy soil." The argument of the entire book could perhaps be crisply captured as: What Montgomery said, except not just about soil, but every stock of capital humanity has ever inherited.

[5] We were tempted to say *Sagans* but did not want to risk alienating the reader. Hopefully this endnote has provided a chuckle.

[6] "You don't like finance? Does that mean you don't like capitalism? What are you, a Marxist or something?" As a matter of fact, we believe this *psyop* has been so phenomenally successful that, in many cases, the most prominent *and accurate* critics are, in fact, Marxists. We quote a few at various places in this book, which is not to say we endorse Marxism, but rather that we respect truth and its insightful analysis regardless of whatever other flaws its speaker may potentially and irrelevantly have.
There is a deeper point to be made here that may well sound like a joke, but only because the insight it captures is contrary to a widespread meme so absurd as to be impossible to analyze without humor: The authors have enormous respect for *actual Marxists* as opposed to the vastly more politically successful proponents of fashionable illiberalism who have culturally colonized most of the Anglophone world. Via the degenerate fiat "capitalism," we will discuss in much more detail in Chapter Three, *This Is Not Capitalism*, that they are making disconcerting inroads in Europe as well. The readers' experience and reflections may differ, but our own are that if somebody tells you they want to seize the means of production because, despite their unease with the violence and mayhem this will likely imply, they think it will be a net gain for society, you can likely have a fascinating conversation with such a person. What will be most interesting about such an exchange will be the surprising common ground: an honest concern for

long-term sustainability and flourishing, yet obviously passionate disagreement on the best means to achieve this end. In contrast, if the reader attempts the same conversation with a fashionable illiberal, they will quickly discover they have no respect for their existence as a human being or their right to engage in discussion. The reader will discover the fashionable illiberal sees them only as an obstacle in their quest for power to be manipulated or, if necessary, destroyed, and that the "conversation" is not an exchange of ideas but is itself a struggle for power. To refer back to Chapter One, *Wrestling with the Truth*, there is an obvious analog to different modalities of martial arts: The reader might naively assume they are in the octagon, bashing truths against one another to see what sticks, while the fashionable illiberal is doing their darndest to play the role of the hero in the movie set, putting on a show not to teach the audience but to manipulate them. And of course, this context shifting will be entirely subversive: They will lie to no end about desiring only to find the truth.

Real Marxists tend not to do this and often to resent that it is done by fashionable illiberals in their name, or by ignorantly and fallaciously co-opting their rhetoric. Ditto, in fact, of *real* conservatives, as opposed to what Matt MacManus has amusingly diagnosed in *The Rise of Post-Modern Conservatism* (a far more accurate, and for that matter *funnier*, name, by the way, than the commonly accepted *populism*, which, as far as we can tell, simply means, *democracy elites dislike*). As Matt McManus points out, Burke, Chesterton, Oakeshott, and Scruton would be unimpressed and irritated by the "deep thinkers" of the "alt-right."

The arguments of Marxists may be entirely unsound, in our opinion, but they are at least committed to arguing with validity, which is encouraging. Perhaps more importantly, they are committed *to the premise and utility of arguing in good faith*. Hence, to return to how this endnote started, we find no issue or contradiction in quoting them favorably when and where it suits. Marxists occasionally have by far the best critiques of degenerate fiat "capitalism" of anybody … besides Bitcoiners, of course. And notice, dear reader, we are eating our own dog food because this is precisely our general thesis: truth by discovery, not by decree. No one school of thought has a monopoly on the truth … besides Bitcoiners, of course.

[7] Available at https://www.federalreserve.gov/econres/feds/files/2021062pap.pdf.

[8] Because Bitcoin fixes everything and this, as a thing, is quantified over by "everything." We hereby propose *Livera's Syllogism*, after Stephan Livera, who coined "Bitcoin fixes this."

[9] Deirdre McCloskey takes issue with how the field ended up in this position in her excellent book, *The Rhetoric of Economics*. She argues that while economists seem to have convinced themselves their topic is so scientific as to necessitate language that is, by unfortunate necessity obscurantist, it is in fact the slide into obscurantism that has convinced them that what they are doing is science in the first place. She writes, "Economics is unsuccessful as social weather forecasting, a role forced on it by the rhetoric of politics and journalism. But it is strikingly successful as social history, or would be if it would stop sleepwalking in its rhetoric. Economics, like geology or evolutionary biology or history itself, is an historical rather than a predictive science. Economics is not widely regarded as an imposing creation of the human mind. But I think it is. It is social self-understanding (a critical theory, indeed, like Marxism or psychoanalysis), as remarkable as anthropology or history. All the more pity that

economists have in the past fifty years become idiot savants of modernism. It's time for them to wake up and get serious about their scientific rhetoric."

[10] "The Microfoundations of Discounting," Alexander T. I. Adamou, Yonatan Berman, Diomides P. Mavroyiannis, and Ole B. Peters, available at https://arxiv.org/pdf/1910.02137.pdf.

[11] We discuss this in much more detail in Chapter Four, *Wittgenstein's Money*. For now, the reader is encouraged to ponder the link between time and many concepts already favorably introduced: process, dynamism, evolution, experimentation, and discovery. All *take time*.

[12] In the following section, we will see that really the cash flows are not "risky" but "uncertain," which makes this problem even worse, but we can stick with "risky" for now as it is bad enough to make the point.

[13] The notorious example of long-term capital management is instructive here. This is essentially what happened to this merry band of Nobel Memorial Prize winners. Their position was "perfectly rational" and "quantitatively hedged" until (shock horror) the real world changed. As celebrated risk theorist Mike Tyson put it, "Everybody has a plan until they get punched in the face."

[14] Strictly speaking, "hedge an uncertain position" is a *Chomsky sentence*: a proposition or, in this case, just a phrase, that is syntactically coherent but semantically empty. Although it obeys the rules of the language's grammar and hence *visually appears* as if it ought to have a meaning, in fact, it does not. We utilize this concept again in Chapter Six, *Bitcoin Is Venice*.

[15] John Maynard Keynes, "General Theory of Employment," *Quarterly Journal of Economics*, 1937.

[16] For a fascinating analysis of this line of thinking from the perspective of a venture capitalist rather than precisely an entrepreneur, see Jerry Neumann's essay, "Startups and Uncertainty," http://reactionwheel.net/2019/11/startups-and-uncertainty.html.

[17] Ross Emmett, "A Century of Risk, Uncertainty, and Profit,"

https://www.econlib.org/library/Columns/y2018/Emmettriskuncertaintyprofit.html.

[18] There is something distinctly Anglophone in the rejection of this fundamental principle — so fundamental it remains untranslatable from French and very possibly diminished on that basis — that it is tempting to blame on the likes of Samuelson, Hicks, Keynes, and even back to Jevons, which Arthur Cole traces even further in *An Approach to the Study of Entrepreneurship*, writing, "In the construction of his economic principles, Ricardo failed to pursue the suggestion supplied by Cantillon and Jean-Baptiste Say that the entrepreneur be distinguished clearly from the other agents of production. This failure is somewhat difficult to understand, since Say had formalized the term 'entrepreneur' and given it definition some fifteen years before Ricardo's *Principles* appeared, and he had repeated the notion several times in the interim, at least one version of which was available to Ricardo in English translation. Not merely is the term itself absent in Ricardo's writings, but no concept of business leaders as agents of change (other than as shadowy bearers of technological improvements) is embraced in

his treatment of economic principles. In neglecting to follow Say, Ricardo seems to me to have rendered a great disservice to economics, and secondarily to economic history."

[19] George Soros, *The Alchemy of Finance* (New York: Wiley, 2015).

[20] Dennis Kneale, "Working at IBM: Intense Loyalty in a Rigid Culture," *Wall Street Journal*, April 7, 1986.

[21] The reader is encouraged to search for "Raghuram Rajan Jackson Hole" online if unfamiliar.

[22] This is an excellent example of how knowledge and competence are necessarily local: The aggregation of "the market" only exists insofar as it is fractional representations of individual companies and entrepreneurs acting on their own initiative. There is no such thing as "a share in a company" that any existence exclusively in aggregate and without reference to *that company*. "The market" is purely an abstraction. It can only exist by *abstracting from* something real. We will utilize this concept many more times but will wait until Chapter Nine, *Global Money, Local Freedom*, to analyze it fully and in isolation.

[23] We note in passing that this commentary is merely intended to provide the intuition that something is amiss with the "equity premium puzzle." It is incomplete as an explanation. In the later section on leverage efficiency, we will cover Peters's and Adamou's more formal proof of the puzzle's "non-puzzliness."

[24] The reader is encouraged to investigate the essay collection *Bounded Rationality: The Adaptive Toolbox*, edited by Gerd Gigerenzer and Richard Selten, and *Heuristics: The Foundations of Adaptive Behavior*, edited by Ralph Hertwig and Thorsten Pachur. For a more popular account, *Reckoning with Risk* by Gigerenzer alone.

[25] As a fascinating aside, there is a standard Marxist critique here for which we admit we have some sympathy: Capital is *not really* homogeneous and, often, entrepreneurs *are* privileged in their access to assets they intend to employ as capital. As was mentioned in a previous endnote, that this critique is essentially correct does not mean Marxism as a whole is, therefore, correct and we have to seize the means of production to fix this. But it is worth contemplating why this is the case, if it is a problem that we think is worth solving, and if it could be solved. Our own take is that this is clearly unfortunate but in a kind of juvenile and utopian sense (i.e., a Marxist sense). Capital is *not homogeneous* because capital is *local*. It can never fail to be local unless we really do *seize the means of production*, at which point we will find ourselves with much bigger problems than imperfectly competitive entrepreneurship.

That said, we don't want to wave the word "local" like a magic wand that ends debate in our favor. "Local" does not mean "predetermined" and "unable to change." To the extent this critique is one worth taking seriously in the first place, it likely follows from highly unequal wealth distribution and social stratification. We will return to various shades of this argument in Chapter Three, *This Is Not Capitalism*, Chapter Five, *The Capital Strip Mine*, and again in Chapter Eight, These *Were Capitalists*, but we do think there is a reasonable case that Bitcoin fixes this, at least a little. Bitcoin doesn't make capital homogeneous, as this is impossible, and it doesn't bring peace and love to all mankind, but it will very probably contribute substantially to reducing the political stranglehold on capital that is clearly upstream of social stratification and wealth inequality.

[26] We note in passing the delightful similarity in the concluding thought of this extract to the argument of Peter Thiel's *Zero to One*, considered by many a kind of spiritual bible for — you guessed it — *entrepreneurship*.

[27] Not to distract from our praise for Arthur, but the exceptionally curious reader is encouraged to dig up *Increasing Returns and Economic Progress* by Allyn Young, written in 1928. This is an old idea, ignored by mainstream academic economics for nearly one hundred years on account of the political inconvenience of where the argument inevitably leads.

[28] The reader is encouraged to look into *Wright's Law*, in particular, *Statistical Basis for Predicting Technological* Progress, by Béla Nagy, Doyne Famer, Quan Bui, and Jessika Trancik, which basically says that Moore's Law happens for everything, just slower, or we learn by doing. Available at https://journals.plos.org/plosone/article?id=10.1371/journal.pone.0052669.

And without diminishing the work of these authors, we would posit that Wright's Law is a special case — although an unusually helpful and parameterized one — of one of our general theses as introduced in Chapter One, *Wrestling with the Truth,* that capital accumulation is the product of hard-earned knowledge.

[29] Nic Carter kindly pointed out to us in reviewing the manuscript that this represents the dominant philosophy behind growth venture capitalist investing from around 2015 until the near-collapse of WeWork in 2019, as if a bunch of zealous, born-again Arthurians were playing a game of non-iterated prisoner's dilemma with other people's money.

[30] We think W. Brian Arthur should almost certainly be better known and respected by Bitcoiners. Arthur's 2013 paper, "Complexity Economics," is an excellent place to start. Likewise, a good argument can be made that complex systems researchers should be a lot more interested in Bitcoin (to be fair, so should everybody, but them especially). Readers may well have picked up on the essence of Arthur's analysis consisting of "network effects." We avoided using the term because Arthur himself doesn't use it. But he is considered the pioneer of their analysis in economics, and when you think about it, the concept of "increasing returns" makes perfect sense in the context of a network. What greater competitive advantage can you have than everybody needing to use your product simply because enough people already use it? And what product do people need to use solely because others are using it more than "money"?

Although we have eschewed the idea of "lock-in" as helpful for the analysis above, Bitcoin surely has among the strongest interdependent network effects of any economic phenomenon in history. Is it not a naturally interdisciplinary complex adaptive system *par excellence*? Is it not a form of artificial life, coevolved with economizing humans in the ecology of the internet? Andreas Antonopoulos claims to have put ants on the cover of *Mastering Bitcoin* because "the highly intelligent and sophisticated behavior exhibited by a multimillion-member ant colony is an emergent property form the interaction of the individuals in a social network. Nature demonstrates that decentralized systems can be resilient and can produce emergent complexity and incredible sophistication without the

354   Bitcoin Is Venice

need for a central authority, hierarchy, or complex parts." Back in the SFI workshop, Arthur writes, "When a nonlinear physical system finds itself occupying a local minimum of a potential function, 'exit' to a neighboring minimum requires sufficient influx of energy to overcome the 'potential barrier' that separates the minima. There are parallels to such phase-locking, and to the difficulties of exit, in self-reinforcing economic systems. Self-reinforcement, almost by definition, means that a particular equilibrium is locked in to a degree measurable by the minimum cost to effect changeover to an alternative equilibrium."

We are not sure anybody can sensibly describe what such a "minimum cost" would be. Particularly because Bitcoin is set up in such a way that any move away from lock-in by one metric causes a disproportionate pull back to lock-in by another. To quote Knut Svanholm's *One-Shot Principle* from *Bitcoin: Independence Reimagined*: "Absolute mathematical scarcity achieved by consensus in a sufficiently decentralized distributed network was a discovery rather than an invention. It cannot be achieved again by a network made up of participants aware of this discovery, since the very thing discovered was resistance to replicability itself." It's Schelling points all the way down.

[31] Which is to say, it would invite Jane Jacobs's scorn like nothing else! See *Cities and the Wealth of Nations*, as well as the discussion in Chapter Four, *Wittgenstein's Money*, specifically the section, "Time, Energy, and the Triangle Game." We refer to Jane Jacobs's body of work in nearly every chapter from this point on, but this particular point of hers is cited where just mentioned.

[32] *According to what norm in the vector space?* The reader is advised not to think about this too hard or for too long, unless she is fully aware it is a joke and in doing so amuses herself.

[33] Nick Szabo, "Money, Blockchains, and Social Scalability," available: https://nakamotoinstitute.org/money-blockchains-and-social-scalability. We discuss this essay in much more detail in Chapter Four, *Wittgenstein's Money*.

[34] Fischer Black, *Noise*, https://onlinelibrary.wiley.com/doi/full/10.1111/j.1540-6261.1986.tb04513.x.

[35] For more on *Ergodicity Economics*, the reader is encouraged to visit the program's website, *https://ergodicityeconomics.com/*, or the primer, "The Ergodicity Problem in Economics," *Nature Physics*, *https://www.nature.com/articles/s41567-019-0732-0*.

We have been led to believe there is a university textbook in the works, but, at the time of writing, it has not been published.

[36] We reference Savory several more times throughout the book, and although this particular extract forms an unexpected and amusing connection, we do not think it is entirely coincidental — or really coincidental at all. It speaks to how highly attuned Savory's thinking is to the importance of *time*, a concept we return to repeatedly as of fundamental importance to understanding *capital*. This obviously comes across more clearly when discussing regenerative agriculture, Savory's direct specialty, in Chapter Seven, *A Capital Renaissance*. But it is not surprising at all to discover his wisdom to be much more widely applicable. Without at all meaning to pathologize (and besides, this is high praise!) we believe this is because, as a farmer and rancher, Savory knows *exactly*

where real wealth comes from. He cannot be fooled by the obscurantist mathematics of fiat finance into believing either that wealth can be manipulated as easily as money can, or, indeed, that wealth even *is money* in the first place. Of course, it is not. Wealth is, if anything, *capital*, and capital *is not money*, a point we discuss in much greater detail in Chapter Four, *Wittgenstein's Money*, in particular in the section, "Money, Capital, and Social Scalability."

[37] https://arxiv.org/abs/1101.4548.

[38] Amusingly, the received wisdom among Bitcoiners — we might even call it a *heuristic* — that: *HODL, don't be greedy, you'll only get rekt,* etc., finds in this material a mathematical proof of its soundness.

[39] Ultimately, the consistency of the stock's return on equity. We will explore in much more detail in Chapter Three, *This Is Not Capitalism*, why *returns analysis* rather than, say, "revenue growth" is actually best understood as following from mindfulness of the need to nurture, replenish, and grow a capital stock, and that "revenue growth" is the borderline meaningless counterpart in finance to "GDP growth" in economics.

[40] It is worth noting for any readers triggered by such terms as *geometric Brownian motion* (GBM) and *normal distributions*, they needn't be. Adamou and Peters acknowledge that GBM is not realistically either necessary or sufficient as a mechanism for stock price movements. But their argument really only depends on the characteristics of an upward drift and random volatility, both of which *are* reasonable to expect. They choose GBM because it is simple to handle, well understood, and prevalent in the literature they criticize, but they also write that "for any time-window that includes both positive and negative daily excess returns, regardless of their distribution, a well-defined optimal constant leverage exists in our computations ... Stability arguments, which do not depend on the specific distribution of returns and go beyond the model of geometric Brownian motion, led us to the quantitative prediction that on sufficiently long time scales real optimal leverage is attracted to $0 \leq l_{opt} \leq 1$ (or, in the strong form of our hypothesis, to $l_{opt} = 1$)."

[41] Andrew Lo, "The Adaptive Markets Hypothesis," https://alo.mit.edu/wp-content/uploads/2015/06/AMHjpm2004.pdf.

[42] There is also a persistent attempt to reconcile the overall argument with behavioral economics, but we are strongly averse to this school, as already described several sections up in this chapter, and think it is likely this is what takes Lo off track, as we describe.

[43] As we will explore in much more detail across Chapter Four, *Wittgenstein's Money*, and Chapter Five, *The Capital Strip Mine*, this is the main distinguishing feature between the Complexity and Austrian schools of economics: Complexity Economics is consistently disappointing in its failure to recognize the un-modellable power of human ingenuity. It often covers enough mathematical groundwork from accurate enough assumptions about economic reality to come as close to a mathematical proof of this insight as can be hoped for in economics before missing it entirely due to a methodological failure to appreciate *what acting humans are and are doing*, for lack of a more straightforward description. Besides this, the schools are perhaps surprisingly

similar in philosophy and conclusions — all the more interestingly so for the dramatic difference in methodology.

Although not a precise *solution* (as desperately sought by the Complexity crowd and rejected as metaphysical nonsense by the Austrians), we do recommend readers inclined towards the mathematical formalisms of Complexity Economics to also look into and take seriously the emerging school of *Ergodicity Economics*, as introduced in the previous section in the context of one of its most important theoretical contributions (in our view): leverage efficiency. We reference this school of thought several times throughout the book, including citing a helpful primer in an earlier endnote to *this chapter*, so we will leave our minimal exposition here besides advertising that we think the school has isolated and successfully addressed a rare corner of economics that *can be* coherently mathematized: that of *time*, which is clearly enormously relevant to Austrianism, arguably much more so than to Complexity. The overlaps here are fascinating and probably ought to be explored elsewhere and in their own right, as we have said, by the way, to Adamou and Peters!

An amusing indication of the connection and the relationship between Complexity and Austrian economics comes from the article in the January 1996 issue of *Reason* magazine by William Tucker, "Complex Questions," in which Tucker quotes Brian Arthur as saying, "Right after we published our first findings, we started getting letters from all over the country saying, 'You know, all you guys have done is rediscover Austrian economics,'" says Arthur, sitting in his book-lined offices at the Santa Fe Institute's sun-drenched hilltop mansion. "I admit I wasn't familiar with Hayek and von Mises at the time. But now that I've read them, I can see that this is essentially true."

[44] We hesitate a little given our primary criticism of *Knowledge and Power* is that Gilder doesn't seem to be entirely aware that this is a metaphor rather than literally true, leading him to occasionally say very silly things about information theory itself, having attempted to transfer insights in the wrong direction across the disciplines.

[45] One might even think to link Lo's "evolution of the speed of thought" in economics to literal biological evolution on the basis that DNA is, in a sense, information that, through mutating replication, adapts to its ecology without the slightest care for what is or is not "rational" (less this being on purpose, of course — so, *randomly* rather than *uncertainly*), but this is a little too outside the academic competence of either author to be worth pushing any further without risking embarrassment.

Should the reader want to tug on this thread a little further, we highly recommend the short paper, "The Economy of the Body" by Michael Ghiselin, in which he argues that economics and biology ought to be considered subdivisions of the same discipline, writing, "If it can be argued that biology is not a wholly economic discipline, I can only answer that actually it is. All the properties of organisms, without exception, are the result of evolution, and the mechanism of evolution, selection, is nothing more than reproductive competition between members of the same species. Competition, of course, is as fundamental an economic phenomenon as can be imagined. Of course, there are differences between natural and political economies. There is no analogue of sec in economics. Biology has nothing strictly equivalent to money. But subdisciplines often have phenomena peculiar to themselves; animals do not photosynthesize sugars, and plants lack nerves." We would argue, in fact, that biology absolutely has the concepts of time and energy and hence a strict analogue to money, and that, as per Lo, economic evolution is far more strictly analogous than just suggested given it too follows a form of mutation – just consciously directed as opposed to purely random. Ghiselin may have an even stronger point than he realizes!

[46] Our homage to *Hofstadter's Law*, from Gödel, Escher, Bach, and after the polymath author Douglas Hofstadter: It always takes longer than you think, even when you take into account Hofstadter's Law.

[47] This, in short, is why we do not subscribe fully to Islamic economics, although we do find it undeniably compelling. We believe that although interest-bearing debt will be enormously diminished in importance under a Bitcoin standard, it will still exist. To exactly (or even *roughly*) what extent is and will continue to be a fascinating question.

[48] Carl Menger, "On the Origins of Money," *The Economic Journal* 2, no. 6 (June 1892).

[49] We hate the expression "the economy" and will endeavor not to use it unless avoiding it would be unbearably clumsy. It is a noun when it should really be a verb, because the way it is commonly used refers to a flow not a stock.

[50] This may also be a helpful framing within which to identify the traits of *financialization* (or even *hyper-financialization*) as the likes of: a financial company financing a financial company to finance a financial project.

[51] Accruals-based accounting exists in the first place to give at least *some* useful information over shorter time periods, but it cannot be considered complete unless it is also reasonable to extrapolate a single year to eternity.

[52] For yet another argument that degenerate fiat finance does not appreciate the relevance of dimensionality, the reader is encouraged to investigate yet another output of the Ergodicity Economics school: Asset management legend Michael Mauboussin interviewed Ole Peters, and in particular, Peters explained the implications of the Sharpe Ratio *not being* dimensionless: http://lml.org.uk/wp-content/uploads/2012/03/Mauboussin2012.pdf.

[53] The simple argument that follows consists of our biggest gripe with the otherwise excellent and provocative *New Institutional* school of economic thought. The school emphasizes the roles of *institutions* in mediating economic activity (unsurprisingly, given the name) and accords well with our insistence that capital and money *literally are* social institutions or, as we will explain in more detail in Chapter Seven, *A Capital Renaissance*, that they are a particular type of social institution which New Institutional economist Elinor Ostrom termed a *common pool resource*. Yet, on the very first page, in the fourth paragraph of Douglass North's and Paul Thomas's *The Rise of the Western World*, they write, "In speaking of economic growth, we refer to a per capita long-run rise in income." Seemingly oblivious to the idea that in a real economy, as opposed to a computer simulation, this measure is unmeasurable.

[54] Luigi Einaudi makes a closely related point in his essay, "The Theory of Imaginary Money from Charlemagne to the French Revolution," which we also quote at greater length in Chapter Six, *Bitcoin Is Venice*. On this point, Einaudi writes, "If these were

functions which actually were or might be filled by imaginary money, it does not seem that a conscious effort was ever made to use it as a means to achieve a purpose — supposing this purpose were desirable and possible — for which it was particularly well suited. That purpose is the utopian idea of price stability, which must be called 'utopian' for a number of reasons.

(1) An acceptable definition of the concept 'the general level of prices' does not exist, since it is uncertain which goods should be included in the preparation of a satisfactory index: Only finished products, or also raw materials and unfinished products? Only tangible goods or also services? Only consumer goods or also capital goods? Furthermore, economists and statisticians are not in accord as to the criteria which should be used in constructing an index for measuring the price level itself, and all are sceptical about the possibility of adhering to those criteria, once they are known.

(2) The idea that it is desirable to stabilize the general level of prices — a naïve and undemonstrable idea — does not have to be accepted. Why should invariability of prices exist in a world where everything else continuously changes? Should we also aim at the invariability of every single price, which is manifestly absurd? Why intend the invariability of something as abstract as the general level of all prices? [...]

(3) The possibility of reaching that end by means of a monetary policy which consists in decreasing or increasing the volume of money in circulation, as prices go up or down, especially if those variations are undesirable, is questionable. The success of such a policy depends entirely upon the assumption that everything else remains equal."

[55] In *The Fiat Standard*, Saifedean Ammous discusses a very similar problem of the immeasurability in dollars of "change" at the micro scale, debunking the politically convenient fallacy of *"consumer price inflation,"* writing, "As prices of highly nutritious foods rise, people are inevitably forced to replace them with cheaper alternatives. As the cheaper foods become a more prevalent part of the basket of goods, the effect of inflation is understated, as was discussed in Chapter 4. To illustrate, imagine you earn $10 a day and spend it all on eating a delicious ribeye steak that gives you all the nutrients you need for the day. In this simple (and many would argue, optimal) consumer basket of goods, the CPI is $10. Now imagine one day hyperinflation strikes, and the price of your ribeye increases to $100 while your daily wage remains $10. What happens to the price of your basket of goods? It cannot rise tenfold because you cannot afford the $100 ribeye. Instead you make do with the chemical shitstorm that is a soy burger for $10. The CPI, magically, shows zero inflation. No matter what happens with monetary inflation, the CPI is destined to lag behind as a measure because it is based on consumer spending, which is itself determined by prices. Price rises do not elicit equivalent increases in consumer spending; they bring about reductions in the quality of consumed goods. The change in the cost of living cannot, therefore, be reflected in the price of the average basket of goods. This gives us an understanding of how prices continue to rise while the CPI registers at the politically optimal level of 2%–3% per year. If you are happy to substitute industrial waste sludge for ribeyes, you will not experience much inflation!"

[56] Ole Peters, "Democratic Domestic Product," *Ergodicity Economics*, February 26, 2020,https://ergodicityeconomics.com/2020/02/26/democratic-domestic-product/#more-3342.

[57] As a fascinating aside, we encourage the reader to contemplate the possibility of a form of technologically supported barter involving minimal currency, sometimes called "neo-barter," re-emerging post-hyperbitcoinization (hence the further obsolescence of "GDP" and an obsession with flows over stocks), an insight we credit to John Ennis. The reader's instinctive reaction may be that this is primitive nonsense belying ignorance of *exactly the problem solved by money*, but upon deeper consideration, we are not so sure. The thinking rests on the assumption of dramatically changed attitudes to consumption in the first place. With truly sound money, consumers will be significantly more interested than currently in the durability of goods they purchase so as to minimize suffering from depreciation and repurchasing. Also, for goods purchased long ago which are no longer needed, consumers will be far more interested in cashing in on them rather than discarding them. Both these subtle differences create optimal conditions for "neo-barter," which is carried out not because money is absent, but, almost the opposite, because money is extremely valuable and the primary concern of all parties is to preserve it. Hence, money (i.e., bitcoin) would surely feature as the unit of account and would likely lubricate trade by forming the residual value to balance exchanges, but the very qualities of bitcoin strongly incentivize preserving purchases in good condition and seeking to trade for them, if possible, rather than sacrifice truly sound money.

In addition to sharing with us his own work in this area, John Ennis kindly pointed us to the work of Ali Haydar Özer and Can Özturan, who have also researched methods to support neo-barter. For more information, please see the research papers, "A Model and Heuristic Algorithms for Multi-Unit Nondiscriminatory Combinatorial Auction" by Özer and Özturan, and "A Double Auction Based Mathematical Market Model and Heuristics for Internet-Based Secondhand Durable Goods Market" for more details.

[58] Figures from United Continental Holdings, Inc., 2019, Schedule 14A, https://ir.united.com/static-files/f9aa8e22-70df-4e54-a112-7903aabb36a2.

[59] The reader is encouraged to contemplate the potential contemporary relevance of the following few passages (among *many more*) in Adam Ferguson's *When Money Dies*, an account of the Weimar hyperinflation: "In November, a year after the Armistice, Frau Eisenmenger wrote that her position was alarmingly worse, the financial situation beyond her understanding. The krone, at 25 Swiss centimes the previous Christmas, was now quoted at one-twelfth of a centime. Her shares, however, were going up. Gambling on the stock exchange had become the fashion — the only way to avoid losing all one's money and perhaps to add to it. [...] Until the Ruhr invasion the reasons for the German inflation could have been put down, first, to the uncertainty of the aftermath of the war, and secondly, to the inexperience and weak acquiescence of the new men in power. Industry wanted neither heavy taxation nor to be hampered in its expansion at home or abroad: so the government gave way and replaced the missing revenue by printing it. Neither the industrialists nor the general public were prepared to pay the true costs of the railways, or of the post office, or even of bread: so the government understood, and printed the money to pay for them. Did Germany's nationals have claims arising out of the war, or, better, out of the peace treaty? Did one of the federal states, or the meanest district, look to Berlin to meet its financial requirements? The government printed notes to satisfy everyone, telling itself that as the granting of credit through cheques had so greatly decreased the actual currency in circulation to be so much greater. The rich and

the strong came off best. [...] Speculation in currency was in no way the exclusive domain of the financially informed. Anyone – banker, politician, businessman or workman – who observed that there were easier ways of keeping one's head above water than the now very problematic one of working for it was ready to indulge as opportunity offered. It was computed that well over a million Germans in early 1923 were engaged in exchange speculation."

[60] Judith Burns, "BB&T Blasts TARP as 'Huge Rip-Off'," *Wall Street Journal*, June 12, 2009.

[61] Adam Levine-Weinberg, "Macy's Is a Real Estate and Credit Card Company Masquerading As A Retailer," *The Motley Fool*, March 4, 2007, https://www.fool.com/investing/2017/03/04/macys-is-a-real-estate-and-credit-card-company-mas.aspx.

[62] Bijan Stephen, "Patreon Will Now Give Creators Cash Advances on Their Subscription Money," *The Verge*, February 18, 2020, https://www.theverge.com/2020/2/18/21142306/patreon-capital-loans-jack-conte-cash-advances.

[63] Larry White, "Defending Dollarization in Ecuador," *Alt-M*, December 4, 2014, https://www.alt-m.org/2014/12/04/defending-dollarization-in-ecuador/.

[64] It is worth pointing out that none of the theory developed from this point onwards in this chapter is original. It is captured at a high level across the primary texts of Classical, Austrian, Complexity, and, increasingly, Ergodicity economics and padded out with a few thinkers so heterodox as to seemingly defy classification.

The Classical texts are standard and the reader will not benefit from our reciting the canon — although we will briefly editorialize in that Turgot, Cantillon, the Salamanca school, and Ibn Khaldoun and the school of the Islamic Arab-scholastics all ought to be better known and celebrated. Beyond these, we credit:

- Carl Menger's *Principles of Economics*
- Eugen von Bohm-Bawerk's *Capital and Interest*, in particular *The Positive Theory of Capital*
- Ludwig von Mises's *The Theory of Money and Credit*, but also the concept of the "evenly rotating economy" best explicated in *Human Action*.
- Frank Knight's *Risk, Uncertainty, and Profit*
- Israel Kirzner's *Competition and Entrepreneurship*
- Andrew Lo's *Adaptive Markets*
- Benoit Mandelbrot's *The (Mis)Behavior of Markets*
- George Gilder's *Knowledge and Power*
- Carlota Perez's *Technological Revolutions and Financial Capital*
- Yochai Benkler's *The Wealth of Networks*
- George Selgin's *Money: Free and Unfree*
- Jörg Guido Hülsmann's *The Ethics of Money Production*
- Joseph Schumpeter's *Capitalism, Socialism, and Democracy*
- Julian Simon's *The Ultimate Resource*

- The brief commentary on economics towards the end of Per Bak's *How Nature Works*
- The remainder of the combined output of the *Complexity Economics* program: most notably the collection *The Economy as an Evolving Complex* System by Philip W. Anderson, Kenneth J. Arrow, and David Pines, but in particular the essays, "Self-Reinforcing Mechanisms in Economics" by Brian Arthur, "The Global Economy as an Adaptive Process" by John Holland, and "The Evolution of Economic Webs" by Stuart Kauffman. W. Brian Arthur's later *Complexity and the Economy* is also recommended.
- Hernando de Soto's *The Mystery of Capital*

- Nick Szabo's "Money, Blockchains, and Social Scalability," "Shelling Out," "Secure Property Titles with Owner Authority," and "Formalizing and Securing Relationships on Public Networks"

We credit all these writers for aiding the development of our own thinking and cite them here for the benefit of the interested reader looking to dig deeper. However, we also think there is merit in keeping mention of these works in an extensive endnote rather than in the main body of text (with the brief exception of de Soto and Szabo) so as to lead the reader through the thought experiment as much as possible from first principles and without appeal to authority.

The reader may be interested to know that, while predominantly Classical and Austrian, our larger thesis also draws on the insights of New Institutional, Post-Keynesian, (German) historical, Islamic, and Marxist economic thought where occasionally relevant. The former two are merely variations of mainstream dissent that we recommend to the curious but about which we don't have much interesting to say. German historical economics is an inspiration more in spirit than in practice. We realize the merit of deep suspicion of "absolute theory" divorced from the reality of economic and human affairs, even if we do not endorse the specific thoughts or programs of those self-identifying as members of the school. We spare the reader too much of a digression on this point given we cover it in more detail in the introduction to Chapter Eight, *These Were Capitalists.* Islamic economics we will likewise spare the reader for the time being given it does not come up in this chapter, but is discussed extensively in Chapter Six, *Bitcoin Is Venice,* and again in a little less detail in Chapter Eight, These *Were Capitalists.* That said, we have also quoted Tarek El Diwany in several places already, where we frankly think his insights go well beyond drawing exclusively on Islamic finance and are simply accurate criticisms of some or other aspect of contemporary finance. We further editorialize that Chapters Two through Four of *The Problem with Interest* are among the best introductory material on banking and finance we have ever read (Chapter One is an extended and questionable opining on *entropy* that we feel has more literary value than economic or physical insight, and Chapter Five onwards is explicitly about *Islamic* finance: still excellent but clearly not general). Marxism we value far less highly for probably obvious reasons; we are staunchly anti-poverty, anti-democide, and anti-collapse of civilization, for example, among our various politically incorrect positions. But, as covered in an endnote to Chapter Two, *The Complex Markets Hypothesis,* we do find Marxism to be valuable on occasion, usually as appropriately and accurately critical rather than as usefully prescriptive — and as much for heterodox honesty as any purely economic insight.

All this said, to be frank, economics as an intellectual pursuit is nothing more than *logic applied to risky and creative human affairs*. Which is to say, if the reader has had any experience with people, any experience taking imaginative risks, and if they know how to think, economics will not be difficult, and in fact will all be rather obvious. Most mainstream economists fail on *all* counts, and the corpus they devote most of their professional time to memorizing adds nothing and likely subtracts whatever little they started with. Should the reader take it upon themselves to indulge in a smorgasbord of anthropology, social and economic history, and literature (for the people part), either become professionally involved in the creative arts or sports (or amateurly but at a high and serious level) or start a business (for the calculated risks and imagination part), and learn some elementary logic and statistics (for the thinking part), they will likely imbibe "economics" by accident and will never need to waste any time, energy, or money on materials exclusively devoted to the subject. Also, they should learn to code. It doesn't have anything directly to do with this, it's just a good idea.

[65] If the reader is at all a fan of action movies or spy thrillers, they might appreciate the following reference: We think an excellent metaphor for the fact of distributed, local knowledge creating fundamental uncertainty that cannot be centrally planned for — in essence, Mises's *socialist calculation problem* — is a scene in the movie *The Bourne Supremacy*. Jason Bourne, played by Matt Damon, plans to meet Nicky, played by Julia Stiles, in the center of Berlin, knowing full well that despite cooperating in arranging the meeting, the CIA is fully intent on catching him. The CIA team led by Pamela Landy, played by Joan Allen, massively outguns and outmans Bourne, and the viewer sees them planning for every conceivable contingency with a vast surveillance operation. Yet they do not possess *local knowledge* that Bourne evidently does: He arranged the meetup at the exact time and place of a huge protest, which throws the surveillance into total disarray and allows Bourne to meet and escape with Nicky with ease. That is socialist planning in a nutshell: All the resources that can possibly be thrown at an exceedingly simple problem are still nowhere near enough and will fail. ☺

[66] The reader may notice this is essentially the same core issue, albeit approached from a different direction, as the endnote in the previous chapter citing Luigi Einaudi's criticism of the idea of "a stable general level of prices."

[67] Readers intrigued by the mechanism alluded to here are encouraged to look into *Complexity Economics*, as mentioned several times as a source of inspiration for our own economic thinking. "The Triangle Game" is a simple and intuitively easy to grasp (even to try for yourself!) example of a *complex nonlinear system*, and also, more specifically, a *self-organizing critical system*, a concept popularized by physicist and later complexity scientist Per Bak. An excellent introductory resource is provided by Ian Johnston of the Open University, https://motivate.maths.org/content/Avalanches.

We would editorialize that none of this is strictly necessary to understand what is fundamentally *economics* but is rather a useful additional toolkit for the more mathematically or mechanically inclined.

[68] This will become more relevant in Chapter Eight, *These Were Capitalists*, but it is worth pointing out a thread connecting a range of totally disparate writers and thinkers,

of which Jane Jacobs and James Scott are exemplars: Those who learn about social systems *by prioritizing the experience of those who comprise them*! We would also cite Alex Gladstein's phenomenal reporting on Bitcoin adoption and use around the world, which we reference several times in the chapters that follow, and the outlook of Ann Sussman and Justin B. Hollander in *Cognitive Architecture*, an excellent short book marrying a subgenre of artistic criticism with advances in evolutionary psychology. The subtitle of the latter, *Designing for How We Respond to the Built Environment*, gives a clearer indication of the source of our praise than does the title. Towards the end of the book, they write, "This book promotes the biophilic approach and focuses on our subconscious human responses to places to most effectively do so. Essentially, we take an inside-out approach to the problem of solving the riddle of how to best design for humanity. We argue that it is best to first look at how people are built – not only mechanically but also mentally, subconsciously, and then design or plan for these requirements and tendencies."

[69] Having sufficiently established the rhetoric of "time and energy" at this point, the reader is encouraged to contemplate the significance of a money that really is *based on energy*, as has been hypothesized across the ages by as diverse a range of brilliant thinkers as Henry Ford, Buckminster Fuller, and John Nash. The sense in which Bitcoin mining uses the unforgeable constant of energy to convert time into money is a little beyond the scope of the present discussion, but will be returned to in Chapter Seven, *A Capital Renaissance*.

[70] Leonard E. Read, *I, Pencil*, https://fee.org/resources/i-pencil/.

[71] In his introduction to Caryl Emerson's translation of Mikhail Bakhtin's *Problems of Dostoyevsky's Poetics*, Wayne C. Booth addresses this point with humorous seriousness, writing, "The *Poetics* has often been called a 'handbook' for writing tragedy; it tells us, in its detailed analysis of the ingredients of the existing tragedies, and its strongly evaluative account of the best ways of mixing those ingredients, just how we might go about making, or improving, other objects of the same kind.

It does not do so, however, my offering any simple rule book or algorithm. Its analyses are all steeped in value judgments, not of technical or formal beauty separable from moral qualities but of a shaped action, a "synthesis of incidents" or events that represent choices made by moral or immoral agents, and thus in consequence deserve, as "plot," to be called the "soul" of the work. Thus what Bakhtin calls ideology is an essential part of the Aristotelian analysis; the forms Aristotle treats are made not of abstract shapes but of values: value sought, values lost, values mourned, values hailed. There is no more of a hint in Aristotle's formalism than in Bakhtin's dialogism of pursuing designs like hourglass shapes or spiraling curves or abstract symmetries or asymmetries of any kind. People in action cannot be reduced to mathematical figures or equations, and neither can 'imitations of action.'"

[72] In the economic realm, this would be quantified by the measure of a positive *return on capital*, a flow-over-stock metrics the importance of which was belabored in Chapter Three, *This Is Not Capitalism*. Poetry is rather more qualitative and likely resists such a measurement to all by the stupidly arrogant high-modernists. That said, "returns to poetry" suggests satirical value we leave to the reader to explore.

[73] This is edging towards a discussion of Elinor Ostrom's conception of *common pool resources*. In Chapter Seven, A *Capital Renaissance*, we will argue that money *literally is* a common pool resource. However, this is just for the reader's interest: The above passage is unaffected.

[74] We discuss in the following chapter, *The Capital Strip Mine*, how deflation is actually not well-defined and can appear to be caused by the financial crises fiat finance makes inevitable, but for the time being this will do.

[75] The semanticist would have serious difficulty explaining Helen Zimmern's observation in *The Hanseatic League* that it was common for a period in the Hanseatic League to use salted herring as money, which, obviously did not store value as it would shortly rot, yet was so ubiquitously popular as a fungible consumption good that it nonetheless served as a medium of exchange; or George Halm's amusing example in *Monetary Theory*, of a primitive tribe using a goat as a standard of value, and of which a judge must decide whether a particular goat, "is not too old and too scraggy to constitute a standard goat," arguing that this shows, "that the medium of exchange may be strictly speaking, a concrete thing." Frederic Lane and Reinhold Mueeller add to this example in *Money and Banking in Medieval and Renaissance Venice* (they quote it themselves in a footnote), "Whether the 'units of the medium of exchange' were practically identical during the centuries when coin was the chief means of payment is questionable, since coins of the same denomination varied significantly one from another and from the standard set for freshly minted coin." Even gold bugs, and some Bitcoiners for that matter, have serious difficulty trying to explain away the prominent role silver has played throughout the history of money.

The course of economics in real life is determined by the interaction of creative humans. Economic history and common sense alike teach us that it cannot be reduced to semantics, to models, to axioms, or to math.

[76] If the reader has had the misfortune of an education in degenerate fiat economics, they will recognize that what we are really saying here is, effectively: Microeconomic supply and demand, then, in the paragraphs that follow, the classical theory of the firm, can only be properly understood via methodological individualism. But then, so must everything be.

[77] Of course, none of this is to mention *real-life circumstances changing* over such a time period, suggesting any attempt to track "the general price level" is utterly futile, and asinine besides. Then again, we have already covered Luigi Einaudi's thorough explanation of this and referred back to it more than once.

[78] Michael McLeay, Amar Radia, and Ryland Thomas, "Money Creation in the Modern Economy," 2014, https://www.bankofengland.co.uk/-/media/boe/files/quarterly-bulletin/2014/money-creation-in-the-modern-economy.pdf

[79] Hyperlink in original text, added here for clarity: https://www.bloomberg.com/news/features/2016-05-30/the-untold-story-behind-saudi-arabia-s-41-year-u-s-debt-secret.

[80] For an even more detailed look at this topic, and with a Bitcoin-specific lens, we highly recommend Alex Gladstein's article "The Hidden Costs of the Petrodollar," *Bitcoin*

Magazine, September 21, 2021, https://bitcoinmagazine.com/culture/the-hidden-costs-of-the-petrodollar.

[81] It would be remiss of us not to mention here that, although the quote is itself a reference to Ernest Hemingway's tongue-in-cheek explanation of the experience of going bankrupt, the title of this section is, for us, a reference to Parker Lewis's astonishing series of blog posts by the same name. Lewis is obviously making the same reference, except more ominously with reference to all of society, not an individual. The series is available at https://unchained-capital.com/blog/category/gradually-then-suddenly/.

Any reader looking for a gentle introduction to Bitcoin for the layman — either for themselves or to recommend to family and friends — is strongly encouraged to carefully read the entire series, in order, one by one. We would posit it is the indisputably joint-best introduction alongside *The Bitcoin Standard* by Saifedean Ammous, *Mastering Bitcoin* by Andreas Antonopoulos, and *The Bullish Case for Bitcoin* by Vijay Boyapati.

[82] The reader may be amused by this unintentionally hilarious extract from Roger Backhouse's *Penguin History of Economics*, "[Josiah Child's] *Brief Observations Concerning Trade and Interest of Money* (1668) opens by asking why the Dutch are so much more successful than the English. He offers fifteen explanations, but claims that the last, a low rate of interest, is the most important, being the cause of the other causes of Dutch wealth ... According to Child, countries are 'richer or poorer in exact proportion to what they pay, and have usually paid, for the interest of money'. This rule, he claimed, never failed. Child recognized that such evidence did not establish that a low interest rate was the cause rather than the effect of prosperity. However, he offered almost no arguments to support his claim that it was. He claimed that reducing the interest rate from 6 per cent to 4 per cent or 3 per cent would double the nation's capital stock, but he did not explore this and turned instead to answering other people's objections to lowering the interest rate."

[83] We return to this point in much more detail and with the specific example of intensive farming in Chapter Seven, A *Capital Renaissance*.

[84] They always are to some degree in terms of the opportunity cost of investing the capital in something *other than* high time preference nonsense, but the following is arguably *even worse*.

[85] James Olan Hutcheson, *The End of a 1,400-Year-Old Business*, *Bloomberg*, April 17, 2007, https://www.bloomberg.com/news/articles/2007-04-16/the-end-of-a-1-400-year-old-businessbusinessweek-business-news-stock-market-and-financial-advice.

[86] Matt Stoller, "A Land of Monopolists: From Portable Toilets to Mixed Martial Arts," July 10, 2020, https://mattstoller.substack.com/p/a-land-of-monopolists-from-portable.

[87] References to individual entries in Parker Lewis's series, *Gradually Then Suddenly*, respectively: "Bitcoin Is Not a Ponzi Scheme," "Bitcoin Does Not Waste Energy," and "Bitcoin Is Not Backed by Nothing." Series available at https://unchained-capital.com/blog/category/gradually-then-suddenly/.

[88] Marc Andreessen, "Why Software Is Eating the World," *Wall Street Journal*, August 20, 2011, https://a16z.com/2011/08/20/why-software-is-eating-the-world/.

[89] It is worth stressing the *ubiquity* point as a common historical fallacy pertaining to the birth of modern capitalism in late medieval Italy in regards to its prevalence, when in fact it was a barely noticed social institution for many hundreds of years. What mattered was the innovation in ideas, not their adoption. Economist and sociologist Werner Sombart put it well in his essay, "Medieval and Modern Commercial Enterprise," "Medieval trade [...] was either occasional or artisanlike, and it had nothing in common with modern capitalism [...] The legal patterns that allowed the rise of the commenda and similar partnerships originated in a spirit of a new age. These partnerships had therefore inevitably a revolutionizing effect: when they kept on expanding, they would in the long run destroy the solid framework of medieval economic institutions and would prepare the way for new relations between businessmen. True, the handicrafts had for centuries used the occasional type of partnership without being damaged. However, the legal forms which the system itself had created became imperceptibly the factor that changed the craft system into a fundamentally different economic pattern. Specifically, the significance of various legal forms of occasional partnerships for the development of capitalism must be sought in their revolutionary impact on basic economic ideas."

[90] Before even making the link to Bitcoin, the following extract from Carlo Cipolla's *The Economic History of World Population* is extremely encouraging in light of software's difference to previous forms of productive capital: "In an industrial society the contribution of science and scientific methods to production is obviously great. Consequently the rate of growth of an industrial society is largely influenced by the amount of resources devoted to research and education and by the efficiency at which these resources are used. This does not detract from the importance of investment in reproducible physical capital, because for much of the new knowledge that becomes available, its incorporation into the productive process requires replacement of existing physical capital goods by new ones. On the other hand, because of the highly dynamic character of an industrial society, its members are under the threat of accelerated obsolescence; vast resources must therefore be devoted to the training and retraining of people just as vast resources are needed for the building and replacement of capital goods." Software clearly benefits both sides of this trade-off: the fixed costs of this class of capital formation are dropped more or less to zero, while the cost, ease, and availability of training and retraining via the internet has improved enormously.

[91] Consider also the following extract from Oscar Gelderblom's *Cities of Commerce*, charting the successive rises of Bruges, Antwerp, and Amsterdam to commercial primacy across 1250 to 1650: "So why could rulers compete through institutional arrangements rather than the use of force? Surely the leading cities were powerful enough to hurt commercial rivals through tariffs, embargoes, or outright warfare — and they probably did, considering the high incidence of violence in the history of European trade. However, there were so many competing states in Europe with one or more important markets in their territory that sovereigns were careful not to prey on merchants in these cities. They not just feared the direct loss of fiscal revenue or a higher cost of capital, but also realized they would play into the hands of their political rivals, as foreign merchants in particular were footloose and would not hesitate to remove their business to ports outside their realm."

[92] See, http://siddiqi.com/mns/AVisionForTheFutureOfIslamicEconomics.htm.

[93] Consider the following extract from the essay, "The Historical Development of the Enterprise" by Gustav Schmoller, "The Rôles d'Oléron also state that sailors were paid partly by portions of the freight and partly by a fixed hire. Laband, in discussing the maritime code of Amalfi (twelfth to thirteenth century), defines the contract columnae communi as an association among the following: part owners of the ship, owners of the commodities on board, capitalists investing money in the undertaking, and finally the seamen, who would serve aboard ship. All these people formed a society, and, after the voyage had been ended, they divided among themselves the gains or losses, according to fixed and predetermined proportions. Nobody, however, could lose more than he invested."

[94] We stress "successful" to properly distinguish and contrast Islamic economics to socialism, of which, the reader might be interested to know, S. Abul Ala Mawdudi's *Mankind's Economic Problems and their Islamic Solutions* provides possibly the most concise and effective refutation we have ever read, fusing Mises and Havel in a two-page polemic).

[95] Consider Satoshi's exhortation in BitcoinTalk, December 5, 2010, that, "The project needs to grow gradually so the software can be strengthened along the way. I make this appeal to WikiLeaks not to try to use Bitcoin. Bitcoin is a small beta community in its infancy. You would not stand to get more than pocket change, and the heat you would bring would likely destroy us at this stage." https://satoshi.nakamotoinstitute.org/posts/bitcointalk/523/

[96] Pierre Rochard, "Speculative Attack," *Nakamoto* Institute, July 4, 2014, https://nakamotoinstitute.org/mempool/speculative-attack/.

[97] Reid Hoffman, Michael McCullough, and Tim Ferriss, "The Oracle of Silicon Valley," *Tim Ferriss Podcast*, https://tim.blog/2015/08/31/the-oracle-of-silicon-valley-reid-hoffman-plus-michael-mccullough/.

[98] Nick Szabo, "Money, Blockchains, and Social Scalability," as also referenced in Chapter Four, *Wittgenstein's Money*.

[99] Einaudi later quotes Le Blanc as writing in 1690, in "Traité historique des monnoies de France" of *ideal money*, "These changes, I admit, are surprising because if there is anything in the world which ought to be stable, it is money, the measure of everything which enters the channels of trade. What confusion would there not be in a state where weights and measures frequently changed? On what basis and with what assurance could one person deal with another, and which nations would care to deal with people who lived in such disorder?" If Le Blanc were to observe degenerate fiat "capitalism," he would no doubt be rather concerned that all the means of measuring time and energy via money frequently changes, and was all imaginary besides!

Einaudi would likely agree. Several pages later he clarifies his overall argument following a historical overview including Le Blanc and others: "Imaginary money — here is my thesis — is not money at all. It is a mere instrument or technical device used to perform some monetary functions." That is not to say it is useless or immoral by any means. Einaudi claims Le Blanc's critique is essentially too purist to be accurate, along with most of the other historical writers he surveys. But Einaudi would certainly argue that a lack of clarity regarding the difference between real money and imaginary money certainly is dangerous. We might extend his analysis to Bitcoin by rather simply suggesting that Bitcoin neither allows nor even needs imaginary money. It is purely real, and so the problems Einaudi describes in confusing the two cannot arise in the first place.

[100] Specifically, a *common pool resource*, as designated by Elinor Ostrom, whom we first mentioned in Chapter Three, *This Is Not Capitalism* and again in Chapter Five, *The Capital Strip Mine*, but will return to in much more detail in Chapter Seven, *A Capital Renaissance*.

[101] At the time of first writing, most clearly evidenced by NYDIG CEO Ross Stevens's remarks at the MicroStrategy Bitcoin for Corporations Conference in February 2021, but it has since been repeated so widely as to defy a solitary source besides Saifedean Ammous himself.

[102] Raymond de Roover, *Money, Banking, and Credit in Medieval Bruges* (Cambridge: Mediaeval Academy of America, c1948).

[103] "Critiquing Bitcoin with Frances Coppola and Nic Carter, What Bitcoin Did," *YouTube*, January 15, 2021, https://www.youtube.com/watch?v=hy8JhNgU8eI.

[104] https://www.gwern.net/Bitcoin-is-Worse-is-Better.

[105] This is a bit of a broad historical sweep, admittedly, and so the curious reader is directed to Abbot Payson Usher's essay, "The Origins of Banking: The Primitive Bank of Deposit, 1200–1600," for a fuller account of the incremental progression from money changing to deposit banking in medieval and early Renaissance Europe.

[106] The reader may be interested to learn that the *offsetting* system perfected in Florence around the same time arguably builds on this from Lane in *also* explaining the institutional mechanics of the Lightning Network remarkably accurately; see Richard Goldthwaite's *The Economy of Renaissance Florence*, pp. 458–463. However, we keep this to an endnote to honor the chapter title and avoid drawing too much attention away from Venice. We will return to this point in much more detail in Chapter Seven, *A Capital Renaissance*.

[107] "CBDCs: An Opportunity for the Monetary System," *BIS Annual Economic Report 2021*, https://www.bis.org/publ/arpdf/ar2021e3.pdf.

[108] Cited in multiple earlier chapters but all pointing to the following more in-depth treatment!

[109] The reader may also be interested in pondering that this schema readily debunks so-called "intellectual property." The standard defense of this legal regime, although clearly never openly advertised as such, is to imply that "ideas" are common pool resources, even though they clearly are *actually public goods*, as ought to be clear from the analysis presented in the main text. Even though this error essentially follows from definitional sloppiness, the proponents nonetheless immediately go further with their slipshod analysis and demand what Ostrom specifically cautions against, even if they had previously been correct in their starting assumption, that the only way to save society

from catastrophe is to *make these common pool resources* private goods that belong to the government, on which legalized monopolies may then be issued to favored patrons. Continuing this train of thought is outside the scope of this chapter and book, but curious readers are encouraged to source *Against Intellectual Monopoly* by Michele Boldrin and David K. Levine, as well as the many writings and talks of Stephan Kinsella, of which a natural starting point might be, "Against Intellectual Property," *Journal of Libertarian Studies*, https://cdn.mises.org/15_2_1.pdf.

Please note, we practice what we preach in this regard: This book has been fully open sourced, meaning the authors retain no nonsensical "rights" to its content. It may be reproduced or referenced by anybody, in any way. We ask only that anybody doing so

properly credit the source material, but of course even this we cannot compel anybody to obey.

[110] This touches on the idea of local knowledge and competence in tension with global authority, that we will discuss in much more detail in Chapter Nine, *Global Money, Local Freedom*.

[111] We are again foreshadowing Chapter Nine, *Global Money, Local Freedom*, in which we dive into the concepts of costs to attack and defend and the returns to violence in much more detail.

[112] The reader is encouraged to look into *Dynamic Stochastic General Equilibrium*, if only for comedic value. Just don't spend too long on it: Time is scarce, after all.

[113] Emerging terminology for "Lightning Network protocol / Bitcoin protocol" in homage to "TCP/IP," which we heartily endorse.

[114] Matt Taibbi, "The Great American Bubble Machine," *Rolling Stone*, April 5, 2010.

[115] Earlier in the essay, Gras defines "petty capitalists" as those engaging in capitalism on a deliberately small scale with no expansive or acquisitive ambitions, and those who may not even think of themselves as "capitalists" but more likely as "merchants" or "artisans" — this is all simply to clarify that Gras implies no moral connotations by this word choice.

[116] It will be fascinating to contrast whatever does emerge along these lines with Carlota Perez's analysis in her excellent *Technological Revolutions and Financial Capital*. We keep this mention to an endnote as we don't want too much of a tangent in the main text. But for the curious reader, Perez's short book — deemed by many a contemporary classic — provides a compelling theoretical overview of the shifting roles of production and financial capital (using essentially the same terminology as Gras). Perez convincingly applies the framework (in our opinion, at least) to the major bursts of investment and output growth since the Industrial Revolution. We don't have a precise prediction in terms of Perez's analysis beyond that it strikes us as reasonable that "financial capital" may come to be permanently disenfranchised given the entire period Perez analyzes (which, recall, is all that has, in fact, existed since the Industrial Revolution) progressed from minimal to arguably non-existent (or certainly, incomparable) central bank intervention in financial markets to its recent all-time high.

[117] Among many others, of course, but given both Elizabeth Stark's position and her bank of knowledge and experience, we are inclined to consider her the intellectual leader of this train of thought.

[118] A natural complement to humbly constrained layering is *openness*: build one thing at a time but make it as simple and well-defined as possible to interact with what you have built externally. This is less technically interesting as it may well be imagined as an obvious design default, but it may equally be thought of as *more* psychologically interesting, and it arguably even better captures *humility*. If you make simple building blocks that are open for others to build on, you never know what they will come up with and, in fact, you incorporate the essence of *a peer-to-peer network* right into the engineering of what may well itself *be a peer-to-peer network*!

In *How the Internet Happened*, Brian McCullough recalls how Marc Andreessen had essentially the above dispute with Tim Berners-Lee over the design of early web browsers. Berners-Lee wanted tight control over how HTTP worked and for what it would be used, very much in line with *his closed design vision,* whereas Andreessen instinctively understood the merits of the above argument and wanted the protocol to be more of a *platform* to which others could contribute with novel insight and experimentation.

[119] See, https://bitcoinmagazine.com/technical/a-monetary-layer-for-the-internet.

[120] Nik Bhatia, *Layered Money* (Self-Published: 2021).

[121] This terminology may quickly become out of date if or when other robust higher layer mechanisms for asset issuance on top of Bitcoin come to fruition. But, at the time of writing, the authors are only familiar enough with sidechains as an example, both of such a mechanism and one we know can be utilized in conjunction with DLCs as we will go on to describe.

[122] Saul Kripke, *Naming and Necessity* (Hoboken, NJ: Wiley-Blackwell, 1991).

[123] From the *Epsilon Theory* blog, first quoted in Chapter Three, *This Is Not Capitalism*, https://www.epsilontheory.com/this-is-water/.

[124] See Alfred Chandler's *Scale and Scope* for a compelling theoretical and historical argument that industrial capitalism naturally gravitated towards bigness and, in turn, catalyzes its own adaptive forms of management that would not have been necessary on a smaller scale — largely indifferent to the circumstances of its being financed. We do not present this argument as either a binary or even a single spectrum of variables. Chandler is almost certainly correct in the crux of his argument and we would not be so arrogant as to brush his incredible work aside. But we see two differences — or, we might say, *two extra dimensions* — he does not analyze: that of the supra-economic and arguably political influence of fiat taken to its contemporary (degenerate) extreme and, therefore, the logic of its unravelling precisely on account of Bitcoin.

[125] Parker Lewis, "The Great Definancialization," *Unchained Capital*, December 23, 2020.

[126] The precipitation of *narcissism*, unsurprisingly.

[127] Earlier, too, *The Organization Man* was published in 1956, *The Culture of Narcissism* in 1979.

[128] A sentiment recaptured recently by the likes of Joel Kotkin's *The Coming of Neo-Feudalism*, already cited in the introduction, and Michael Lind's *The New Class War*.

[129] Whyte hilariously notes a few pages later: "It is quite obvious, nevertheless, that [a corporate trainee manager] must pursue the main chance in a much more delicate fashion. To get ahead, he must cooperate with the others — but cooperate better than they do."

[130] We leave it as an exercise to the reader to figure out how this squares with encountering Bitcoin for the first time. Having sufficiently pondered it on her own, we can highly recommend Croesus's short piece, "Why the Yuppie Elite Dismiss Bitcoin," https://www.citadel21.com/why-the-yuppie-elite-dismiss-bitcoin.

[131] There are plenty other such entirely empty technologisms, by the way, that function in exactly the same way. We just happen to have chosen one that is pertinent to the topic of this book.

[132] One sentence has been removed from this extended quote in which Lasch picks up on a criticism he makes of Ludwig von Mises that he began earlier in the chapter, and which reads as jarring without that earlier context. But the criticism as a whole is fascinating: Lasch qutoes Mises's *Bureaucracy*, as emblematic of what he calls "the conservative critique" of bureaucracy, as opposed to his own more communitarian critique. In this case, we side against Mises and find Lasch's critique incisive and persuasive. Lasch writes of Mises, "This argument suffers from the conservative's idealization of the personal autonomy made possible by the free market," and while the discussion runs for four pages or so and we don't intend to reproduce it here in its entirety, we think it is fair to interpret this as very similar to a claim we make several times but will analyze in much more detail in Chapter Eight, *These Were Capitalists*: that economic capital requires social capital. This is similar also to de Soto's thesis of the importance of capital over freedom: Freedom alone is necessary but insufficient for flourishing.

[133] They won't go quietly, mind you, but on a long-enough time horizon they will become insignificant. Or so we can hope.

[134] This section has been adapted from an article by Allen Farrington that originally appeared in the online magazine *Areo*, titled, "Towards a Free and Open Internet." Many thanks to Helen Pluckrose and Iona Italia for their permission to use this material here.

[135] Most concisely presented in the *Medium* post, "Here's How We Can Break Up Big Tech," https://medium.com/@teamwarren/heres-how-we-can-break-up-big-tech-9ad9e0da324c.

[136] As an entirely irrelevant aside, a fun parlor game is to think of the X in "Big X" that makes the least sense and is the most incongruous with the intended perception of menace and corruption. Our favorite is "Big Paint." Credit also to the writer Ben Sixsmith, who asked on Twitter, "Do you actually need 'rest days' from the gym or is that a conspiracy by Big Sofa?"

[137] Tellingly, Adam Back's Hashcash, which introduced *proof of work*, was an early attempt to counter precisely this problem.

[138] Encapsulating IP, TCP, UDP, HTTP, TLS/SSL, SMTP, IMAP, DNS, and so on.

[139] There is a good argument that what this demonstrates is that, actually, the current legal regime is hopelessly outdated rather than that the technology itself is somehow morally suspect. This is probably far enough down this rabbit hole, but readers whose interest we have piqued are encouraged to read Boldrin and Levine's *Against Intellectual Monopoly*, as highlighted in an earlier endnote, but also Lawrence Lessig's *Remix* and *Free Culture*, for arguments that are less philosophically and more culturally minded.

[140] Credit to Clay Space for the gist of the idea explicated here. Although originally discussed with us in conversation, his thinking has since appeared on *Medium*, https://clayspace.medium.com/c21b582d4e90.

[141] Dhruv Bansal and Ryan Gentry, "The Bitcoin Stack," presentation at Bitcoin 2021 Miami, https://www.youtube.com/watch?v=qlV5_udJkC0.

[142] The economic futility of the converse can be grasped by realizing that it boils down to the following radical innovation in corporate finance: The good that emerges from capital formation should also be a security in the enterprise owning and operating the capital, such that there are strong incentives for the price to go up *and* down, both of which are necessary to avoid failure. For a far longer analysis, see "Only the Strong Survive," by Allen Farrington and Big Al, https://www.uncerto.com/only-the-strong-survive.

[143] Around eleven minutes in, same link provided in endnote 141.

[144] Rather amusingly, this does not capture, or even come close to capturing their "carbon footprint," either direct or indirect: It is purely a question of *cost*.

[145] "UK Fires Up Coal Power Plant as Gas Prices Soar," *BBC News*, September 7, 2021, https://www.bbc.com/news/business-58469238.

[146] Vaclav Smil, "World History and Energy," *Encyclopedia of Energy, Volume 6* (Elsevier, 2004).

[147] Although perhaps this is unfair, Cipolla rightly points to two bursts of dramatic change in how humans utilized energy to which all other periods pale in comparison. But we can point to first, the Commercial Revolution and, now, what we might call the Information Revolution, as bursts of dramatic change in how humans *incentivize* energy utilization rather than how energy itself is generated and consumed. We make the case in the following chapter, not all in life — not even all in *economics* — is monetary or *calorific* exchange. Arguably what is good in life is *everything else*. After all, *the Renaissance* followed not the Agricultural Revolution, but the Commercial Revolution — and it is looking like the Bitcoin Renaissance will follow not the Industrial Revolution, but the Information Revolution. The Industrial Revolution may have changed the forms of energy we generate, but Bitcoin is changing how we are *incentivized* to generate energy at least as much, if not more so.

Admittedly, Cipolla acknowledges as much later on, writing, "Man needs capital to trap energy. And still more capital to exploit obtained energy for productive purposes. Capital accumulation is a necessary condition for any society's survival and progress is in a way a measure of that society's capacity to accumulate capital and use it efficiently."

[148] Saifedean Ammous, "Bitcoin Mining: Energy and Security," *The Bitcoin Standard Research Bulletin* 1, no. 3 (November 2018), p. 21.

[149] Roughly correct at the time of writing, but of course, Bitcoin will almost certainly incentivize people all over the world to find ways to drive these costs down. We look forward to these stats being wildly out of date in the near future.

[150] One might even be tempted to sarcastically argue that Bitcoin is, therefore, the *least wasteful* use of energy, by definition. We do not argue this, given we recognize, as per Chapter Two, *The Complex Markets Hypothesis*, that value is subjective. But we gladly contribute it to the pool of sarcastic comebacks to disingenuous pseudo-environmentalists.

[151] Credit to the work of Hass McCook, Selene Lindstrom, and Hodl'n Caulfield for helping us understand this and much of what follows.

[152] To be clear, there are other uses of stranded energy such as desalination, aluminum smelting, fertilizer production, battery charging (to whit, see two endnotes down) and even, in places such as Norway, repurposing excess energy towards pumping water back uphill in hydroelectric facilities. We do not mean to discount these industrial uses, but the key difference is that none trade in natively global markets, and all require vast physical infrastructure. It is even plausible that all will be usurped by Bitcoin mining by the same operators due to these economic disparities.

[153] Nick Szabo, "Money, Blockchains, and Social Scalability," referenced in several chapters, previously and still to come, but focused on most in Chapter Four, *Wittgenstein's Money*. See, https://nakamotoinstitute.org/money-blockchains-and-social-scalability/.

[154] What this really all points to is that energy *production* as opposed to *consumption* is a distinction without a difference. "Energy" isn't just lying around, waiting to be scooped up; it must be harnessed and directed mechanically. That is to say, it must be *capitalized upon*. Literally, we must devote capital to its mechanical harnessing and direction. It is the fact of *using* energy — simultaneously producing and consuming — that creates *power*. And it is power — energy at the margin — that we really want. We will explore this idea in more detail in Chapter Nine, *Global Money, Local Freedom*, but the creation of capital is a necessarily local phenomenon. This ought to make clear in this context that "total energy," in the sense of, *all the energy in the world*, is a numerical fiction. Scott in particular would likely argue specifically that it is a high-modernist numerical fiction.

In fact, we have come to suspect that there is a more widespread and *pathological* high-modernist fallacy at play here: That because the subjects of two or more measurements have the same dimensions and the same physical units, it must be true that they can be meaningfully added or subtracted without further thought. Of course, this is nonsense: Precisely the kind of nonsense that lands us with useless metrics like "GDP growth," as discussed in Chapter Three, *This Is Not Capitalism*. We would call this the *Farrington-*

374   Bitcoin Is Venice

Meyers Fallacy, except that we are honor-bound to credit Saifedean Ammous as having brought it to our attention in this exact case of energy and power. If Saif understandably objects on the basis that *Ammous's Fallacy* too strongly suggests, *the fallacy committed by Ammous*, then we will happily name it after Elizabeth Warren instead.

[155] Hence the monopoly on production and management of the currency used to globally price oil is an exorbitantly valuable privilege.

[156] This chapter and section are focused more on economic reasoning, whereas we save social theorizing for Chapter Eight, *These Were Capitalists*, and political theorizing for Chapter Nine, *Global Money, Local Freedom*. But the reader is encouraged to ponder that the non-localism described here also represents a political attack vector against which Bitcoin incentivizes creating resilience, arguably for the first time in history.

[157] Note this does not mean "Bitcoin is a battery," as we have noticed seems to have become a popular saying. We are frankly unsure what people think they mean by this given there is no circumstance in which bitcoin could be used "as a battery" in which a battery could not also be used *as a battery*. But of course, this is almost certainly likely to be the least economical choice and hence distracts from why Bitcoin is both new and useful in the first place. In fact, the reality is very nearly the opposite: The digital infrastructure we claim *extends the physical infrastructure* is extending the market for the *product* of energy consumption — in this case hashes — not energy consumption itself. You can't send natural gas over the Bitcoin network, but you can send the valued-by-others product of consuming natural gas. If you want to store energy, use a battery. If you want to store money, use Bitcoin. Precisely the innovation here is that Bitcoin mining creates a market for these two to be digitally exchanged. If they are really the same thing, then what are we talking about?

[158] An insight we credit to Ross Stevens, although others have surely written and spoken similarly.

[159] We actually went back and forth on the terminology we even wanted to adopt. On the one hand, "the environment" conveys an unfortunate arrogance with respect to our total inability to *manage* such a system. But on the other hand, "natural resources" — meaning something like, *that tiny subset of the environment that is economically relevant* — sounds exploitative in precisely the manner we are trying to avoid. If the reader could do us a favor and coin a new expression that has the benefits of both and the drawbacks of neither that would be grand.

[160] Just in this extract, to be clear. Later in *The Problem with Interest*, El Diwany provides a thorough debunking of the lunacy of fiat money and banking, from which we have already quoted in numerous other chapters.

[161] It is the kind that is relevant to the capital stock of *capital*! Or, to be less cute, *financial and production* capital, as opposed to the more abstract and intangible varieties discussed in this chapter and the following.

[162] There are conceptual reflections here of comments made in Chapter One, *Wrestling with the Truth*: Why simulate the entire universe when the universe will happily simulate itself? We run experiments precisely because we cannot just deduce or model the answer.

Note also experiments require upfront costs and take time. As we tried to impress upon the reader explicitly in Chapter Two, *The Complex Markets Hypothesis*, but also throughout the book, this is much more than just an analogy or a metaphor; it is literally true: Entrepreneurship *is* experimentation.

[163] Always metaphorically but sometimes literally, too! It is also worth noting here that soil erosion plays a key role in each of emissions, pollution, deforestation, and biodiversity loss, and so in some sense is the ur-example of an environmental problem.

[164] The reader may be amused by this unintentionally hilarious assessment of Simkhovitch's (lack of) contribution to academic economics in Eli Ginzberg's *Economics at Columbia: Recollections of the Early 1930s*, which note, was a hotbed of early degenerate fiat economics: "The hard core of the old department in addition to Seligman, Saeger, and Moore included Vladimir G. Simkhovitch who offered courses on socialism and economic history. Russian by birth and German by education, Simkhovitch, even with the perspective of time is not easy to characterize and even harder to evaluate. A collector of Chinese art and a grower of delphiniums in Perry, Maine, he was recognized as an expert in both fields. Most students, the bright as well as the dull, considered his lectures somewhat tedious distraction from serious work on contemporary economics; they had little interest in his exhaustion of the soil explanation for the decline of Rome or his Edward Bernstein-modified critique of Karl Marx." Of course, they did.

[165] See, https://theecologist.org/2014/apr/28/glyphosate-found-breast-milk.

[166] Stephen O. Duke, John Lydon, William C. Koskinen, Thomas B. Moorman, Rufus L. Chaney, and Raymond Hammerschmidt, "Glyphosate Effects on Plant Mineral Nutrition, Crop Rhizosphere Microbiota, and Plant Disease in Glyphosate-Resistant Crops," *J Agric Food Chem.* 60, no. 42 (October 24, 2012): 10375–10397.

[167] Anthony Samsel and Stephanie Seneff, "Glyphosate, Pathways to Modern Diseases II: Celiac Sprue and Gluten Intolerance," *Interdiscip Toxicol.* 6, no. 4 (Dec 2013): 159–184.

[168] See, https://www.scientificamerican.com/article/soil-depletion-and-nutrition-loss/.

[169] Whom we may as well bucket as *degenerate fiat environmentalists*, given their cause is a degenerate-fiat-money-enabled anti-human LARP.

[170] Jared Diamond makes a provocative Devil's Advocate case against agriculture and for the hunter-gatherer lifestyle in his essay, "The Worst Mistake in the History of the Human Race." The thesis may seem ridiculous on the face of it, but Diamond is meticulous and compassionate, not to mention an excellent writer. We obviously disagree, but we encourage the curious reader to take the piece completely seriously and to make up their own mind. https://www.discovermagazine.com/planet-earth/the-worst-mistake-in-the-history-of-the-human-race.

[171] We may as well call it a degenerate fiat error. It's not like we aren't in deep enough at this point!

[172] An excellent example not only in historical fact but in terms of its historiographical

characterization is to be found in Mary Lindemann's *The Merchant Republics*, writing of seventeenth century Hamburg, "It was also expected that such governors would seamlessly stitch together their private and public lives and acknowledge no difference between their own good and the good of the commune; each secured the other. Good government in Hamburg supposedly rested on just these pillars of the community whose willingness to sacrifice their time, their leisure, and occasionally their fortunes sustained the whole and underwrote Hamburg republicanism. Their wealth was believed to ensure probity in office; their reputations to prevent the abuse of authority. Repeatedly, observers found in this system where 'citizens govern citizens' the surest guarantees of civic harmony and liberties. If the real situation glowed less rosy, contemporaries and many historians praised it as able to avoid the rampant and destructive corruption they saw in every monarchy even in fellow republics, like Amsterdam. In Hamburg, voluntary government formed a safely banked middle road between the tyranny of absolutism and the anarchy of mob rule."

[173] There is an obvious link here to, again, Szabo's "Money, Blockchains, and Social Scalability": Dunbar's number (~150 manageable relationships per adult) as an evolved psychological trait could be thought to act as a ceiling for direct, pairwise social capital accumulation, whereas Szabo argues that markets — and trust in the institution of markets rather than in the pairwise participant, necessarily — enable the scaling required for substantive *economic* capital accumulation.

Credit to Kelly Lannan for the intriguing observation on reading earlier drafts of this chapter that the internet, and to some extent Bitcoin also, enables far more rapid and disparate creation of what he amusingly called *Dunbar eTribes*: Spontaneous organizations of networked individuals that can emerge and disband ad infinitum for the purpose of nurturing, replenishing, and growing social capital. Arguably, Bitcoin development is a perfect example of such behavior.

[174] Note that "peer-to-peer" and "client/server" work just as well here, but given the domain is so far removed from computer networking, we didn't want to impose terminology that read as too jarring. While "centralized" and "distributed" means roughly the same thing, we prefer "top down" and "bottom up" for this chapter as we believe this best captures the crucial image of the *direction* of idea transfer. In the following section on *urban capital*, this image takes on additional resonance with respect to the manner in which things are actually, physically built that we deliberately foreshadow. What literally follows in the discussion of urban capital could even be thought of as an effective metaphor in this section.

[175] Galatians 3:28.

[176] He doesn't say "toxic bigness" but then his is a kind of anthropological study, not so arrogantly sweeping as our own finance-oriented theory of everything.

[177] We referenced Whyte's scathing mockery of precisely this attitude in Chapter Two, *The Complex Markets Hypothesis*.

[178] The reader may recall an endnote near the beginning of Chapter Two, *The Complex Markets Hypothesis*, making a very similar point about fashionable illiberals. If the reader is not entirely comfortable with the religious overtones of calling such people *devilish*, that is quite alright, but know at least that they are undeniably totalitarian at

heart. They will operate in the mode of the Grand Inquisitor, and the reader should engage with them fully aware of this and at their own clear and obvious risk.

[179] See, https://pjmedia.com/instapundit/106691/.

[180] Of even more insidious varieties in addition to those commonly cited in terms of physical intimidation, one example of which only fairly recently starting to receive mainstream attention being "redlining." This is the practice of enforcing, centrally and by fiat, worse terms for credit on collateralized properties in neighborhoods known full well to be majority black. The effect (almost certainly bigoted and intentional) was to prevent black Americans from even *beginning* to accumulate capital. For an excellent popular account of emerging evidence of the extent of this injustice, see Whet Moser, "How Redlining Segregated Chicago and America," *Chicago*, August 22, 2017,https://www.chicagomag.com/city-life/august-2017/how-redlining-segregated-chicago-and-america/.

[181] Edited by Clayborne Carson.

[182] Attributed directly.

[183] Edited by Carson.

[184] Edited by Carson.

[185] Edited by Carson.

[186] See, http://www.katarxis3.com/Alexander_Eisenman_Debate.htm.

[187] Scott touches on the fallacy of transferring this attitude, skillset, and approach too readily from one space to another, having merely — if accurately — witnessed its success in the first realm, but without proper consideration as to *what about that realm made it successful.* He writes in *Seeing Like a State,* "When are high-modernist arrangements likely to work and when are they likely to fail? The abject performance of Soviet agriculture as an efficient producer of foodstuffs was, in retrospect, "overdetermined" by many causes having little to do with high modernism per se; the radically mistaken biological theories of Trofim Lysenko, Stalin's obsessions, conscription during World War II, and the weather. And it is apparent that centralized high-modernist solutions can be the most efficient, equitable, and satisfactory for many tasks. Space exploration, the planning of transportation networks, flood control, airplane manufacturing, and other endeavors may require huge organizations minutely coordinated by a few experts. The control of epidemics or of pollution requires a center staffed by experts receiving and digesting standard information from hundreds of reporting units."

[188] An excellent example can be found in the *Freakonomics* documentary series: https://www.youtube.com/watch?v=aFYlgqv3T-w.

[189] As flagged in a much earlier endnote, the subtitle of this book is far more telling of its message: *Designing for How We Respond to the Built Environment.*

[190] Note again the applicability of Reynolds's comments cited in the previous section.

[191] *Congrès Internationaux d'Architecture Moderne*, or the International Congress of Modern Architecture, the organization founded by Le Corbusier in 1928 to promote his preferred style across the world. N.B. endnote ours, not Scott's.

[192] Indeed, it is well-told that Marcel Duchamp meant *The Fountain* as an actual joke. Despite the nuanced and reasonable (if nonetheless objectionable) thesis Duchamp was working from and the satire of the artistic establishment he produced to convey this thesis, the primary influence of his work seems to have become as an anti-symbol of art itself, championed by those who didn't and still don't get the joke.

[193] Harold Bloom, *The Anxiety of Influence: A Theory of Poetry* (Oxford University Press, 1996).

[194] An amusing and, for balance, less than flattering *Goodreads* review by M. D. Hudson of Bloom's later *Shakespeare: The Invention of the Human* describes the history of Bloom's peddling this concept as follows: "This theory was elaborated from the late-1950s to the early-1970s, when a Freudian reading of literature was pretty much ala mode in American letters. By the 1970s, his 'anxiety of influence' theory had made Bloom's reputation, and Bloom probably thought he had the culture by the balls. But as it turns out, by the 1980s, the French and the feminists and the post-structuralists were deconstructing and whatnot while Freud became increasingly debunked. Bloom had secured Ivy League tenure by then, but intellectually he'd backed the wrong horse." See,https://www.goodreads.com/review/show/341667861.

We would caution in addition that, among a vast array of contrary views, Wimsatt and Beardsley's *The Intentional Fallacy* and *The Affective Fallacy* in particular are philosophically stronger than Bloom's furious dismissal of their theses. We cite Bloom more for his passion than his coherence, which is arguably suspect anyway given his apparent internalization of Freud.

We find Bloom's legacy best neutrally characterized and helpfully explicated by Professor Paul Fry as lecture number fourteen in his "Open Yale Course, Introduction to the Theory of Literature," which we highly recommend. Fry says, "The contributions of Bloom to Theory, in my opinion – and I hope to bring this out in the long run, have primarily to do with the fact that he can legitimately and authentically be called an important literary historiographer. That is to say together with people like Tynyanov and Jakobson earlier in the course, and Hans Robert Jauss later in the course, Bloom does seriously deserve to be considered a literary historian, that is to say, a person with a *theory* about literary history on a par with those other figures." See, https://www.youtube.com/watch?v=vui_MuI0HU0.

[195] Arthur de Gobineau, *Religions and Philosophies of Central Asia.*

[196] And worryingly find it to be increasingly relevant to comprehending social and cultural reality in the degenerate fiat West.

[197] See, https://soundcloud.com/washington-post/jazz-artist-wynton-marsalis-says-rap-and-hip-hop-are-more-damaging-than-a-statue-of-robert-e-lee/s-TRkFv.

[198] It is interesting to note, for example, that the ratio of unique words used to total words used in each artist's corpus is *far higher* for Aesop Rock, Busdriver, GZA, and Jedi Mind

Tricks than it is for Shakespeare, Marlowe, Milton, Dickens, or Joyce (more than double in every pairwise case). On the other hand, the gross unique words used seems to peak for rappers with Jedi Mind Tricks at 7,879, a decent amount below Marlowe's 13,544, the lowest on the previous list. The ratio is arguably fairer, however, or at least *as fair*, as most rappers do not top 50,000 total words due to the nature of the art form, whereas the lowest on the previous list of authors is Milton's 137,318, while Shakespeare wrote 882,515. Sources for the interested reader, https://github.com/ianmiell/word_counts/commit/f863e0ccd65c5192726dc436355f1cd e424c555f and, https://pudding.cool/projects/vocabulary/index.html.

[199] Virginia Postrel, *The Future and Its Enemies: The Growing Conflict Over Creativity, Enterprise, and Progress* (New York: Free Press, 1999).

[200] Frequent collaborator with Marc Andreessen, whom we have referenced several times already.

[201] See, https://www.youtube.com/watch?v=29CpBEOhTi0.

[202] See, https://a16z.com/2014/03/02/the-legend-of-the-blind-mc-2/.

[203] As poetry has become a far smaller share of the total output of literary culture, we tend to forget that most poetry ever composed was awful and that we only tend to remember, and preserve, the brilliant poems.

[204] We should also flag that Newton's and Searle's social program and outlook was very nearly the opposite of Martin Luther King Jr.'s. Nonetheless the legacy and influence of the Black Panther Party is far clearer on the early development of hip hop than is that of the Civil Rights Movement and so this is a contextually relevant reference for Anthony to make.

[205] See, https://www.youtube.com/watch?v=cHGu11GL9qw.

[206] See, https://quillette.com/2021/08/18/the-language-of-sex/.

[207] See, https://wtfhappenedin1971.com/.

[208] See, www.facebook.com/wyntonmarsalis/posts/10156215049577976.

[209] There is arguably even literary significance and intrigue in this "misreading," by which Bloom would no doubt be fascinated.

[210] Richard Goldthwaite, *The Economy of Renaissance Florence* (Baltimore, MA: Johns Hopkins University Press, 2009).

[211] Scholars of monetary history usually insist on ticking off such additional desirable or necessary traits as durability, fungibility, divisibility, and portability, but we skip these in the interest of focus given the obvious competition to gold in any remotely advanced or complex society were other precious metals that also had these traits.

[212] Or, at the most removed, a government-granted private right, liable to be revoked at a moment's notice.

[213] Garfinkel and Skaperdas make an interesting observation in the essay quoted just above about why we aren't used to thinking in these terms. In developed Western

societies, what are in fact threats of violence (if we are being keenly analytical) are couched in such superficially civil procedures that this is put entirely out of mind for most (who are not being keenly analytical but simply going about their affairs). They write, "In Brazil and elsewhere, however, violent conflict remains mostly in the background, as a distant threat and, more frequently, it has been completely supplanted by more civilized and controlled forms of conflict in the legal and political sphere. Within the modern state, and especially in prosperous countries, we don't observe the assembly of rival armies of soldiers. Rather, we observe the lining up of lawyers aided by assistants and expert witnesses or of lobbyists, mass mailers, and campaign consultants."

[214] Given we have now favorably quoted Oakeshott more than once, we would be remiss not to include an endnote from *Seeing Like a State*, lest the reader get the impression there is nothing in Oakeshott to criticize: "It is in fact impossible for most modern readers to take in the vast complacency with which Oakeshott regards what the past has bequeathed to him in its habits, practices, and morals without wondering if Jews, women, the Irish, and the working class in general might not feel as blessed by the deposit of history as did this Oxford don."

[215] Recall Scott insists there are some areas in which it is necessary and hence *must be* attempted, although we do not.

[216] There is an interesting objection to be made to our argument here in that, if capital is so much more mobile, won't economic existence becoming increasingly nomadic, undermining the cultural capital we have claimed throughout is key to the creation of every other kind, but in particular in Chapter Eight, *These Were Capitalists*? In *Deforestation, Investment, and Political* Stability, Robert Deacon alluded to "the marked difference in how the land and its forests, soil, and other resources are used by nomads versus settled agriculturalists. To the latter, future well-being of immediate family and descendants depends on maintaining the land's productivity. Nomadic pastoralists, on the other hand, occupy the land in a transient manner; so there is little impetus to form cultural norms that would favor long-term investments in the conservation of a specific site."

Our response would be that we must be careful in precisely what we mean by "mobile" and *of what* we are claiming this characteristic. So, for example, that Bitcoin is arguably maximally mobile capital means that *it* can be moved out the way of attack without its holder any physical production capital having to move. Physical capital, and the social capital that derives from physical proximity, can remain very much sedentary, yet its monetary wealth as stored in savings can, in effect, run away infinitely quickly. That said, it is a good point. What it seems to point to is basically that, for all the wonderful good Bitcoin does, one thing it will have a hard time fixing entirely is bad people taking your stuff!

[217] As explained previously in Chapter Eight, *These Were* Capitalists, by "voice," Hirschman essentially means "politics": expression of opinion, debate, lobbying, and social maneuvering as a decision-making procedure rather than market clearing.

[218] Arguably, more importantly, the Federal government in particular.

[219] Interestingly, Ostrom has what might be called the "inverse" of this concern in *Governing the Commons*, as explained in the main body of Chapter Seven, *A Capital Renaissance*: She assumes the default of her academic discipline is to assume that government (i.e., downward flowing credible threats of violence) can solve everything and considers herself to be fighting against this notion on the basis that it is morally and intellectually lazy but also, more importantly, unrealistic.

[220] And what does "legible" mean in Scott's usage if not precisely "tractable" in that of Garfinkel and Skaperdas? We might once again employ the metaphor of information to

Scott's general critique of high-modernism: That it tries to compress information beyond its most already least entropic state, hence necessarily destroying some or all of its signal.

[221] A short and delightful book on exactly this topic, as the name suggests.

[222] For an application of this line of legal and philosophical thought to the digital sphere both fascinating and amusing, see Elaine Ou, "A Lockean Theory of Digital Property," https://elaineou.com/2018/08/07/a-lockean-theory-of-digital-property/.

[223] A. A. Allchian, and W. R. Allen, "Exchange and Production," in *Theory in Use*, 1st ed., pg. 158. N.B. Citation not ours but in the original text we quote.

[224] Ostrom would almost certainly disagree with this specific claim with respect to most *common pool resources*, as discussed at length in Chapter Seven, *A Capital Renaissance*, and of which we would argue money, and hence Bitcoin, are examples. Referring back to Chapter One, *Wrestling with the Truth*, inherent human goodness can be a perfectly good motivator in place of credible threats of violence. In the cases Ostrom discusses, a sense of community engendering an appreciation of the depreciability of the common pool resource leading individuals to forego the opportunity to risklessly profit because they understand that, if scaled to all individuals, this behavior would lead to suffering for all in the long run. This is a subtle argument but note it hinges on communitarianism and empathy given it is strictly rational, in the sense of a Nash Equilibrium, for individuals to "cheat" in spite of this realization and regardless of the behavior of others.

[225] Unrelated to the present discussion but of extraordinary relevance to Chapter Four, *Wittgenstein's Money*, is the following throwaway line a few pages later in the essay from the extensive quote that follows above: "The concept of violence, or the use of physical force on another individual, is ambiguous. It could include the actual use of guns, knives or fists, or merely the threat of their use. It could also include the building of a fort to other protective structures. To clarify the concept as it will be used here, and to simplify the analysis, violence will be defined as the labor time allocated to excluding other individuals from a piece of land."

[226] There is an amusing irony in all this that it would be unfair of us not to bring to the reader's attention: This "capital formation" was essentially completely socially useless and in fact parasitic. Gold had value due to its monetary premium. Hence what was really happening here was vast capital misallocation to facilitate newly profitable inflation. The real wealth that poured into California was buying the rights to seigniorage, and nothing of real value was being exported beyond the illusory.

[227] Having already more or less explicitly identified fiat money with violence, the authors cannot help but notice the uncanny similarity between this observation and the common social media trope that the "deplorables," *grow the food, produce the energy, and the fight wars*, of urban "educated" elites — that is, high-modernist, all-decreeing, all-modelling, closed-source-insisting, consent-resisting, censorial client/server types, "educated" primarily in degenerate fiat economics and its various bullshit offshoots.

[228] See, https://bitcoinmagazine.com/culture/bitcoin-a-currency-of-decolonization.

[229] See, https://blog.chainalysis.com/reports/2021-global-crypto-adoption-index.

[230] See, https://bitcoinmagazine.com/culture/can-bitcoin-bring-palestine-freedom.

[231] Erik von Kuehnelt-Leddihn, *Liberty or Equality: The Challenge of Our Times* (Auburn, AL: Ludwig von Mises Institute, 2014), and Hans Hermann Hoppe, *Democracy: The God That Failed* (Piscataway, NJ: Transaction Publishers, 2001).

[232] "Elect me, and I will do nothing! I might even do less than nothing!" This is actually highly appealing to the authors, so please note we are not dismissing it as a political position, merely remarking that the comical tragedy of hoping for freedom to prevail in contemporary democracy necessarily relies on making this seemingly farcical argument and hence, obviously, consistently fails.

[233] An excellent example of this would be the likelihood of rapid uptake of state-of-the-art nuclear power by local administrations that has for decades been blocked by centralized politics on entirely spurious grounds that primarily rely on the carrot of corruption and the stick of fearmongering. We could have mentioned this in Chapter Seven, *A Capital Renaissance*, but we feel that this teased out explication of localism and power in this chapter was necessary to appreciate it fully.

Authors

Allen Farrington and Sacha Meyers are professional investors living in Edinburgh.

Allen holds a First in Mathematics and Philosophy from the University of St Andrews. His writing has appeared in *Quillette*, *Areo*, and *Merion West*. You can follow him on Twitter @allenf32.

Sacha holds a First in Physical Geography from King's College London, an MSc in Environmental Systems Engineering from University College London, and an MSc in Water Resources Management from Imperial College London. He is a CFA Charterholder. You can follow him on Twitter @sacha_meyers.

Made in the USA
Coppell, TX
31 March 2022

75823360R00225